Cuisine

Cuisine Bon Marché

Hugh Fearnley-Whittingstall

M

MACMILLAN

LONDON

First published 1994 by Papermac

a division of Pan Macmillan Publishers Limited
Cavaye Place London SW10 9PG
and Basingstoke

Associated companies throughout the world

ISBN 0 333 59032 5

9 8 7 6 5 4 3 2 1

A CIP catalogue record for this book is available from
the British Library

Typeset by Spottiswoode Ballantyne Printers Ltd
Printed and bound in Great Britain by
Mackays of Chatham plc, Chatham, Kent

For Mum and Dad, a great cook and an expert shopper. Many thanks for letting me make a mess in your kitchen, tidying up after me, and for saying nice things about the results.

Contents

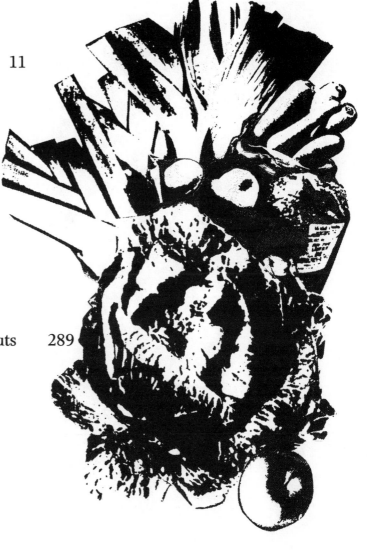

Acknowledgements

In no particular order, I would like to thank the following:

All the chefs who contributed recipes to this book (about whom more in the Introduction), but especially Adam Robinson, for his cooking at The Brackenbury, which inspired the article which inspired this book, and for his willingness to pass on his knowledge and understanding of good ingredients. His wisdom, which all too often I have shamelessly passed off as my own, has informed many of the chapters, particularly those on fish and meat.

My agent, Carol Heaton, for going far beyond the agent's call of duty. In particular, for her intelligent comments on my text, and for her unflagging encouragement throughout.

Everyone at Pan Macmillan who worked on the book, especially Judith Hannam, for her good humour and elastic application of deadlines, Tanya Stobbs, for her patience and politeness under duress, Peter Ward for his excellent page design and accommodating attitude, and Helen Dore, for her kind remarks and extremely accurate copy-editing.

Andrew Palmer and Lindsay Baroloni for their brilliant cover design and Akio Morishima and Rosie Reeve for their illustrations (and Andrew especially for giving so much time, for so long, for so little).

John Lanchester for his many helpful comments on the text, and Michael Day of the Huge Cheese Company, for his help with the chapter on Cheese.

Lisa Freedman and Mark Hughes Morgan on the *Sunday Telegraph*, for supporting *Cuisine Bon Marché* through the pages of that newspaper.

I am also immeasurably indebted to those friends who have cooked for me, for whom I have cooked, who have tested my recipes, either by eating them, or cooking them, and whose hospitality and generosity has helped to keep me sane during the writing of this book. They are many, but I must mention Aurea Carpenter, Jaimie D'Cruz, Tom Faulkner, Sarah and Adam Nicholson, Kate O'Sullivan, Jane Raven, Pots and Ivan Samarine, Carron Staplehurst and Charlie Taylor.

Introduction

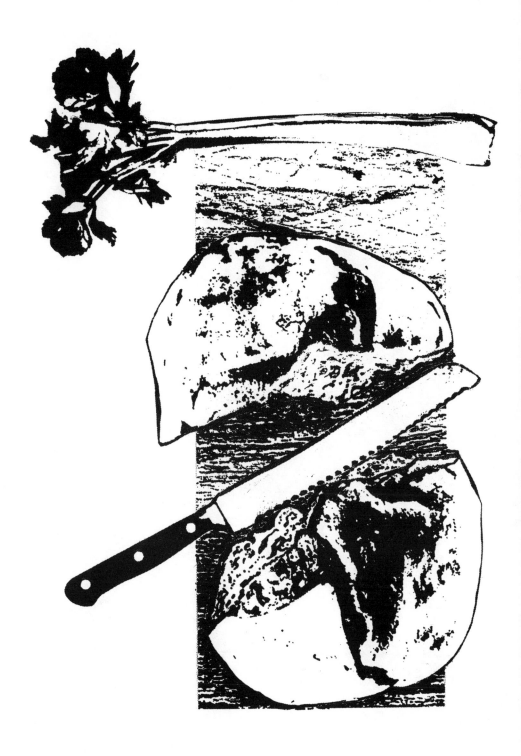

This is a recipe book with a difference. It takes as its starting point the place where every endeavour of every home cook begins, but which few cookbooks stop to consider: the market-place. Much of the text is about shopping for food – in the butcher's, the fishmonger, the grocer, the deli or the supermarket. I am confident that it is the first book of its kind.

Those who know the market for food books will point out that there has recently been a spate of books which deal with the problem of where to find certain foods. Such foodie directories are certainly useful, but I have not attempted to join their ranks. This is not a listings book, there is no directory of addresses, and very few retailers are mentioned by name. If you have bought this book hoping for this kind of information, then I'm afraid you may be disappointed. But if you would like to know *how* to shop for food rather than *where* to, then read on.

You might wonder if such a book is really necessary. Most of us assume we are competent shoppers; we know how to get to the supermarket, fill a trolley, and hand over a credit card at the till. Is there really much more to it than that? I am convinced there is. If you regard shopping for food as a chore, or even a bore, then what you choose is unlikely to be the best example of its kind. The food that ends up in your basket is hardly likely to inspire you when you unpack it in the kitchen, and chances are that your time spent cooking will be similarly gloomy. But when shopping is an exciting search for something truly delicious, it is no longer a chore but an adventure; handling and cooking this lovingly chosen produce becomes positively therapeutic; eating it, of course, with family or friends, is the final reward.

So why *Cuisine Bon Marché*? Finding a title for a cookery book is a hazardous business these days. We food writers have an inordinate fondness for neat culinary neologisms, not a few of which begin with the word *cuisine*. In cookery publishing, the last few years have given us *Cuisine Terroir*, *Cuisine Naturelle*, *Cuisine Actuelle* (as opposed, perhaps, to *Cuisine Imaginaire?*). At the same time the restaurant scene is buzzing with fancy phrases to describe the latest edible fashion: from 'Euro-rustic' to 'Pan-Asian eclectic', 'one-pot dining' to 'American retro', 'neo-classical French' to 'haute canteen'.

On one level this naming game does no harm. It at least reflects the unprecedented diversity of cooking styles now on show in this country, and draws attention to the depth of talent and imagination now at work in our restaurant kitchens. But for those who like to cook as well as eat out, the vast number of culinary pigeon holes can begin to sound like a daunting catalogue of specialist skills which will take years to master. The sheer diversity of today's food culture can be so baffling as to undermine the kitchen confidence of home cooks: they want to be more adventurous, but don't know where to start.

This book is partly intended to help those who feel the horns of this dilemma. I have chosen the phrase *bon marché*, not in order to add to the long list of named culinary styles, but to cut across them – the words are French, but culinary influences are felt in this book from all over the world. What they all have in common is that they make the best possible use of ingredients that have been carefully chosen from the increasingly bewildering array of produce available in the market place. For the chefs who have contributed recipes to this book, such insistence on quality is second nature. For you, the reader and home cook, it is not hard to learn.

Most dictionaries translate the phrase *bon marché* with the stigmatized English word 'cheap'. But the French means much more. *Bon marché* is not just about price, it is about quality and value. It denotes the skill of the shopper, as well as the 'goodness' of the produce bought. In fact the English phrase 'a good buy' is probably the best translation we have – which gives a literal translation of the title of this book as 'Good Buy Cooking'!

Apart from the unfortunate ambiguity of this English phrase, there is another good reason why the title of this book should be in French. For centuries, French housewives have been great experts in the art of shopping for food. One of the aims of this book is to help English home cooks (of both sexes) to catch up.

But this book is not just about shopping. It also has plenty to say about the second part of the adventure, the cooking. Many cookery books offer the home cook exciting and original recipes. But in the minds of most cooks, such books are for special occasions, for entertaining. The rest of the time . . . well, they just cook. Although I would be proud to prepare any recipe in this book and serve it to guests, my main aim is not to help in the planning of dinner party menus. It is to enrich the lives of readers, by increasing the range and quality of their taste experience at every mealtime.

It sounds like a grand aim, and in some ways it is. It can be summarized in the following three principles:

1 *Improve the quality of the ingredients which you currently buy.*

2 *Increase the range of ingredients with which you currently cook.*

3 *Expand your current repertoire of cooking methods.*

Adopt any one of the three principles, and you will instantly improve your cooking and eating life. Adopt all three, and you will never have to eat a dull meal again.

Finally, there is one more reason for becoming a Bon Marcheur* – perhaps the best of all. It is often said of the people of this country that 'we get the press we deserve'. I'll leave that for the media analysts to debate. But an analogous theory, and one to which I wholeheartedly subscribe, is that, as a nation of shoppers, we get the food we are prepared to put up with. And if we're not prepared to put up with the second rate, we will eventually be offered something better.

Anyone who thinks the consumer never fights a winning battle is wrong. A decade ago free-range eggs were a loss-leading gimmick on sale in a handful of smart supermarkets. Today you can buy them in every corner grocer. Once you would have been lucky to find three types of apple in a greengrocer's. Now the adventurous shopper can find dozens. By boycotting the second rate in favour of the first rate, we strengthen the market for quality. Even by avoiding a tired lettuce or a wrinkled pepper on the supermarket shelf, we increase the vigilance of suppliers in maintaining their standards. Be a Bon Marcheur, and you help create a Bon Marché.

* A French friend tells me that bon marcheur *actually means 'stout walker'. Since this is undoubtedly a skill required also of the best food shoppers, I have decided to let it stand.*

How to use this book

Different people use cookery books in different ways. Some will use them to choose recipes for an occasion, and then go out and shop for the ingredients. Others, finding themselves landed with a seemingly random selection of produce, will scour the kitchen bookshelf for a recipe that brings them all together. Still others – me, for example – will read cookery books in bed, while salivating and hatching grand plots for future feasts.

I suspect, however, that all but the most avid readers of cookery books are browsers – of one sort or another; and that the way in which they generally approach a cookery book is through the index.

This book has been structured very much with the browser in mind. The index is intended to be thorough. The entries in bold script correspond closely to the hierarchy of headings and subheadings that divide up the main text of the book. This is intended to make it easy to access specific information and advice (about, for example, choosing, storing or cooking) both for generic types of produce (such as game, fruit, or herbs, etc.) and for particular items (such as pigeons, papayas, or parsley).

The index entries in light script are recipes – not only the fully written-up recipes that make up the second part of each chapter, but also many of the more informal recipe ideas and cooking tips that crop up throughout the book. Some of these 'mini-recipes' have, for the sake of even greater accessibility, been printed as separate marginal notes. Others you will find (easily enough, I hope) incorporated into the flow of the main text.

I hope, therefore, that those who know more or less what they are looking for will be able to find it with a minimum of delay. Those who are taking a more leisurely approach (and I hope there will be a few) should find that each chapter is pretty much self-contained, and moves, on the whole, as the shopper moves – from the market to the table, via the kitchen and the cooker.

About the recipes in this book

Around half the recipes in this book are 'my own'. By that I don't wish to imply that I invented them all: many have been stolen or adapted more or less shamelessly from books, articles, chefs and friends. These sources I have tried to acknowledge wherever possible, but I fear some of the victims of my burglary will have to go unrecognized.

The remaining recipes have been generously contributed by a number of restaurants. They are not necessarily among the most written-about restaurants in the country. Certainly they are not the most expensive. But those who have eaten in them will probably already know why I asked them to contribute. They seem to me to exemplify the understanding of produce and technique which is the spirit of Bon Marché cooking.

The chefs involved are not household names, but wise and well-informed shoppers in today's increasingly confusing market place. They not only understand but enjoy their raw ingredients, and can transform them, with a maximum understanding of their inherent qualities and a minimum of fuss, into truly excellent dishes bursting with flavour, interest and integrity. They have chosen not to compete with the clutch of so-called star chefs for guide accolades and Michelin stars not because it is a competition they could not win, but because they realize it is a competition in which honest food, good taste, and sane pricing are so often the losers.

In the text, contributed recipes are marked with the name of the restaurant from which they come. To make these labels meaningful there follow brief profiles of the restaurants who contributed. I am greatly indebted to them all.

THE ARK

The Street, Erpingham, Norfolk NR11 7QB

Tel: 0263 761535

The Norfolk village of Erpingham is almost too pretty to have a good restaurant – day trippers and weekenders could easily be fleeced by a second-rate establishment. It is a credit to Mike and Sheila Kidd that their hospitality and food at the Ark set examples not just for Erpingham but for the whole county.

Sheila, who runs the kitchen, is modest about her cooking and quick to acknowledge her debt to Elizabeth David. A little too quick, perhaps, and a little too modest: her daily-changing menu shows a wide knowledge of many cooking traditions, and a strong streak of originality too. She makes her own 'Gravad-mackerel' with flappingly fresh, locally caught fish, and uses the best local vegetables, many from her own lovingly tended garden. There are always vegetarian options; not merely a sop, these are often enticing enough to tempt confirmed carnivores away from the meaty elements of the menu.

Puddings are a strength (there are no weaknesses), especially fruit tarts, greedy cakes, and delicious fools, mousses and ices.

The restaurant now offers accommodation, and the weekend crowds can be avoided by taking advantage of bargain prices for mid-week stays.

THE BRACKENBURY

129–131 Brackenbury Road, London W6 0BQ

Tel: 081-748 0107

If anything gives the little backwater of West London that surrounds this restaurant the right to call itself Brackenbury Village, it is the warm hospitality and stunning food that emanates from Adam Robinson's kitchen. Since Adam and his wife Katey opened the Brackenbury in 1990, their eminently reasonable prices have hardly budged. The cooking here is generous – in quantity and, more importantly, in taste. The range of flavours and textures encountered on the short menu, which changes every day, outdoes most restaurants that charge double the price.

'I'd rather charge less and retain the right to make mistakes,' Adam once told me, 'otherwise I wouldn't develop as a chef.' In fact, mistakes are rare, though 'development' is apparent at each new visit. Adam takes no short cuts, salting his own cod, pickling his own tongues, and doing most of the butchery himself. At the same time he, along with his loyal sous-chef Toby Gush, has proved to have a ceaseless curiosity and boundless energy for finding interesting dishes, and by the time this book is published there will no doubt be a whole host of new recipes worth stealing from the Brackenbury.

BRASSERIE DU MARCHE AUX PUCES

349 Portobello Road, London W10 5SA

Tel: 081-968 5828

At the top of the eponymous flea market in the Portobello Road, in the heart of the Spanish and Portuguese quarter, is a haven for anyone searching for food that is highly innovative and a touch sophisticated without being decadent, flashy or overpriced. Proprietor and occasional chef Philip McMullen works with his young and enthusiastic kitchen team to produce a monthly changing menu that reflects the multi-ethnicity of this lively part of London. Mexican salsas and West Indian fish dishes may be found alongside hearty English stews and classic French bistro dishes. Vegetables are a particular forte, in risottos, pulsy stews, soups and salads, and a bold use of spices and fresh herbs makes many such dishes wonderfully aromatic.

I am especially indebted to Noel Ashbourne, who was chef at the Brasserie at the time I began to compile the recipes for this book. He has since moved on, but his influence is still strongly felt in the kitchen and on the menu, and his recipes in this book are a delight.

THE BUT 'n' BEN

Auchmithie, Tayside DD11 5SQ

Tel: 0241 77223

Margaret Horn is an accomplished home cook who invites passers-by to pop into her kitchen and sample something delicious she just happens to have bubbling on the stove. At least, that's how it feels to eat at this small Tayside cottage in Auchmithie, just a few miles north of Arbroath (try the smokies). She doesn't roam far for her ingredients, but knows exactly what is best locally. Much of this is fish, which is cooked so simply that I could not persuade Margaret to give a recipe, beyond 'take a fresh herring, clean it, roll it in oatmeal, and fry it in butter'. You will sometimes find lobster on the menu, simply grilled or boiled, at a price you will think is a mistake. But it is not a mistake, simply a great bargain and a rare treat.

Margaret is also a dab hand with the stock pot and her Scotch broth, stews and other slow-cooked dishes are appreciated when a chill wind blows, as has been known in this part of Scotland. Equally comforting are her high teas – the But 'n' Ben is open all day – which might comprise the above-mentioned herring, followed by a hefty slice of fruit-laden, treacly clootie dumpling.

THE FOX AND GOOSE

Fressingfield, Suffolk IP21 5PB

Tel: 037-986 247

Fressingfield is a charming if unexceptional Suffolk village. Roughly in the middle is a pub called the Fox and Goose. It looks like a pub and it feels like a pub, a warm and comfortable pub. But it eats like a gastronomic tour of five continents. Proprietor Ruth Watson and her co-chef Brendon Ansborough cook with enthusiasm verging on the fanatical. They are passionate, and you can taste their passion in the food. Behind the undisguised joy there is also skill and considerable attention to the quality and freshness of ingredients.

Eclecticism can be a dangerous game, but here such a mixed bag as grilled halloumi (Greek cheese), Peking duck, ceviche of scallops and salmon, and tempura of vegetables are carried off fearlessly and with complete success. Seasonal game, robust stews, meat braises and roasts ensure that the best of English produce is also given an outing. 'Pub' is too small a word; gastronomically speaking, the Fox and Goose is a palace.

JEMIMA'S

Nash Grove, Freystrop, Haverfordwest,
Dyfed SA62 4HB
Tel: 0437 891109

There is no great fanfare to announce the existence of this restaurant at the top of a hill just outside Haverfordwest. Just take the Burton Road south and stop when you get to the delicious smell.

That Ann Owston might ever stop cooking seems unthinkable. But how she finds time to do all she does is something of a mystery. On Friday and Saturday mornings she sells her homemade cakes, breads and jams, and is back at the stove in time for lunch. She also finds time to cure her own hams and make her own charcuterie. And then there's the vegetable garden . . .

When the food arrives it is as if Ann has been cooking only for you. She is bold in her experimentation with global influences, and dishes such as Szechuan prawns, Indonesian pork and escabèche of mackerel testify that she is also very successful. There are plenty of original touches, and some dishes – lamb's liver with Dubonnet, rabbit with Riesling – sound unlikely. Those intrigued enough to try them will realize they should never have doubted.

THE WHITELEAF AT CROYDE

Croyde, Nr Braunton, N. Devon, EX3 1PN
Tel: 0271 890266

It is hard to know how to describe the Whiteleaf Hotel. Bed and breakfast? Country Inn? I'd settle for 'home from home'.

Right on the Devon coastal path, just a few minutes' walk from the beach, this is a place to know and love. David Wallington does the cooking, practically unaided, while his wife Flo pampers the guests front of house. Dinner is a five-course affair, and the price might not strike you as unreasonable, even if bed and breakfast were not included!

David's repertoire takes in Italy and France, but is rooted in traditional British cooking. Whatever he is up to, you can be sure the ingredients will be of the best and freshest, and the results irresistible. Game pies and hearty stews are a speciality, and roasts are exemplary. But pasta and risottos are also an abiding love. Fans of Italian wine will find no one better than David to share and feed their passion.

CHAPTER ONE

The Bon Marché Kitchen

Most of this book is about the pursuit, use and consumption of the very best ingredients that this country's market-place has to offer. All three activities can and should give the cook a great deal of pleasure. But if the last two are really going to afford maximum satisfaction then an extra ingredient is required – *a well-run kitchen.*

This doesn't mean that you have to become a gastro-despot, commanding the kitchen domain with military authority, according to a list of rules nailed to the wall. If you are a relaxed cook, then you will want to run a relaxed kitchen. But if you are the chief cook in a household – and this book largely aims to address people in that position – then it makes sense for your kitchen to be organized in such a way that when you are in it, cooking, your mood is one of contentment, if not outright joy. If, on reflection, the current state of your kitchen is more likely to bring on a fit of despair, then it may be time for some changes.

The basic step towards making your kitchen a happier place to cook in could hardly be more simple: think of all the ways, however big or small, in which alterations or additions to your culinary practices, kitchen layout or battery of equipment could improve the time you spend cooking. You will probably be amazed at how many small and inexpensive adjustments can be made almost at once, and how dramatic their effect is. You may be so pleasantly surprised that the larger projects no longer seem so urgent. You can take months, even years, to plan them at your leisure. If and when they come to fruition, then, truly, your kitchen will be a paradise.

The rest of this chapter looks at the key aspects of kitchen life, and considers possible means of improvement.

The Larder

I have a game I like to play in other people's larders and kitchen cupboards. I ask them to guess how far past the sell-by date the oldest can, packet or jar will be. 'A few months,' most of them say, 'a year at most.' Invariably I find something that shocks them – a can from when flares were in fashion (the first time round), or a jar of chutney from a summer fête five years earlier.

The issue here is not particularly one of health or hygiene – many canned and preserved foods remain safe long after statutory use-by dates have expired – but one of psychology. If your larder is full of ancient cans, it is because they are full of things you don't want to eat. And if you are surrounded by things you don't want to eat, you will hardly be inspired to cook.

The proper purpose of larders and food cupboards is to store any fresh produce that does not require refrigeration (including meat and cheese – see pages 192 and 383) and to keep to hand a ready supply of non-perishable ingredients used regularly. These may include flour, sugar, rice, pasta, pulses, nuts and spices. No doubt there will also be cans, jars and bottles; but these should at least contain things you actually like and use – why buy canned tomato soup 'for an emergency' if in reality you know you hate the stuff? Similarly, there is little point in filling your larder with specialist ingredients that you use only once in a blue moon. If you require them so rarely, they are probably used in dishes which are planned well in advance, in which case they can be bought as and when you need them.

So when you have some time on your hands, take a look at everything in your larder, and ask yourself, 'Am I really likely to eat this in the next month?' If the answer is no, throw it, or give it, away.

The Fridge

All that I have said about the larder applies equally to the fridge, only on a shorter time-scale. If a fridge is anything like full, then it is practically inevitable that some of its contents will be eaten in a condition that is far from optimum. A fast turnover of food in the fridge and larder indicates a confident cook who shops intelligently and wastes little. On the other hand, savers of perishing produce, and hoarders of useless cans and jars, are permanently haunted by a ghastly feeling, conscious or unconscious, that there is something lurking in the fridge or larder which they should be using up.

In the light of this theory, the uses of the fridge can be summarized thus:

○ To maintain the optimum condition of fish, meat, vegetables, dairy products and other perishables which you intend to eat in the immediate future.

○ To store leftover cooked foods that require refrigeration to avoid decline – *but only those you really intend to eat.*

○ To cool foods, drinks and prepared dishes which are most palatable when served chilled, including fruit and vegetables that would not normally benefit from refrigeration (see page 36). Such items should be refrigerated for only as long as it takes to chill them through.

○ To store opened cans and jars whose contents would deteriorate if not refrigerated. (It is worth noting that this includes pots of mustard.)

NOTE: the storage requirements and reaction to chilling and freezing of particular foods are discussed in the appropriate chapters.

Work surfaces

One of the greatest aggravations in the kitchen is a lack of space in which to work. Force of habit means that certain things are kept in certain places, but it is worth considering the possible benefits of revising the allocation of your kitchen space. For example, are there potential work surfaces that are more or less permanently covered by movable items such as jars, pans, flower-pots, etc? Perhaps one small shelf or an extra cupboard could accommodate these things, leaving you with more clear space to work in.

Even large kitchens do not always have adequate work surfaces – but they may well have space for an old-fashioned butcher's block. Free standing, on three sturdy legs, these are inexpensive second-hand, immensely satisfying to use and can, at a stroke, solve the space problem in many kitchens.

In very tiny kitchens space will always be at a premium. I have had to cook in my fair share of London galley kitchens, and have found that an extra large chopping board which can be placed right over the sink or even on top of the cooker can make life a little easier.

The Cooker

The relationship between the cook and his or her cooker is a vital one. If you hate your cooker, it will sense your hostility and fear, and do everything within its power to spoil what you are cooking – at least it will seem that way. And if you are at peace with it, you will be surprised how tolerant it can be of your errors. Choosing a new cooker therefore offers a great chance to improve your kitchen performance permanently.

Although it is possible to dent your finances to the tune of thousands of pounds to find a reliable and user-friendly cooker, good design and simple functionality are still available for a three-figure sum. Essential requirements, in my view, are as follows:

1 A minimum of four hobs which will give stable support to pots and pans of all shapes and sizes.

2 At least two of the hobs should be capable of bringing a large (say, 10-pint/5-litre) pan of cold water to the boil in less than 10 minutes.

3 At least two of the hobs should be able to keep even a relatively small pan at a very gentle simmer, preferably without (and certainly with) the aid of a heat diffuser.

4 When the hobs are turned down, the heat should drop immediately.

5 The oven should be spacious enough to take the largest thing you are likely to cook in it, *without a dramatic drop in temperature.*

6 The oven should reach a temperature of at least 230°C/450°F/Gas Mark 8.

7 The oven should have no heat spots (i.e. the temperature should be the same in all parts of the oven).

These seven points are not much to require of a cooker, but it is surprising how many brands fall short, sometimes on all seven. Until a few years ago only gas hobs were responsive enough reliably to fulfil points 2), 3) and 4), but with today's technology many electric cookers are now sufficiently sensitive to compete and even win against gas on these requirements. My own preference is still for gas, but I am not prepared to embrace the blanket condemnation of electric hobs that many old-school chefs still go in for.

As far as ovens are concerned, fan-assisted electric ovens are probably the most reliable and user-friendly in the lower price range. Cheap gas ovens tend to have heat spots.

When buying a new cooker it is not always easy to be sure that all the points listed above (and others *you* may feel are important) are satisfied – ask the sales person for a written assurance that the cooker will perform on all the parameters that you have insisted on. Should it fail to deliver on any of these points, then, even if there is nothing actually *wrong* with it, you will be entitled to a full refund.

Of course Gas versus Electric is not the only choice. I have always been a great fan of the Aga. Rather than sing its praises here, I would suggest that anyone who is interested contacts the company and asks for a full demonstration. This is the only way to get the full picture of this characterful cooker.

Microwave ovens

Although a microwave does not feature in my current kitchen line-up (hence its use is not specified in the recipes in this book), I have owned one, and found it very useful in a number of limited applications. Successful deployment depends on understanding the exact nature of the microwave cooking process. The microwaves are absorbed by the food and produce heat by the agitation of water molecules: effectively microwaved food is being steamed from within. You cannot therefore expect the microwave to be an adequate substitute for any cooking process that requires some evaporation of the water content of the ingredients. Nothing can be browned or cooked crisp in a microwave oven. Another drawback is that the speed of microwave cooking does not allow time for tougher cuts of meat to tenderize – so it is no substitute for slow-cooking techniques such as braising and stewing. In my view, these two factors practically rule out cooking any meat dishes in the microwave, along with bread, cakes, tarts, gratins and pastries.

However, fish, and fresh and frozen vegetables can be cooked very successfully in a microwave oven, if you are looking to achieve a steamed effect. Sauces, soups and fruit also cook well, and the microwave is particularly useful for reheating cooked food without any further loss of moisture.

The Hardware

There are few things with greater power to affect the cook's mood than the tools of the trade – and the cooker is only the start of it. If there is one shopping expedition that I anticipate with an even greater thrill than a food-buying trip, it's a foray in search of a few choice items of kitchen hardware. Good kitchenware shops make me drool with covetousness. Along the wall-lining shelves glints the cold steel of professional pots and pans. From the ceiling hang sieves, colanders and balloon whisks with perfect functional contours. Then there are the small, simple gadgets – things you never knew existed but which, once purchased, you would never be without: an olive stoner, a miniature garlic grater, a tiny birch twig whisk for salad dressings.

So is this where we crack? Defences down, we think, 'Pay now, grovel to the bank manager later.' Shouldn't we rather remember our Bon Marché principles, put away the cheque book, and continue to make do with blunt knives and battered aluminium until they fall apart?

Not necessarily. Good kitchen economy is not just about buying cheaply, it's about buying cleverly. And sometimes it's clever to spend a bit more. There is no point in buying a plastic spatula that melts at egg-frying temperature – especially if you fry a lot of eggs. And there is no point in buying a cheap 'non-stick' frying pan that buckles and blisters when you turn up the heat, and thenceforward burns, curdles or otherwise messes up the carefully chosen produce which you put in it.

Equipping your kitchen with tat is not only a false economy, it also takes away the immeasurable satisfaction of pursuing your culinary passion with well-designed tools that were made to do the job properly. A well-crafted utensil gives a small buzz of pleasure every time you use it: the potato peeler which effortlessly skins a spud and never sticks; the can opener so robust and ruthless you could use it to make your car a convertible; an ordinary wooden spoon, a simple sculpture in beechwood, the design perfect for the application.

There is no knowing what psychological barriers are created by unsatisfactory hardware. Could it be that the only thing between you and a perfectly puffed, golden-brown, creamy cheese soufflé is that you can't bear to remove that finger-mincing, buckled bastard of a cheese grater from the back of the kitchen cupboard? So remove it now, stamp on it, toss it away with glee . . . and go and buy one that works.

Pots and Pans

The more you use a particular piece of kitchen equipment, the more its inadequacies are going to haunt you – or the more its fine design is going to thrill you. The choice is yours. As you are likely to use your pots and pans on a daily basis, their selection is worth taking some trouble over.

If you've never cooked with top-quality stainless steel saucepans, then you have a great treat in store. They don't tarnish, they don't stain, they don't dent, they don't buckle and, unless you abuse them in an imaginative and powerful way, they will last you a lifetime. Two of the best makes are Cuisinox and La Pentole, but other professional brands intended primarily for the catering trade are likely to be as good.

Stainless steel is expensive. A good-sized stock-pot, with lid, can cost well over £100. But after a few years of daily use, when it is still coming up as shiny as new after every scrub, you may regard that as a bargain.

If steel does not appeal, the heavy-duty Le Creuset range in enamelled cast iron is an excellent alternative – and now available in lots of jazzy colours as well as the traditional warm orange and deep blue. Their frying pans are particularly recommended, and the larger saucepans are ideal for casseroles.

Other essentials

The list below is not intended to be comprehensive, but the following items are things which, over the years, I have come to depend on. If you are going to explore the recipes in this book at length, you will find them useful too.

Balloon whisk

Choose a good heavy model in all steel or steel with a wooden handle. They are ideal whenever you are mixing by hand – sauces, mayonnaises, cake batters – especially when you are aiming to get some air into the mix. If you can be bothered, use it to whip heavy cream and to whisk egg-whites – you can judge the consistency to perfection, and avoid the risk of over-beating. It's also very good for your triceps and biceps, and immensely satisfying when you've finished – like coming back from a long walk. A smaller whisk for sauces and dressings may also be useful.

Food processor

I used to spurn the Magimix (and similar food processors or 'kitchen robots'), on the grounds that they instilled laziness in the user and encouraged the taking of short cuts. Then I went to work in a restaurant kitchen and realized that all the best chefs use them *all the time*. The Bon Marché chef is required to do a lot of chopping and slicing, particularly of vegetables, and not a little mixing. Perhaps the most under-used feature of the food processor is the grater – particularly handy if you are preparing industrial quantities of grated Parmesan, Gruyère or Cheddar cheese, as I often seem to do. The slicing blade is also extremely useful for preparing vegetables, especially potatoes and celeriac, for deep-frying and making gratins. A food processor also produces a far better mince than the butcher's grinder – see page 199.

I mentioned the Magimix, and that is my preferred brand. It used to have a clear edge over other makes of food processor, some of which were lacking in power, others in precision or design. But recently when I have had occasion to use rivals to the Magimix, I have been more impressed. Braun and Kenwood certainly have good models. I leave the final choice to you.

The only thing you really need to know about a food processor is when NOT to use it. Here are a few key guidelines:

○ Do not chop vegetables in a food processor if the size and shape of the resulting pieces is important to the end product – i.e. if you require regular bite-size pieces of carrot, parsnip, onion, etc. to be identified and enjoyed in your stew, soup, tart or whatever.

○ Do not expect a food processor to add much air to anything – for example, a cake batter. If I am making a cake I will use the processor to blend all the ingredients *except* the eggs. These I will beat into the mixture in a separate bowl, using an electric whisk, a rotary beater or balloon whisk.

○ Do not over-process in a food processor any mixture containing flour. Anything you mix in a processor takes a real pounding, and a pastry mix or cake batter processed for too long will contain too much gluten released from the flour. The resulting pastry or cake will not be as light and melting as it should be. So process only until it is well mixed, i.e. do not leave it mixing merrily away for ages while you perform other tasks.

○ The food processor is not a blender, and is therefore unsuitable for making really smooth purées out of cooked vegetables and fruit. It *can* be done, however, if you separate the solid bits (lumps, leaves, vegetables, etc.) from the liquid, and process only the solids to begin with. When the solids are finely puréed, trickle in the liquid through the pouring tower on the lid. Even then, it may be necessary to pass your purée through a fine sieve.

○ Do not attempt to purée vegetable mixtures with a high proportion (more than one-third) of potatoes. The result will be sticky and starchy and not very palatable. Best to separate the potatoes, rub through a sieve with a wooden spoon, then recombine with the rest of the purée.

Gratin dish

Gratins, especially of vegetables, are a delight. Not only do they make much of the flavours of their main ingredients, they are also (generally speaking) *crispy on top* – and let's face it, we all like things which are crispy on top. A shallow, white ceramic dish, oval or rectangular, is ideal. Never make a gratin too deep – a high ratio of surface area to depth gives more crispiness.

Griddle pan

Perhaps the single most treasured item in my kitchen. This is what used to be called, simply, a grill, before that word was hijacked and used to refer to the overhead grill, which cooks by heating from above, that is now a feature of most domestic cookers. Griddle pans come in a number of shapes and sizes: square, rectangular, or round with a handle like a frying pan. The vital feature is that it is made of heavy cast iron with raised ridges on the cooking surface. It is the ridges that perform the magic. On a steak or slice of aubergine they produce those tempting, zebra-like charred stripes that so impress in a restaurant.

Grilling on a griddle is infinitely preferable to grilling under an overhead grill. Instead of being sealed by a blast of searingly hot air, which has a dehydrating effect, the meat, fish or vegetable in question is seared on contact, and the moisture and flavoursome sugars of the produce are retained. A griddle pan is also extremely easy to use. You just stick it on the hob (preferably gas) and wait for it to get *very* hot.

A griddle pan will cost between £20 and £45, depending on size. A small price to pay for such a great stride forward in the taste mission.

Steamer

Useful for steaming vegetables (and small portions of fish) and generally avoiding the 'tea-bag effect', see page 44. For some vegetables improvisation is possible, but a steel steamer is not expensive and does the job properly.

Tart tin

Obviously essential if one is to be making tarts (and one should). Ideal is a light steel or tin model with a fluted edge and – essential, this – a loose (removable) bottom. This means the tart can then be turned out on to a plate or board, and shown in all its glory. Not because we're that fussed about presentation. But because the humble tart generally gets a raw deal, stuck to the bottom of unsuitable ceramic or Pyrex dishes, and deserves better.

Gismos and Gadgets

There are other, less basic items of kitchen equipment (some I have mentioned above) that can hardly be regarded as essentials, but can none the less add greatly to both your repertoire and the pleasures of preparing food. Here is an eclectic selection of items I would hate to be deprived of, with brief notes for their use.

Chinois

This conical-shaped strainer with a fine metallic mesh is ideal for straining stocks, purées and sauces – indeed, that is precisely what it is designed to do. It is preferable to an ordinary sieve because the mesh is finer and the structure is sturdier. The liquid can be pressed through with the back of a ladle or some such, with considerable pressure and without any danger of buckling the implement, so that a maximum of liquid is extracted with a minimum of impurities. For an absolutely 'clean' stock or sauce, a second straining should be made, the chinois lined with a piece of muslin or cotton cloth.

Fish kettle

This long, deep container, in aluminium or stainless steel, is extremely useful for poaching and steaming whole large fish, or several smaller ones at the same time. See pages 141–2 for more details.

Ice-cream machine

You really can't make the best ice-cream without one. Whether or not you feel a need to make the best ice-cream is entirely a matter for you, but nothing you can buy in the shops, not even Häagen-Dazs, comes close to what you can produce at home if you get your own machine. If you grow your own fruit, you'd be mad not to have one. For more on ice-cream making, see pages 363–6.

Mezzaluna

The crescent-bladed (*mezza-luna* literally means half-moon), double-handed chopping knife is extremely useful for finely chopping just about everything, but especially herbs, chillies, garlic, shallots, etc. It is quicker than using a knife, and more precise that a food processor, allowing you to decide just how fine the chopped material should be. A wonderful invention, it is as therapeutic as it is effective. Double- and even triple-bladed varieties are available, but they require greater expertise in the handling, and save time only when very large quantities are involved. Avoid miniature mezzalunas (with a blade of less than 6 in/15 cm); they are a gimmick and do not do the job properly.

Nylon sieve

A modern substitute for the old-fashioned horse-hair sieve (if you find one of the latter, please let me know), the nylon sieve is very useful for straining purées, particularly of soft acidic fruits (mainly currants and berries), which discolour and suffer a taint in flavour if passed through a metal sieve.

Olive/cherry-stoner

This may sound like a whimsical item, and using it is indeed rather like playing with a favourite toy. Kitchen-oriented children could be allowed 'a go' as a special treat. The reason it is so useful is simply because olives are so useful – and the key ingredient of a number of recipes in this book. Pre-stoned olives, especially black (which are the more useful) are usually unsatisfactory in taste, so buy unstoned and stone them yourself. Most olive-stoners are in fact a feature incorporated into another useful item, the garlic press. When you see one, you won't believe the stoning feature is going to work, but it does. Also very handy for preparing cherries for a tart or clafoutis.

Skimmer/slotted spoon

The best device for skimming the scum from the top of stock-pots, etc. is a large, round, perforated spoon, very shallow – almost flat, in fact – with a long handle like a ladle's. It takes off the scum without disturbing or removing the precious liquid underneath. It can also be used for removing delicate items such as eggs and gnocchi from their poaching liquid, though a slightly deeper slotted spoon of conventional shape can also be used for this. For deep-fat frying you will need a curved spatula or slotted spoon with an insulated handle (of wood or plastic) to remove fritters, etc. safely from the hot fat.

The Kitchen Library

As far as inspiring the cook is concerned, even the finest *batterie de cuisine* that money can buy is no substitute for the written wisdom of the best cookery writers. A good selection of cookery books is therefore an essential feature of any successful kitchen. This doesn't mean you have to have hundreds, or even dozens of volumes. Like the over-stocked larder, the over-stacked bookshelf can do more harm than good, stifling rather than releasing the cook's sense of possibility.

Hundreds of thousands of cookery books must have been written, and no doubt almost all of them have had at least one or two worthwhile things to say. One could say the same of just about everybody one ever meets – but that doesn't mean you want them all to become your friends. In the course of using this book the reader will soon find out, from the numerous references and 'borrowing' of recipes, which cookery books have, over the years, become *my* friends. By way of a combined bibliography and acknowledgement, I will list the key influences now.

For their mastery of technique, extraordinary scope, and insight into the fundamentals of good cookery, I would regard the following classic books as verging on the essential:

The Book of Household Management by Mrs Beeton (Ward Lock)
Make sure you get hold of a copy of the original (published 1859–61), and not some updated and bastardized modern version. Hardback facsimiles of the first edition are available in good bookshops, published by Chancellor Press (1986).

The Constance Spry Cookery Book by Constance Spry and Rosemary Hume (J. M. Dent)
First published in 1956, this volume was intended to be a companion to the now extinct Winkfield Place school of cookery and flower-arranging and the recently revived Cordon Bleu School in London. As a written course in the basics of cookery it has never been bettered. It is particularly useful in covering matters of technique, such as filleting of fish, jointing of meat and poultry, liaison of sauces, etc, and in this capacity the comprehensive index can solve a great many kitchen problems as they arise.

French Provincial Cooking by Elizabeth David (Penguin, 1964)
This was the book that lifted British home cooks out of the post-war doldrums
and brought them, as an alternative to the fierce discipline of French *haute
cuisine*, the often simple but always inspiring culinary traditions of the
provinces – the original *cuisine bon marché*. The recipes are genuinely
inspirational, and the book is quite beautifully written.

Besides these excellent general works, my three *sine qua non*s, the following
books deal particularly brilliantly with the special areas on which they focus.

North Atlantic Seafood by Alan Davidson (Penguin, 1979)
As far as our native fish and shellfish are concerned, this is the bible. Scholarly
and comprehensive, yet not only readable but positively entertaining, no fish-
lover should be without it.

English Seafood Cookery by Richard Stein (Penguin, 1988)
Rick Stein runs one of the best fish restaurants in the country, the Seafood
Restaurant in Padstow, Cornwall. His book contains an impressive repertoire
of highly original recipes for just about every fish that is landed on our shores,
as well as a wealth of wisdom on the subject of buying and preparing fish in the
current market-place.

Jane Grigson's Fruit Book (Penguin, 1983)
Much more than just an A–Z of the world's fruit, the range of recipes and depth
of information in this book are staggering. Her other books, particularly the
ones on fish and vegetables, are also excellent, but this one happens to be my
favourite.

The Essentials of Classic Italian Cooking by Marcella Hazan (Macmillan, 1993)
Despite its rather arid title, this is one of the most sumptuous and exciting
works about a nation's regional gastronomy since *French Provincial Cooking*.
Marcella Hazan must take a lot of the credit for the boom in real Italian cooking
in this country in recent years.

On Food and Cooking: the Science and Lore of the Kitchen by Harold McGee
(HarperCollins, 1991)
Not a conventional recipe book, but a critique of our whole food culture, and a
fascinating investigation of the physics and chemistry of cookery. It's not just
for eggheads, though: its demystification of many cooking processes makes it a

riveting read for anybody interested in the 'why' as well as the 'how' of cooking.

This short list of eight completes, at the time of writing, my collection of Desert Island Cookbooks. Though diverse in subject and style, they all, I feel, have something in particular to offer the Bon Marché chef: each, in its own distinctive way, seeks to celebrate the richness and diversity of produce, and to promote cooking to the greater glory of the ingredients, and not of the chef.

CHAPTER TWO

Vegetables

Vegetables are the Bon Marché cook's greatest asset. I say that despite the fact that many home cooks consider the vegetable element to be the most tiresome in preparing any meal. The fact is that vegetables, along with their vegetative relations, herbs, fruits and spices, offer an infinite range of flavours, aromas and textures for the Bon Marcheur to explore.

The number of vegetable species is astounding, the differences between them boundless. How can you compare a cabbage leaf with a fresh garden pea in terms of taste or texture? A cucumber and a carrot? A sweet potato and a head of chicory? A cauliflower and an avocado? If selecting a vegetable accompaniment presents a problem to the home cook, it is simply this: which solution, from the many hundreds so readily available, should be chosen?

Shopping for vegetables

Compared to buying meat or fish, little skill or knowledge is necessary to shop successfully for vegetables. The only basic requirement is a sense of adventure. With close inspection, just about anybody can see whether a particular item is good and fresh or past its best. The more subtle indicators of quality, or the lack of it, will be dealt with under individual entries in the alphabetical guide to vegetables below. Apart from that, successful vegetable shopping is merely a question of getting access to quality vegetables and avoiding a few obvious pitfalls.

Where to buy vegetables

Greengrocers

Top-quality greengrocers with a wide range of seasonal fruit and vegetables are, like good butchers and fishmongers, a rare and threatened breed. If you're lucky enough to have one locally, the alphabetical guide at the end of this chapter will help you take full advantage. If, on the other hand, your most convenient local greengrocer falls into the 'distinctly shabby' category, then you have a problem. Effecting a remedy can be hard, but it is not impossible. If alternative outlets are only to be found at a tiresome distance, and you plan to put down roots where you are living, it is well worth a try. Once you have shopped there often enough to establish yourself as a valued customer, start dropping hints to your greengrocer that the condition of his produce leaves a bit to be desired: 'These cabbages look a bit tired,' you might say. 'I don't suppose you have any fresher out the back?' If it is the limited range that irks you, try politely asking for things you're pretty sure he hasn't got – radicchio, celeriac, fennel, sweet potatoes, etc. Perhaps you will be told that 'there isn't much call for it'. Ask if he can get some anyway, just for you – it is not inconceivable that he will take your individual order, provided that you want a reasonable quantity of whatever it is. The chances are it will only cost him the price of a phone call.

The best tactic of all, if you can find the allies, is a joint attack. I once conducted a most successful campaign in league with a neighbour. I had asked my local greengrocer near Shepherd's Bush, who was otherwise excellent, why he didn't sell Savoy cabbage. He replied that he was convinced it wouldn't sell. I mentioned this to my neighbour, a keen cook herself, and suggested that she should innocently ask for Savoy cabbage the next time she went into the shop. She said she not only would, but she'd pass the message on to a friend who lived round the corner. This little tripartite conspiracy was enough to convince the doubting grocer: the following week I was delighted to see a dozen crisp heads of emerald-green Savoys taking pride of place at the front of his display. He had no trouble shifting them either, and has continued to sell them ever since. A few months later we pulled off a similar coup with butternut squash.

Food markets

As you would hope, there are few better places to buy good fruit and veg than a good fruit and veg market. There are also few places more fun to shop. Competition can literally be between neighbouring stalls, so that elegant displays of fresh produce piled high in neat rows or towering mounds compete spectacularly for your attention. The visual appeal is often backed up with a rowdy cacophony of vocal advertising, bringing to your attention the bargains of the day – and occasionally less practical information, such as the fact that a rival stallholder is sporting a toupee!

Such markets are the happiest of hunting grounds for the Bon Marché shopper: if you don't like the look, or the price, of the asparagus on one stall, you can try another. And if you want to buy in bulk, then you can bargain for a deal on, say, a crate of oranges, a sack of potatoes or a bag of onions.

The timing of your trip is also worth a little thought; if you want to have the pick of the best produce, go early; but if you want to take pot luck with the giveaway bargains, go near the end of the day. The stallholders are loath to take away with them half-empty boxes of ripe fruit and veg that are likely to get battered and bruised on the way to the warehouse – so instead they'll let you have them at knock-down prices.

Supermarkets

Vegetables are the one example of fresh produce where the quality and range on offer in the big supermarkets are often as good, or even better, than that generally available in specialized outlets. Supermarkets also tend to be more thorough in providing information about the origin and possible culinary uses of the vegetables they sell. The fact that these are clearly marketing ploys – nobody is going to buy a vegetable they have no idea how to cook – is no reason to disregard them.

The three main reasons – all related – why buying vegetables in the supermarket is not always satisfactory, are packaging, price and an over-reliance on produce imported from abroad. The first two I will consider here, the third further down (see 'English versus Imported', below) as it applies to vegetables wherever you buy them.

The packaging policy of supermarkets over recent years has been a work of sly genius. Take French beans (actually almost always Kenyan). Ten years ago you would have found these loose in a tray on the counter, picked up a few handfuls, popped them into a polythene bag and wheeled the trolley on. Then came those handy polythene boxes, covered in cellophane. They meant you didn't have to grope around in the tray, and risk getting a little dirt under your nails. They also meant that there was no need to weigh the beans at the checkout – the price on the packet could be keyed straight into the till. A few extra pence was all you had to pay for this extra convenience. True, it meant you couldn't choose exactly how many beans you wanted (funny how those packs always contain slightly too much for two, not quite enough for a family of four) – and when you got home you would still have to top, tail and wash the beans. But it was progress.

Once we had got used to this little luxury, it was again superseded: these days you can buy your French beans in even neater little polythene packs. The beans inside are of uniform length, topped and tailed, and entirely ready for cooking. Okay, they're a bit pricey for French beans – but so much effort saved!

The supermarkets would argue that this is what the customer wants. Many of them would also point out that they present a choice: and sure enough, a good number do offer an alternative of self-selection in the 'old-fashioned' manner. But this is the really sneaky bit. Have you ever noticed how close in price the self-service vegetables are to the ones in the handy polythene packs? Just close enough, in fact, to make most people think, 'Why not spend the extra cash? This little pack is so clean and neat and handy, after all.' The fact is that if the price of the convenient pack genuinely reflected the extra costs involved – making and transporting the packaging, trimming and washing the vegetables, filling the pack, labelling it, and arranging it on the shelves – then the price would be so extortionate compared to that of the loose vegetables that nobody would dream of buying the pack.

So what happens is that the price of the loose vegetables is artificially raised, and the price of the packaged version slightly lowered, so that the difference is not too alarming. The result is that customers buying loose vegetables are under the reassuring illusion that they are getting them at bargain prices, whilst for just a few extra pence, the pack-pickers can distinguish themselves from the *hoi polloi* who are getting their hands grubby.

This is one reason I am proud to be one of the grubby-handed who are content to top and tail and wash their beans at home – the more of us there are, the smaller the percentage of produce that will be overpackaged, and the fairer the price we will all pay.

There is another reason. Choosing loose vegetables by hand allows me to select the best of the bunch: the smallest, firmest courgettes; the tightest, greenest cabbages; the fleshiest, freshest mushrooms – all of which are all the better for not being suffocated in cellophane.

Use-by dates

What used to be 'sell-by dates' are no longer permitted – just as well, as they were confusing in the extreme, saying, for example, 'Sell by 11 Feb' on the top, and 'Eat within 3 days of purchase' at the side. Practical logicians were baffled by the seemingly contradictory advice they were being given: say they bought the item on the 7th, well, they were supposed to eat it within 3 days, i.e. by the 10th. But the supermarket would have been happy to keep it on the shelf until the 11th, and had they bought it then, it should have been good until the 14th! This deeply disturbing situation was then remedied by the less ambiguous 'use-by' date. Phew!

However, just when you thought it was safe to go back into the supermarket, along comes a whole new concept – the 'display until' date. This is applied primarily to fruit and vegetables. I assume the logic is as follows: the supermarket has deemed that the product in question will remain in a satisfactorily fresh and attractive condition, and therefore on the shelf, until the date in question. Once you, the punter, have taken it out of the supermarket, you're on your own.

Well, actually that suits me fine. I am more than happy to be the judge of when my vegetables are no longer fit for the pot. I have two eyes and a nose, after all.

Organic vegetables

There are people who swear they can taste the difference between organically grown vegetables and those which have been cultivated with the benefit, or otherwise, of chemical fertilizers and pesticides. I do not count myself among them. I do not say this to discount the importance of the organic farming movement: it has my full support. I say it because I believe it does the movement no good if we get side-tracked into a 'Stork versus butter' type of argument, when the real, and urgent, reason why the organic movement needs to be heard is because of the environmental threat posed by intensive farming methods in general, and the ill-considered use of hazardous chemicals in vegetable farming in particular.

Having said that, the organic vegetables I have cooked with have been of the highest quality, with excellent flavour. If you can afford the few extra pence, and you believe in the cause, then you can do no better to further its aims than buy organic produce when you see it. Only with widespread support will the range of organic produce be able to expand, and the prices come down to compete with the wider market. The presence of the Soil Association symbol can be taken as a guarantee that produce is organically grown.

English versus Imported

There can be no doubt that vegetables and fruit of the same kind, from different places, can have markedly different flavours. An enormous number of factors contribute to this: climate, soil, fertilizers, the selected strain of the plant in question, time of harvesting, method of transport, time of transport. Often it is impossible to tell by inspection how good an example of its kind, from a flavour point of view, is the specimen you are looking at. So how do you choose?

If your choice is entirely uninformed by previous experience, then there is not a lot to go on. Some vegetables may be worth a sniff – tomatoes, fennel and celeriac, for example, should all have a pleasing aroma. Others may present specific visual clues to quality – see notes in the alphabetical guide to vegetables below. Otherwise you can do no better than choose whatever is most visually appealing. The important thing is to note the salient details of what you do eventually choose: anything distinctive about its shape or colouring might be relevant but, most importantly, note the country of origin (it should be marked; if it isn't, the stallholder/shopkeeper should be able to tell you). That way, if you don't like your Dutch tomatoes, you can make a point of looking for Italian ones next time, and gradually build up a databank of personal preferences and dislikes.

For what it is worth, I will mention a few of my own preferred sources for imported vegetables in the alphabetical guide below. Others may not always agree, but one thing I am convinced about is the reliably high quality of most home-produced vegetables – provided they are in season. This is not just patriotism. In this country we have a tradition of growing top-quality vegetables that goes back hundreds of years and still thrives – from the huge market gardens of Kent or the Vale of Evesham, right down to the tiniest city allotment on which a pensioner is trying to grow a record-breaking marrow.

Besides the fact that the British are simply good at growing vegetables, there is the travel factor: British fruit and vegetables destined for British shops do not have far to go. The Bon Marché shopper can therefore find home-grown vegetables not long picked that have lost none of their goodness and flavour to the stresses of travel and the natural processes of ageing. I mentioned earlier that I wouldn't be able to tell an organically grown specimen from an ordinary one. But I would like to think I could taste the difference between an English carrot just plucked from the earth, and one grown in Holland under glass and pulled 5 days earlier.

For this section I am indebted to the thorough appraisal of the subject in Harold McGee's *On Food and Cooking: The Science and Lore of the Kitchen.*

Most fresh fruits and vegetables remain alive after they are harvested, in the sense that cell activity within the plant attempts to carry on as normal, though it now has to do so without the benefit of water or nutrients from the soil. A bought vegetable is, in a sense, dying, but not dead. Correct storage is therefore a matter of 'keeping it alive' for as long as possible, always bearing in mind that the sooner you eat it, the more full of life, and therefore taste, it is likely to be.

Vegetables lose condition – and therefore become inedible – for two main reasons:

1   infection from external sources (microbes, moulds, etc.)

2   actions by enzymes within the plant itself.

Any method of storing vegetables to prolong their usable life must therefore be aimed at preventing 1, and delaying the inevitability of 2.

Any physical damage to a plant is likely to increase its vulnerability to 1: cuts and bruises will break cells which can then leak nutritious fluids for the opportunistic mould spores to feed on. I understand perfectly why so many supermarkets choose to have their fruit and vegetables displayed at the entrance to their store: it is to create that 'feel-good moment', when customers walk through the door and find themselves surrounded by a huge display of colourful fresh produce – it gets their spending juices flowing. Unfortunately, it also encourages them to load up with fruit and veg before they move on to the cans, jars, packets and bottles – heavy weaponry to mount an assault on the vulnerable produce beneath. Much more sensible to wheel your trolley to the far end of the store, and shop backwards, leaving fruit and veg to the end. Similarly, it is common sense to pack delicate vegetables and fruits separately and carefully at the checkout, and to try to ensure they do not roll around in the boot of your car on the way home.

When you unpack at home it is worth quickly checking the produce to see what damage has been done. Any badly cut or seriously damaged leaves or stalks on cabbages, lettuces, celery heads, etc. should be removed at the base before the item is put away.

Many spores and microbes are naturally present in the air. You might think it would help to protect your vegetables from these if you wrapped them in clingfilm. The only problem with this is that, whilst helping to combat 1, it also starves the plant (which remember, is still trying to breathe) of oxygen. This in turn leads to cell damage, and the acceleration of the problems associated with 2. Better to store fruits and vegetables in paper bags or perforated cellophane, both of which are gas- and water-permeable.

Refrigeration

A refrigerator is an appliance designed specifically for slowing down the natural decline of vegetables (2, above) as well as other foodstuffs. But before I discuss its proper deployment, it is worth mentioning that a number of vegetables (and many fruits, see next chapter) do not benefit from refrigeration – generally speaking, those which are used to a warm climate. At the low temperatures of a refrigerator (3–4°C), cell activity in such plants is not merely slowed down, it is halted, and the plant starts to deteriorate. For this reason, the following vegetables should *not* be kept in the fridge:

* Red and yellow peppers can benefit from refrigeration, perhaps because they have finished ripening, and the cells are less active.

aubergines	cucumbers	potatoes
avocados	green peppers*	tomatoes
courgettes		

The ideal temperature for storing the above is about 8–12°C – the temperature of a cool larder. If you wish to ripen avocados or tomatoes further they should be kept in a warm, airy and well-lit place. A windowsill is ideal in summer, and in winter also if it is not too draughty.

Most other vegetables, especially those comprised of leaves and stems, will benefit from refrigeration, at as near 0°C as possible (because the moisture content of the cells in such plants contains a solution of salts and sugars, it will not actually freeze until the temperature drops several degrees below zero). However, as we tend to keep other foods in the fridge that would be damaged at freezing point, the standard compromise is 3–4°C. All the best modern fridges have an accurate temperature gauge.

Freezing

One way to counteract the natural decline in the condition of vegetables is to halt it altogether. Freezing stops the respiration of plants in its tracks, thereby killing the plant tissues and crystallizing their water content, so that chemical activity comes almost to a complete standstill.

As with meat (see page 192), the formation of ice crystals damages the cell structure of vegetables when they are frozen, but the extent of the damage varies according to the type of vegetable, the speed at which it is frozen, and at how many degrees below freezing it is then stored.

Freezing at home

Even deep-freezing, however, does not halt the activity of enzymes altogether, which means that over weeks and months vegetables stored in a freezer can spoil, losing colour, flavour and vitamin content. To minimize this, fresh vegetables which are to be frozen at home should first be blanched: this involves immersing the vegetables in boiling water for just long enough to inactivate the enzymes – 1–2 minutes will suffice – then cooling them rapidly (by plunging them in iced water) to prevent further damage to the cell walls. When cold, the vegetables should be thoroughly dried, and frozen in a bag that is as air- and watertight as possible. This is best achieved by using your lungs to 'vacuum-pack' the vegetables, by placing them in a polythene bag and sucking the air out, then twisting and sealing the bag with a wire tie. Then place the vegetables in the freezer, which should be turned to the coldest possible setting.

In my experience only a few vegetables survive the freezing process sufficiently well to be worth serving *au naturel*, i.e. whole and simply steamed or stir-fried. They are:

artichokes (hearts only)
broad beans
peas
spinach (which should be squeezed as dry as possible after blanching)
sorrel (ditto)
sweetcorn
leafy herbs (see page 424 for details)

Runner and French beans retain good flavour and a passable, though slightly flabby, texture. If you grow vegetables and are prone to gluts, then obviously it makes good sense to freeze some, but if they are not on the above list then the best policy may be to make them into a simple purée or, if you have the time, a finished soup, and freeze that. Soups, especially smooth creamy soups (there is no texture to spoil), freeze extremely well, and would be likely to pass as fresh to even the most refined palate, especially if they have only been in the freezer for a month or so.

Buying frozen vegetables

Even in the dead of winter there is still a wide choice of fresh home-grown vegetables – not just roots, but cabbage, cauliflower, greens, sprouts, curly kale, broccoli and many others. To supplement these, just about everything we grow here in the summer, and more besides, is imported from all over the world. What need is there to have recourse to the freezer?

You might reply that there are always emergencies, and you would have a point. The greengrocer may close at 6 p.m. and the supermarket at 8 p.m., so what happens when you miss them both? You go to the corner shop and fish around in the deep-freeze. From what you are likely to find there, all I can recommend, tentatively, are peas, broad beans and spinach. Peas and beans that are labelled 'baby', 'young' (or are alleged to be a member of some unlikely country club) may be marginally preferable to those that are not. Spinach is probably the best bet of all, especially if it is then creamed (see SPINACH in the alphabetical guide below).

Canned, pickled and dried vegetables

Each of these methods of preserving vegetables exploits a different principle to the same basic end: destroying micro-organisms and halting the action of enzymes that would break down the structure of the vegetable. Canning does this by heating a can containing the vegetable to a point where the dangerous agents are deactivated – the contents are protected from further contamination by a hermetic seal. Canning is still the most common of the preserving techniques, but it has been in steady decline ever since the freezing of food became industrially viable. In general, canned vegetables are inferior to either fresh or frozen, in taste, texture and nutritional value. But there are some canned vegetables of interest to the Bon Marché cook, either as a very usable standby, or because they offer a particularly distinctive taste. These include tomatoes, French petits pois (see page 83), some types of beans, and other pulses; they will be covered in more detail in the alphabetical guides, both here and under pulses in Chapter 7.

Pickling works by changing the ph value of foods, making them so acidic that potentially harmful microbes become ineffective. A variation on the pickling theme involves fermentation; the action begins by treating the vegetable with a brine; at the right temperature this encourages a natural cultivation of acid-producing bacteria (this is what gives sauerkraut, or pickled cabbage, its distinctive flavour). Everyone recognizes the distinct taste of vegetables pickled in vinegar. In my view, most pickled vegetables taste more of vinegar than vegetable. Though I wouldn't begrudge anyone a penchant for pickled onions, or pickled anything else, the pickled vegetables I find most worthwhile are those which retain or develop a flavour or texture uniquely their own. I would include beetroot, gherkins, wild mushrooms and capers on my short list (although salted capers* have the best flavour).

Drying quite simply starves bacteria and mould spores of one of the essential ingredients for their destructive activities: water. Chillies, peppers, tomatoes and mushrooms are among the more worthwhile dried vegetables.

* salting, a technique only rarely applied to vegetables, is a highly effective way of preserving meat and fish. See the respective chapters for details of the procedure.

Growing your own

This is not a gardening book, and I am not an expert gardener. However, I am lucky enough to have been brought up in houses with excellent kitchen gardens, and I am convinced that the taste of home-grown, fresh-picked vegetables and fruit is significantly better than anything you can buy in a shop. Many people regard this as a sentimental view, but there is sound scientific evidence to support my contention. Harold McGee writes:

> It has been shown that the composition of vegetables changes radically in only a few hours after harvest . . . [Sweet]Corn and peas, for example, lose up to 40 per cent of their sugar in six hours at room temperature, either by converting it to starch or using it for energy to stay alive. Bean pods and such stem vegetables as asparagus and broccoli begin to use their sugar to make tough, indigestible, lignified fibres. The sweetness, flavor, and even texture of many vegetables deteriorates quite rapidly, then, and it's no sentimental illusion that corn picked one minute and dropped into boiling water the next just can't be matched.

Besides those vegetables that McGee mentions, I would further argue that root crops and tubers – carrots, parsnips, potatoes, turnips, kohl rabi, swede –

have a wonderful earthy-fresh flavour if cooked within a few hours of being dug up, which is entirely lost if they are stored for any length of time. Best of all, and worlds apart from their cousins in the supermarket and greengrocer, are young broad beans and peas, steamed for just a couple of minutes within an hour of being picked.

Cooking vegetables

The aim of cooking vegetables, historically speaking, has been primarily to render them safer, and more digestible. Boiling vegetables to disintegration point will undoubtedly fulfil both these objectives, but at the price of flavour, texture and nutritional value.

Most vegetables have the highest nutritional value in their raw state, although some have elements which would, in this state, render them indigestible or even toxic. But many raw vegetables have an excellent, crunchy texture, and fine flavour. Do we need to cook them at all? There are purists who insist that we don't, who maintain that every boiled carrot, every braised head of celery, every deep-fried floret of cauliflower, is a criminal waste of vitamins. I can't agree. My view is that if something does you no harm, and particularly if it does you some good (even if that's not the most good it can do you), and if it also happens to taste delicious, then eat it.

This brings me to my main point about cooking vegetables: different techniques applied to the same vegetable can produce vastly different and exciting experiences in both taste and texture – and applied across the whole range of available vegetables the possibilities are almost limitless. I hope anyone who is inclined to think that vegetables are the boring part of cooking a meal will find some relief from their torpor on the pages that follow. To begin with I will consider the general effects of basic cooking techniques, presented in alphabetical order, before moving on to an alphabetical guide to vegetables in which I make appropriate suggestions for particular types.

Boiling

Boiling vegetables is an extremely effective way of heating them through and thereby tenderizing the tougher tissues. Providing they are not overcooked, many boiled vegetables also show an improvement in intensity of flavour. This is because the aromatic molecules and sugars are more active at high temperatures: they 'buzz about' on your tongue, if you like. However, the downside of boiling is what I call the 'tea-bag effect'. The breaking down of the cell walls releases juices that run out of the vegetables and into the cooking water, like the aromatic oils running out of a tea-bag into the hot water in a teapot.

This is obvious when you observe that water in which vegetables are boiled will take on the colour of that vegetable. But as well as colour, the water will also steal flavour and vitamins. And the longer the vegetables are boiled, the more flavour and vitamins will be lost. Eventually the vegetables will have little more going for them than a spent tea-bag.

We cannot eliminate the tea-bag effect altogether: all vegetables, when heated, will lose juices. But we can cook vegetables so that the beneficial effects of eating them hot – tenderness and buzzing flavour molecules – are not outweighed by the negative. This means that if we must boil them, we should do so only until they are just tender, and even still a little crunchy (*al dente*).

In fact very few vegetables need anything more than a few minutes in boiling water, so fast is the transfer of heat to the inside of the vegetable. Leaf vegetables, such as spinach, sorrel and cabbage, need 2–4 minutes. Root vegetables, like carrots, parsnips and turnips, will take 5–15 minutes, depending on the size of the pieces they are cut into. (Only potatoes in large pieces are likely to take upwards of 20 minutes; they, admittedly, may take over half an hour.)

The tea-bag effect can be partially alleviated, and a little extra flavour retained, if vegetables are steamed (see page 44).

If you want to discover just how dramatic the tea-bag effect can be, gently simmer 2 sliced carrots, 2 celery sticks, 1 large onion, 1 parsnip and 1 turnip in 1¾ pts/1 litre boiling water for 1 hour. It's the water that will be worth keeping – a delicious vegetable stock, in fact.

Braising

Braising is an excellent way of cooking many vegetables, particularly those with tough fibres and a high water content, such as fennel and celery. The technique is to cook the vegetables in a moderate heat, either on top of the stove or in the oven, with just enough water or stock to prevent them from sticking – very little liquid is needed, as the vegetables will soon leach out some of their own water content. During braising, as during roasting, much of the water is evaporated from the vegetables, concentrating sugars and other flavours, both in the vegetables themselves and the juices that collect around them. Ovenproof dishes, wide saucepans and even deep frying pans can be used for braising.

CARAMELIZING: at the end of braising, the juices can be allowed to boil dry, and the surface of the vegetable burn just a little, as you push it around the dish with a wooden spoon. This 'caramelizes' some of the sugars in the vegetable, giving a pleasant, toffeeish taste. The effect is rather like roasting, but no oil is necessary to achieve the caramel effect (though a little will certainly help).

Baking

In cooking vegetables, the distinction between baking and roasting, and even braising, is somewhat blurred. We all know what a baked potato is. Other vegetables, notably aubergines, peppers, tomatoes and squashes, can be cooked in the same way – unadulterated except perhaps with a little salt, and placed whole in a hot oven. It is currently fashionable to describe this procedure, when not applied to potatoes, as roasting. I prefer to stick with baking, reserving roasting to describe the process of cooking vegetables in hot fat, with which they are also basted, in a hot oven.

Baking also appropriately describes a very easy and convenient technique that produces particularly delicious results with courgettes, leeks and celery (in each case cut into 2–3-in/5–7.5-cm batons). The vegetables are placed in a greased baking dish or small casserole dotted with butter or trickled with a little olive oil and seasoned with salt and pepper (a crushed garlic clove is an option). This is covered with foil or its own close-fitting lid, and placed in a moderate to hot oven (190°C/375°F/Gas Mark 5) for 30–35 minutes (25 minutes may be enough for small courgettes). The result, not unlike braising, is tender, flavourful pieces of vegetable in a delicious buttery juice. Celery cooked like this is an excellent accompaniment to roast game birds.

Frying (shallow and deep)

Hot fat will affect different vegetables in different ways. Some, such as aubergines, will absorb vast amounts of it into their porous tissues, and become quite saturated. Others, such as courgettes and potatoes, may absorb a little fat into the surface before forming a crispy coating that resists further penetration. Still others, such as French and runner beans, are likely to burn on the surface before they are tenderized in the centre (the dynamics of stir-frying are a little different – see page 45). This means that it is hard to generalize about the effects of frying vegetables, but individual details are given in the alphabetical guide below.

Generally speaking, deep-frying is a more versatile and efficient way of cooking vegetables than shallow, and produces particularly delicious results when the vegetables in question are first dipped in batter. Detailed instructions for a dish of deep-fried vegetables appear on page 119. Cooks enamoured of this technique, as I am, might want to consider investing in a deep-fat fryer. They are safer, cleaner and easier to control than a saucepan full of boiling oil. Various oils can be used for deep frying; sunflower oil is perhaps the healthiest, and groundnut oil is recommended by all the best chippies. For some dishes, the special flavour of olive oil is appropriate, but it cannot be heated to too high a temperature (max 170°C/335°F).

Gratins

Gratin is a loosely applied term which many take to imply the presence of cheese and cream. In fact, it is derived from the French *gratter*, meaning to scrape. This originally referred to the scraping of the delicious burnt crispy bits that always accumulate around the edge of a good gratin.

To my mind there are three essentials that define a gratin: 1) it is baked in the oven in a fairly shallow dish; 2) it has a crispy top; 3) it is invariably delicious. Whilst either grated cheese or breadcrumbs (or both) can be sprinkled on top of a gratin, the crisped surface of the main ingredient itself often produces all the 'gratination' one could want.

Grilling

Along with roasting, grilling is one of the most exciting yet under-explored ways of cooking vegetables, although it is gaining familiarity through the large number of fashionable restaurants that now serve char-grilled vegetables. At home the best, or rather the *essential*, tool for the job is a cast-iron griddle pan, the basic principle of which is explained on page 21. Though vegetables can be roasted under a conventional, overhead, eye-level domestic grill, the results are nothing like as satisfactory. The recipe for a salad of grilled mixed vegetables on page 120 suggests the type of vegetables that are classically brought together in the Italian version of such a dish, but others, in particular leeks or French beans, are delicious if grilled after par-boiling – for details, see the alphabetical guide below.

Roasting

Cooking in shallow oil in a fairly hot oven has given us one of the most widely loved of all English vegetable accompaniments, the roast potato. But for many cooks that's where the roasting of vegetables begins and ends. This is a pity, because roasting brings a rich sweetness and concentration of flavour to a whole host of vegetables. In particular, members of the onion family – garlic bulbs and shallots, as well as onions of all sizes – are delicious if roasted whole in their skins. Roots, including artichoke, celeriac, parsnip, turnip and sweet potato, are also excellent. All kinds of oil can be used for roasting. Sunflower is probably best if you want the flavour of your vegetables to speak entirely for itself, but good olive oil produces fine results with a distinctive flavour. You can also roast vegetables in the fat around a joint of meat, but you will probably have to add extra fat – goose or duck fat is ideal – for really good results. With the exception of potatoes and eddoes (see page 69), it is not necessary to parboil vegetables before roasting.

There are two vital tips for successful roasting of vegetables: the first is that the oil or fat should be thoroughly pre-heated in the oven before you begin. The second is that you should not stint on the quantity of oil or fat. It should be at least ½ in/1 cm deep when all the vegetables are put in, though remember, the level will rise as the oil is displaced by the vegetables. Roasting times vary from vegetable to vegetable, so it may be appropriate to add different vegetables at intervals (or cut those that take a long time, such as potatoes, into smaller pieces). The recipe for winter vegetables roasted in goose fat on page 122 will act as a reliable guideline for roasting vegetables in general. Varying times for different vegetables (in a fairly hot oven) are suggested in the alphabetical guide below.

Steaming

Steaming, like boiling, is a simple method of tenderizing vegetables without adulterating them with any foreign flavours, except perhaps salt and pepper. For many vegetables steaming is preferable to boiling because it reduces the severity of the tea-bag effect (see BOILING above). However, you need to be just as vigilant about cooking times when steaming vegetables: over-steamed, mushy carrots are no more appetizing, and probably no more nutritious, than over-boiled ones.

The water in your steamer should be boiling rapidly when you add your vegetables, and you should steam with the lid on. Follow this procedure and steaming takes no longer than boiling – for leaves and baby vegetables 2–3 minutes are often enough. Always let your mouth be the final arbiter of 'doneness'.

Stir-frying

This traditional Oriental method of cooking brings out the best in a lot of vegetables, releasing their sugars and aromatic qualities while retaining a good crunchy texture and excellent colour. The wok is the key: a high, even heat is conducted right up the sides of the pan, which, because they are sloping, ensure that the contents tend to fall back down to the middle when stirred or, in the hands of a skilful operator, dextrously tossed. This means that as long as the contents of the wok are kept on the move, everything will cook fast and evenly without staying put on the surface long enough to burn.

The skill of cooking in a wok is easily acquired. The first important rule to learn is that nothing should be so large that it requires more than a few minutes to heat through. Celery and carrots are therefore best chopped into thin slices or sticks, broccoli or cauliflower cut into small florets, mushrooms sliced, etc. There are not many vegetables that cannot become part of a stir-fry, but a good general rule is that vegetables which are not palatable when cooked *al dente*, such as potatoes, turnips and other roots, are best avoided.

It is almost impossible to use a wok on an electric hob unless you have the special flat-bottomed variety. You can, however, attempt to stir-fry in a conventional frying pan, but you should allow 1–2 minutes extra cooking time. You will also have to be very vigilant about keeping the vegetables on the move in the pan, tossing and stirring to prevent them from sticking and burning.

Trifolati

The Italian word *trifolati* describes vegetables, usually courgettes or aubergines (onions and tomatoes can be included), that have been cooked in olive oil until they are completely tender, but too slowly to brown or burn. A large amount of the vegetables' naturally high water content is thus cooked out, and they become soft and creamy with a wonderful intensity of flavour. Garlic is practically *de rigueur* as a flavouring, and a little fresh chilli adds a delightful piquancy. The recipe on page 107 shows how courgettes cooked in this way can be adapted to make both a soup and a pasta sauce.

Wilting

Somewhere between braising, steaming and stir-frying, 'wilting' is a fast and simple technique which gives delicious results with leaf vegetables such as spinach, greens, Swiss chard, pak-choy and sorrel. The leaves, which should be perfectly fresh, are trimmed and washed, then thrown into a saucepan or wok on a high heat, with just a tiny amount of water to ensure they don't burn on initial contact with the pan. The leaves will quickly release a little of their own juice, and should be turned and stirred for just 1–2 minutes until they have all wilted, i.e. become wet and floppy. Any excess water should then be drained off (in the case of spinach there is likely to be quite a lot) and the vegetables can then be tossed in a little butter.

Wilting should be done at the last possible minute before serving and the vegetables eaten at once. Leaves cooked in this way are sweet and tender, with the stems still crunchy.

ALPHABETICAL GUIDE TO VEGETABLES

The cooking suggestions in this guide are not intended to be comprehensive, merely to indicate the wide range of possibilities for each vegetable.

Where vegetables are suitable for freezing, this is indicated in the text. Vegetables that are commercially grown in this country are indicated with the word '*native*', followed by the months they are in season. So '*native*: May–June' under Asparagus indicates that you can expect to find English asparagus in the shops in May and June.

Artichoke
(Globe)

The globe or leaf artichoke is the flower-bud of a member of the thistle family. There are a great many varieties, from huge round green artichokes to small pointy purple ones, but the basic preparations are the same. Most commonly the stems are cut off ½ in/1 cm or so below the head, and whole globes are boiled and served hot with melted butter, hollandaise sauce or a vinaigrette. The edible parts are the fleshy bases of the leaves, and the heart to which they attach. The leaves are traditionally plucked one by one, dipped in the sauce, and the edible part bitten off, the rest of the leaf being discarded. When all the leaves are eaten the 'choke' (which is a mass of rather hairy strands, in fact the florets of the bud) must be scooped out before the real prize – the tender flesh of the heart – can be tackled with a knife and fork.

In Italy and France, where artichokes are highly regarded, plentiful and cheap, many recipes use the hearts only, in salads, or cut up and cooked in any number of ways. I think it is very extravagant to throw away the leaves: the edible parts of bigger ones can be snipped off with kitchen scissors and incorporated into the dish (as in the Artichoke and Thyme Tart on page 427), or dressed separately and served as a salad – or, at the very least, munched as chef's perks as you go along!

Choosing artichokes

Choose globes with firm, glossy leaves, avoiding those which have shrivelled or browning tips.

Basic preparation

Before boiling, artichokes should be thoroughly rinsed to remove dirt and bugs. Better still, soak them upside down in a bowl of salted water for 1 hour. Any cut surfaces of raw artichokes should be rubbed with lemon juice to prevent discolouration and spoiling.

Cooking methods

BOILED: 20–35 minutes, depending on size, in plenty of water acidulated with a little lemon juice. Boiled artichokes are done when one of the inner leaves can be plucked without too much resistance. Do not attempt this test without first removing the artichokes from the boiling water.

BRAISED: cooked artichoke hearts can be braised, in a little meat juice, stock or wine, then finished with a sprinkling of chopped fresh parsley and a generous dollop of double cream.

COLD/SALAD: the most common way of serving cooked hearts. A mixed salad of cubed artichoke hearts and new potatoes, with a mustardy vinaigrette, is particularly good.

DEEP-FRIED: slices of cooked heart can be battered and deep-fried.

GRATIN: slices of cooked heart and leaf trimmings are tossed in oil or melted butter, mixed with chopped hard-boiled eggs, double cream or béchamel sauce, topped with fresh breadcrumbs and grated Parmesan or Gruyère cheese, and browned under the grill.

Native: June–July.

Asparagus

To be enjoyed at its absolute best, there is no doubt that asparagus must be cooked the same day it is cut – preferably within a few hours. Only those who grow their own are likely to enjoy this privilege. Making the best of what is available in the shops is a good challenge for the aspiring Bon Marcheur. There are a number of varieties available – long thin spruce, fat white American purple. Freshness is more important than type, but I tend to avoid the huge, woody spears imported from the USA.

Choosing asparagus

If your greengrocer stocks locally grown asparagus, then you have a reasonable chance of finding a bunch not too long cut and in decent condition: the sensible thing is to quiz him about the origin of his stock and the times of delivery, and coordinate your shopping accordingly. Examining the cuts at the base of each stem will give you some idea of how recently it has been harvested. Stems which are beginning to lose their rigidity, or whose tips are in the least dry or withered, are useless.

Imported asparagus, which comes mainly from Cyprus, Israel and the USA, is a great disappointment for the price. It is perhaps worth including a few stems in a plate of grilled mixed vegetables, where the added hint of charcoal, and the companionship of other noble vegetables, will restore some of its dignity.

The best asparagus deserves to be a course on its own, and can be served with melted butter, hollandaise sauce, vinaigrette or, a personal favourite of mine, with top-quality olive oil, coarse black pepper, and a few shavings of fresh Parmesan cheese.

Basic preparation

If the bases of the stems are tough and woody, they should be further trimmed. Some cooks like to peel off the tougher skin at the base end in an attempt to make the whole stem edible. I am quite content to leave whatever is tough on the side of my plate.

Cooking methods

BOILED: there are tall pots designed specifically for the purpose of boiling asparagus – the bound bunch of stems is placed tips uppermost in boiling water, which should be about 2–3 in/5–7.5 cm deep in the pot, so that the tips are left to cook in the steam. If you don't possess such a saucepan, careful placing of the stems in a normal pan may still keep the tips out of the water. Otherwise steaming is a good method. Cooking will take from as little as 8 to as many as 25 minutes, depending on the size, age and type: the fresher and thinner the stems, the shorter the cooking time – you will have to test by tasting. Asparagus is ready when the tips are tender, but not disintegrating, and the stem just on the soft side of *al dente*.

STEAMED: 8–25 minutes, test as above.

STIR-FRIED: tips only, of very fresh asparagus, can be included in a stir-fry.

Native: May–June.

Asparagus pea

Not commercially available at the time of writing. I mention this curious pod with okra-like ridges because it is catching on among enthusiastic kitchen gardeners and appears very occasionally in restaurants. I wouldn't be surprised if we start seeing it on the shelves of the larger supermarkets. The vital tip is that the pods should be harvested when no more than 1 in/2.5 cm long; after this they become tough, fibrous and quite unpalatable. They are eaten, pod-and-all, like mangetout, and should be simply steamed or boiled for just 5 minutes, then tossed in butter.

Aubergine

The aubergine has the reputation of being a 'difficult' vegetable. This is true only in the sense that, unlike most vegetables, it cannot be boiled. That seems a feeble reason for excluding it from one's repertoire, and a number of very simple treatments can give the most delicious results.

Choosing aubergines

The skin of a good aubergine is shiny, purple (though whitish-green and yellow varieties are available on the Continent), and tight-fitting, unblemished by bruises or wrinkles. It should feel firm to the touch and not too light or hollow. When cut, the flesh should be creamy-white. There is no reason not to pick the largest aubergines, provided they conform to these specifications.

Basic preparation

Most recipes recommend that aubergines are cut, sprinkled with salt and left for an hour or so before cooking, in order to leach out the bitter juices. This is probably advisable, but only essential to my mind if you are grilling or frying thin slices of aubergine. Long, slow cooking seems to neutralize any bitter taste.

Cooking methods

(For Sheila Kidd's Aubergines Three Ways, see page 103.)

BAKED: whole, in a fairly hot oven (200°C/400°F/Gas Mark 6), for 35–40 minutes. The flesh can then be scooped out and eaten hot with salt, pepper and a generous trickle of olive oil; or puréed with garlic, lemon juice and olive oil and served cold as a dip. Or halved and stuffed – for example with coriander pesto (see page 105).

DEEP-FRIED: thin slices, salted, then wiped dry and dipped in batter (see pages 119–120 for more details). If you are cooking aubergine fritters to be enjoyed on their own, rather than as part of a dish of deep-fried mixed vegetables, the palaver of deep-frying can be avoided if you have a large frying pan: shallow-fry the aubergine slices in ½ in/1 cm good, very hot olive oil. A lighter fritter can be made if coated not with batter but a light dusting of seasoned flour. A purée of roasted garlic cloves is an excellent accompaniment.

GRATIN: the classic gratin is the *parmigiana di melanzane*, in which aubergine slices are layered with tomato sauce and topped with melted mozzarella and Parmesan cheese. Elizabeth David's *Italian Food*, and Jane Grigson's *Vegetable Book* both have exemplary recipes.

GRILLED/GRIDDLED: aubergines are an essential part of the grilled mixed vegetable dish on page 120, but are also delicious on their own, dressed with olive oil, slivers of garlic and a squeeze of lemon. Cut into slices or sticks, sprinkle with salt, leave for 1 hour, then wipe thoroughly before grilling.

Avocado

The avocado, which is technically a fruit, has a uniquely high fat content – about 20 per cent – which has earned it the nickname in its native tropics of 'poor man's butter'. Lower than most other fruits in vitamins A and C, it is nevertheless high in the B vitamins and minerals, making it a nutritious part of any diet.

Peculiarly, avocados are incapable of ripening on the tree, hence leaving them there is the most practical way of storing them, enabling commercial growers to stagger their crop over more than half the year. A hard avocado will soon ripen if kept in a warm kitchen. Never attempt to slow the process or prolong the life of a ripe avocado by refrigeration; the fruit is very susceptible to chilling injury, becoming discoloured and losing its proper flavour. Avocados should not be kept in polythene for any length of time – this will deprive them of oxygen and the ripening process will be halted. In short, always keep them at room temperature, unwrapped.

Choosing avocados

Although we import avocados from all over the tropics, as well as from Israel and California, there are, with a few minor variations, two basic kinds in our shops: the bright green-skinned variety, often distinctly pear-shaped; and the slightly smaller Hass variety with a rough, knobbly, purplish-brown skin, sometimes almost black in colour. It is a matter of personal taste, but I think the Hass variety has a rather better flavour.

To test both kinds of avocado for ripeness, squeeze them gently with the finger tips – the surface should be slightly yielding, especially around the narrower end. In the winter, watch out for avocados that have been stored in the cold for too long: their shiny skin becomes dull, and they will never ripen properly.

Very ripe avocados, perhaps with some bruising, can often be had at knock-down prices from market stalls and greengrocers. Any badly blackened bits can be removed, and the rest of the flesh used in any recipes where mashed or puréed avocados are required.

Basic preparation

I am not a fan of cooked avocado, though numerous recipes exist. In my opinion avocados are best eaten raw, and quite plain, with a dressing made

One of the best uses of over-ripe avocados is in a simple but delectable guacamole, made by mashing the flesh with garlic, fresh chilli, a squeeze of lemon, salt and pepper and (optionally) soured cream.

from the finest olive oil, a squeeze of fresh lemon, salt and black pepper. There are other pleasing combinations: avocado with chicory, with grapefruit, with smoked salmon, with prawns or crab and, of course, in a *tricolore* salad with tomatoes and mozzarella.

Once puréed and acidulated with lemon juice, avocado flesh can be refrigerated and kept for up to 24 hours. Soon after that it will start to discolour.

Bamboo shoots

Chiefly available canned, as used in most Chinese restaurants. They have a curiously acidic, nutty flavour, and can make a handy addition to a stir-fry, though their flavour is improved if they are briefly blanched first in freshly boiled water.

Fresh bamboo shoots can be found in the Chinese markets in London's Soho and, who knows, they may spread further afield. There are two types, spring and winter. The winter ones are smaller and sweeter. After brief blanching they can be eaten crunchy and cold in salads, or incorporated into stir-fries.

Bean sprouts

Technically a pulse. See pages 104 and 296 for bean sprout recipes and how to sprout your own beans.

Beetroot

Until recently beetroot has had the reputation in this country of being a rather plebeian, even barbaric vegetable, somewhat lacking in finesse. Inevitably, as peasant cooking has become fashionable, the lurid purple root has found a few champions, and become almost trendy. It is sweet and distinctive in flavour, and there are many ways to cook it, so why not?

Choosing beetroot

Beetroot can be bought fresh and raw, pre-cooked and vacuum-packed, or pickled in jars. Whilst all forms have their uses (pickled beetroot is particularly delicious with cold pork, cold beef and pastrami), the best flavour comes from carefully chosen fresh roots. Pre-cooked beetroot is convenient if you are in a hurry, and makes a handy standby as it can be kept for several days in the fridge. Avoid brands with a great profusion of E-numbers and preservatives: I have even seen some with artificial sweeteners, which seems a horrible idea.

Fresh beetroots should be bought unwashed, with their whiskery roots intact and a good few inches of unbroken stalk at the top. Beetroots bruise and bleed very easily, so avoid those which are soft, beginning to wrinkle or clearly losing some of their juices. Choose roots the size of an eating apple or larger: the smaller ones can be almost too sweet, lacking the earthy taste that comes with maturity.

Basic preparation

Most recipes involving beetroot specify that it should be pre-cooked. This can be done by boiling or baking; either way, the vegetables should be delicately rinsed to remove dirt (harsh scrubbing will cause them to bleed during cooking) and the stalks and roots should be left intact. They can then be gently simmered in well-salted water for about 1½ hours or baked for 3 hours in a slow oven (150°C/300°F/Gas Mark 2), in a baking dish covered in foil, with a little water in the bottom to stop them drying out. When cool, beetroot thus prepared can be kept covered, or wrapped in clingfilm, in the fridge, but they should not be peeled or trimmed of stalk and root until it is time to use them.

Cooking methods

Prepared as above, beetroot can be peeled and sliced or chopped while cold or still warm, heated through with a little butter or cream and served as an accompanying vegetable. It is particularly good with white fish. When cold it can be sliced and tossed with a sharp vinaigrette and finely chopped fresh parsley, and served as a salad.

DEEP-FRIED: thin slices of cooked beetroot are remarkably good deep-fried in batter.

GRATIN: slice cooked beetroot, layer with cream and a good sprinkling of grated Parmesan and Gruyère cheese, top with fresh breadcrumbs and bake in a hot oven (220°C/425°F/Gas Mark 7) for 12–15 minutes until browned.

For my own version of Bortsch, a quick beetroot soup served with slices of salt beef, see page 105.

Native: June–November.

Breadfruit

This large, heavy fruit, up to 10 in/25 cm in diameter, is a native of the South Pacific, but also grows in the West Indies, and is often encountered in ethnic markets over here. Breadfruit is an appropriate name, as the fruit is starchy and very calorific.

Choosing breadfruit

Breadfruit travels and keeps well, and usually reaches market in fairly good condition. Its thick rind, with a mosaic-like pattern, turns from yellow to greenish-brown when ripe.

Cooking breadfruit

Peeled and cut into pieces, breadfruit can be treated pretty much like the potato, and added to soups, stews and curries. A traditional West Indian pudding is made by mashing cooked breadfruit with coconut milk, dark brown sugar and cinnamon, and baking it in a moderate oven (180°C/350°F/Gas Mark 4) for about 35 minutes, until browned on top.

Cooking methods

BAKED: whole in its skin in a moderate oven (180°C/350°F/Gas Mark 4) for at least 1 hour.
BOILED: for about 20 minutes in salted water, then toss in butter or mash like potatoes.
FRIED/DEEP-FRIED: thickish slices can be shallow-fried; thin slices make delicious crisps when deep-fried.
ROAST: par-boil first, then as for potatoes.

Broad beans

I have already mentioned the delights of freshly picked baby broad beans, lightly steamed (see page 40). Those who do not grow their own will be dealing with larger, tougher beans, but they can be worthwhile none the less.

Choosing broad beans

Choose small, undamaged, fresh-looking pods, avoiding large ones that are tough or leathery, with very obviously fat beans bulging out like rabbits swallowed by a python. There is considerably more pod than bean, and to be generous you will need about 12 oz/350 g pods per person for a decent portion.

Larger beans, and commercially frozen brands, are less bitter if their grey-green skins are removed after cooking.

Cooking methods

BOILED/STEAMED: 2–6 minutes, depending on age. Besides being served *au naturel* as an accompanying vegetable, cooked beans can be served puréed, as a soup, or cold in salads.

COLD/SALAD: tiny beans, and even very young whole pods, can be eaten raw. The sweet green kernels of cooked beans are delicious mixed with crispy bits of bacon, pancetta, ham or chorizo, and tossed in olive oil with a squeeze of lemon.

Native: May–August.

FREEZES WELL.

See also page 297 for uses of dried broad beans.

Broccoli

This flowering shoot of the cabbage family was given a bad name when Barbara Bush banned it from the White House. It never deserved such ignominy, for it is an excellent vegetable that stands out on its own for its fine flavour and texture.

Choosing broccoli

There are two principal kinds of broccoli in the shops: the purple sprouting variety which is grown in this country has small flower-heads with a purplish tinge, and a leafy stem; the brighter green variety, also known as calabrese, has fatter stalks, fewer leaves and a much larger flowering head. Both are good, though I prefer our own purple variety when it is in season. Whichever you choose, make sure you pick broccoli with dark, tightly packed, fresh-looking flower-heads. Broccoli which is beginning to look limp, or whose flowers are turning a yellowish-brown, should be avoided.

Basic preparation

Some recommend that broccoli stalks should be stripped of their leaves. I imagine this is because when broccoli is over-cooked, the leaves will be conspicuously mushy. But provided broccoli is kept *al dente*, there is no need to remove the leaves; indeed, they are particularly delicious. All that is required, then, is a quick rinse, and trimming of damaged leaves and tough stalks. Larger heads of broccoli can be cut into smaller florets to speed up cooking time.

Cooking methods

Simply boiled, or steamed, broccoli makes a fine course on its own served with hollandaise sauce or, even better, the Anchovy Dressing on page 165.

BOILED: 6–10 minutes, until the stalks are just tender.

DEEP-FRIED: small florets, pre-blanched and patted dry, can be deep-fried in batter.

GRATIN: I prefer Broccoli Cheese to cauliflower; blanch until just tender, place in a dish, cover with a thick béchamel sauce flavoured with good Cheddar cheese, top with a little more cheese and fresh breadcrumbs, if liked, and brown in a hot oven (220°C/425°F/Gas Mark 7).

STEAMED: preferable to boiled as the delicate flower-heads are less likely to be damaged.

STIR-FRIED: tiny florets make an excellent addition to a stir-fry.

Native: February–mid May.

Brussels sprouts

Many people groan at the mention of Brussels sprouts. I think there are two reasons for this: first, sprouts are often sold in a pretty shabby state; second, they are all too often over-boiled to a mushy, bitter pulp. When both problems are remedied, sprouts come into their own.

Choosing Brussels sprouts

Pick only tightly packed, hard little sprouts, as near round as possible – these are less inclined to become waterlogged during cooking than loose, spongy ones. Avoid sprouts with yellowing or flaccid outside leaves. If you grow your own, you will know that sprouts are best after the first frost.

Basic preparation

Trim a little off the base of each sprout, taking with it one or two of the outside leaves. You should be left with a shiny, clean, even more compact little ball. It is not essential to cut a cross in the base, as some texts recommend, though it may reduce the cooking time by a minute or two.

Cooking methods

BOILED: in just enough salted water to cover, for 7–10 minutes.
GRATIN: as for broccoli above.
STEAMED: the best method of simple preparation, 7–10 minutes.
STIR-FRIED: an unusual but rewarding way to cook sprouts; shred or roughly grate them, and stir-fry for 5–6 minutes with 2 tsp of finely chopped fresh ginger root. Add 1 tbsp sesame oil towards the end of cooking.

Boiled and steamed sprouts are delicious if mashed with cream and plenty of freshly ground black pepper; bacon bits, broken chestnuts or toasted almonds can be added for a little luxury.

Native: October–March.

In February and March, sprout tops are on sale. For cooking guidelines follow suggestions for SPRING GREENS and WINTER GREENS below.

Cabbage

Whole books could, and probably have, been written about cabbage, perhaps the most versatile, certainly the most common, of our leaf vegetables. I will restrict my comments to the problems most often associated wtih selecting and cooking it, and suggest some simple solutions.

Choosing cabbage

A number of varieties are widely available in this country, all of which are good at their best. The hard, Dutch white cabbage keeps well (though not as long as some would have it). Primo is a good dark grey-green variety, which must be bought at its eponymous prime. Hard to beat, for flavour as well as looks, is the crinkle-leaved emerald-green Savoy. There are other varieties too, locally grown and seasonally available. (The CHINESE LEAF is also a cabbage, but sufficiently distinctive in character and application to merit an entry on its own – see below.) Red cabbage which lends itself to very different cooking techniques is a separate entry on page 91.

Whichever you opt for, choose a head which still has the dark green outer leaves surrounding it (unless of course it is a white cabbage); the leaves should be firm and still stiff: basically a good cabbage is one that looks healthy and alive, as if its roots were still feeding in the ground. Avoid cabbages which have been cut in half and wrapped in clingfilm – they quickly lose condition and become flaccid.

Basic preparation

The first mistake most English people make when preparing a green cabbage is to peel off and discard the dark green outer leaves. With Savoy cabbage in particular this is criminal – there is more flavour in these leaves than in the rest of the cabbage. In Italy it is often the pale heart which is discarded, while the chlorophyll- and sugar-rich outer leaves are lovingly trimmed, carefully rinsed, then perhaps blanched for a couple of minutes before being tossed in a pan with olive oil, a little garlic and pancetta to accompany a roast partridge or rabbit.

Inevitably the very outer leaves may be damaged or browning at the edges, but even these can be trimmed so that what is still succulent is saved for cooking. I use all the outer leaves, trimmed of the tougher, thicker stalks, sometimes keeping back the very pale hearts, of weaker flavour, for stir-frying or for use raw in a salad.

The all too distinctive odour of boiled cabbage, redolent of school and hospital corridors, is the result of boiling too fast and too long. The secret of sweet and succulent cabbage is short steaming or a quick plunge in already boiling water, and no waiting around before you serve it. It can be cut and washed in advance, but should not be cooked until the last possible moment.

It is possible to cook cabbage for a very long time, but it should be done slowly. This is the way with the classic soups and *garbures* of southern France – see page 117 for a simple version.

Cooking methods

BOILED: 3–5 minutes in already boiling salted water.

BRAISED: roughly shredded cabbage can be braised with meat juices, and is particularly delicious if cooked slowly in the liquid surrounding a braising game bird; with partridge this would give you the classic *perdrix aux choux*.

COLD/SALAD: crisp hearts of Savoy or white cabbage can be used for coleslaw, but Chinese leaf is preferable.

FRIED: previously blanched cabbage can be fried with onion and cooked potato to make the ever-pleasing bubble-and-squeak.

GRATIN: see the recipe for Colcannon on page 106.

STEAMED: 3–5 minutes over rapidly boiling water.

STIR-FRIED: the finely shredded hearts can be mixed with bean sprouts, carrots, bamboo shoots and other stir-fry vegetables and flavoured with soy sauce at the end of cooking for a simplified chop suey.

Native: Savoy: March–July. Primo: September–November. White: November–February.

Cardoon

This relative of the artichoke is popular in southern France and the Piedmont region of Italy, less so in this country, though it is easily grown. The cardoon resembles a cross between a head of celery and a thistle (to which it is related).

Choosing cardoons

Buy juicy, crisp young ones, avoiding those with hard or stringy stems.

Basic preparation

Cut away and discard the prickly outer stems – only the inner leaf stalks and firm hearts are eaten. Cut the stalks into lengths of 3–4 in/7.5–10 cm and slice the heart into pieces of a similar size.

Cooking methods

Cardoons should be steamed (for about 25 minutes), or gently braised in stock or acidulated water until tender (30–35 minutes). They are then served with plenty of melted butter or, classically, with an anchovy sauce (see the Anchovy Dressing on page 165). If very young, they can be eaten raw, again dipped in anchovy sauce.

Carrot

Choosing carrots

Despite the wild enthusiasm among chefs in recent years for baby carrots, these are often disappointing unless very freshly picked. You will generally get more flavour from a decent-sized donkey carrot, 1 in/2.5 cm thick at the base and at least 4–5 in/10–12.5 cm long, and these are what I choose in the shops. Really huge carrots, on the other hand, can be dry and lose condition fast, especially if they have split and the central core has become woody – then they are good for little except lending what flavour they have left to a stock. Dutch carrots, especially the long thin ones with pale, almost translucent tips, have always seemed to me watery and insipid. I avoid them if I can.

Basic preparation

Young carrots straight from the garden need only a quick scrub to remove loose dirt, then topping and tailing, and they are ready for the steamer. Larger carrots have tougher skins, which should be peeled with a potato peeler, or at least scraped. They can be cut lengthways into batons or across into discs – I prefer batons, as the discs remind me of the tasteless, watery, overcooked carrots we used to get at school.

Cooking methods

BOILED: in just enough salted water to cover, for 5–15 minutes until tender. Boiled carrots are delicious puréed with a knob of butter and a few twists of black pepper.

COLD/SALAD: grated, with vinaigrette, or in sticks as crudités.

DEEP-FRIED: thin strips can be deep-fried in batter.

ROAST: chunks of larger carrots are surprisingly good roasted around a joint, or with other vegetables (see page 122).

STEAMED: 5–15 minutes, depending on size.

STIR-FRIED: in thin sticks or discs.

Native: April–November.

Cauliflower

The theme may be getting a little tired, and I realize we've only got to 'C' in the alphabet, but here is yet another vegetable for which overcooking spells disaster. A fresh specimen, cooked *al dente* and tossed in butter with plenty of freshly ground black pepper, is an entirely different and delectable animal.

Choosing cauliflower

Look for creamy-white, tight-headed flowers, unblemished by grey-brown patches or black spots; then pick up your proposed purchase and have a good sniff. If it smells in the least tainted – a whiff of old cabbage is a giveaway – reject it.

Basic preparation

If you want to cook a whole head in one piece, which is rather majestic, you should trim off all the leaves, then cut the base of the stalk straight across so that it will sit flat on the bottom of a saucepan. The cauliflower can then be simmered in 1 in/2.5 cm or so of salted water, with the lid on, so that the flower part, which is clear of the water, is steamed. Alternatively you can cut the head into smaller florets and simply steam them.

Cooking methods

BOILED: 12–20 minutes (above method).

COLD/SALAD: small raw florets of very fresh cauliflower make excellent crudités.

DEEP-FRIED: small, pre-blanched florets, in batter (see page 119).

GRATIN: see Broccoli Cheese under BROCCOLI above. Instead of a cheese sauce you can use a béchamel flavoured with a few spoonfuls of the tomato sauce described on page 100, then top with grated Parmesan cheese and brown under the grill.

STEAMED: 8–12 minutes for medium florets.

STIR-FRIED: thumb-sized florets can be added to a stir-fry, particularly good with garlic, chopped fresh chilli and finished with soy sauce.

Native: mid-September–May.

Celeriac

This rooty relation of celery is a more versatile vegetable than it is widely given credit for.

Choosing celeriac

The grubby, convoluted exterior of celeriac is not a pretty sight, but before you select a root you should pick it up and examine it closely. Make sure there are no bruised or slimy patches, and that the root is firm on all sides. If it has soft patches, parts of it will be dry and hollow inside.

Basic preparation

The gnarled, rooty surface must be trimmed away before the creamy interior can be cut to the required size. The cut surface of celeriac will quickly brown; this can be prevented by rubbing it with a lemon wedge, or putting the cut pieces into a bowl of cold water acidulated with 1 tbsp lemon juice or vinegar.

Cooking methods

BOILED: 15–20 minutes until tender. Then mash with butter. This can be mixed with mashed potato.

BAKED: in fat sticks, as for CELERY below.

BRAISED: a good braising base for meat and game.

COLD/SALAD: as a classic *rémoulade*, thickly grated or in a very thin julienne strips in a mustard mayonnaise.

FRIED: slices can be sautéed in butter until tender; very thin slices, deep- fried, make delicious chips to go with game.

GRATIN: the best celeriac dish of all – see page 106.

ROAST: in chunks, either around a roast or in a separate dish of hot fat or oil –
see Roast Mixed Vegetables (page 122).
STEAMED: 15–20 minutes until tender.

Native: September–May.

Celery

The distinctive aromatic qualities of celery are rightly regarded as essential in
many soups and stocks, but it deserves a better reputation as a vegetable in its
own right.

Choosing celery

Imported green celery heads of reliable quality, mainly from Israel, are
available all year round. English white or 'self-blanching' celery comes into
season in the late summer, but is at its best after the first frosts of autumn. It is
often rather grubby, and can be tough and stringy, but it has excellent flavour
and is well worth choosing, especially for braising as an accompaniment to
seasonal game.

Basic preparation

Tough outer stems should be removed and set aside for flavouring stocks. The
wide end of even the inner stalks can also sometimes be hollow and fibrous – if
so, they should be trimmed. Leaves can be chopped finely, and used to garnish
a dish of celery at the end of cooking, or kept back for stock, as you wish.

Cooking methods

BAKED: cut into 2-in/5-cm lengths, place in a covered dish or casserole, dot
with butter, season with salt and pepper, and bake in a moderate to hot oven
(190°C/375°F/Gas Mark 5) for 30–35 minutes. Do not forget the juices when
serving.
BOILED: not recommended as so much flavour is lost.
BRAISED: around braising meat, with or without other vegetables, and
especially when braising or casseroling older, tougher game birds.
COLD/SALAD: raw celery is, of course, delicious with cheese, especially a salty
blue cheese like Roquefort.

Native: August–November.

Chayote

Also known as christophene or cho-cho, this pear-shaped member of the pumpkin family has a very mild flavour, verging on the bland, and benefits from being well spiced. Originally from South America, it is now grown throughout the tropics and is particularly popular in Creole cookery. You will come across it here in ethnic markets, and occasionally in larger supermarkets. It is very good in curries or heated through in a piquant tomato sauce.

Choosing chayote

You are unlikely to have the choice, but you should be aware that chayote comes in a number of varieties: spiny and smooth-skinned, round or more or less pear-shaped, heavily or lightly ridged, from very pale green to bright emerald. The smooth-skinned, ridged variety is the one most commonly encountered in this country. The smaller ones are best; they should be shiny, unblemished and completely firm to the touch.

Basic preparation

Unless they are being cooked in a flavoured liquid which is part of the dish, for example in a curry, chayotes should be simmered whole in their skins until tender, then peeled and cut up according to the recipe. The large seed at the base should be discarded. For soups, stews and curries, peel and cut up the chayote first.

Cooking methods

BAKED: pre-boiled chayotes can be cut in half, scooped hollow, stuffed and baked.

BOILED: 30–40 minutes if whole.

COLD/SALAD: if blanched first.

DEEP-FRIED: thin slices of blanched chayote, in batter.

FRIED: cooked chayote is excellent fried with onions, garlic, chilli and a few chopped sun-dried tomatoes.

Chicory

There is some confusion about the name of this plant: in this country chicory refers to the forced, whitish-green, tightly packed torpedo-shaped heads of a member of the dandelion family. Its close relative, the curly-leafed endive, which looks like a rather wild and spiky Webb's lettuce, is known as *chicorée* or *frisée* in France, whilst our chicory heads are called *endive* – this is the source of the confusion. What is commonly called radicchio is in fact a red type of chicory, rather more bitter than the white variety. It can be used in a similar way or cooked with chilli and cream to make my favourite of all pasta sauces – see page 114 for the full recipe.

Choosing chicory

The darker the green of the leaf tips, the more bitter the chicory will be. I happen to like it fairly bitter, especially if I am having it raw or grilled. Choose small, tightly packed heads, particularly if you are intending to cook them whole, rather than separating the leaves. Avoid chicory with flaccid outer leaves and brown leaf tips or edges.

Basic preparation

It is usual to discard a few of the outside leaves, though if they are perfectly stiff and unblemished this is not necessary. Cut a thin slice off the base.

Cooking methods

BAKED: whole, halved or quartered heads (split lengthways) of chicory are baked in a covered dish as for celery above, though good olive oil is preferable to butter.

BRAISED: stew gently in a little olive oil until tender.

COLD/SALAD: particularly good with slices of avocado and a hazelnut oil vinaigrette, flavoured with a squeeze of fresh orange juice.

GRATIN: lay whole or half heads of chicory in a generously (olive-) oiled baking dish, pour over cream, and season with salt, pepper and 1 tsp brown sugar. Bake, covered, in a moderate to hot oven (190°C/375°F/Gas Mark 5) for 10–15 minutes, then sprinkle with grated Gruyère and/or Parmesan cheese, and/or fresh breadcrumbs, and continue cooking for a further 10–15 minutes until browned and bubbling.

GRIDDLED/GRILLED: individual leaves, or heads split lengthways into quarters, should be placed on a very hot griddle pan until striped but not dried out. Grill on both sides. Dress while still warm with olive oil, lemon juice, salt and black pepper. Radicchio leaves can be grilled and served the same way, but wither very quickly on the griddle pan and so take less time.

Chinese leaf

A delicately flavoured member of the cabbage family which is excellent both raw and cooked.

Choosing Chinese leaf

Go for tall, tightly packed, heavy heads with clean, unwilted leaves.

Basic preparation

The outer leaves can be tough and a little dry – if so, discard them. The ends of the leaves are more tender, and it may be appropriate to slice the top off the cabbage and use the tips for salad, keeping the end with the thicker stalks for cooking.

Cooking methods

BRAISED: slices of stalk from the very thick end can be braised in a little stock for 5–6 minutes until tender.

COLD/SALAD: endless possibilities – try shredded with red and yellow peppers, cucumber and a dressing made with toasted sesame oil (as you will find it described on the bottle – it is extracted from the toasted seeds).

STEAMED: shredded leaves will steam in 2–3 minutes. Then toss in sesame oil or butter and 1 tsp caraway seeds.

STIR-FRIED: for half a head of Chinese leaf, finely shredded, stir-fry a crushed garlic clove and a grated 1-in/2.5-cm piece of fresh ginger root in hot oil (preferably sesame) in your wok. After a minute add the leaves, stir or toss well, then add 2 tsp soy sauce, and cook for another minute. You can do this in an ordinary frying pan, but make sure it is a large one and cook for a minute or two longer.

Courgette

Once the privilege of those who grew their own and knew to pick them young, the baby marrow (for that is what a courgette is) now appears in practically every greengrocer's and supermarket in the country. Yet they still might be picked a little smaller. Courgette flowers (see page 119) are easy enough to acquire if you grow your own and can even be bought, though not cheaply, at some specialist greengrocers'.

Choosing courgettes

Select the smallest you can, choosing firm ones only, and steering clear of any that are bendy, bruised, or in any other way damaged. The round end is the first to soften; give a squeeze, and reject the courgette if it is already going soft.

Basic preparation

Wash well, top and tail. Courgettes that are to be grilled, shallow- or deep-fried will benefit from being sliced, then salted and left to sweat for 30 minutes, then wiped dry.

Cooking methods

BAKED: as for celery above, with the addition of a crushed garlic clove.
BOILED: a pretty desperate measure as most of the flavour is lost and the flesh becomes waterlogged. Sliced courgettes will be tender in 5–10 minutes.
COLD/SALAD: very small, garden-fresh courgettes can be added, sliced, to a salad.
FRIED: sauté in hot oil until browned and crispy – but they are better if deep-fried, with or without batter.
GRATIN: gently sweat most of the water out of thinly sliced cougettes, then transfer to a greased baking dish, top with breadcrumbs and Parmesan, dot with butter and bake in a moderate to hot oven (190°C/375°F/Gas Mark 5) for 15–20 minutes until golden-brown.
GRILLED: on the griddle pan, in thin slices or batons, until nicely char-striped.
STEAMED: for purists who don't want to use any fat, 5–10 minutes; not for me.
STIR-FRIED: in thin slices, by themselves with garlic and soy, or with bean sprouts, carrots, cauliflower, Chinese leaf, etc. in a general stir-fry.

Native: July–October.

Cucumber

Always valued in a plain green salad, other possibilities for the cucumber are sadly under-explored.

Choosing cucumbers

Avoid cucumbers that are at all bendy, or whose skins are beginning to wrinkle. To be entirely sure of freshness, press the thin bit at the stalk end. This, like the rest of the cucumber, should be absolutely firm.

Basic preparation

There is no need to peel cucumbers – the skin is the most aromatic part. Just wash gently before cutting up.

Cooking methods

Most recipes involving cucumber use it raw, but there are some delicious soups and sauces which require cooking. A recipe for Chilled Cucumber and Gooseberry soup (which is not as bizarre as it sounds) appears on page 110. For more ideas see Jane Grigson's *Vegetable Book*.

Curly kale

Usually subsumed under the general heading of 'greens', I choose to give curly kale a separate entry because it is a personal favourite of mine, especially when served, with the formality normally reserved for asparagus and broccoli, as a course on its own accompanied by Anchovy Dressing (page 165).

Selection, preparation and cooking

As with greens, the leaves must be in prime condition, crisp, stiff and dark, with the curls still sharp, as if just picked. It is cheap, so when you find the best quality you can afford to buy generously, and improve the quality further by discarding any damaged or withered leaves and trimming the toughest and thickest of the stalks. Having done that, 4–5 minutes in the steamer will cook it through. With butter and plenty of pepper it is fine, but a real pauper's treat with anchovy sauce.

Native: January–April.

Eddoe

A recent addition to the market-place, and a welcome one, this hairy tuber looks rather unapproachable, but once peeled it is like a slightly slippery potato. Provided you can get a grip it can be treated similarly. Eddoes are fairly indestructible, and keep well, but when choosing you should handle them to make sure they are firm and heavy none the less. Mashed with butter, roasted around a joint, or deep-fried as chips, the slightly sweet eddoe makes a change from potatoes that is better than interesting – it is very tasty. It is also a good addition to a vegetable curry.

Endives

see LETTUCES AND SALAD LEAVES *below.*

Fennel

Its aromatic aniseed flavour and crunchy texture make fennel one of the most exciting of all vegetables.

Choosing and preparing fennel

Fennel bulbs are pretty tough, but they are often treated as if they were indestructible; avoid those with bruised, damaged or cut surfaces. Fennel is not cheap in the first place, and since you generally have to trim away a lot of stalk from the top, and a hard and stringy outer layer, what you have left is often half the weight you paid for. The fatter and rounder the bulb, the less wastage there will be. Once trimmed, wipe the bulb with a clean damp cloth, but don't bother to wash it unless it is to be eaten raw.

Cooking methods

BAKED: as for CELERY above.

BOILED: only to blanch for 3–4 minutes as a preparation for gratins, etc.

BRAISED: the best way to cook fennel as an accompaniment to fish or meat is to stew quarter bulbs slowly in olive oil and a little stock or water, until tender; then turn up the heat, allowing the water to evaporate and the fennel to caramelize (burn) a little.

COLD/SALAD: toss wafer-thin slices of raw fennel with salad leaves (*not* chicory, whose bitter flavour is incompatible), or serve them on their own in a mustardy vinaigrette made sweet with a little brown sugar.

DEEP-FRIED: thin slices in batter.

GRATIN: put blanched quarters or thick slices into a buttered ovenproof dish, pour over a little cream, dot with butter, top with grated Parmesan cheese, then bake in a moderate to hot oven (190°C/375°F/Gas Mark 5) until bubbling and brown.

GRILLED/GRIDDLED: thin slices on the griddle pan, then dress in olive oil and lemon juice.

ROAST: in hot olive oil for about 40 minutes; salt during cooking.

STEAM: quarters, 5–8 minutes; season and toss in butter.

French bean

Along with French beans I include the now ubiquitous Kenyan dwarf beans and the rather irregularly shaped climbing green beans. They are all closely related, and can be similarly prepared (though cooking times may vary). English-grown French beans are still the best, if you can get them.

Choosing French beans

I prefer to buy French beans loose, as a protest at the unnecessary premium charged for packing (and sometimes even washing, topping and tailing). Even if you prefer the more 'convenient' packages, choose beans which look fat and fresh, and are as stiff and crisp as possible. Avoid those which are floppy and wasting at the top end, or otherwise wrinkled or blemished.

Basic preparation

Topping and tailing is traditional, but if your beans are really fresh they certainly don't need tailing. Otherwise a quick rinse to dislodge any dirt is all that is required.

Cooking methods

BOILED: in well-salted water at a rolling boil. Add the beans and boil with the lid off for 6–8 minutes, until tender but just *al dente*. Toss in butter and a little chopped parsley.

COLD/SALAD: the freshest, tiniest beans from your own garden are quite palatable raw in salads. Cooked French beans make an excellent salad: dress while still hot with a mustardy vinaigrette, with *tapenade* (finely chopped black olives, anchovy, garlic and chillis) or simply extra virgin olive oil and a squeeze of lemon juice. Try making a salad with French beans, new potatoes, artichoke hearts and blanched baby leeks, dressed with walnut oil vinaigrette.

GRILLED: French beans blanched for 2–3 minutes in boiling water can then be griddled or barbecued and incorporated into a dish of char-grilled vegetables.

STEAMED: 6–8 minutes.

STIR-FRIED: a useful addition, in short lengths, to any mixed stir-fry, particularly a 'green' one including spring onions, broccoli, courgettes, mangetouts, bean sprouts and garlic.

Jerusalem artichoke

These knobbly little roots are fiddly to prepare, but inexpensive and rewarding for their unique taste.

Choosing Jerusalem artichokes

Pick out the smoother, larger ones, if only for the sake of convenience in preparation.

Basic preparation

Peel as thinly as possible, dropping straight into acidulated water to prevent discolouration.

Cooking methods

BOILED: simmer until soft, 15–20 minutes. Can then be mashed – excellent mixed with an equal amount of mashed potato, a knob of butter, and a little cream.

FRIED: sauté in shallow oil or, better still, deep-fry as chips.

ROAST: scrub well, then roast in their skins (see page 122).

Native: November–May.

Kohl rabi

Kohl rabi means 'cabbage turnip' in German, an apt description of the other-worldly appearance of this vegetable – it looks as if some mad scientist has grafted a few cabbage stalks on to a pale green turnip. In fact it is no hybrid, but a *bona fide* member of the cabbage family with an edible swollen stem. The taste, not surprisingly, is somewhere between cabbage stalk and turnip. That may not sound like a recommendation, so I should add, 'but better than either'.

Choosing kohl rabi

Kohl rabi should be no larger than an eating apple, and completely firm. It is sold with the trimmed stalks still attached – make sure these are not starting to wither.

Basic preparation

Trim back stalks to the surface of the kohl rabi and rinse well, then cut into 1-in/2.5-cm cubes or thick slices.

Cooking methods

BAKED: in chunks, as for celery above.

BOILED: 12–20 minutes. Should still be a little crunchy.

COLD/SALAD: grated in salads, or as for CELERIAC *rémoulade* above.

GRATIN: cooked pieces covered in a cheesy béchamel sauce, topped with fresh breadcrumbs and browned under the grill.

ROAST: very small ones can be roasted whole around a joint.

STEAMED: the best method – 12–20 minutes.

FREEZES WELL, if blanched first.

Leek

This dependable winter stalwart, which is essential in so many soups, stews and stocks, also deserves an occasional solo outing. Try the Leek and Gruyère Tart on page 401.

Choosing leeks

For grilling, salads and dishes in which leeks are to be served whole, choose the smallest possible. Otherwise size is unimportant, though you should avoid the real monsters. Try to choose leeks with a high proportion of white part along the stem.

Basic preparation

Leeks should be trimmed of the coarse, dark green leaves at the top, but it is not true, as some texts suggest, that only the pure white part can be used – the paler green parts are fine too. If your leeks are not absolutely fresh and the outer layer is a little dry and loose, it can be slit with the point of a knife and peeled away. Leeks can gather a lot of dirt under their layers, particularly at the leafy end. If the recipe requires them to be sliced fine, then you should give them a thorough rinsing, changing the water once, after they have been cut up. If the leeks are to be served whole, then, after trimming the dark green leaves, make a slit a few inches long in the top – enough to let you fan out the layers under a running cold tap and flush away any grit.

Cooking methods

BAKED: sliced thinly into discs, then as for CELERY above.
BOILED: not recommended, except for blanching whole small leeks which are then to be barbecued or cooked on a griddle pan.
BRAISED: stew ¼-in/5-mm slices of leek in 1 tbsp butter or olive oil until soft.
COLD/SALAD: if steamed until tender, young leeks can then be served cold in a vinaigrette, or a dressing of olive oil, lemon juice, salt and black pepper. Raw leeks occasionally appear in salads, but I don't much care for them.

DEEP-FRIED: in batter, baby leeks the size of spring onions, split down the middle and fanned a little to collect more batter.

GRATIN: baked or braised leeks can be finished with a topping of cheese and browned under the grill.

GRILLED/GRIDDLED: small, whole leeks can be blanched, griddled until well charred, then dressed in olive oil and a squeeze of lemon.

ROAST: 2-in/5-cm chunks can be roasted around a joint; see also page 122.

STEAMED: 8–15 minutes until tender, then toss in butter.

STIR-FRIED: baby leeks only, sliced like spring onions.

Native: September–May.

Lettuce and salad leaves

The variety available in our supermarkets seems to grow by the week, so it is sometimes difficult to know what to choose. Most importantly, you should go for whatever is in good condition, looks pretty and, from experience, tastes good. I think it is always nice to have something a little piquant and peppery, such as rocket or watercress, in a salad, or something sharp like sorrel, and/or some aromatic leafy herbs such as chervil, coriander, parsley or dill. Bitter endive (frisée) mixes well with plainer lettuces, rocket and watercress but not, I find, with herbs, or with fennel.

Lettuces are tastiest, and actually most nutritious, when grown out of doors rather than in hothouses. The home-grown lettuces of spring and summer are therefore the best. The condition of the outside leaves is not always the key indicator – they are naturally fragile and can always be stripped off and thrown away. Check the inner leaves and make sure they are crisp and not beginning to tire. Earthy roots mean a lettuce will have to be thoroughly washed, but may also indicate that it is locally grown and fresh.

Lettuces and other leaves should be washed and dried thoroughly but gently – the leaves break and bruise easily. A salad spinner is ideal for drying, but should never be over-crammed with leaves.

Any lettuce that is beginning to look a bit tired can be salvaged by transforming into a fine soup: fry some onions, add a medium diced potato, cook in chicken or vegetable stock. Add the lettuce last of all, liquidize and serve hot, or chilled with a blob of cream.

Cos (aka ROMAINE): king of the English lettuces, crunchy with a fresh, bittersweet taste. Essential in a Caesar salad, also makes excellent soup.

ENDIVE (aka *FRISÉE*, see also CHICORY above): a curly-leafed member of the dandelion family, and therefore cousin of chicory, this slightly bitter leaf is very popular in France, especially in a salad with *lardons* (crispy bits of smoked pork belly) and croûtons. Can also be cooked, for example replacing radicchio in the recipe on page 114. Batavian endive, sometimes known simply as batavia, is an excellent broader-leafed version, approximately cabbage-shaped, of milder flavour.

ICEBERG: a crunchy but watery and tasteless lettuce, bred mainly for its shelf-life. I avoid it.

LAMB'S LETTUCE (aka CORN SALAD, *MÂCHE*): very mild, succulent little leaves, with a slightly spinachy taste, excellent dressed with aromatic oils (hazelnut, walnut or sesame seed).

MUSTARD AND CRESS: always an excellent peppery addition to salads, and of course you can grow your own.

OAK LEAF: an attractive lettuce with purplish-brown edges to the curled leaves.

POUSSE D'ÉPINARDS: a pleasantly nutty-tasting type of baby spinach grown specially for salads.

ROUND LETTUCE (aka BUTTER LETTUCE): the most common kind of lettuce, though it is in danger of being overtaken by the ubiquitous and rather dull iceberg (see above). It is good at its best – grown out of doors in spring and summer – less good grown under glass in Holland and imported in the winter months.

SORREL: the sharp, lemony tang of sorrel leaves is not to everybody's taste, but very much to mine. Besides being used raw in salads, it makes excellent soups and sauces. Wilted in butter, it is especially good with fish. See page 421 for how to grow your own.

SPINACH: salad of spinach with bacon, avocado and croûtons has become a staple in many restaurants. It is not always done well – the spinach should be young, tender and thoroughly washed of grit – but at its best, with a strong, mustardy vinaigrette, it is very good indeed. See also separate entry for SPINACH below.

WATERCRESS: I love these mildly astringent leaves; they seem to combine particularly well in a salad with orange and chicory. Watercress soup has become fashionable to the point of ubiquity, but is none the worse for that.

Mangetout

Mangetout was perhaps *the* restaurant vegetable of the 1980s. It is now so common that it is not always treated with the care it deserves. Cook it a minute too long and it loses most of its considerable charm.

Choosing mangetout

I often see mangetout in greengrocers and supermarkets in a very sorry state – dull grey-green, speckled with black spots, bendy with the feathery stalks beginning to wither. Only buy them when they are bright green, unblemished, fresh and crisp-looking.

Preparation and cooking

Top and tail the pods, stripping the slightly stringy edges as you go.

I have seen and tasted recipes for mangetout in various creamy and cheesy sauces, but I can see no point to them. I think they should be cooked as simply as possible, either steamed (5–8 minutes) or stir-fried.

Mooli

An impressively large member of the radish family (it is also known as white radish). Julienne strips of mooli, watery and crisp, are a classic accompaniment to Japanese *sashimi*, but can give a good clean crunch to any salad.

Choosing mooli

Mooli should be a clean creamy-white, and completely hard to the touch.

Preparation and cooking

Thinly peeled, it can be sliced like cucumber, grated or cut into julienne strips. It has barely enough flavour to be worth cooking, but is delicious 'raita-style' dressed with yoghurt, crushed garlic and finely chopped fresh coriander. The clean crunch means that, like celery, it goes well with cheese.

Mushroom

There are literally hundreds of kinds of edible fungi, most of which can be had for free by those in the know, and some of which can be bought at vast expense from specialist suppliers. If you want to find out more about wild mushrooms, I would refer you to three excellent books: Jane Grigson's *The Mushroom Feast*, Antonio Carluccio's *A Passion for Mushrooms*, and Roger Phillips's definitive field guide, *Mushrooms*. In this section I will deal only with the common cultivated varieties readily available in our shops.

Choosing mushrooms

The first decision to make is what size. Although button mushrooms the size of a large marble and still tightly closed make attractive little morsels to encounter in a soup or stew, they have far less taste than the open variety. For most purposes, especially when mushrooms are called upon to deliver their full fungal flavour, I choose the larger, open-cupped field variety, as open as possible in fact, showing plenty of feathery gill underneath. The fresher the better – fresh mushrooms should have a firm, creamy-white surface, without wet slimy bruises, and no signs of drying or wrinkling. The stalk should be firm and clean, neither dry and woody nor soft and mushy. The gills under the cup can vary in colour from a pale pinkish-brown to very dark brown, almost black, in the very large umbrella-shaped mushrooms. Colour is less important than condition: the gills should be fresh-looking and preferably undamaged – neither dry nor bruised and mushy. Fresh mushrooms should have a good earthy aroma – the better they smell, the better they will taste.

CHESTNUT MUSHROOMS, which have a pinkish-brown, slightly flaky skin, have a good flavour and are worth investigating.

OYSTER MUSHROOMS are also now being farmed; they have a slippery texture when cooked, which can be pleasing, especially with some fish dishes, but the farmed versions I have tried are not strong on flavour.

DRIED PORCINI, or CEPS, are easy to find in delicatessens, but not cheap. However, their very strong fungal flavour means a little goes a long way, and a packet of porcini, reconstituted in a cup of boiling water, makes a fine addition to any mushroom dish, especially soups or risottos. Once reconstituted, porcini must be thoroughly washed – in a sieve under a cold running tap is easiest – to remove any grit. The water in which they are soaked will also be full of mushroom flavour, and should be strained through a cloth or coffee filter paper and added to your dish.

Basic preparation

There is no need to wash mushrooms, but they should be wiped or scraped free of any dirt. If they are very dirty, and are to be eaten raw, they can be peeled.

Cooking methods

BAKED: large flat mushrooms can be baked underside up on an oiled baking tray, sprinkled with fresh breadcrumbs, chopped garlic and black pepper, and dotted with butter.

BRAISED/FRIED: sliced open cup mushroons should be sweated in a generous amount of olive oil, then reduced in their own liquid until it has almost boiled away, by which time they will be dark and intensely flavoured. A crushed garlic clove, a sprig of thyme and a squeeze of lemon can be added halfway through. Mushrooms cooked like this can be served on toast rubbed with garlic or on grilled polenta. Finished with a little cream they make a fine pasta sauce, served with freshly grated Parmesan cheese, of course.

COLD/SALAD: I am not mad about raw mushrooms, preferring the concentrated flavour of cooked ones, but don't let that stop you, if you like them in a salad.

DEEP-FRIED: I find small raw mushrooms deep-fried in breadcrumbs remain too watery, but sweated first until completely cooked, both whole small mushrooms and thickish slices of big mushrooms are delicious deep-fried in batter.

GRATIN: mushrooms half-braised, half-fried, as described above, can be put in individual ramekins, with or without a little cream, topped with fresh breadcrumbs and baked in a hot oven (220°C/425°F/Gas Mark 7) until brown. STIR-FRIED: mushrooms to be included in a stir-fry should be sliced thinly.

Nettle

In April and May the top, bright green leaves of young nettles can be gathered (wearing gloves, naturally) and used as an economical alternative to spinach. Nettles make excellent soup. The leaves should be thoroughly washed and trimmed of stalks before cooking. See page 429 for a definitive nettle soup recipe.

Okra

Okra, or lady's fingers as they are curiously known, are the edible pods of a member of the hibiscus family.

Choosing okra

Go for the smallest, brightest pods, avoiding those with shrivelled tips or browning ridges.

Basic preparation and cooking

The little pyramid cap at the stalk end of each pod should be cut away, but if the okra are to be cooked whole, be careful not to expose the inside of the pod and its seeds: okra exude a slimy juice when cooked which is not to everybody's taste – certainly not to mine. This can be minimized by soaking them in well-acidulated water – one part vinegar to 4 parts water – for an hour before cooking. Even then they will still be a little gluey. Shallow- and deep-frying (in batter) are the methods that best combat this tendency, and therefore the ones I most often employ. Stewed in oil with garlic and spices, okra are the *bindi bhaji* of every curry house. They can also be simply steamed (4–6 minutes) and tossed in butter, or added to curries. In the southern states of the USA they are added to spicy gumbos.

Onions

(including SPRING ONION and SHALLOT)

One could hardly say that onions are under-used in English cooking – or indeed anywhere in the world – but they are too rarely appreciated as a vegetable in their own right. Two simple ways of preparing them that are particularly worth adding to your repertoire are in a confit, or onion 'marmalade' see page 112, and roasting them whole in their skins in olive oil (garlic bulbs can be done in the same way).

Choosing onions

Onions are readily available throughout the year in all shapes and sizes – larger onions tend to be slightly milder in flavour, and are therefore probably better for eating raw (though I have never much cared for raw onions in salads – except spring onions, and even then only grilled). It is worth hanging up a few strings of good English onions to last you through the winter. Eventually they may start to sprout shoots but this is no reason to discard them, and in fact the green shoots can be snipped and used like chives. Unlike grown-up onions, baby spring onions lose condition quickly. Those with withered tops and a dry, filmy outside layer should be avoided. The 'red' and 'silver' varieties of onion (which are actually purple and white respectively) have a slightly sweeter, milder flavour. They are particularly good raw in salads.

Basic preparation

I have no great tips to avoid the sniffles when chopping onions, except that, in recipes where it is not important to have nicely shaped slices or pieces you can always use a food processor. For fine, even chopping, it is best to use a knife or mandolin. For the confit on page 112, and for an onion tart, very fine slices are required: the fine-slicing blade of a food processor does this beautifully – for best results feed in ½ onion at a time, on its side.

Cooking methods

BRAISED: sliced onions, with or without other vegetables, make an excellent braising base for all kinds of fish and meat. Very small whole onions, peeled, can be cooked around a braising joint of pork or lamb, and served with it. FRIED: when shallow-frying onions, I prefer to do it slowly until they are tender, then turn up the heat to caramelize them slightly. Rings of raw onion are classically deep-fried in batter.

GRIDDLE: whole spring onions, charred on the griddle pan, can be added to a dish of grilled mixed vegetables.

ROAST: small onions, shallots and even whole bulbs of garlic can be roasted whole in their skins, in hot olive oil (or duck/goose fat), until the inside is soft, sweet and pulpy. Choose a dish into which the onions will fit together closely, pour in a good ½ in/1 cm of olive oil and pre-heat this for 5 minutes in a fairly hot oven (200°C/400°F/Gas Mark 6). Then add the onions, peeled, if at all, only of the loosest outer layer of skin, and roast for 45–60 minutes until tender. (Small to medium sized are best.) Serve whole on the plate – the soft, sweet insides can be squeezed out from the charred, crisp outer skin.

Native: July–October.

Pak-choy

Pak-choy (or bok-choy), sometimes known as mustard greens or celery cabbage, is a cabbage-like leaf vegetable that does not form a closed head, and looks rather like a cross between spring greens and Swiss chard, with slightly smaller leaves than either. It is well worth seeking out for its clean, peppery taste.

Choosing pak-choy

It can be found throughout the year in Asian and Oriental markets, occasionally in supermarkets, and is usually bought in stems, with 8–12 large leaves attached. The leaves should be separated before cooking, and the end of the stalks trimmed. Choose firm, undamaged leaves which show no signs of wilting.

Cooking pak-choy

DEEP-FRIED: the finely shredded leaves of pak-choy, quickly deep-fried, are what you often get when you order crispy seaweed in a Chinese restaurant.

STEAMED: 5–7 minutes.

WILTED: in a wok or saucepan, this the best method of cooking (see page 45); it may take a minute or two longer than, say, for spring greens, before the thick stalks are cooked through.

Parsnip

This versatile root is, I think, more aromatic and delicious than its cousin the carrot.

Choosing parsnips

If possible always select parsnips by hand, preferring the smaller ones and making sure that the thin end is not bendy or flaccid and that the stalk end is not starting to soften.

Basic preparation

If the parsnips are small and very fresh, it may be unnecessary to peel them: simply wash off any dirt and nip off any whiskery rootlets. If you do peel them, do so thinly with a potato peeler. Very large parsnips develop a tough, woody core. This will have to be removed – an operation more easily accomplished if you blanch the parsnips first. But best to avoid the giants altogether.

Cooking methods

BOILED/STEAMED: 12–20 minutes, then drain and toss with butter and chopped parsley. Or purée with a little stock and finish with cream.

FRIED: dip slices of par-boiled parsnip in egg, then fresh breadcrumbs, then shallow or deep-fry. Plain par-boiled parsnips can be deep-fried as chips.

GRATIN: as for CELERIAC above.

ROAST: in hot fat or oil, or around a joint. They will roast quicker if par-boiled first, though this is not essential.

Native: September–March.

Peas

The ubiquity of frozen peas meant that for years very few greengrocers could be bothered with selling fresh peas in season. The situation seems to be improving ever so slightly, and we should encourage it with our custom.

Choosing peas

Select young, green pods, avoiding any that are greyish and withered. You will lose almost half the weight of your peas after shelling.

Basic preparation

When podding bought peas you inevitably come across a few cannonballs whose taste will be coarse and starchy. Set these aside to use for making a pea soup, or at least for supplementing a soup made with green split peas (see recipe on page 323).

Cooking methods

Fresh peas should be boiled or steamed with a sprig of fresh mint for 2–8 minutes according to size and freshness, then served with a knob of butter and a twist of black pepper. Very young peas fresh from your own garden are delicious steamed whole in their pods (which should first be stringed like mangetout) and eaten pod and all.

Native: June–September.

FREEZE WELL.

Canned petits pois

Tiny peas are one of the few vegetables which are pleasing after being canned. Not that canned petits pois are remotely comparable to fresh peas; they are a different thing altogether, but, I happen to think, a rather delicious one – sweet and soft, almost creamy on the palate. The French make the best petits pois, but there is no need to buy the expensive jars that you sometimes find in delicatessens. The cans, provided they come from France, are just as good.

To prepare, heat the peas in a saucepan with all the liquid from the can. Bring them just to the boil, then drain them of *almost* all the liquid, and add a generous knob of butter. Serve with roast beef, lamb or venison (a good strong gravy, into which the peas can be mashed, is essential).

A can of petits pois makes an excellent standby pasta sauce with garlic, pancetta and cream.

Pepper
(Capsicum)

Peppers appeared in Britain only about thirty years ago. Now, happily, they are as easy to find as cabbage, and people are beginning to discover more interesting ways of cooking them – with a little help from our more fashionable restaurants. The recipes on pages 113, 118, and 171, illustrate well the versatility of this vegetable.

Choosing peppers

The first decision to make is which colour you want. Green peppers are simply unripe red ones, but the flavour is certainly different – much less sweet, with a slight bitterness. The choice between yellow and red is largely an aesthetic one, which may be governed by some thoughts of colour coordination in the dish you are planning – both are sweet and mellow in flavour. I have found orange, purple and near-white peppers in the shops recently, all of which are mild and sweet, though not always as flavourful as the best red peppers. Whichever peppers you use they should be firm and glossy, not in the least withered or wrinkled.

Basic preparation

I find the best way to remove the cluster of seeds in a pepper is to cut round the stalk with the point of a sharp knife, then pull it out. With a bit of luck the pale, pithy part to which the seeds are attached will come with it. You can then slice up your pepper, trimming away any more of the pithy part that remains as necessary.

The crunchy freshness of raw peppers, particularly red ones, is always valued for salads and crudités. An olive oil vinaigrette containing finely chopped anchovies and garlic is a great way to dress a salad of mixed raw peppers.

BRAISED: sliced peppers can be stewed in a little olive oil until soft and practically a purée. Spiked with a little chilli powder, this is an excellent accompaniment to sausages and mash or fish and chips – a welcome change from ketchup.

GRILLED/ROAST: it is not hard to produce those deliciously soft, succulent strips of pepper so popular in trendy restaurants when marinated with olive oil, paper-thin slivers of garlic, and anchovies. The peppers – of any colour but a mixture is always pretty – should be cooked whole and uncut either under a grill, on a griddle pan, in a hot oven or, best of all, over charcoal. Turn them occasionally until the skin is blistered and blackened all over. Then place them in a pan or bowl, covered with a lid, until they are cool enough to handle. The next step is a little messy but not difficult: with your fingers peel away and discard the blackened skin and wipe away the seeds, then tear or cut the skinned peppers into thick strips and place in a clean dish. The peeling operation should be done over the bowl so that the juices are not lost. When you have peeled all the peppers, strain the juice that has collected in the bowl. It can then be added to your marinade, salad dressing or, in the case of the recipe on page 113, soup.

Skinned peppers can be used in all kinds of ways – in salads, as a filling in omelettes, served on grilled bread rubbed with garlic and trickled with olive oil (*bruschetta*), chopped or puréed to make *salsa rossa* (see page 118), even in sandwiches (very good with avocado).

Plantain

There are dozens of varieties of this cooking banana, a few of which are increasingly available in shops and supermarkets in this country.

Choosing plantains

Plantains vary in colour from green to yellow to almost black, according to variety and ripeness, but as long as the skin is not broken and the plantain feels firm, it will be fine. If you are buying several plantains make sure they are all approximately equally ripe, as ripeness affects the time they will take to cook. Plantains, like bananas, should not be stored in the fridge.

Basic preparation

Plantains can be baked whole in their skins. Otherwise, simply peel and slice them. Very green plantains are harder to peel – you may have to slit sections of the skin with the point of a knife. Thin slices for frying should first be soaked in salted water for 30 minutes, then thoroughly dried.

Cooking methods

BAKED: whole in their skins in a moderate oven (180°C/350°F/Gas Mark 4) for 1 hour.

BOILED: 20–30 minutes until tender, then toss in butter or mash with butter and milk.

FRIED: slice to the thickness of two 10-p pieces, soak in salted water, dry thoroughly, then sauté or deep-fry until crisp and golden.

GRILLED/GRIDDLED: par-boil, then cook slices on a griddle, or barbecue whole in their skins for 20–30 minutes until blackened and soft, then split open, season with salt and pepper and add a knob of butter.

Potato

For a comprehensive review of all the classic potato preparations, plus a good number of more unusual recipes to boot, I would refer you to the section on potatoes in Jane Grigson's *Vegetable Book*. The tips and suggestions I make below merely cover what I consider to be some of the more common blind spots among home cooks where choosing and cooking potatoes is concerned.

Choosing potatoes

As far as their cooking qualities are concerned, the many varieties of potato are broadly divided into two categories: floury and waxy. In fact most varieties of potato will start off fairly waxy, as is implied by the very loosely used word 'new' in describing certain types. Traditionally waxy or new potatoes are served boiled whole and buttered, or cold in salads, whilst the later crop of mealy, floury potatoes are used for mashing, baking, roasting and most recipe preparations. The distinction is, on the whole, a useful one, but should not be taken as law. Most varieties of small new potato, for example, are delicious roasted whole and unblanched, preferably in good olive oil, with a few sprigs of rosemary thrown in halfway through cooking time. Larger potatoes of the waxy varieties are also very good for making chips.

If you find yourself with raw potatoes on your hands whose cooked texture you are uncertain of, Harold McGee suggests a simple test. Make a brine of one part salt to 11 parts water, and put one of your potatoes in it. Waxy potatoes will float, while the denser, floury potatoes will sink.

The very wide variety of potatoes grown in this country, with their various distinctive tastes, are not reflected in the limited choice on offer in most greengrocers and supermarkets. All too often the variety of the one kind of potato on offer is unknown to the shopkeeper as it is to you. I like to know what variety I am buying, if only so that I can avoid it in the future if it turns out to be disappointing. It is pleasing, therefore, to note that several of the leading supermarket chains are now offering a wider choice of varieties, and even providing information about their different cooking qualities. The problem with supermarket potatoes, however, is that, as they are usually thoroughly scrubbed, they do not keep as well as unwashed potatoes with a little dry earth clinging to them, and will gradually lose flavour through their exposed skin.

The following varieties are particularly worth looking out for:

WAXY POTATOES
Aura: a yellowish (sometimes known as lemon-fleshed) small potato, excellent for salads.
Kipfler: the kidney-shaped new potato, also good for roasting whole (see above).
Pink Fir Apple: my parents have always grown this strange, knobbly potato, tinged with pink. It is my favourite of all waxy potatoes, never better than when simply boiled with a sprig of mint and served with generous amounts of butter. Also excellent in salads.

FLOURY POTATOES
Croft
Désiree: also good for salads when young.
Golden Wonder
King Edward: especially good for baking.
Maris Piper
Redskin: good flavour.

If you are a potato-lover – and a taste for the best spuds is worth cultivating – you might consider ordering, either through your greengrocer or direct from a farmer, a sack of 'old' potatoes of a variety that you particularly like. Stored unwashed in a cool dark place, they will keep their condition and flavour for a good few weeks. New potatoes, on the other hand, do not keep as well, and should be bought at regular intervals.

Cooking potatoes

Potatoes are peeled far more often than is necessary. Most of the vitamins and minerals are found in and just under the skin. Boil them in their skins, well-scrubbed, and not only will they keep their shape, they will retain more of their goodness. If you prefer not to eat the skin, or want to mash the potatoes without it, it is easily removed with a fork once the potatoes are cooked.

PERFECT CHIPS: A deep-fat fryer with a built-in temperature gauge is easier to use for frying chips and less hazardous than a chip pan, loose basket and oil thermometer.

The secret of good chips is good potatoes, good oil (groundnut or sunflower is recommended), and close attention to the following procedure.

The size of chips is a matter of personal taste; I like them thickly cut with the skins still on. When you have cut your chips to size, rinse them thoroughly in clean fresh water – this helps to reduce the starch. They must then be thoroughly dried, with kitchen paper or a clean cloth, before frying. Chips need to be cooked twice; the first time they are 'blanched' in fairly hot oil to tenderize them; the second frying, over a higher heat, crisps them up.

Heat your oil to 170°C/325°F, and fry your chips in uncrowded batches, stirring very gently with a wooden spoon after the first few seconds to prevent the chips from sticking together. Fry at this temperature for a few minutes (not more than 10), until the chips are a pale golden colour. Carefully remove one chip with the wooden spoon, and test it with a fork; it should be just tender right through, *but only just*. Shake out the chips into a big tray lined with several sheets of greaseproof paper. When all your chips have been blanched, turn up the heat and bring the oil temperature to 190–200°C/375–400°F. Fry the chips again – you can probably get away with slightly larger batches this time – until they are golden-brown and crispy (2–3 minutes). Tip out the chips into a warm tray lined with fresh paper, sprinkling each batch with salt as you go along.

You can, if it suits you, leave the chips after the initial blanching and before the final frying, but not for more than a few hours.

PERFECT MASH: Boil good, floury potatoes, cut up but with their skins still on, until completely tender (about 25 minutes). Drain and remove the skins. Heat a generous knob of butter and a little milk in a saucepan until the milk is hot and the butter melted (I like my mash rich and creamy, and quite runny, so I use plenty of both, but it is a matter of personal taste). Rub the potatoes through a wire sieve with a wooden spoon (or better still, press them through that handy gadget, the potato ricer) directly into the milk and butter. Beat well so the milk and butter are well absorbed and season with salt and pepper.

GARLIC AND OLIVE OIL MASH: for a variation on the above, use olive oil instead of butter. Crush 2 garlic cloves into the milk and simmer for 1–2 minutes. Then add the olive oil (the best you have) and sieve in the potatoes.

See also recipes for Colcannon (page 106) and Potato Gratin (page 214).

Pumpkin and squash

These vine-growing members of the gourd family were once of little more than decorative interest to the British. Now we are beginning to catch on to their traditional culinary uses in America and south-west France, and discovering that there is much to enjoy in these versatile vegetables: see for example, the recipes on pages 105 and 114.

Choosing pumpkins and squashes

Besides the large orange pumpkin there are several types of squash, both winter and summer varieties, to be found in our shops. All are good, but for my money the best of all is the light-bulb-shaped, buff-coloured butternut squash. As long as they are unbruised and unblemished, with a good hard skin, both pumpkins and squashes can be kept for several months without spoiling.

Basic preparation

Peel the tough skin reasonably thickly, scrape out the seeds with a spoon, then cut the flesh into pieces. Alternatively cook with the peel still on – it is more easily removed afterwards.

Cooking methods

BAKED: season chunks or large slices with salt and pepper, wrap in buttered foil, bake in a moderate to hot oven (190°C/375°F/Gas Mark 5) for 45 minutes.

BOILED: simmer gently, with only enough water to prevent from burning, until tender (10–20 minutes). Drain off any excess liquid, then season well and mash with butter.

FRIED: shallow-fry floured slices gently in butter until lightly browned; thinner slices (¼–½ in/5 mm–1 cm) are delicious deep-fried in batter.

GRATIN: layers of pumpkin, shallow-fried as above, can be topped with fresh breadcrumbs and grated Parmesan cheese and browned under the grill.

ROAST: in chunks in hot oil, or around a joint, for 1 hour at 180°C/350°F/Gas Mark 4 or less at a higher temperature.

STEAM: 10–20 minutes until tender.

Soup freezes well, otherwise freezing is not recommended.

Radicchio

see CHICORY above, and recipe on
page 114.

Radish

The small round radish, scarlet with a white tip, should be bought as fresh as possible, ideally with its leaves still attached. Radishes do not, in my view, work as part of a composite salad, but should be enjoyed on their own, with perhaps a little warm Anchovy Dressing (page 165) to dip them into, or just plain rock salt. Radishes should be topped and tailed, well washed, and served bobbing in a bowl of cold water. See also MOOLI above.

Red cabbage

The nutty flavour and succulence of red cabbage, often sharpened with the addition of vinegar and sweetened with a little brown sugar, or perhaps apples, goes particularly well with game, such as hare or pheasant, and also with smoked meats and salt pork.

Choosing red cabbage

Red cabbages keep well, and any damaged or slightly wilted outer leaves can be trimmed away until crisper, fresher layers are revealed. It's best, however, to avoid those which are badly bruised or appear very wilted.

Cooking methods

BRAISED: the leaves of red cabbage are thick and fleshy, and require long, slow cooking to become tender. Red cabbage should never be cooked in boiling water – it will lose colour, flavour and texture and end up limp and drab. The best way to cook it is to braise it in a covered pot, over a very low heat or in a slow oven (150°C/300°F/Gas Mark 2), for at least 2 hours. Here is a classic and reliable preparation, using one large red cabbage (serves 8–10 – leftovers can be eaten cold):

In a large casserole or saucepan, sweat 1 large or 2 small onions, sliced, in 1 oz/30 g butter or lard for a few minutes until softened but not brown. Add the cabbage, shredded but not too finely, 4 tart eating apples such as Cox's Orange Pippin, peeled and sliced, 3 tbsp good red wine vinegar, a wine-glass of red wine, 2 cloves, 2 tsp brown sugar and ½ tsp salt. Mix gently but thoroughly, cover and set over a very low heat, or in the oven at 150°C/300°F/Gas Mark 2. It will take about 2½ hours to cook, but will come to no harm if you leave it for 3 hours. If you are cooking on the hob, occasional stirring may be necessary to prevent burning.

The addition of salt pork, pieces of bacon, boiling sausages and even confit of duck or goose makes this dish into a robust meal. Add bacon or salt pork at the beginning of cooking, sausages and confit for the last hour only.

COLD/SALAD: red cabbage can also be eaten raw in salads – see recipe on page 104.

Rocket

see LETTUCE AND SALAD LEAVES **above,**
and page 418 for how to grow your own.

Salsify

These distinctive-tasting roots have been grown by enthusiastic kitchen gardeners since the seventeenth century. They are just beginning to catch on in the best supermarkets and specialist greengrocers. A close cousin of salsify is the similar-looking but dark-skinned SCORZONERA. It can be prepared in all the same ways, but is a little tougher, and takes slightly longer to cook.

Choosing and preparing salsify

Choose firm, stiff, straight roots, avoiding those that are bendy or flabby. Top, tail and scrape the roots clean – they tend to bleed if you try and peel them. Cut into 2–3-in/5–7.5-cm lengths, and immerse at once in acidulated water to prevent them from turning brown.

Cooking methods

Salsify soup: sweat 1 onion, 1 garlic clove and 1 sliced celery stick in a little butter, then add 1 lb/450 g salsify, scraped and sliced, cover with good stock (preferably chicken) and simmer until tender. Liquidize, add 4 fl oz/100 ml single cream, season well and, if necessary, thin with more stock or water. Garnish with finely chopped parsley.

BOILED: simmer gently for 15–30 minutes until tender but not mushy. Drain, then toss in butter or, better still, dress with 'wet' *gremolata* (see page 416).

COLD/SALAD: grate when raw, and dress with a lemony mayonnaise. Cooked salsify dressed with *gremolata* (see page 416) is also excellent cold.

FRIED: sauté cooked salsify in butter until lightly browned, or coat in batter and deep-fry to make salsify fritters.

GRATIN: my favourite method – coat the just-cooked salsify (boiled or steamed) while still warm with double cream, transfer to a baking dish, sprinkle over grated Parmesan or Gruyère cheese (or a mixture), and bake in a fairly hot oven (200°C/400°F/Gas Mark 6) until bubbling and brown.

STEAMED: 15–30 minutes until tender.

Native: October–April.

Samphire

A summer delicacy, samphire from the marshes of Norfolk and Suffolk is more often found in the fishmonger's than the greengrocer's. They don't charge much for it – some of them even give it away. The strange, fleshy emerald stems are unlike any other vegetable. Everyone should try samphire once.

Basic preparation

Rinse thoroughly, then pick over, trimming off any wispy, wiry roots and discarding any tough, woody stems, then rinse well. Samphire needs to be cooked, but only for a few minutes – any longer and it becomes mushy and loses its bright green colour. Steam or boil, without salt, for 2–5 minutes until tender, then drain and toss in butter. Excellent with poached salmon. If ever you come across pickled samphire, snap it up. It is delicious.

Spinach

Though frozen leaf spinach is a handy standby, in taste and texture it does not compare with fresh leaves.

Choosing spinach

Select bright, bushy bunches of crisp-looking leaves, avoiding those that are wilting, yellowish, or beginning to brown at the edges. Many supermarkets sell bags of spinach leaves that have already been picked over and trimmed. Providing the leaves look good and fresh, this may be a sensible buy if preparation time is likely to be short. Bear in mind that fresh spinach leaves will shrink to at least half their weight when cooked. I allow about 6 oz/170 g per person of fresh, which gives a 2–3-oz/60–85-g serving of cooked spinach.

Basic preparation

Spinach should be thoroughly picked over and any withering leaves discarded, along with the thicker and tougher of the stems. At this stage you may wish to set aside especially tender young leaves for using raw in salads. Wash very thoroughly in several changes of clean cold water – any traces of grit in your cooked spinach and it is totally spoiled.

Cooking methods

BOILED: spinach can be blanched for a couple of minutes, then drained and pressed as dry as possible in a sieve or colander, but wilting is easier and just as effective: see below.

COLD/SALAD: see SPINACH under LETTUCE and SALAD LEAVES above. Balls of cooked spinach are delicious cold and dressed with 'wet' *gremolata* (page 416).

DEEP-FRIED: whole leaves, dipped in a very light batter and deep-fried for barely a minute.

GRATIN: roughly chop 1 lb/450 g lightly cooked, well-drained spinach, and place in a well-greased shallow gratin dish. Beat 2 egg yolks with 5 fl oz/150 ml double cream, season well, and pour over the spinach. Top with grated Parmesan cheese and bake in a moderate to hot oven (190°C/375°F/Gas Mark 5) for 20–25 minutes.

WILTED: pile the leaves, still wet from washing, into a large saucepan over a moderate heat. Push down with a wooden spoon, then put the lid on for a minute or so to help contain the heat. Give the spinach a stir, then cook for another couple of minutes before giving it a final stir. It should not take more than 5 minutes, unless there is a huge amount. Turn the spinach into a colander or sieve, and press well with the back of a spoon to drain. It can then be left to cool, and later squeezed even drier with your hands. It is important to get as much water out of the spinach as possible, especially if it is then to be used in a recipe. To serve plainly as a vegetable, the cooked, drained spinach should be heated through in a generous amount of melted butter, and seasoned with salt and freshly ground black pepper.

PERFECT CREAMED SPINACH: into 1½ lb/675 g cooked spinach, thoroughly drained and chopped, stir a scant 5 fl oz/150 ml béchamel sauce (see page 399), 1 tbsp double cream, and 1 oz/30 g freshly grated Parmesan cheese. Season well with salt, pepper and a pinch of freshly grated nutmeg.

Spring greens, winter greens and sprout tops

The legendary reluctance of young British children to 'eat up their greens' has given these vegetables a bad name. Even Jane Grigson, as broad-minded a vegetable-eater as there has ever been, described greens as one of the 'nastier aspects of the cabbage family'. I have to disagree. If you can buy greens or sprout tops that are really fresh, with leaves still stiff and succulent, they can be delicious.

Judicious cooking is the key. Washed and trimmed of thick stalks, the leaves can be wilted whole for 2–4 minutes, until the dusky green turns bright emerald. Served tossed in butter and well peppered, with the stalks still a little crunchy, they will be eaten up most readily. Alternatively, shred the leaves (but not too finely) and steam, again for just 2–4 minutes.

Squash
see PUMPKIN AND SQUASH *above.*

Swede
see TURNIP AND SWEDE *below.*

Sweetcorn (Corn-on-the-cob)

The importance of maize as a dietary staple and fodder crop rather overshadows the use of the young sweet kernels of just-picked corn. I have always found eating corn-on-the-cob, with lashings of melted butter, a joyful, if messy business.

Choosing sweetcorn

Only those who grow their own cobs will know the joy of corn boiled or steamed within minutes of being picked. The rest of us will have to make do with the freshest cobs we can find, avoiding those with dried or browning outside leaves or shrivelling kernels. Imported frozen corn-on-the-cobs can be better than fresh local ones, perhaps because they have had more sunshine and have been processed and frozen very soon after picking. There is also a vacuum-packed product of 'long-life' pre-blanched cob, which is surprisingly good. Frozen niblets, corn-off-the-cob if you like, are less impressive, and canned niblets very much a last resort.

Basic preparation

For corn-on-the-cob, the outer green leaves in which the corn is often sold must be stripped away, and the silky threads pulled off. If your recipe, for example a soup or chowder, requires niblets off the cob, they can be sliced off with a sharp and heavy knife. Stand the cob on its end on a chopping board, and slice downwards, away from yourself, as close to the hard core as you can. Turn the cob and slice again. Five or six slices should take off all the niblets, but it is worth scraping the core to get at any bits of kernels that are still clinging to it.

Cooking methods

Sweetcorn fritters are a delight, and the best possible way to use canned corn (though they are even better with fresh). For 8 oz/225 g cooked or canned corn niblets you need 5 fl oz/150 ml thickish pancake batter, seasoned with a good pinch of chilli powder. Fry tablespoons of the mixture in hot butter or oil, turning once,

BAKED: whole cobs, wrapped in well-buttered foil, in a fairly hot oven (200°C/400°F/Gas Mark 6) for 30–40 minutes.

BOILED: whole cobs, 8–15 minutes until tender. Not recommended for loose niblets.

GRILLED: par-boiled cobs, finished on a griddle pan or barbecue, have a delicious charred taste.

STEAMED: feasible only if you have a very large steamer, though a fish kettle (see page 22) will accommodate 5–6 large cobs.

PERFECT CREAMED CORN: for 1 lb/450 g corn to serve 4 people you will need 4–6 cobs, depending on size. Scrape off the niblets as described above. Add to a saucepan with just 1 tbsp cold water and 1 oz/30 g butter. Cook over a moderate heat for 4–5 minutes until the corn is tender. Stir it well with a wooden spoon, add 1 generous tbsp double cream and simmer for another minute or so.

Native: July–October.

FREEZES WELL, if blanched.

until golden-brown. Add fried onions, a crushed garlic clove, and 2 tsp garam masala to the batter, and you have delicious curried corn fritters. They make a fine snack or starter served with mango chutney.

Sweet potato

The sweet potato is now widely available, yet I am always encountering people who have never tasted it. Some plead ignorance of how to cook what they consider to be an exotic item. That's easy to counter – there's precious little you can do to an ordinary potato that isn't also suitable treatment for a sweet potato. If anything, the sweet potato is even more versatile, as it is widely used in making cakes and desserts as well as all its savoury applications. A recipe for one of the best of these – Portuguese *batada* – appears on page 115.

Choosing sweet potatoes

Choose completely firm tubers showing no signs of wrinkling or softness. The variety with pinkish-orange flesh is particularly delicious, and some greengrocers and market stallholders will cut a few on their display to reveal this characteristic.

Cooking methods

Cooking and preparation of sweet potatoes are as for ordinary potatoes, but particularly recommended are:

SWEET POTATO CHIPS: see 'Perfect chips' (page 88).

SWEET POTATO GRATIN: see page 106.

LEEK AND SWEET POTATO SOUP: as an alternative to vichyssoise: add 1 good tsp curry powder, serve hot or cold.

MASHED SWEET POTATOS: see 'Perfect mash' (page 89).

Swiss chard

This member of the beet family is prized not for its root but for its succulent spade-like leaves with their enlarged middle stems, known as ribs. LEAF BEET, another kind of chard, has a thinner stalk, which does not need to be cooked separately. It is used much like spinach, and is particularly good wilted with butter.

Choosing chard

The leafy part should be crisp, glossy and dark green, the thick central stalk smooth, creamy-white and undamaged.

Basic preparation

The green leafy parts will cook much faster than the thick stalks, so they are usually trimmed off and cooked separately – they are good wilted, like spinach, and finished with a little cream and grated Parmesan cheese. The stems should be washed and, if very long, cut into shorter lengths. If they seem a little tough and stringy, they should be stripped of the outer skin, which should take a few stringy bits with it.

Cooking methods

BOILED: simmer for 8–15 minutes until tender, then toss in butter.

GRATIN: cover blanched stalks in a cheesy béchamel sauce (use Gruyère or Parmesan cheese, or a mixture) and brown under the grill.

SWISS CHARD TART: as for the Leek and Gruyère Tart on page 401, substituting cooked chard (stalks and leaves cooked separately) for the leeks.

Native: all year round.

Tomato

For years one of the great shopping challenges has been to find tomatoes with real flavour. Jane Grigson, in her *Vegetable Book* published in 1978, complained eloquently of 'the dreaded Moneymaker and similar varieties, whose only virtues are regular size and vast yield'. She issued a call to arms: 'We all have to shove,' she said, '... to save the tomato from the dragon of commerce.' The ears her message fell on were not completely deaf, though they may have been a little slow to hear. At last we are beginning to see tomatoes in our shops and supermarkets which can rightfully brag of their breeding: Melrose, Gardener's Delight, and Marmande, for example. Even plum tomatoes from Italy and Spain can be found, though they are sometimes sadly underripe.

Choosing tomatoes

Such are the skills of the genetic engineers that there are no visual clues to indicate which tomatoes have particularly good flavour. Tasteless tomatoes picked early for a longer shelf-life can be artificially reddened by exposure to certain gases. Smell is a better clue: sniff tomatoes, even through the holes in their polythene boxes, and the very best will reveal themselves by their rich, flowery aroma. Labels can also be a guide: look for ones which actually name the variety of tomato. Failing that, pick those which say 'grown specially for flavour'. Although this sounds faintly absurd (for what else would tomatoes be grown for?), it at least indicates that someone is on the case.

Vigilant, or vigilante, Bon Marcheurs, might like to continue to carry forward the late Jane Grigson's good work. If you find a greengrocer who sells exceptionally good tomatoes, make a note of the origin and, if possible, the brand on the box. Spread the gospel: recommend it to other greengrocers; do so tactfully and they won't bite. They may even sell more – especially if they invest in labels saying 'grown specially for flavour'! Unfortunately the best tomatoes are often more expensive, but if we care enough to pay a little more today, then tomorrow the price will come down.

If you can't find good tomatoes, then canned are better for cooking with than tasteless fresh ones. Whole, peeled plum tomatoes are the best canned kind; avoid those which have herbs added, as they tend to be bitter.

Basic preparation

Large tomatoes that are destined for salads are nicer, I think, if skinned; pour boiling water over them and drain after 20 seconds, then flush with cool water and peel with a knife. Small cherry tomatoes and Gardener's Delight do not need peeling.

Cooking methods

Apart from as tomato sauce, and an ingredient in many dishes, the only way I cook tomatoes is by grilling (preferably on a griddle pan) or frying (preferably in bacon fat). A good tomato sauce, however, is a crucial skill for any cook to acquire.

PERFECT TOMATO SAUCE: skin 2 lb/900 g ripe, tasty tomatoes, and cut them up, discarding the tough, stalky ends. In a large frying pan heat 2 tbsp best olive oil, and add to it 2 finely chopped garlic cloves. Just as the garlic begins to take colour (do not let it brown), add the chopped tomatoes. Cover the pan with a lid or foil and cook for 1–2 minutes, to encourage the juices to run from the tomatoes. Remove the lid again, and allow the tomatoes to bubble and reduce, stirring occasionally, until they are completely soft and pulpy and the sauce is rich and thick. On no account allow the sauce to catch on the bottom of the pan. You can then, and only then, season the sauce, with freshly ground black pepper, a pinch of salt and, only if you think it needs it, 1 tsp sugar. Tear up a few basil leaves and add just before serving. Like almost all tomato sauces, this one freezes extremely well.

If you can't find really good tomatoes for this sauce, then use 2 × 14-oz/400-g cans of peeled Italian tomatoes.

There are many richer variations to this sauce (Ann Owston's creamy sauce on page 109 is a fine example), including those that begin with sweated onions, to which is added a wine-glass of white wine. They are all good, but the secret of success is in not adding any salt, or salty ingredients such as bacon or pancetta, until the sauce has reached a fairly advanced stage. Otherwise the natural sweetness can be lost.

A wonderfully simple pasta sauce can be made by sweating a can of anchovies in olive oil until they break up into a purée, adding the completed but unsalted tomato sauce described above, and finishing it with a little cream. It is a sauce that, perhaps surprisingly, also goes very well with cauliflower.

For Roast Tomato and Red Pepper Soup, see page 113.

SUN-DRIED TOMATOES: now widely available, these are an extremely useful ingredient, besides being delicious in their own right. Chopped very fine, they will enrich any dish in which fresh or tinned tomatoes are being included. The sun-dried tomatoes that come in oil can be used straight from the jar, but the completely dry kind should be soaked in hot milk for one hour before using.

Turnip and swede

Since both these roots are fed in abundance to farm animals, they hardly bear much gastronomic cachet. Treated disdainfully, they will indeed disappoint, or worse. But if care is taken to bring out their best qualities, they will delight the democratic diner, if not the snob.

Choosing turnips and swedes

Baby spring turnips undoubtedly have a less coarse, more appealing taste than the winter giants. Baby swedes are not something I have ever encountered, though I always choose the smallest I can find.

Basic preparation

Both turnips and swedes need to be peeled, though turnips any smaller than a golf ball can forgo this. If you want them to cook quickly for mashing, cut them into small dice, but not too small if you are boiling rather than steaming them, or too much flavour will be lost into the water.

Cooking methods

BOILED/STEAMED: baby turnips make an excellent addition to stews. Bringing out the best of plainly cooked swedes and turnips (i.e. cut up into pieces and steamed or boiled for 10–30 minutes until tender) basically means lavishing butter generously on them. A squeeze of lemon also helps to bring out the flavour, and plenty of freshly ground black pepper is essential. For 'bashed neeps' sieve or mash cooked swedes or turnips with plenty of butter and pepper, and finish with a little double cream. These are a must, of course, to accompany haggis, but also go well with rich, meaty, wintery stews.

ROAST: baby turnips can be roasted whole; larger ones, and swedes, should be cut into pieces, blanched for 3–4 minutes, then roasted as for potatoes.

Native: Turnips: May–December. Swedes: September–February.

Watercress

see LETTUCES AND SALAD LEAVES *above*.

Yam

In itself, the yam is a little blander, more starchy, and less exciting than the sweet potato. However, lifted with spices it makes a pleasing contribution to a curry or stew.

FRIED: for delicious spicy yam croquettes, mash 1 lb/450 g boiled or steamed yams with a knob of butter, 2 egg yolks, a crushed garlic clove, 1 tbsp chopped fresh coriander and 1 tsp chilli powder. Form into balls, roll in seasoned flour, dip in beaten egg, roll in fresh breadcrumbs and deep- or shallow-fry until golden-brown.

Recipes

Aubergine Three Ways
THE ARK

Sheila Kidd writes: 'There are many variations on this theme. The essence is to keep variety of texture and colour in each combination. Use what is ripest and readily available. We sometimes make a trio of other vegetable mixtures such as sweet and sour onions, courgettes and pinenut salad, and one of the aubergine dishes.'

Sweet and Sour Aubergine Salad
Serves 6 as a starter

Layer the aubergine with generous sprinklings of salt in a colander and leave for at least 30 minutes. Rinse and squeeze as dry as possible in a clean cotton cloth.

Take a cast-iron pan for preference and cover its base with oil. Cook the onion until golden, add the garlic and stir for a few minutes. Add the aubergine and stir for 3–4 minutes, then put everything else into the pan, mix well and allow to bubble gently for 30–40 minutes, stirring regularly to ensure nothing catches on the bottom of the pan.

The dish is finished when the aubergine is completely tender and the sauce rich, purply and reduced. Taste for seasoning and adjust if necessary. Cool, and serve at room temperature.

3 medium aubergines, cut into
1-in/2-cm cubes
salt
olive oil
1 large onion, chopped
2 garlic cloves, crushed
14-oz/400-g can peeled
tomatoes, chopped small
a handful each of chopped fresh
parsley and mint
3 tbsp red wine vinegar
1 tbsp sugar
black pepper

Marinated Aubergine Slices
Serves 6 as a starter

Layer the aubergine slices with salt in a colander and drain for 30–40 minutes. Rinse and pat dry. Heat the oil in a frying pan and fry the aubergine slices a few at a time until golden-brown on both sides. Place in a dish as they are cooked and sprinkle each layer with garlic, parsley, freshly torn basil, pepper and a few drops of vinegar. Set aside to cool and infuse in the herbs and vinegar for 1 hour. Serve at room temperature.

3 medium aubergines, peeled
and cut into ¼-in/5-mm
slices
salt
6 tbsp olive oil
2–3 garlic cloves, crushed
2–3 tbsp chopped fresh parsley
a few sprigs of fresh basil
black pepper
balsamic vinegar

Aubergine Purée
Serves 6 as a starter

3 medium aubergines
2 garlic cloves, crushed
juice of 1 lemon
3–4 tbsp extra virgin olive oil
8–10 fl oz/250–300 ml thick
  natural yoghurt
salt and black pepper

To garnish
chopped fresh parsley
black olives
fine-cut strips of red pepper
a few broken walnuts

Either grill the aubergines until blistered all over and soft right through or bake them in a pre-heated hot oven (200–220°C/400–425°F/Gas Mark 6–7) for 25–35 minutes, turning them from time to time. Leave until cool enough to handle, then peel and drain off any bitter juices. Mash with a fork or purée in a food processor with the garlic, gradually mixing in the lemon juice and oil. Beat in the yoghurt and season to taste with salt and pepper. Serve at room temperature. Garnish with parsley, olives, pepper strips and walnuts.

Bean Sprout Salad with a Japanese Dressing
Serves 4 as a starter or salad course

Made with home-sprouted mung beans, this is one of my favourite salads – well worth serving as a course on its own. The recipe is adapted from one served at the Croque en Bouche restaurant in Malvern Wells. You can vary the lettuce leaves according to what is available; the bean sprouts and red cabbage are constants. If you don't have or can't find Mirin (a kind of sweet saké), use ordinary saké and a pinch of sugar or, failing that, sherry.

8–10 large leaves cos or other
  good lettuce
a small bunch of rocket
4 heaped tbsp sprouted mung
  beans (see page 296)
4 oz/115 g red cabbage

For the dressing
2 tbsp Mirin
4 tbsp toasted sesame oil
2 tsp soy sauce
1 tbsp chopped fresh coriander
black pepper

Wash the salad leaves and dry in a salad spinner. Wash the bean sprouts and shake dry in a clean cloth. Shred the cabbage (very finely) and the lettuce (less finely). Shake all the ingredients for the dressing together in a closed jar, until emulsified.

You can simply combine all the vegetables in a large salad bowl, and toss with the dressing. I prefer to mix together the cabbage and bean sprouts, dress these, and serve them on top of the other leaves, undressed.

Baked Butternut Squash with Coriander Pesto

Serves 4 as a starter or light supper dish

I don't know if the Italians would approve of coriander pesto, but I have found it goes well with a number of vegetables. Besides baked butternut squash, you can add it to a soup made from the same vegetable, or from pumpkin or carrot. Or try it with grilled or baked aubergines. To make a classic pesto, substitute basil for coriander, and add 1 oz/25 g of fresh-grated Parmesan.

Cut the squash in half and scoop out the seeds with a spoon. Brush the cut surface of each half generously with oil, put a garlic clove in the cavity and season well with salt and pepper. Place cut side up on a baking tray and cover loosely with foil. Bake in a pre-heated fairly hot oven (200°C/400°F/Gas Mark 6) for 35–40 minutes. Test for doneness with a skewer – it should slip easily through the squash.

    To make the pesto, pound together the coriander, garlic and pinenuts with a pestle and mortar to make a smooth paste (or do this in a food processor), then stir in the oil and season to taste with salt and pepper. Serve the piping hot squash, one half per person, with a spoonful of pesto in each cavity.

2 small butternut squash
a little olive oil
4 garlic cloves
salt and black pepper

For the pesto
2 oz/60 g fresh coriander
  leaves, washed, trimmed of
  stalks and dried
4 large garlic cloves
2 oz/60 g pinenuts
3 tbsp olive oil
salt and black pepper

Bortsch with Salt Beef

Serves 4 generously

The salt beef is an optional extra in this dish, but it does make for a more substantial soup, turning a starter into a supper.

Peel the beetroot and grate it on the coarse blade of a cheese grater. Peel and similarly grate the carrots and onion. Put the grated beetroot, carrot and onion into a saucepan with the potato, stock, bay leaf and a pinch of salt and pepper. Bring to the boil, cover and simmer gently for 45 minutes. At this point you can decide what kind of a texture you want your soup to have. For a thin, consommé-like soup (elegant and less filling, therefore good as a starter) you can simply strain the liquid through a sieve and discard all the bits. For a thicker but smooth soup, you can liquidize it. Or you can simply leave it as it is, country-style with all the bits still in it.

1 lb/450 g beetroot, uncooked
2 carrots
1 small onion
1 small potato, diced
1½ pts/850 ml beef or veal
  stock
1 bay leaf
salt and black pepper
6 oz/170 g salt beef
a little bacon fat, beef dripping
  or frying oil
soured cream, to serve

When the soup is almost ready, fry thin slices of the salt beef in the fat or oil for a few minutes until crispy. Divide the beef among 4 warmed bowls, and ladle the soup over. Serve with soured cream.

Colcannon

Serves 4

This lovely Irish dish can be made with leftover potatoes and cabbage, providing the cabbage has just been lightly steamed and is not over-cooked. It is very delicious, and certainly worth starting from scratch. Serve on its own, or as part of a fry-up with bacon, sausages, black pudding and egg.

I lb/450 g mealy potatoes, cooked
10–12 oz/285–350 g cabbage, lightly steamed
salt and black pepper
I large *or* 2 small onions, thinly sliced
a little bacon fat, beef dripping *or* frying oil

Sieve or mash the potatoes and mix with the cabbage. Season well with salt and pepper. Fry the onion in the fat over a moderate heat, until it is soft and beginning to brown. Using a spatula, press half the potato and cabbage mixture in an even layer on to the onion, and fry for 4–5 minutes until it is well browned and crispy underneath. Cut the mixture into 4 quarters with the spatula or palette knife, and turn them over carefully so that the crispy bit is uppermost. Press the remaining potato and cabbage mixture on to the first layer, and after a few more minutes, cut and turn again. When the bottom is again browned, you will have a crispy top, a crispy bottom, and a crispy layer in the middle.

Celeriac Gratin

Serves 6

Exactly the same procedure can be followed using sweet potatoes or a mixture of sweet and ordinary (not new) potatoes. If you want to bulk out the celeriac, you can make this dish with equal quantities of celeriac and sliced floury potatoes.

Peel the celeriac, cut in half, then slice each half as thinly as possible (about the thickness of a 10p piece is ideal). Or you can use the slicing blade of a food processor. Put the slices into a basin of water acidulated with the lemon juice as you go. When you have cut up all the celeriac, drain the slices and shake in a clean cotton cloth, or pat with kitchen paper, to dry.

In a large mixing bowl, toss the celeriac slices with 2 tbsp of the oil and all the other ingredients. Transfer to a lightly oiled gratin dish. You do not have to layer the gratin piece by piece, but try to ensure that the celeriac slices are mostly lying flat. Pour over any cream remaining in the bowl, and trickle the remaining oil over the gratin. Bake in a pre-heated fairly hot oven (200°C/400°F/Gas Mark 6), for 45–50 minutes, until the celeriac is completely tender and the top is browned and crispy. For extra crispness you can finish under the grill for 1–2 minutes.

I large (about 2 lb/900 g) or
  2 small celeriac
juice of ½ lemon
cold water
3 tbsp olive oil
3 garlic cloves, finely chopped
I small fresh green chilli, finely
  chopped
5 fl oz/150 ml double cream
salt and black pepper

Courgettes *Trifolati* with Four Finishes

Courgettes give out a lot of water when they are cooked. Stewed gently in olive oil until all the water has evaporated, they become soft and pulpy and wonderfully aromatic. The Italians call this method *trifolati*, and serve the pulp on pieces of grilled bread rubbed with olive oil (finish 1). But the pulp can also be used as the basis for a pasta sauce, a soup or even a soufflé (finishes 2, 3 and 4).

Wash, top and tail the courgettes, and slice them into thin discs (use a food processor if you have one). Heat the oil in a large heavy frying pan over a low heat and add the garlic. Cook for just 1 minute, and before it takes any colour add the sliced courgettes. Cover the pan for 1–2 minutes to encourage the courgettes to release their liquid, then remove the lid and turn up the heat a little. As long as there is liquid in the pan, the courgettes can bubble away without any danger of burning.

After 10 minutes or so, when most of the liquid has evaporated, lower the heat again, and let the courgettes stew in the oil until they are completely soft. Stir regularly with a wooden spoon or spatula, making sure they do not catch on the bottom of the pan. As the courgettes become soft you can start to break them up with the spoon. Eventually you will have a rough but creamy purée, which should not be at all watery. Season to taste with salt and pepper. At this stage the courgettes can be served as an accompanying vegetable

Basic recipe
2 lb/900 g small, firm
  courgettes
3 tbsp olive oil
3 garlic cloves, finely chopped
salt and black pepper

with any number of dishes – they are particularly good with roast lamb or simply grilled fish. Alternatively, you can go on to prepare any of the following dishes.

1. Bruschetta con zucchini
Serves 6

Additional ingredients
6 slices good white country
  bread
1 garlic clove
olive oil
2 oz/60 g fresh Parmesan
  cheese in one piece

Toast or grill the bread and rub the surface of each slice with a garlic clove. Trickle a little oil over each slice, and spoon on the courgettes. Pass around the Parmesan with a grater to grate directly on to the courgettes.

2. Spaghetti with courgettes
Serves 4 as a main course, 6 as a starter

Additional ingredients
12 oz/350 g spaghetti,
  tagliatelle or other preferred
  pasta
2 tbsp double cream
4 oz/115 g fresh Parmesan
  cheese, grated

Cook your chosen pasta according to the instructions. When the courgettes have finished cooking as described above, add the cream and half the Parmesan, and bubble for just a minute so that the cream is incorporated and reduced a little. Drain the pasta, toss in the sauce, and serve. Bring the remaining Parmesan to the table.

3. Courgette and milk soup
Serves 5-6: this soup is rich,
so portions need not be huge

Additional ingredients
up to 1½ pts/850 ml full-
  cream milk
4 oz/115 g fresh Parmesan
  cheese, grated
salt and black pepper
a few fresh basil leaves

When the courgettes are cooked as described above, mash them with a potato masher to make sure the purée is fairly smooth. Pour in the milk, stirring well, until the soup reaches the desired consistency (I like it fairly thick). Bring the soup just to the boil, stir in half the Parmesan, season to taste with salt and pepper, and serve at once, with a few torn basil leaves strewn over each bowl, and the remaining Parmesan on the table.

4. Courgette soufflé
Serves 6

Sieve the cooked courgettes into the béchamel sauce and mix well. Stir in both cheeses. Separate the eggs and beat the yolks into the béchamel–courgette mixture. Whisk the egg whites to stiff peaks and fold gently into the mixture (which should not be too hot, preferably room temperature). Pile the mixture into a large (at least 2 pt/1 litre), well-greased soufflé dish. (It should not be more than three-quarters full, so you may have to use 2 smaller dishes.) Bake the soufflé in a pre-heated moderate to hot oven (190°C/375°F/Gas Mark 5) for 30–35 minutes. It should be well-risen and golden-brown on top but still a bit creamy in the middle. If you use 2 smaller soufflé dishes, reduce the cooking time by 5–6 minutes.

Additional ingredients
5 fl oz/150 ml thick béchamel sauce (see page 399)
3 oz/85 g Gruyère cheese, grated
1 oz/30 g fresh Parmesan cheese, grated
3 eggs
butter *or* oil for greasing

Courgette 'Pudding' with a Creamy Tomato Sauce
THE ARK
Serves 6

This is a simple baked savoury custard of the kind you normally find inside a tart shell – indeed you could cook it inside one, if you love pastry, but it does not need it.

Top and tail the courgettes and grate them coarsely. Mix with the salt, sugar and vinegar, then leave to 'bleed' in a colander for about 30 minutes. Transfer to a clean cotton cloth and squeeze out as much water as you can with your hands.

Beat the eggs with the cream, adding a little basil or tarragon if used. Season to taste with salt and pepper and stir in the cheese. Thoroughly stir in the courgettes, turn into a reasonably deep, lightly buttered gratin or soufflé dish of 1½–2-pt/850-ml–1.1-litre capacity, and bake in a pre-heated fairly hot oven (200°C/400°F/Gas Mark 6) for 20–25 minutes until just set.

1½ lb/675 g small firm courgettes
1 tsp salt
1 tsp caster sugar
2 tsp tarragon vinegar
2 eggs
5 fl oz/150 ml double cream
a few fresh basil or tarragon leaves, chopped (*optional*)
2 tbsp freshly grated Parmesan or Gruyère cheese, *or* a mixture of the two
salt and black pepper
butter for greasing

For the tomato sauce
2lb/900 g full-flavoured
   tomatoes
2 tbsp olive oil
1 small onion, finely chopped
salt and black pepper
sugar
8 fl oz/250 ml crème fraîche

Wash the tomatoes and place in a foil-lined grill pan. Grill under a moderate heat, turning occasionally, for 15–20 minutes until lightly charred (alternatively, you can do this on a griddle pan). Rub the cooked tomatoes through a sieve, discarding the skin and pips.

Heat the oil in a pan and sweat the onion gently until completely soft and translucent. Add the sieved tomato and simmer for 7–10 minutes to reduce to a thick pulpy sauce (take care it does not catch on the bottom of the pan). Now (and not before) season with salt and pepper, and a pinch of sugar if required. Finish by stirring in the crème fraîche, off the heat.

To serve, pour a generous pool of tomato sauce on to each of 6 warmed plates, spoon portions of the 'pudding' on top and serve at once.

NOTE: Sheila Kidd writes: 'I bake flat mushrooms at the same time in the oven with olive oil, a little garlic, seasoning, lemon juice, chopped parsley and summer savory. They make a good accompaniment.'

Chilled Cucumber and Gooseberry Soup
Serves 4

This recipe is rather cheeky, as I invented it by stealing and combining recipes from two distinguished cookery writers, Elizabeth David and Jane Grigson. The former observed, in *French Provincial Cooking*, the remarkable similarity in flavour between sorrel and gooseberries. The latter, in her *Vegetable Book*, gave an excellent recipe for Russian Cucumber and Sorrel Soup. My experiment was to substitute gooseberries for sorrel in the Grigson recipe, and to my delight it worked. You can, of course, return to the original recipe – use 8 oz/225 g sorrel leaves, with the tough stalks removed, instead of the gooseberries; shred them, wilt in a pan (see page 45–6) and stir to a purée. Then proceed as below.

Cook the gooseberries in a pan with just enough water to prevent them from burning. Do not boil vigorously, but simmer gently for 5–10 minutes until the juices have run and the fruit is soft and pulpy. Rub through a nylon sieve to get a smooth, seedless purée. Leave to cool.

If the beef stock is set firm, warm it very gently to liquefy it, but do not allow it to become hot. Add it with all the other ingredients to the gooseberry purée, mixing well and seasoning to taste with salt, pepper and lemon juice. Chill thoroughly in the fridge before serving, and garnish each bowl, if you like, with a few more chives and a sprig of dillweed.

8 oz/225 g gooseberries
a little water
15 fl oz/450 ml good beef stock *or* good canned consommé
10 fl oz/300 ml single cream
10 fl oz/300 ml natural yoghurt
8 oz/225 g cucumber, cut into small dice
3 hardboiled eggs, chopped
1 tbsp chopped fresh chives
1 tbsp chopped fresh dill *or* fennel leaves
salt and black pepper
squeeze of lemon
extra chopped fresh chives and dillweed sprigs, to garnish (*optional*)

Fennel and Parmesan Risotto

THE BRACKENBURY

Serves 4 as a main course, 6 as a starter

When you trim the fennel bulbs, retain as much of the feathery fronds as you can – they dramatically increase the aromatic qualities of the risotto when added at the end of cooking. You can discard the tough stalks (and outer layer of the bulb if it is also tough). Slice the fennel as finely as you can (using the slicing blade of a food processor).

Sweat the onion and garlic in the oil in a heavy-based saucepan for a few minutes until softened. Add the fennel and cook for a further few minutes until softened. Add the rice and the wine and allow to bubble for 1–2 minutes. Add half the stock, then bring to a simmer. Cook gently, adding more stock whenever the liquid in the pan has almost been absorbed. You probably won't need all the stock. The final result should be smooth and creamy, with the rice still a little *al dente* – just chalky in the middle.

At the end of cooking, stir in the finely chopped fennel leaves, the Pernod and half the Parmesan. Take the remainder to the table for sprinkling on the risotto.

2–4 fennel bulbs (1 lb/450 g after trimming)
1 small onion, finely chopped
2 garlic cloves, finely chopped
2 tbsp good olive oil
8 oz/225 g arborio rice (see page 307)
1 wine-glass white wine
1 pt/575 ml warm chicken stock
a dash of Pernod
6 oz/170 g fresh Parmesan cheese, grated

Horseradish Mash

Serves 4

1½ lb/675 g floury potatoes
4 fl oz/100 ml milk
2 oz/60 g butter
1 tbsp freshly grated
  horseradish root
salt and black pepper

Add the unpeeled potatoes to well-salted boiling water, bring back to a simmer and cook until tender. Meanwhile, put the milk, butter and horseradish into a separate pan and heat to melt the butter. Keep hot, but not boiling, over a low heat or in a slow oven (150°C/300°F/Gas Mark 2) to infuse the flavour of the horseradish. Drain the potatoes when they are completely soft, then rub them through a sieve or potato ricer directly into the hot milk mixture, stirring well over a low heat. Season to taste with salt and pepper.

This is the purist's method of mashing potato, giving an extra smooth, creamy result. You can, of course, mash your potatoes in the usual way, pouring on the milk/butter/horseradish mixture as you go along.

Sweet Onion Confit

Makes about 1 lb/450 g

Long, slow cooking reduces the onions to a sweet, jammy pulp. The confit is delicious with grilled liver, or with cold meats, charcuterie and rough country pâtés. Start with plenty of onions or by the end of cooking time you will be left with nothing.

3 lb/1.3 kg medium to large
  onions
3 tbsp olive oil
2 tbsp red wine vinegar
10 fl oz/300 ml red wine
a few twists of black pepper

Peel the onions and slice them as finely as possible – you can use the fine slicing blade on a food processor. Heat the oil gently in your largest frying pan or a wide, heavy-based saucepan. Add the onions and cook very gently, stirring occasionally, so that they do not brown at all but merely sweat in their own juices. After 30 minutes or so the onions should be nice and soft, and considerably reduced in volume. Most of the liquid in the pan will have evaporated. Add the vinegar and half the wine, and allow to simmer gently until this liquid too has evaporated. Then add the remaining wine and repeat the process, continuing to cook the onions until they are very tender and sweet, and there is no liquid left in the pan. So long as you do not burn the onions you can hardly over-cook them, so just keep going until you think the risk of burning is too great – 1½ hours is about normal, 2 hours not excessive. You do not have to attend the pan constantly, but do stir the onions regularly and make sure they are not catching on the bottom.

When the onions are cooked, leave to cool, then transfer to a bowl and cover, or store in screw-top jars. The confit will keep for a week in the fridge.

Roast Pepper and Tomato Soup
Serves 4

The roasting of the vegetables adds a wonderfully rich flavour note to this dish, but what really makes it is the quality of the tomatoes – they must be fresh, aromatic and sweet, so avoid the thick-skinned and tasteless Dutch monsters. The bacon also adds flavour, but can easily be left out if you are vegetarian.

Put all the vegetables (including the garlic and onion) and the bacon into a roasting tin and place in a pre-heated fairly hot oven (200°C/400°F/Gas Mark 6). Remove the bacon after 10–15 minutes (before it gets crispy) and set aside. Cook the remaining vegetables for a further 15–20 minutes (30–35 minutes in all), until the peppers are blackened and blistered, then remove from the oven and set aside to cool. (If the onion is on the large side, it may take a further 10 minutes to become soft right through.)

When the peppers are cool enough to handle, peel away and discard the blackened skin, and scrape out and discard the seeds, but do this over a bowl so that you retain all the juices. Sieve the tomatoes, discarding the seeds and skin. Squeeze out the soft flesh from the onion or shallots and from the garlic cloves, and place, together with the skinned peppers and their juice, the sieved tomatoes and the bacon in a liquidizer and blend until smooth. Pour into a clean pan and season well with salt and pepper. Stir in the cream and heat through, but do not allow to boil for more than a moment.

1½ lb/675 g best fresh tomatoes, halved
3 large or 4 medium red peppers
1 small onion *or* 3 shallots, unpeeled
3 garlic cloves, unpeeled
2 bacon rashers, chopped (*optional*)
salt and black pepper
2 tbsp double cream

Pumpkin and Basil Risotto

BRASSERIE DU MARCHÉ AUX PUCES

Serves 4 as a generous starter

1 small onion, chopped
2 tbsp olive oil
6 oz/170 g arborio rice (see
  page 307)
15 fl oz/450 ml vegetable *or*
  chicken stock
a thyme sprig
1 bay leaf
8 oz/225 g pumpkin *or*
  butternut squash, diced small
2 oz/60 g butter
salt and black pepper
12 fresh basil leaves
2 oz/60 g Pecorino cheese,
  grated

Sweat the onion in the oil in a heavy-based saucepan until soft but not browned. Add the rice and mix well for a few seconds, pour in half the stock, add the thyme and bay leaf and bring to a merry simmer. Cook until almost all the stock is absorbed. From then on add more stock a little at a time, until the rice is almost tender. Add the pumpkin or squash and cook for a few further minutes until the rice is tender, or just *al dente* according to your taste, and the pumpkin cooked. Remove the bay leaf and the stalk of the thyme, then stir in the butter, and season well with salt and pepper. Divide into 4 servings and sprinkle with thin ribbons of shredded basil and the grated cheese.

Radicchio and Chilli Pasta Sauce

Serves 4 (with 12 oz/350 g uncooked weight
of preferred pasta)

A piquant and bitter pasta sauce, with a very distinctive taste that may not be everybody's cup of tea, though I think it quite divine. It is very quick and easy to prepare. Put your chosen pasta (try using penne, ridged pasta quills) on to boil just before you start to fry the pancetta, and by the time the sauce is finished the pasta will be ready.

2 medium radicchio heads
4 oz/115 g pancetta (Italian
  smoked belly of pork), in 2
  thick slices, *or* streaky bacon
1 tbsp olive oil
2 garlic cloves, finely chopped
1 small fresh red chilli, finely
  chopped
½ wine-glass red wine
5 fl oz/150 ml double cream
salt and black pepper

Wash and shred the radicchio, as you would a cabbage. Trim the rind off the pancetta and cut into thick matchsticks. Fry in the oil in a large frying pan for a few minutes until lightly browned, then throw in the garlic and chilli. Cook for just 1 minute, then pile in the radicchio, stirring so that it sweats and wilts but does not burn. The pan will seem overloaded at first, but the radicchio quickly reduces in volume. Add the wine and let bubble for a few minutes to reduce. Add the cream and reduce a little further, until the sauce is thick and glossy. Season to taste with salt and pepper. Add the cooked, drained pasta (or add the sauce to the pasta dish, if your frying pan is too full), mix well and heat through for 1 minute before serving. I prefer not to serve Parmesan cheese with this dish, but you can if you like.

Sweet Potato Batada
Serves 6

A simple and delicious pudding from Portugal, for those with a sweet tooth.

Rub the sweet potatoes through a sieve. Dissolve the caster sugar in the water in a saucepan over a low heat. Turn up the heat and boil vigorously for 4–5 minutes to form a syrup. Stir the potato into the syrup and cook over a gentle heat, stirring all the time, to get a smooth, sticky and slightly translucent paste – like wallpaper glue.

Remove from the heat and allow to cool. When the pan is cool enough for you to rest your hand against it, beat in the egg yolks, one at a time, to get a smooth, glossy cream. Return to a gentle heat and stir constantly, as if making a custard – on no account allow the mixture to boil. It is ready when rather thicker than custard – you should be able to part the mixture with your spoon to see the bottom of the pan. When this point is reached, dip the base of the pan in cold water to prevent further cooking. Stir in 1 tsp of the cinnamon and divide the mixture among 6 ramekins or glasses. Chill in the fridge. Just before serving, top each pot with a blob of cream and a sprinkling of icing sugar mixed with the remaining cinnamon.

scant 8 oz/225 g sweet potatoes, peeled and boiled until tender
4 oz/115 g caster sugar
5 tbsp water
10 egg yolks
1 1/2 tsp ground cinnamon
5 fl oz/150 ml double cream, whipped
2 tsp icing sugar

Yam Cakes with Chilli Dressing

BRASSERIE DU MARCHÉ AUX PUCES

Serves 4–5 as a generous starter, or 2 as a
light supper

I large or 2 small onions, finely
  chopped
sunflower *or* other oil for
  frying
I lb/450 g white yam, cooked
  and mashed
2 eggs
2 oz/60 g plain flour
salt and black pepper
a pinch of chilli pepper

For the dressing
4 tbsp olive oil
I tbsp wine vinegar
I small fresh green chilli, very
  finely chopped
a few sprigs of fresh coriander,
  finely chopped

Fry the onions gently in a little of the oil until completely soft, but not brown. Add them to the yam, with the eggs and flour, and mix to a smooth paste. Season to taste with salt, pepper and chilli.

Form the mixture into small patties and shallow fry in the oil for 5–7 minutes, turning occasionally, until crisp and golden brown. This quantity should give you 8–10 cakes.

Combine the ingredients for the dressing and serve in a saucer or small bowl as a dipping sauce.

Andalucian Garlic Soup with Poached Eggs

THE BRACKENBURY

Serves 4

A warming and very economical supper dish – so good it can easily be elevated to the status of dinner-party starter.

2 tbsp good olive oil
2 thick slices white country
  bread *or* ciabatta
4–8 garlic cloves, depending on
  size, very finely chopped
2 pts/1.1 litres good, strong,
  clear chicken stock
4 fresh eggs
vinegar

Heat the oil in a heavy saucepan and gently fry the bread with the garlic. Do not let the garlic brown, but just as it is on the point of taking colour, transfer the mixture to a blender with a cup of the stock, and blend until smooth. Return the mixture to the saucepan, add the remaining stock and bring to the boil. Simmer gently for just 1 minute, until the soup thickens.

In a separate pan of water acidulated with a little vinegar, lightly poach the eggs, and place each in the bottom of a warmed soup bowl. Ladle in the hot soup and serve with ciabatta.

A greedy but delicious way to enjoy this soup is to dip your ciabatta into a little pool of olive oil and then into the runny yolk of your poached egg.

Garbure
(French Cabbage Soup)
Serves 6-8

This hearty dish is a complete meal, and a carnivorous one by anybody's standards. I include it in the vegetable chapter because cabbage is the one essential among ingredients which vary, in France, from region to region. I suggest as the meat elements a bacon hock, a piece of salt pork and a few sausages, as these are easily available from any good butcher. The adventurous cook could replace or supplement these with a breast of mutton, a few pieces of duck or goose confit, or even a pig's head.

Shred the cabbage, not too finely, and blanch in boiling water for 2 minutes. Drain well and put into a large stock-pot with all the other ingredients except the sausages and potatoes. Pour in enough boiling water to cover the ingredients by 1 in/2.5 cm or so, cover and cook at a very slow simmer (barely a tremble) for at least 3 hours. You can do this in a very slow oven (130°C/275°F/Gas Mark 1) if you like. About 40 minutes before you are ready to eat, brown the sausages quickly in a frying pan and add with the potatoes to the pot. Cook until the potatoes are tender.

When you serve the soup, it may be helpful to remove the pieces of meat and cut them up, so that you can make sure everybody gets some.

1 large or 2 small green cabbages (e.g. Savoy or Primo)
2 lb/900 g bacon hock, on the bone
1 lb/450 g salt pork (belly or ribs)
8 oz/225 g carrots, peeled and cut into large batons
½ celeriac, peeled and cut into large dice
4 small turnips, quartered
4 oz/115 g dried haricot beans, soaked overnight
a bouquet garni (including bay leaf and parsley)
salt and black pepper
8 oz/225 g good butcher's sausages
1 lb/450 g mealy potatoes (e.g. Désirée or Golden Wonder), peeled and thickly sliced

Parsnip and Pheasant Soup
Serves 6

I often make this lightly curried, nourishing soup when I have prepared some pheasant stock, but you can just as well use chicken, beef, or even vegetable stock. The finished soup freezes well.

2 lb/900 g parsnips
1 onion, sliced
2 garlic cloves, finely chopped
2 oz/60 g butter
1 small, tart eating apple,
  peeled, cored and sliced
1 small or ½ large floury
  potato, peeled and diced
1 tbsp garam masala
½ tsp dried chilli flakes
salt and black pepper
2 pts/1.1 litres pheasant stock
2 tbsp double cream (optional)

Trim, peel and cut up the parsnips into large dice. Sweat the onion and garlic gently in the butter in a large saucepan until softened but not coloured. Add the parsnips, apple and potato, and sweat for a further few minutes. Add the spices, season with salt and pepper, mix well, and cook for a further 2 minutes. Pour over the stock and bring to the boil. Cover the pan and cook at a gentle simmer for 20–25 minutes until the vegetables are completely tender.

Sieve or liquidize the soup and return to the pan. Adjust the seasoning, thin with a little water if you feel this is necessary, and reheat thoroughly without boiling. If you wish to enrich the soup with a little cream, stir it in just before serving.

Salsa Rossa
(Red Sauce)

The ingredients given below are a rough guide only. The idea is to get the sweetness of the red pepper, the aromatic flavour of tomatoes and the pep of chilli and garlic. Exact quantities are not important. You could use chilli powder instead of fresh chilli. Or, for a milder sauce, you could scrap the chilli, and add a few fresh basil leaves.

1 garlic clove, peeled
1 small shallot, peeled
2 anchovies
2 red peppers, roasted, skinned
  and de-seeded
2 fresh plum tomatoes,
  blanched, peeled and de-
  seeded
3 sun-dried tomatoes in oil
½ small fresh red chilli, or less
  depending on heat
1 tbsp olive oil
1 tsp balsamic or red wine
  vinegar

On a large chopping board, finely chop together the garlic and shallot (preferably with a mezzaluna, see page 22), followed by the remaining ingredients except the olive oil and vinegar, until you have a rough purée. (This can be done in a food processor, but the texture will not be quite as good.) Transfer to a bowl and stir in the oil and vinegar. Serve with grilled sausages or lamb chops.

NOTE: this can be adapted as a pasta sauce if heated with a little cream.

Deep-fried Vegetables in Batter

This is one of my favourite ways of eating vegetables. You can make this dish as a light snack or starter, or cook enough vegetables to make a whole meal. A domestic deep-fat fryer makes this operation safer, easier and cleaner than an old-fashioned chip pan. The quantities given below make enough batter to coat vegetables for 6 people.

Make a well in the centre of the flour in a mixing bowl, break in the egg and mix to a paste with a fork. Stir in the oil, then the water, and mix to a smooth cream. Season with a pinch of salt. Leave the batter to stand for at least 1 hour before using.

    If you want a particularly light and crispy batter, you can withhold the egg white from the initial blending. Then, just before you coat the vegetables, whisk it to stiff peaks and fold it into the batter.

For the batter
4 oz/115 g plain flour
1 egg
3 tbsp olive oil
5 fl oz/150 ml tepid water
salt

There is a great range of vegetables you can use, and the alphabetical guide pages 46–103 indicates whenever a vegetable is suitable for this treatment. Here are some suggestions for vegetables which, together, make a particularly good selection:

For the vegetables

COURGETTES: cut lengthways into thin slices or batons, sprinkle with coarse salt and leave in a colander to drain for 1–2 hours. Dry thoroughly by patting with kitchen paper or a clean cloth just before frying. Tiny courgettes with the flowers still attached can be deep-fried whole.

AUBERGINES: cut into thin slices down the length of the fruit, then salt and pat dry as for courgettes.

FENNEL: cut across the bulb from top to bottom into slices no thicker than a 10p piece.

CAULIFLOWER and BROCCOLI: small florets of either should be blanched for 3–4 minutes in boiling water and removed while still just crunchy. Leave to drain in a colander, then toss in a cotton cloth to make sure they are quite dry.

SPRING ONIONS and BABY LEEKS: use specimens barely thicker than a pencil. Wash and dry, trim the dark green tops, then split with a knife to about 1 in/2.5 cm from the bulb. Feather out the leaves just before dipping in the batter, for maximum coating.

CARROTS: no need to blanch if you cut them thin enough – into slices no more than $\frac{1}{16}$ in/1 mm thick down the length of the peeled carrot.

BASIL PARCELS: choose large, plump basil leaves. Roll up a whole anchovy fillet (canned) in the leaf and tie up the roll with a chive or a strip of spring onion.

Procedure

It is essential to use a good deep-frying oil – I prefer groundnut (peanut) oil, but you can use corn oil or sunflower oil. Olive oil can be used, though it should not be heated higher than 170°C. Heat the oil in your pan or deep-fat fryer to 190°C/375°F (170°C/340°F if you are using olive oil). Dip the vegetables in the batter just before frying, shaking each piece gently as you remove it so that any excess batter falls back into the bowl. Fry the vegetables in small batches, for 3–4 minutes, until crispy and golden-brown. (The basil leaves will take barely a minute.) Remove each batch as it is ready, shaking the wire basket over the pan to drain off excess oil, and transfer to a large warmed dish lined with absorbent kitchen paper. The finished fritters should not wait around for too long, so once you have prepared enough for your guests to get started on, delegate an assistant to take them to the table straight away.

Accompaniments

Sea salt, black pepper and a few lemon wedges should be on the table. No other condiments are essential, but a purée of soft, roasted garlic cloves (see page 81), mixed with a little olive oil and a pinch of salt and black pepper, is a rather delicious accompaniment.

Grilled Mixed Vegetables

Serves 6 as a starter or accompanying
vegetable

Only a barbecue or griddle pan will produce the perfectly succulent, char-striped vegetables that make this dish such a delight. The dish can be prepared in advance, and the grilled vegetables left to marinate in their dressing, but not for more than a few hours.

Cut the courgettes and aubergines lengthways into thin slices or batons, sprinkle with salt and put into a colander to drain for 1–2 hours. Trim the spring onions or baby leeks and blanch in boiling water for 2 minutes, then drain well and pat dry. Cut the fennel bulbs from top to bottom into slices the thickness of a 10p piece.

Pre-heat your griddle pan over maximum heat for at least 5 minutes. Grill the vegetables one at a time, in batches if necessary. It is a good idea to start with the peppers, as these have to be left to cool before they can be skinned. (You can save time, if you like, by roasting the peppers in a hot pre-heated oven (220°C/425°F/Gas Mark 7) until the skins are blackened and the flesh tender.) If you use a griddle or barbecue, grill them whole, turning frequently, until they are charred and tender. Put the finished peppers into a covered dish to cool.

The courgettes and aubergines should be pressed dry with kitchen paper or a clean cloth just before grilling. Lay them across the bars of the griddle pan or barbecue, and cook for 2–3 minutes on each side, until nicely striped and tender. You may want to taste one or two pieces to make sure they are neither too burnt nor too raw. You will soon get the hang of it. Transfer to a large dish as they are done. Cook the spring onions or leeks and the fennel slices in the same way, turning only once if possible.

When you have grilled all the vegetables, return to the peppers which should now be cool enough to handle, and peel off the charred skin with your fingers. Cut or tear each pepper into 5–6 strips, scraping out the seeds, and add the strips of pepper to the other vegetables in the serving dish.

Cut the garlic as thinly as possible into slivers and distribute over the vegetables. Mix the lemon juice and olive oil, season with salt and pepper and pour this dressing over the vegetables. You can serve the vegetables still warm, or at room temperature, but do not refrigerate. Garnish with a few torn basil leaves just before serving.

This dish can be served as a course on its own, accompanied by thick slices of crusty white bread, grilled on the barbecue or griddle pan, rubbed with a piece of garlic, and with a little olive oil trickled over each slice.

4 medium *or* 6 small
 courgettes
I large *or* 2 small aubergines
salt
12 spring onions *or* baby leeks
2 fennel bulbs
3 red *or* yellow peppers

For the dressing
2 garlic cloves
I tbsp lemon juice
4 tbsp best olive oil
salt and black pepper
a few fresh basil leaves

Winter Vegetables Roasted in Goose Fat

THE BRACKENBURY

Serves 6 as an accompanying vegetable, 4 as
a light supper

The fat saved from roasting a single goose, or even a large farmyard duck, should be ample for cooking the quantity of vegetables given below. You can, of course, roast the vegetables around the bird as it cooks, but you will probably have to omit some of them for the sake of space. You can also roast these vegetables in ordinary fat or olive oil, but the goose fat makes them particularly delicious.

1 lb/450 g potatoes
1 lb/450 g parsnips
½ large *or* 1 small celeriac
3 large carrots
3 leeks
6 whole shallots *or* pickling onions
8 oz/225 g small Jerusalem artichokes
at least 10 fl oz/300 ml goose *or* duck fat
salt and black pepper

Only the potatoes need to be par-boiled – for about 6 minutes in boiling salted water, with the skins still on. Then drain them, peel off the skins, and cut them into usual roasting-sized pieces. Roughing up the surface with a fork will help them to become extra crispy.

Peel and cut up the parsnips, celeriac and carrots into approximately 2-in/5-cm long chunks. Wash the leeks and cut into similar lengths. Rub off any papery outside skin from the shallots. Scrub but do not peel the artichokes.

Pour the fat into a large roasting tin to a depth of at least ½ in/1 cm. Pre-heat the oil in a fairly hot oven (200°C/400°F/Gas Mark 6) for 10 minutes. The potatoes will take rather longer than the other vegetables (about 50 minutes) so put these in first. Add all the other vegetables, except the leeks, after 20 minutes. Add the leeks 10 minutes later, and continue roasting for a further 20 minutes. Each time you interrupt the cooking to add another batch, turn and baste the other vegetables in the tin. Ten minutes after the leeks are added, give a final basting, and season all the vegetables with salt and pepper. After 50 minutes all the vegetables should be well browned and tender. Remove them from the fat with a slotted spoon, and transfer to a serving dish lined with kitchen paper. Serve at once, so that the vegetables do not lose any crispness.

NOTE: turnips, swedes, whole garlic bulbs and butternut squash could also be incorporated into this dish. They will all take about 30 minutes, so should be added to the potatoes after 20 minutes.

CHAPTER THREE

Fish and Shellfish

'I'm allergic to fish!' was a phrase commonly heard in my primary school dining hall at lunch-time on a Friday. Some of the grumblers were even able to brandish letters from their mothers. This would excuse them from having to partake of a sodden, sorry portion of nameless off-white fish, plastered with a layer of glistening floury paste. This suspect emulsion was sparsely speckled with grey-green flecks, alleged to be herbaceous, which apparently justified the name of 'parsley sauce'.

Though I envied my friends their exemption from, as Nigel Molesworth put it so beautifully, 'the piece of cod which passeth all understanding', I had the deepest sympathy with anyone who was physically intolerant of fish. For they would never know (as I, at the age of six, already knew) the briny freshness of self-caught prawns boiled in sea-water, or the incomparable taste of flappingly fresh mackerel simply grilled.

It is a sad truth that, for an island nation, we make a poor job of introducing our children to the pleasures of eating fish. To many youthful palates fish is something that, unless it comes in Dayglo orange breadcrumbs with a dollop of tomato ketchup, is to be avoided at all costs. It's a state of affairs for which school canteens bear only partial responsibility. The way some parents market fish to their children can only add to their perception that it's one of those evils which adults prescribe and should, if at all possible, be avoided. Like carrots, which help you see in the dark, and spinach, which makes you grow big and strong, fish, so they told us, is good for your brains. That always sounded pretty spurious to me and, true or not, it certainly didn't help to increase its appeal.

So my first plea in this chapter is to parents (I'm assuming that school caterers are beyond the reach of my mission): nurture your children's interest in food with care and, when it comes to fish, with *extra* care. Make out, if you wish, that fish is a greedy and rather unhealthy treat, like ice cream. Reward them, on occasion, with prawns instead of sweets. When you go to the seaside find the freshest mackerel you can and grill it for them. Serve them up a stale fish in formative years and you may find that they join the unhappy band who announce themselves to be 'allergic'. You'll know, of course, that this is nonsense. But the task of persuading them of that will be a hard one.

Buying fish

A good motto for the Bon Marché cook in search of a fish for supper might be 'Every fish has his day'. The problem with too many fishmongers in this country is that most of their fish have already had theirs. But even the sloppiest and least switched-on of fishmongers is liable to have the odd specimen in reasonable condition accidentally slipped into his order. The Bon Marché cook will find it.

For me, buying fish is a bit like going fishing. I never know what I'm going to return home with – on a bad day it may be nothing at all. And like any fisherman, when I do land a prize catch, I will generally spend a good while gloating over it before I turn my thoughts to how it will be cooked.

So how do we arrive at our chosen fish? The person in a particularly good position to help, if he should so choose, is the fishmonger. A good relationship with a scrupulously honest and highly discerning fishmonger is an enviable feather in any cook's cap – most of your problems are solved before they have even begun. 'What's good today?' is all you need to ask.

Unfortunately few of us have it so easy. Even a good fishmonger has to make a living, and that means off loading as much from his slab as he possibly can. Whilst it makes no business sense at all to foist a lame fish on to a valued regular customer, anyone who has shown contentment with the merely adequate is not likely to be steered towards the truly superb. That will be kept for the more discerning shopper.

But a fishmonger who cares is certainly a good start. His shop need not be big, nor need his slab display one of those elaborate piscine collages. Cleanliness, civility and a lack of bad smells are much keener indicators. A willingness to answer questions is more likely to be a sign of reliability and confidence in his product than of a shameless ability to tell fishy tales. 'Where does your fish come from?' is always a good opener. If you can establish whether deliveries are daily, or less frequent, so much the better. The next step is to make sure your fish-buying day is a delivery day.

Provided you are respectful and don't insist on poking everything in the shop, every decent fishmonger should let you touch his fish. It is, however, polite to ask. If permission is refused, there is not a lot you can do, though it is always worth asking, 'Why not?'. 'Because you might catch something,' was an answer I once got from a sympathetic fellow-customer who witnessed such an exchange at the fish counter in Selfridges.

Clues to freshness

Handling a fish will quickly tell you whether it is in good condition. Look for a bright, clear eye, as opposed to a sunken, cloudy one. Look behind the gill covers at the gills, which in most species should be pink, wet and possibly (in a very fresh fish) bloody. As the fish loses condition the gills become dull, grey-brown and gummed up with slimy mucus. Sniff behind the gills too. Any whiff of tainted fishiness, and you should look for another specimen.

Press your finger gently but firmly into the thickest part of the fish. It should be firm and resistant to pressure, springing back without leaving an indentation. This is a particularly good test for flat-fish: plaice can look quite decent even when they are rather past it; soles and dabs, on the other hand, often appear drab and unhappy even when they are still quite fresh. Incidentally freshness, as in 'how long dead', is not the only issue. Badly treated fish will rapidly lose condition, whereas a well-packed, carefully transported, firm-fleshed white fish, such as turbot or even cod, will still be worthwhile after 4 or 5 days. The press test is a good test of pot-worthiness, not just age.

A dry skin is no indication that a fish is past its prime, just as 'the wet look' does not guarantee freshness. Fishmongers are adept at cosmeticizing their slabs with a regular splash of water; this is why it is important to examine the fish closely. Once you have inspected a good few fish, including some that are less than fresh, you will soon become adept at discarding doubtful specimens and returning home with a catch to be proud of.

The price of fish

If the herring was a rare fish which swam around in tiny shoals in far-flung corners of the globe, then I suspect it would fetch a rather higher price than it does now. There would probably be a cult for eating it raw, and the world's most extravagant party-throwers would have it jetted in on ice, boasting to their guests that it was only hours since the fish swam free. Rollmops would be a much prized delicacy, and gourmets would vigorously debate the relative merits of kippers and bloaters. All three would be available in airport duty-free shops in special gift-wrapped packages with half a bottle of second-rate champagne, and by mail order at vastly inflated prices. Herring roes would be sold salted or smoked on the black market and people would kill to get hold of them fresh. Tiffany would design jewel-encrusted 24-carat gold 'herring roe forks' and connoisseurs would claim, quite ludicrously, that the flavour of the roe was tainted if it came into contact with any metal other than gold. The people who controlled the herring market would be very rich, very fat, and under investigation for tax evasion. Next time you find a nice fresh herring at your fishmonger, or cook a fine kipper for your breakfast, think of that, and enjoy it all the more.

What I am getting at is that the price of fish is a reflection not of quality but of supply and, to a slightly lesser extent, demand (or fashion). Consequently fish prices go up and down all the time, and will vary greatly from region to region. This is actually to the advantage of the Bon Marcheur. A regular fish-shopper who is observant will soon know what a good price is, at his fishmonger at least, for any number of species he is interested in.

The chances are you will have set your own upper price limit when you walk into the shop. All I would say about that is that it should be your *only* pre-set condition. You may not be prepared to spend more than £8 on enough fish for two. But do, I implore you, be prepared to spend less. Those who go looking for a treat, prepared to splash out on something a bit luxurious, have a long way to fall if it disappoints. If, on the other hand, you walk out of the fishmonger's with a couple of plaice or whiting, or the aforementioned herring, then provided they are really fresh you have indeed found something truly luxurious. And the change in your pocket will be enough to buy an appropriately luxurious wine to go with it.

As I have said, fish prices fluctuate on a daily basis and from place to place. It would be pointless, and entirely against the Bon Marché spirit I have just expounded, to suggest prices at which any particular species becomes 'a bargain'. However, I do feel it is worthwhile to mention a few species which tend to be on the cheaper side and which, when in fine condition, are worth whatever you are happy to pay for them. Consequently I include an alphabetical guide to fish and shellfish at the end of this chapter.

Shellfish

A friend of mine refuses to eat crustaceans on the grounds that they are really just giant insects adapted to marine life. If lobsters lived on land, he argues, no one would dream of eating them. And if one crawled out from behind the fridge, the sensible thing to do would be to club it to pieces with a large stick. Whenever he encounters someone enjoying a plate of prawns he delights in explaining to them, 'You realize that what you're eating is in fact a cockroach that has learnt to swim.' He is right, of course. Crabs, lobsters, prawns and shrimps are, like insects and spiders, all members of the family *Arthropoda*. But his argument can easily be turned around. Perhaps we should really be looking more closely at the culinary possibilities for those arthropods that live on land, indeed even behind our fridges.

Shellfish, be they crustaceans or molluscs, are of great interest to the Bon Marché cook. Many of them can (like insects) be had in plentiful supply for nothing; gathering your own shellfish has the added advantage of guaranteeing freshness. However, if you are paying good money for them you have to be extra vigilant. Most shellfish, especially bivalves (mussels, oysters, clams, etc.) and gastropods (winkles, whelks, etc.), need to be bought alive to be really worthwhile. Unless kept moist and cool, they are forced to consume internally stored nutrients to stay alive – they effectively shrink, and quickly become unpalatable. They are therefore even more susceptible than fish to ill-treatment and inappropriate storage.

Buying shellfish

Because they are so vulnerable, shellfish are best bought close to their point of exit from the sea. Besides being in better condition, they are also likely to be far cheaper. A seaside holiday may be the one time that Bon Marché cooks allow themselves the luxury of a couple of live lobsters to boil at home. The best shopping strategies for different shellfish are suggested in the guide at the end of this chapter.

Fish in the supermarket

Until recently the range of fish available in supermarkets was severely limited – various cuts of cod, haddock, coley, plaice and trout might be found frozen. Fresh fish, if it was sold at all, generally came as a fillet or cutlet pre-packaged in a sealed cellophane tray, making any assessment of its freshness something of a challenge. Most of the smaller supermarkets, and the food departments of Marks and Spencer's stores, still present fresh fish in this way. I don't condemn it, because I don't see what else they can do – and they have to cater for the great number of shoppers who like to do all their shopping in one place.

There is, of course, one clue to freshness that the supermarket offers on its packaged fish which you will not find in any fishmonger – the use-by date. Although this is a very useful guide for the shopper, it is worth bearing in mind what the primary purpose of a use-by date really is. On the one hand it allows the shelf-packers to clear the shelves of produce that is past its best – undoubtedly a good thing. But – and this is probably the key factor for managers wishing to run a profitable business – it also helps to ensure that produce which has been deemed to have a certain shelf-life is not removed and disposed of prematurely. So just because you find a product before its use-by date has expired, that doesn't mean it's in tip-top condition. It merely indicates that it is in an adequate condition, in which – according to exhaustive market research – a sufficiently small percentage of shoppers will find it so objectionable as to shop elsewhere in future. In other words, it won't harm you to eat it, but it may not be delicious.

When buying pre-packaged fresh fish it is not merely handy to bear these factors in mind, it is essential. Personally I would never hand over money for fish on the same day as the use-by date, and would be reluctant to do so the day before. A 2-day leeway is probably worth thinking about, a 3-day margin a very good bet, and 4 days the best you are likely to find. In fairness to supermarkets I should say that when I have found packaged fish well within the use-by date I have often been impressed by its condition.

If, as is the case in an increasing number of the larger stores, a supermarket actually has its own fresh fish slab, then one might think that the Bon Marché cook is effectively back at the fishmonger's, and everything I said earlier on that score applies. If only life were that simple.

In fact, shopping at the fishmonger-within-a-supermarket has a set of problems all its own. The first, and worst, of these, is that there is no fishmonger. Certainly, there is always someone there in a white coat and dairy maid's hat, to pick up your chosen fish (usually with polythene gloves, as if that could somehow rescue or protect a fish from decay), weigh and wrap it for you. But in my experience these people are rarely able to answer any of my questions. They have clearly had nothing to do with the ordering of the fish; they know little, and care even less, about the product they sell. Far from being fish-lovers, these are unfortunate sales assistants who have drawn the short straw and been posted on fish for the week. They are longing to get back to the deli counter. And if you try to touch the fish they don't like it one bit.

Persistence can have its rewards, however. When informed that 'hygiene regulations' strictly stipulated that customers could not touch the fish, I once countered, 'But *you're* touching the fish.' 'Yes, but *I'm* wearing these special sterile gloves' came the reply in a tone of false patience. 'Perhaps you would be very kind and lend me a pair?' I chanced. Rather to my surprise, she did, and I left with a cutlet from a pleasingly fresh haddock. I think it may be some time before supermarket fish slabs offer their patrons a disposable prodding glove as a matter of course, but I live in hope.

Gloveless and forbidden to prod, however, the Bon Marché cook has a problem. All he or she can really do is go by the various visual clues outlined above.

There is one further tip, which I would hesitate to cast in stone, but which may prove useful. The old tradition of eating fish on a Friday has a residual but dependable following in this country. Most supermarkets will expect to sell significantly more fish on a Friday than on any other weekday. They will also expect to sell a fair bit on a Saturday, simply because it is a busy shopping day. Most supermarkets therefore take their largest delivery on a Friday morning – probably of enough fish to last for Saturday as well. Buy your fish on a Friday and the chances are you will have a wider choice of fresher fish.

Freezing fish

The flesh of fish, as of meat, changes when it is frozen. To summarize briefly, crystals form, cells are damaged and fluid is lost on thawing – thus both flavour and texture are affected. Once flavour and texture have been lost from a fish, or from any food come to that, there's not much left worth hanging on to. Frozen fish is therefore probably best thought of as a standby and a filler, particularly useful in recipes where the texture of the fish is not being preserved anyway, such as fishcakes, soup, soufflés or mousselines; or when the fish flavour is strongly supplemented by powerful herbs or spices, or a rich sauce.

Having said that, some fish freeze better than others, and some ways of freezing do less harm. The condition of the fish when frozen is also a factor; if fish is to be frozen at all it must be frozen when fresh. A fast dry-freeze will limit the damage. Frozen fish that end up in the supermarket are generally earmarked for freezing from the start. With luck they have been filleted and frozen on board the ship on which they were landed. Faced with the unenviable choice, you would probably be better off with a piece of frozen cod from the supermarket than a stale fillet from the fishmonger. Whatever you cook may not be as well flavoured as it could have been had you used fresh fish, but at least it won't taste bad. *Never* refreeze defrosted fish – there is no point in threatening your health as well as your palate.

Whole fish, and even ungutted fish, survive freezing better than fillets or portions – this is worth bearing in mind if you have a surplus of fresh fish and want to freeze some yourself. Oily fish, such as salmon, mackerel, sardines and eel, freeze rather better than white fish, and fish that have a tendency to be watery in the first place, such as pollack, pouting or whiting, fare worst of all. By the same token, most smoked fish, which have already lost much of their moisture, survive freezing remarkably well.

Of the shellfish, which I will discuss in more detail in the alphabetical guide below, cooked whole prawns in their shells freeze well, as do whole raw squid. Another frozen shellfish product often available in fishmongers is cooked crab, the white and brown meat often available separately. Neither is worth much on its own, but both, the brown meat especially, retain some crabby taste, and are handy bulkers for any fishy bisque or soup. I wouldn't want to encourage you to use frozen crabmeat for my Crab Ramekins (page 177), but you might get away with it!

Smoked fish

Haddock, cod, trout, salmon, eel, mackerel, herring – every fishmonger will stock some or all of these fish smoked. The British, particularly the Scots and Irish, have been smoking fish for centuries. No surprise, then, that we've got rather good at it.

Smoked fish are a great boon for the Bon Marché chef. They are naturally preserved products which travel well and have a long shelf-life; consequently there is little even the most slapdash fishmonger can do to ruin them. They are also extremely versatile, as you will discover from the recipes ahead. The wide availability of smoked fish means that you need never leave the fishmonger's entirely disappointed, though I wouldn't want to imply that smoked fish is always a last resort.

When shopping for smoked fish, be aware that the techniques for curing vary greatly. Many large-scale operations use dyes, chemical preservatives and an excess of salt to increase the shelf-life of their product. Such additives, of course, have no benefits in taste. It is therefore always worth enquiring about the origin of smoked fish products, and requesting kippers and smoked haddock, in particular, that are undyed and additive-free. Here are some smoked fish products to look out for:

ARBROATH SMOKIES: a smokie is to a haddock what a bloater is to a herring; a whole one (smaller fish are used) smoked without being split or gutted. Smokies have a strong oaky flavour all their own. Very popular in Scotland, they are harder to find in England, especially in the south, but well worth seeking out. Try them poached in milk and served whole with butter melting on them. The head and bones will make a lovely smoky fish stock.

BLOATERS: bloaters are smoked whole herrings, unsplit and ungutted, and usually have the added bonus of roe in their cavities. Shrivelled and brown, you may think they look less than appetizing – I avoided them for years. They are in fact quite delicious, and highly economical. See page 165 for Adam Robinson's Three Uses of a Bloater – now, *that's* Bon Marché.

KIPPERS: originally the word kipper referred to smoked salmon and trout. The split herring, brine-soaked and then smoked, originated on the Northumbrian coast at the beginning of the last century. By 1900 it had stolen the name 'kipper' and become ubiquitous as a classic British breakfast dish. Now they are produced wherever herrings are landed – mainly in Scotland and the north of England. The saltiness and flavour vary greatly, according to the exact 'recipe' for the cure. Loch Fyne kippers are said by many to be the best.

Besides being delicious grilled, or poached in milk, kippers make an excellent pâté or even soufflé, and a cheap but rather classy starter when marinated in olive oil, lemon juice and chopped shallots. I must confess to a weakness for Bird's Eye boil-in-the-bag frozen kipper fillets – the ones that come with that ridiculous star-shaped piece of butter frozen inside the vacuum pack. They are incredibly easy to cook, even with a hangover, and a very good cure for that condition to boot.

RED HERRINGS: yet another variation on the kipper theme, the red herring is the product of an extra strong cure, and keeps well even unrefrigerated. Red herrings are very hard to find in England now. Although still produced in fairly large quantities, most are exported to Africa and the West Indies where they are extremely popular. They are actually the original ingredient for The Brackenbury's West African Fish Soup (page 166), though Adam Robinson more often uses bloaters. Intrepid Bon Marché cooks might like to look out for red herrings in the ethnic markets of our larger cities. There is a stall in Balham Market, south London, that usually has them.

SMOKED COD: can be substituted for smoked haddock in most recipes. As with haddock, however, avoid the fish which has been dyed a lurid yellow.

SMOKED COD'S ROE: some good fishmongers (and some well-stocked delicatessens) will sell you a piece of smoked roe in an untreated state. It's not expensive, and very worthwhile, as it allows you to discover the very special taste of taramasalata as it should be (page 164). The result is a world away from the frightening pink gunge of the mass-marketed product. Good smoked roe is delicious entirely unadulterated, served with wedges of fresh lime and brown bread. A Russian friend of mine insists it must be served with shots of ice-cold vodka – which has always been fine by me.

SMOKED EEL: available as fillets (usually vacuum-packed) or on the bone in sections. Quite delicious on its own with brown bread and a little grated horseradish, or in a salad with rocket leaves (a rocket and smoked eel sandwich is another great treat).

SMOKED HADDOCK: a very versatile ingredient and, when of the finest quality, delicious simply poached, perhaps on a bed of spinach. The best smoked haddock is called Finnan haddock and comes from Scotland – it is the classic ingredient for Cullen Skink (page 158), and is best bought still on the bone. Failing that, always ask for undyed smoked haddock – it has a much more subtle flavour than the bright yellow variety, which also tends to contain extra preservatives. You should note, however, that although it will keep for a few days in the fridge, smoked haddock – undyed and Finnan in particular – has a shorter shelf-life than most other smoked fish. If it starts to smell 'fishy' then you will have to throw it away.

SMOKED MACKEREL: perhaps the most ubiquitous of all smoked fish, smoked mackerel has now found its way into the chilling cabinet of practically every corner shop in the country. A decade ago smoked mackerel pâté was a stalwart starter at many a Sloane supper party. These days it hardly seems such a treat. I find the fish on its own very rich and, in many cases, none too subtly smoked. A heavy, buttery pâté is more than I can take, but mash smoked mackerel with fromage frais and a squeeze of lemon, and you get a lighter pâté with a nice tang. Besides the familiar hot-smoked product, you may occasionally encounter cold-smoked mackerel. This is quite delicious, more like smoked salmon, and definitely worth seeking out. If your fishmonger cannot get hold of some for you, try calling the Cornish Smoked Fish Company on St Austell (0726) 72356. They can supply mail order, or tell you where it is available.

SMOKED SALMON: the most celebrated of all smoked fish – and one of the most expensive. The increasing availability of cheap, farmed fish has brought the price down a little, though certainly not as much as one might have hoped. More predictably, it has also led to a rash of new and large-scale smoking operations which are no doubt hoping to take advantage of an expanding market. Consequently the quality of the product varies hugely, and buying smoked salmon has become a hazardous business. I tend to avoid it, finding cheaper smoked fish as interesting and more consistent. If you do buy smoked salmon, don't be taken in by the marketing ploy that likes to insist Scottish is always best. Many Scottish smokers are new to the game, cashing in on the proximity of cheap, farmed salmon and using huge patented steel kilns whose faster smoke imparts a much less subtle flavour than traditional brick kilns or smoke-holes. Much of this smoked salmon ends up ready-sliced in vacuum packs, which is fine if the product is a good one, but how can you tell? Bon Marcheurs who find a brand they like should stick to it. I like to buy smoked salmon from a fishmonger who still keeps whole sides for slicing to order. It shows a dedication to service that is unlikely to go hand in hand with a shoddy product – but you can always ask for a little taste before you commit yourself. A company which sells smoked salmon by mail order, and still uses a traditional brick kiln, is Coln Valley Fish and Game in Winson, Gloucestershire (Fossebridge [0285] 720400). All their products, which include *gravadlax*, smoked eel and smoked cod's roe, are excellent.

SMOKED TROUT: this is not my favourite smoked fish, perhaps because farmed rainbow trout are almost always used. These fish are at best somewhat bland and at worst muddy-tasting – the resulting smoked product suffers accordingly. There are exceptions. The Coln Valley smokery, who buy their fish well, do a superior smoked trout, and the Cornish Smoked Fish Company's cold-smoked trout is better than a lot of mass-produced smoked salmon. Whole smoked trout are often better than fillets. Horseradish is a good accompaniment.

Salt fish

Salting, like smoking, is a method of preserving by dehydration of the potentially harmful microbes (again, see Harold McGee's *On Food and Cooking*). Most of the smoked products mentioned above are in fact salted prior to smoking, either by immersing in brine, or covering in dry salt. The texture of salted fish flesh is rendered closer and drier and so makes for an entirely different eating experience. Fish that is salted until it is entirely dehydrated is literally stiff as a board (and will keep about as long). Just about the only unsmoked, salted fish products you are likely to encounter in this country, apart from fish and shellfish canned in brine (see below), are salted anchovies and salt cod. Both are potentially delicious.

Salted anchovies come in jars, plastic tubs or tins. Once opened they will keep for a long time, but not for ever – they should be kept in the fridge. Whole (they are generally headless) salted anchovies, especially the kind known as 'red' anchovies, are superior in flavour to the more readily available fillets canned in olive oil (though these will always do). Salted anchovies can be removed from their container as needed and require a good rinse under a cold tap. The body will begin to soften, which should allow you to split the fish with your thumb and pull out the backbone. A quick dry with kitchen paper and they are ready for use. You can buy them in cans of up to 11 lb/5 kg, which is very economical if, like me, you are an anchovy freak. They can be found in the best delicatessens, especially ones that are run by Italians or Portuguese. Using the very best anchovies makes all the difference in a dish where they are presented as whole fillets.

Salt cod is available in various stages of dehydration. In Spain and Portugal strips of slightly moist salt cod fillet are packed in paper-bound layers in cardboard boxes, in which state, as long as they are refrigerated, they will keep for several months. Such a product can occasionally be found in Spanish or

Portuguese delicatessens over here. It will need to be soaked in cold water, which should be changed several times, for at least 24 hours. It is then ready for use.

Totally dry salt cod is available in sides or thick slices of variable shapes and sizes which often include skin, bone and even fins. Some look like failed attempts at *papier mâché*, others resemble dried-up dish-cloths. If properly prepared, they can be considerably more appetizing than either. They need to be soaked for at least 3 days, in plenty of water which should be changed twice a day. You may be able to remove the backbone, skin and fins about halfway through day 2. The resulting fillets are fine for *brandade*, fishballs and that sort of thing but probably not ideal for the Brackenbury's Salad of Marinated Salt Cod (page 170).

Salting your own fish allows you to prepare a delicately judged 'cure' for immediate or short-term use, as well as keeping indefinitely fish which you have chosen with your own skilled eye – or even caught with your own skilled hand. The basic technique for salting is outlined on page 170, along with Adam Robinson's recipe.

Canned and 'pickled' fish

Canned fish products do not necessarily deserve to be sneered at. Canning and bottling of fish, in oil, vinegar or brine, are practices which have for a long time enabled good cooks to use fish which would otherwise be past their sell-by date by a matter of months, or even years. They are techniques for preservation every bit as valid as smoking and salting and, like these methods, they change the character of fish in both taste and texture. There is a huge variety of such products, many of which will be familiar to everyone, and some of which – for example, canned anchovies – are respected and used by even the most puritan of chefs. I will not attempt an exhaustive listing or analysis. You probably already know whether you like canned sardines, tuna or dressed crab, jars of rolrollmops or shrimps in brine. I would only add that it is always worth experimenting with unfamiliar products and that, for those who have never tried them, canned pilchards in tomato sauce are something of a revelation.

Ordering fish

If you want a particular kind of fish or shellfish, and you want to maximize the chances of getting it in top condition, it is often a good idea to order it from your fishmonger. He should not charge extra for ordering, but should be able to quote you a price in advance. If you are not satisfied with the quality of what turns up, you are under no obligation to take it. I would always order shellfish, except possibly mussels, as I would not generally be confident that the turnover was fast enough to guarantee the freshness of anything in stock.

If you require large quantities of expensive fish and shellfish – lobsters, scallops, langoustines, oysters, sea bass, wild salmon – ordering from a wholesaler or trade supplier can save you a small fortune. One way to find a fish wholesaler is to look in Yellow Pages. Possibly a better way is to ring a local restaurant which you know serves good fish, and ask the owner or chef who supplies them. As with a fishmonger, it is worth striking up a rapport with a fish wholesaler. The first time you make contact, emphasize just how special the occasion is for which you require your order. Even when a fish is delivered right to your door, you have every right to send it away if you are not impressed.

Cooking fish

Having landed a prize catch at the fishmonger's it would be a shame to spoil it by subjecting it to some wholly inappropriate and calamitous kitchen treatment. Fortunately this is easily avoided. Keep it simple, and if you have really found a beautiful fresh fish it will be rewarding eating just about however you prepare it, on one condition – YOU MUST NOT OVER-COOK IT.

How to avoid over-cooking fish

There are, I believe, only two reasons why fish are so frequently over-cooked. Coincidentally they are the same two reasons that account for most failures of human endeavour: *fear* and *ignorance*. Specifically: fear of fish that is raw, and ignorance of when fish is cooked.

The first of these problems, being psychological, is hard to counter with purely rational argument. One can but try. First, provided it is reasonably fresh, a fish that is not cooked all the way through is not likely to harm you at all. That's no consolation for those who find that under-done fish is simply not to their taste. If they encounter a little flesh towards the middle of their Dover sole which is not quite opaque, and still perhaps a little tenacious of the backbone, what can they do? Two things, I would suggest: leave the bit they don't like, which is hardly difficult as it is usually more than happy to remain clinging to the skeleton of the fish; or return the sole to the pan, grill or oven from whence it came, until the offending morsel is done.

As for the question of when a fish is done, there is no great mystery, no magical transformation that occurs at some elusive point (unlike, for example, the mysterious thickening of egg or tenderizing of tough meat). A fish is cooked, quite simply, *when all of it is hot.* That is to say, the moment the last bit of a fish – inevitably the middle – gets too hot to touch (just), it is ready to serve. The corresponding visual clue is that the flesh of the fish, which is always slightly translucent when raw, will be opaque.

This is all very well, but there remains the problem of being aware of what is happening in the middle of a fish which may, after all, be several inches thick. The obvious thing to do is to look. Take a sharp, thin-bladed knife and, on the lateral line where the fish is thickest, make a small incision through to the bone. Part the flesh with a fine knife blade or even a needle, just enough to enable you to see whether the flesh at the bone is still translucent, or fully opaque. If this test reveals the fish to be *almost* done, then simply cover the fish and let it rest for a minute or two. This is all it will take for the heat transference to be completed.

Basic techniques

Wherever possible, fish should be cooked whole and with the skin on. A skinless fillet has lost two of a fish's greatest culinary assets: a bone full of flavour, much of which will be released during cooking; and a natural basting system – the skin of a fish protects the flesh from moisture loss, as it traps a layer of fat beneath it.

When it comes to selecting your method of cooking, just ask yourself a few simple questions. Do I want crispy skin? In which case fry or roast. Do I want to end up with a sauce? In which case braise, bake or poach. Am I in a hurry? In which case griddle or fry. Do I want to pretend I'm at Harry Ramsden's? In which case deep-fry in batter and serve with mushy peas.

BAKING: this is a beautiful way to cook whole fish and very large fillets. It can be done in a pot, with or without a lid, in which you will want to put some vegetables and/or herbs to add flavour to the fish. You should also add a little liquid, such as wine, fish stock or plain water, to help keep the fish moist. When a lot of liquid is added, and the lid remains on, baking effectively becomes BRAISING. This can also be done on the top of the stove. In either case the liquid left at the end of cooking should be served with the fish. It can be strained and reduced, and thickened with a little butter or cream to make a sauce. The oven temperature for baking and braising is moderate: 180°C/350°F/Gas Mark 4.

Another simple baking technique is to wrap a well-seasoned whole fish in a sealed parcel of buttered foil (not too tightly wrapped, or it might burst), enclosing perhaps some fresh herbs, more butter in the fish's cavity, and a splash of white wine or lemon juice. With the fish protected thus, a hotter oven is appropriate – about 220°C/425°F/Gas Mark 7. Again, the juices should be saved and served with the fish. I often cook sea trout like this.

BOILING: I have already talked about the 'tea-bag effect' in the vegetable chapter (page 40–1). This applies equally to fish. If the flavour's in the water, then it's not in the fish. Boiling fish is therefore not a good idea, unless you are making a dish such as a fish stew or soup where the liquor is the main point of the dish. Lobsters, crabs and prawns are an exception, of course – their shells seem to help keep in the flavour – and it is not practical, and certainly not kind, to cook them in any other way.

FRYING: shallow-frying, in oil or clarified butter, is an excellent way to cook smallish whole fish. It gets the skin nice and crispy, something which can be accentuated by rolling the fish in seasoned flour or polenta before frying. Fillets can be similarly floured, or breadcrumbed. The pan for shallow-frying should be very hot, as the fish needs to be sealed instantly to prevent loss of moisture. For the same reason, do not try to fry too many fish at once.

Deep-frying fish is something of an acquired skill, and most easily accomplished with a professional deep-fat fryer. However, domestic models are available. If you really know what you're doing, you can get by with a large saucepan of boiling oil. But, as they say in those terrifying public information films, 'Don't leave it unattended'. Properly conducted, deep-frying can produce fabulous results. A piece of cod or haddock, deep-fried in a light crispy batter, is something close to the heart of many a Brit – as anyone who's holidayed on the Costa del Sol will know.

For success in deep-frying battered fish, temperature is critical. This is why a deep-fat fryer, with its own temperature gauge and thermostat, is so handy. If you are using an ordinary saucepan you will need a special thermometer. The correct temperature, i.e. that at which the fish will be cooked by the time the batter is the desired golden-brown, is about 180°C/350°F, though smaller fillets can be fried at a slightly higher temperature (say 190°C/375°F) for a shorter time.

Always use good clean oil, and plenty of it. Good chippies swear by groundnut (which is, of course, another name for peanut).

GRIDDLING: I have already extolled the virtues of the griddle pan or cast-iron grill plate (page 21). For fish they are quite excellent, sealing the flesh instantly and searing the surface with fabulous carbonized stripes – it's like having a barbecue in your kitchen. Cutlets, fillets and whole small fish can be cooked on a griddle. They should be only lightly oiled (oily fish like mackerel not at all) and seasoned towards the end of cooking (salt will encourage the juices to run). Larger fish can be slashed two or three times in the thicker part of the body to speed up cooking times. A few fresh herbs – thyme and rosemary work well – can be sprinkled on the griddle before and during cooking. They will aromatize the fish as it chars.

GRILLING: I have practically stopped using the overhead, eye-level grill since I bought my griddle pan, except for browning and crisping the tops of tarts and gratins, and *brûlée*ing the occasional *crème*. But cooking under a grill is a perfectly good way to deal with small whole fish and fillets. Larger fish will tend to dry out on the outside before they are cooked through.

MARINATING: I count marinating as a form of cooking, albeit a slow one, as it radically transforms the character of fish flesh in both texture and taste. It's a bit like cold poaching, the marinade taking the place of the court bouillon, and slowly transferring its flavours to the fish. Short marinades, such as the one on page 172, are a delightful way of celebrating a really fresh herring or mackerel. Marinating works better with oily fish on the whole, although some white fish also respond well, especially if salted first.

POACHING: this is a more gentle technique than boiling, but there is still a danger that the 'tea-bag' effect I described in Chapter 1 will come into play. Poaching is therefore usually done in a well-flavoured stock or a court bouillon (which might contain leeks, carrots, celery, onions, white wine and herbs). The idea is to give more flavour to the fish than you are taking away. This is a good way of cooking fish which is to be eaten cold. It can be brought to the boil in a cold court bouillon, then taken off the heat and left to cool. It is not such a good way of cooking fragile white fish such as plaice and whiting, which have a tendency to become pulpy and waterlogged, or very oily fish such as mackerel and herrings. Salmon, sea bass and monkfish could all be profitably poached – monkfish turns out particularly well when red wine is used in the court bouillon. Very large fish can be poached in a fish kettle. Kippers and smoked haddock are best poached in milk which takes the edge off their saltiness. The liquor from poaching is not to be wasted, but should be strained, reduced, thickened if you like (with cream or butter) and served with the fish.

ROASTING: an excellent way to present a whole fish, or a section of a larger fish, with a lovely crispy skin, roasting is much favoured at the Brackenbury (see Adam Robinson's words of wisdom on page 174). The basic technique is to seal a fish on both sides in hot oil or clarified butter to start the skin crisping, then transfer to a very hot oven (230°C/450°F/Gas Mark 8). Basting with oil once or twice during cooking helps achieve that all-important crispiness. In contrast to poaching or steaming, it is an excellent method for whiting, plaice and hake, as it contracts the flesh just a little, improving the texture without making the fish dry.

STEAMING: the purest method, which allows a piece of fish, usually a fillet, to be cooked with minimum loss of moisture and no interference from other flavours. Only the firmest-fleshed fish, such as turbot, halibut, bass and monkfish, are really worth steaming – frailer fish, such as cod, whiting, etc. will tend to become watery. Incidentally it is a complete waste of time, not to mention valuable ingredients, to steam above an elaborate court bouillon of wine and herbs. It will still be plain old H_2O, in vapour form, that does the cooking, and your precious flavours will barely transfer.

Bream

Red bream is landed in the South of England and Ireland in the summer months and tends to be at its cheapest from July to October. Fish on sale outside these months generally come from the Mediterranean, and are likely to be more expensive as well as in poorer condition. Bream is increasingly popular with restaurants, and prices are rising, but great bargains can be had when catches have been good – particularly for those who live near to the point of landing. The smaller black bream is at least as tasty as the red, but rarely seems to find its way to inland fishmongers. Find some at the quayside and you are likely to get it at knock-down prices. Simply grill, or pan-fry in butter, and you have discovered a great treat.

Brill

Once one of the great bargains, the brill is now being devoured in ever-increasing quantities by the restaurant trade, and prices have risen. A medium-sized, oval-shaped flat-fish, the brill became very popular in the mid-1980s when the price of halibut and turbot went through the roof. It is still cheaper than either and, gourmets will delight in telling you, '*almost* as good'. I would maintain that it is every bit as good, though different. It flakes a little more finely and is not so densely textured, but has great flavour and roasts, grills and griddles, in chunky on-the-bone portions, quite beautifully.

Clams

There are many kinds, and many different sizes, of clam. Despite their prevalence around the shores of Britain they are not often encountered on the fishmonger's slab in this country. However, they are gathered, and even farmed, on a commercial basis, both for the restaurant market and for export. A good fishmonger should be able to get some for you, if you ask him nicely. It's well worth it, as the sweet flesh of clams is uniquely sea-fresh and succulent. They should not be too expensive. If you manage to get some that are not just alive, but kicking, then they are delicious raw, with a squeeze of lemon or a splash of shallot vinegar. Otherwise, heat for just a minute or two in a large pan, with a glass of wine, a little butter or olive oil and some garlic and parsley if you like. As soon as they are opened they are ready – any that don't open should be discarded. Serve with the liquor from the pan, or a separate and generous quantity of garlic butter.

Look out also for razor clams, the long thin, variety, which appear occasionally in fishmongers and can also be specially ordered. They are large enough to be griddled or barbecued for barely a minute, and are delicious with a dipping sauce made from fresh chilli, garlic and parsley, all finely chopped and bound with a little olive oil.

Cockles

Like clams, cockles are hard to find on sale, but you should be able to order some. Those within striking distance of the coast should know that they are easily dug from sandy beaches all around the British Isles – cockles are the bivalves with the fat, ribbed, heart-shaped shells. Eat them raw, cook them as for clams or, better still, make Adam Robinson's excellent Cockle Chowder (page 158).

Cod, Haddock, Hake, Ling

I lump these four together, not because they are *exactly* the same, but because they are all extremely versatile, white-fleshed round-fish which, when found in prime condition, are a great asset for the Bon Marché cook, as you will see from the recipes that follow. I would not hesitate to substitute each for any of the others, but would more than hesitate to steam or poach any of them – they can get a bit pulpy and waterlogged. They all 'salt' well (see instructions on page 170). Note, of hake, that it invariably looks miserable on the slab, with its dull grey skin quickly becoming flaccid. But a hake that passes the finger-test will not have been dead long, and is a fish well worth taking home.

Coley

(aka COALFISH, SAITHE)

One thing you can say about this grey-fleshed, rather unappetizing-looking fish, generally considered inferior to all of the above, is that it is always cheap. Unfortunately fishmongers have an irritating habit of filleting it before putting it on the slab, which probably further shortens its slab-life and makes its condition harder to assess. If you can ascertain that it is fresh then it is a perfectly good base for my Coriander Fishcakes, or Chillied Fish with Sweet Potato (pages 159 and 160). If ever I found, or caught, a whole one of 2–4 lb/900 g–1.8 kg (and a good Scottish fishmonger might easily furnish you with just such a fish) I would happily roast it (see page 174), or fillet it, then crumb it and fry it. A *salsa rossa* (page 118) would go well with it.

Crab

One of my favourite things to eat. The large brown (or 'edible') crab remains cheap and in plentiful supply, and is a sane alternative to the insanely priced lobster. You can buy a cold cooked crab, or even a dressed crab, with the white meat separated from the brown, from a good fishmonger whom you really trust (many over-cook their crabs, others freeze and then defrost them). But if at all possible, buy a live crab, preferably one which is still defiantly waving its claws.

If you have the luxury of choice, take a while to select your crab. Big is best – the bigger the crab, the better the ratio of meat to shell. Look for one with a hefty pair of claws – this is where the choice meat is. In late summer and early autumn the hen crabs, whose claws are generally smaller, may have large amounts of red roe under their tail flaps – a bonus not to be missed.

Nothing beats a really fresh crab served cold with a lemony mayonnaise. But if you want a change, or find yourself in possession of a pre-cooked crab, then the recipe on page 177, for gratinated Crab Ramekins, is a winner.

Dab

A small flat-fish often reasonably priced and, I think, of slightly superior texture to plaice. Fry, grill or roast if large (see Adam Robinson's recipe for Roast Plaice on page 174).

Eel

Like Jane Grigson, who enthuses wildly on the subject, I rate eel highly. Any Londoner who possesses a stout fishing rod has a remarkably good chance of catching one at high or low tide in the Thames at any time during the coarse fishing season (mid-June to mid-March). A piece of bacon on a size 10 hook ledgered on the bottom is all you need. Otherwise, eel may have to be ordered from fishmongers, but they should have no trouble getting them, and the eels should be *very* fresh: eels are often transported alive in wet sacks, in which condition they can survive for several days. Londoners can buy them alive in Soho's Chinatown market. They can be cooked almost anyhow. Fillets of larger eels are fabulous fried in plenty of butter: when the fillets are nearly done add a slosh of white wine and a handful of chopped fresh herbs (parsley, tarragon, sorrel, even rocket). Reduce, add a spoonful of double cream or crème fraîche, and reduce again. If you've caught the eel yourself then you can feel truly smug. I certainly did. Smoked eel is an excellent product (see page 134).

Grey mullet

A fine and often fairly priced round-fish. Adam Robinson tells me that some batches are suspect, as they are netted near sewer mouths where they are known to congregate, and can consequently taste less than clean. I have never been unlucky. They cook well almost anyhow, and are a particular treat barbecued. They are beginning to become trendy, and I predict will go up in price over the next few years, though I'd love to be wrong.

Gurnard

A personal favourite (see my recipe on page 161). The French, who call this fish *la Tombe* (because it is coffin-shaped, not because it is lethal), rightly hold it in high esteem. Plenty are landed on the south coast of Britain in the summer, but few make it to London, although it is firm-fleshed and travels well. I'm always hoping it will catch on.

Herring

Every year many thousands of tons of unsaleable herrings are industrially processed to produce oil, fishmeal, animal food and even fertilizer. What a sad fate for such a fine eating fish! And what is now sad may soon become tragic, as a supply of protein that was once thought to be inexhaustible is already showing signs of being depleted. Although it is naturally a robust fish, the herring has to endure considerable abuse. Herring trawlers are often out for a week at a time (factory ships, which can herrings on board, for months at a time). Vast quantities of herring are dumped in the hold, then sucked out at port by a giant vacuum-cleaner. No wonder so many are in such poor condition by the time they reach the fish slab.

Every fishmonger sells them. And almost every time I visit a fishmonger I check out his herrings. But I don't buy them that often. When I do find a really fresh one I will always take it, and eat it simply grilled, or occasionally rolled in oats and fried. On the rare occasions when a whole batch is fresh, I will marinate some (see recipe on page 172). To test the condition of a herring, place your thumb and forefinger either side of the thickest part of its body, a couple of inches behind the head. Squeeze firmly. The chances are that you will squash the rotten thing. But if you should meet with firm resistance, you're in business.

John Dory

This freaky-looking fish, with its large head and other-worldly spines, which the French call *St Pierre*, is beginning to catch on – but no more than it deserves. It's tasty, versatile and lends itself well to all simple cooking techniques. Its well-shaped fillets have long been popular among the *nouvelle-style* chefs, who like to serve it with fine sauces and fancy garnishes of julienned vegetables.

Lemon sole

Often a good buy, and for flavour and texture not far short of its far higher-priced cousin the Dover sole. It is best if simply cooked, either grilled or fried, and whole rather than filleted. Fish of around 1 lb/450 g make a generous portion per person.

Mackerel

With its rich, oily flesh the mackerel is comparable to, and every bit as good as, the herring. Happily it has not been so industrially abused. In plentiful supply when vast shoals are inshore during the summer months, it does not keep well, and is best bought close to the point of landing. When mackerel are being brought in in abundance by the pleasure-fishing boats you will find skippers practically giving them away on the quayside. It's a gift you'd be mad to refuse. In winter, larger mackerel are netted further offshore. They keep a little longer but can be subjected to the same time delays and heavy-duty handling as herrings. Test them the same way, and cook them the same way. When mackerel is *really* fresh I like to eat it raw, or marinated for just an hour or so in lemon juice and olive oil. A freshly caught mackerel grilled over a fire on the beach is an unforgettable experience which every fish-lover should get acquainted with.

Mussels

For the Bon Marché cook, mussels are the friendliest of all shellfish. Widely available, cheap and easy to prepare, they provide an instant fix of sea flavour when steamed open in a little wine, butter and garlic. Slices of French bread to soak up the juices complete the idyll. If mussel-lovers should ever tire of this simple but delectable preparation, then Adam Robinson's spicy mussel broth (page 179) should revive their interest in this feisty bivalve.

Most fishmongers sell mussels. If all the mussels on the slab are closed or almost closed when you buy them, you have little to fear. However, if even a few are gaping open, the whole lot are best avoided. Often mussels are encountered packed up in polythene bags in batches of 4½–11 lb/2–5 kg. Such mussels are likely to have been mechanically cleaned in a machine like a cement-mixer, which removes their beards and any barnacles or bits of seaweed that have become attached to the shell. This is a vigorous process which has its casualties. You should therefore examine the mussels closely through the polythene. The best way to ensure your batch is fresh is to find out on what days your fishmonger has his mussels delivered, and buy only on those days.

There is, of course, a plentiful supply of fresh mussels all around our coastline. The larger ones are generally found nearer the low-water mark (because they are submerged for longer, and hence have more time in which to feed). It is not a good idea to gather mussels from a polluted area. Inquire locally and you should be steered clear of unsafe beaches.

Oysters

You will find two species of oyster on sale in this country. The cheapest, which is fast-growing and widely farmed around our coast, is the Pacific oyster, sometimes confusingly called the Rock oyster, or Portuguese oyster. The native or European oyster, which is rounder and much flatter on one side, is usually about twice as expensive. Connoisseurs regard it as superior, but I think that if availability led to the prices being suddenly reversed, their views would be swiftly reversed too.

Not all fishmongers stock oysters and those that do always seem to have only a few. This suggests to me that their turnover in oysters is on the slow side, and hence that any they do have may not be in peak condition. Unfortunately there is not much you can do to find out how fresh they are, until you get them home and open them. In fact, if oysters are properly stored (at 2–4°C/37°F in plenty of wet seaweed), they will keep (i.e. stay alive) for quite a while. I was once told by a Frenchman who runs an oyster bar that properly stored oysters are good for over a month – though he quickly assured me that his own supply was delivered twice a week.

However well stored they are, it is always desirable to have oysters as fresh as possible. Once removed from the sea they are unable to feed, and have to survive on their fat reserves and the liquor (which is basically sea-water) they retain in their shells. Over time they will become smaller and lose some of this liquor. Ordering your oysters well in advance should help to ensure they are plump and liquor-laden. If you want to buy oysters in larger quantities – say 5 dozen or more – you could try contacting a fish wholesaler who supplies the trade or, better still, your nearest oyster farm. You are likely to get a very competitive price, and they may be able to include you on their delivery round (see 'Ordering Fish', page 138).

Plaice

Held in great contempt by 'smart' chefs, the reputation of this fish has been destroyed by the worst kind of fish and chip shops, which often buy frozen fillets, which are then battered and frazzled to disintegration point in the deep-fat fryer. Overcooking, and freezing, are lethal to many fish, but none more so than to this pretty and delicate flatty. If you find a good one, try roasting *à la* Brackenbury (page 174). Rick Stein, author of *English Seafood Cookery* (Penguin), says that plaice are best avoided in the spring, when they can lose condition after spawning, and his word's good enough for me.

Pollack, Pouting and Whiting

Fast-deteriorating members of the cod family, these three are rarely found in the fishmonger's for that reason. Whiting, if exceptionally fresh, is perhaps a cut above the other two and a fresh one is certainly worth roasting (see page 174). Should you happen on (or catch) very fresh specimens of any of them, then treat as for COLEY above. Smoked pollack, cheaper and almost as good as smoked haddock, has its supporters.

Prawns

The prawn is one of the very few shellfish whose taste and texture seem to survive freezing – the cooked prawns which you see in their shells in fishmongers have always been frozen. These are the Bon Marché cook's best bet, if only because fresh or live prawns are almost impossible to find. The deep-frozen, packaged peeled prawns that are widely available in supermarkets are very variable in quality. They are generally less sweet, and of poorer texture, than the shell-on kind. Some seem to me to be absolutely tasteless, though the better varieties may make a passable addition to a soup, fish pie or seafood pasta dish.

If you're feeling a bit cheeky, you might ask your fishmonger if you can taste one of his prawns. Otherwise the best shopping strategy is to have a good close look. If there are a lot of broken bodies and severed heads, then the prawns have lost condition and suffered from excess man-handling, probably on their way to and from the freezer. If you can get close enough to have a good sniff, then any hint of tainted fish in the smell should tell you all you need to know: avoid.

If you use prawns regularly, and like to have them ready to hand, you could store a quantity of shell-on prawns in your freezer. If you decide to do that, ensure that the prawns you buy have not been defrosted since their initial freezing. Both fishmongers and supermarkets often sell 2¼-lb/1-kg packs of shell-on North Sea prawns, salt-water-cooked and frozen on board ship. These are perhaps the best buy of all.

If ever you do get an opportunity to beg, steal, buy or catch some live English prawns, it should not be passed up. Freshly boiled, preferably in seawater, and dipped in a little melted butter ... if I was a condemned prisoner, that would be my last request.

Salmon

A wild salmon is a rare treat these days, as most are snapped up by the restaurant trade. Relative bargains can be had close to rivers and estuaries where they are netted or angled. My advice to Bon Marché cooks who do not have such privileged access but want to splash out, is to order a wild salmon from your fishmonger. Specify that you want a really fresh one, ask him for a price, and bargain if it sounds extortionate.

Farmed salmon is an entirely different matter, cheap and readily available. Since fishmongers sell a lot of it, it is usually quite fresh – certainly any fishmonger selling out of condition farmed salmon should not expect to stay in business for long. I have mixed feelings about farmed salmon. It is not so much the quality of the product that worries me: farmed salmon is not as good as wild – it lacks the richness and depth of flavour of fish recently returned from the sea, where they feed on crustaceans and small fish – but it is a legitimate product that is better than many fish of comparable price. What worries me is the way fish farms are being run, often without regard for their environmental impact, and their effect on the stock of wild fish. The waste from huge numbers of caged fish is contaminating lochs, and diseases against which farmed fish can be inoculated are passed on to wild fish. I know that many Scottish fish-farmers are working to improve the situation, but until I am confident that the good guys are in the majority I will remain a reluctant and occasional buyer of farmed salmon.

Sardine

(aka PILCHARD)

Let's settle one debate before it gets out of hand: a pilchard is an adult sardine. This lovely fish has received similar industrial treatment to the herring, though to the best of my knowledge stocks are not seriously threatened. Pilchard are canned on a huge scale, and rarely make the fishmonger's slab. Happily sardines are often encountered, and are often cheap. I disagree with purists who say that sardines that have been frozen are no good. In fact most sardines that are sold fresh have effectively been frozen at least once, when they are packed in ice on the boats. What one hopes is that the sardines are then defrosted and sold quickly. Some fishmongers have a very nasty habit of refreezing sardines every night, then thawing them out in the morning – a hazard to health, as well as to the eating quality of the fish. Such fish will be be identified by the Bon Marché shopper on gentle application of the squeeze test (see HERRINGS above). Those that pass should be grilled or barbecued without delay.

Scallops

Scallops are rarely cheap; gathering them is costly business, involving divers or dredging nets, and they continue to be in high demand from restaurants all over the country. Though unlikely to be on the shopping list of the bargain hunter, some caveats are appropriate if those who splash out are not to pay over the odds. Scallops can often be found in fishmongers already prised from their shells – sometimes at surprisingly low prices per pound. The chances are these have been separated from their shells for some time, and soaked in water to retain their fresh, juicy look. Soaked in water to dilute their flavour, add to their bulk, and ruin their texture, more like. Frozen scallops are likely to be even worse, having almost always undergone the same process, to boost their weight, before freezing. Ask your fishmonger to order scallops in their shells. If you don't feel like cleaning them yourself – though the task affords much job satisfaction – ask the fishmonger to do it when you get there. You may have to wait, but at least you'll know he's not fobbing you off with some he 'prepared earlier'.

Like oysters, you will get a much better price for a quantity of scallops if you can contact a trade supplier (see page 137).

Having obtained your unsoaked, sea-fresh scallops, it would be a pity to ruin them by overcooking. Seared on a very hot pan or griddle, a bare minute each side, is a simple but exquisite preparation, and a light dressing of olive oil, lemon juice and chopped green herbs, all that is required to lift the flavour.

Sea trout
(aka SALMON TROUT, SEWIN)

I am sentimental about this fish, which I love to catch and adore to eat. A sea trout is in fact a brown trout which has decided, for reasons best known to itself, to go to sea. It has always struck me as an eminently sensible thing for a young brown trout to do. They come back to the river a little older, a little wiser, and a lot tastier. I would question whether sea trout is any less excellent than wild salmon, and as it is often less than half the price it really is a fish for the Bon Marché cook to cherish. The season for sea trout begins in late March or April and runs sometimes as late as early November. I almost invariably bake it in buttered foil, with more butter in the cavity, as well as salt, black pepper and a trickle of lemon juice or white wine. Overcook it, however, and you might as well make fish cakes. (For the definitive guide on how not to over-cook fish, see above.)

Sprats

Even fish as small as sprats deserve a quick squeeze to test their freshness. Best to do this while the fishmonger is not looking, as a sprat that is past its prime is easily bisected when pinched between finger and thumb. Even though it is really the fishmonger's fault, he may not take kindly to such wilful mutilation. Fresh sprats are, as they say, delicious and nutritious – and, as they sometimes forget to add, cheap. (See the recipe on pages 176–7).

Squid
and Cuttlefish

Delicious when fresh, horrible when not, inexpensive either way, these two cephalopods are perfect subjects for Bon Marché exploitation. Cuttlefish are the wider-bodied creatures with fatter 'wings' and shorter tentacles, but the two are just about interchangeable as far as recipes are concerned. Fortunately they are easy to test for freshness, provided you can get your hands on them. Ideally you should slip a finger just inside the body cavity and pinch the body between finger and thumb. If it is firm, rubbery and resistant, then it is fresh, if it is soft and gives way, then it is not for you. A lot of slime and mucus on the outside is a bad sign. Fresh squid and cuttlefish have a strange, almost soapy smell. 'Off' squid smell very bad indeed, but it is not unusual to encounter them in second-rate fishmongers.

Frozen squid can be perfectly pleasant if cooked slowly and gently in a well-flavoured liquid, but it is hopeless for frying or grilling. You need the freshest possible squid or cuttlefish for the recipe on page 181, Griddled Squid with Chilli and Garlic.

Whitebait

Whitebait might be the tiny young of any number of shoal-fish, usually herrings, sardines or sprats. If more than about 10 per cent appear to be broken up, they are probably past their best. If not, then toss in flour, deep-fry, and serve with lemon wedges and black pepper.

Winkles

A free feast for anyone who can be bothered to scrabble around for half an hour or so among weed-covered rocks. Some may dispute whether the resulting rubbery morsels are really worth all the trouble. Such doubters should try boiling winkles for exactly 3 minutes in a strong fish or chicken stock, made piquant by the addition of Tabasco, cayenne or lots of black pepper. Eat when cold, or at least cool enough to handle, by removing the spiralling flesh from the shell with a pin. The last thing to emerge from the shell, a little trail of muddy slime, is quite harmless, but best discarded.

Recipes

Whiteleaf Fish Chowder
THE WHITELEAF AT CROYDE

Serves 6

David Wallington writes: 'The essentials of a chowder are pieces of fish, potatoes, and optionally salt pork in a flavourful broth based on fish stock with added milk and cream (New England) or water and tomatoes (Manhattan). In America the fish are usually clams or scallops but haddock or other firm flaky white fish are also used. Sometimes it is a main course with large pieces of previously fried fish, sometimes a soup with small pieces of fish poached in the broth. At the Whiteleaf it is offered as a soup, the fish being either salmon or haddock and occasionally smoked haddock with "green" sautéed bacon. The soup is finished either with tomatoes, or with cream. I give instructions for both so the choice is yours.'

To make the stock, rinse the fish bones and vegetables in clean water. Place in a large saucepan with the herbs and water, bring to the boil and simmer very gently, uncovered, for not more than 40 minutes, skimming occasionally as necessary. Leave to cool, then strain through muslin or a clean cotton cloth. Return the liquid to the pan, add the wine and simmer gently until reduced by up to half. Taste and season with salt, pepper and a dash of lemon juice or vinegar.

Place half the tomatoes in a saucepan with the fish stock, cook gently until soft, pass through a sieve or whizz briefly in a food processor. Or add the milk–cream mixture and simmer with the stock until heated through. Add the onion and potatoes and simmer until the potatoes are cooked but still firm. Add the fish and remaining tomatoes, if used, bring gently up to a simmer and cook for not more than 5 minutes. Do not boil. Ladle into 6 warmed bowls and garnish with chopped herbs.

For the fish stock

1–1½ lb/450–675 g fresh fish bones and heads, from salmon or white fish
1 onion
1 large carrot
2 celery sticks
2 leeks, white parts only
2–3 mushrooms, chopped or 2 oz/60 g mushroom trimmings
a few sprigs of parsley, fennel and dill, as available
3 pts/1.75 litres water
4–5 fl oz/100–150 ml dry white wine
salt and black pepper
a little lemon juice or white wine vinegar

For the chowder

14-oz/400-g can of tomatoes, de-seeded and chopped, with the juice, or 8 fl oz/250 ml each milk and double cream
1 small or ½ large onion, finely chopped and sautéed until golden in a little butter
4 medium potatoes, peeled and cut into ¼-in/1-cm cubes
6–8 oz/170–225 g skinned and trimmed white fish, salmon, or smoked haddock, cut into similar-sized pieces to the potatoes
chopped fresh parsley, fennel or dill, to garnish

Cockle Chowder

THE BRACKENBURY

Serves 8

Adam Robinson writes: 'Not strictly a chowder, but a good version of the classic shellfish and cured pork combination.'

1 pt/575 ml dry white wine
1 large onion, finely chopped
3 lb/1.3 kg washed cockles
1 leek
4 celery sticks
2 large carrots
1 fennel bulb
2 oz/60 g butter
1 lb/450 g good smoked bacon
  or pancetta, diced
2 garlic cloves, crushed
1-in/2.5-cm piece ginger root,
  peeled and grated
1 pt/575 ml fish stock
2 potatoes, peeled and cut into
  ½-in/1-cm dice
salt and black pepper

Bring the wine to the boil with half the onion, and add the cockles in batches, removing them with a slotted spoon as soon as they are open (2–3 minutes). Strain the liquor through a clean cotton cloth when all the cockles are cooked, and reserve. Shuck (shell) two-thirds of the cockles, leaving the remaining third in their shells.

Cut the remaining vegetables into ½-in/1-cm dice, and sweat them in the butter, along with the bacon or pancetta, garlic and ginger, in a large saucepan. Cook gently without allowing the vegetables to brown, until they are just tender. Add the liquor from the cockles, the fish stock, the potatoes and the cream, and bring to the boil. Simmer gently until the potatoes are tender. Season with pepper and salt if needed. Divide the cockles among 8 warmed bowls, so that each has a few with shells, and some without, and ladle the soup over.

Cullen Skink

Serves 4 as a main course

This hearty Scottish soup is really very basic indeed, but none the less delicious. My recipe is adapted from one I found in a thorough and fascinating appraisal of the history of Scottish food, *Broths to Bannocks*, by Scottish food writer Catherine Brown. For an authentic Cullen Skink you should use unskinned finnan haddock on the bone, which adds extra flavour. If you can't find such fish, use undyed smoked haddock, with the skin still on.

Peel the potatoes and cut into halves, or quarters if they are large. Sweat the onion in half the butter in a large saucepan until soft but not brown. Add the water and bring to the boil. Add the potatoes and simmer for 20 minutes or so, with the pan half-covered, until the potatoes are almost tender.

Lay the fish on top of the potatoes and replace the lid. Simmer for 5–6 minutes until the fish is cooked, then remove it. Pick out the bone and skin from the fish and discard. Roughly flake the flesh and divide among 4 warmed bowls. Drain the cooking liquid from the potatoes and reserve. Mash the potatoes with the milk and the remaining butter until smooth. Stir in enough of the reserved cooking liquid to get a thick, soupy consistency. Season with black pepper, and salt if you feel it is needed. Reheat the soup (but do not allow to boil), then ladle into each bowl over the fish, and serve.

1½ lb/675 g floury potatoes (see page 87 for recommended varieties)
1 large onion, thinly sliced
4 oz/115 g butter
1½ pts/850 ml water
1 lb/450 g smoked haddock, ideally finnan, on the bone
5 fl oz/150 ml milk
salt and black pepper

Coriander Fishcakes
Serves 6 (makes 12 x 4-oz/115-g fishcakes)

You don't have to use coriander in this recipe – for a more traditional fishcake chopped fresh parsley is appropriate, and you can leave out the garam masala. Dillweed is another alternative, but in that case I would substitute farmed salmon for the white fish.

By 'fresh' breadcrumbs I simply mean to suggest that you should avoid using the orange packet variety. Stale bread, either white or brown, will do fine.

Scrub the potatoes (there is no need to peel them) and cook in plenty of lightly salted boiling water until tender. Drain well, leave for a few minutes for the steam to evaporate, then rub through a sieve or pass through a potato ricer. The skins will be left behind. Leave to cool.

While the potatoes are cooking, put the fish into a food processor with the shallot or onion, coriander, garam masala and one of the eggs. Process until the fish is roughly minced but not a completely smooth paste.

Add the fish to the potato, mixing the two together in a large bowl until they are well combined (do not do this in the food processor as

1 lb/450 g floury potatoes
2 lb/900 g cod, haddock, coley or other white fish, skinned and filleted
1 shallot or small onion, very finely chopped
2 tbsp finely chopped fresh coriander
2 tsp garam masala
2 eggs
salt and black pepper
1 tbsp milk
plain flour for coating
4 oz/115 g fresh breadcrumbs
oil (ideally olive or sunflower) for frying

the potato will become starchy and sticky). Season the mixture well with salt and pepper, divide into 12 equal portions, and shape into round, flat cakes, about ¾ in/2 cm thick.

Whisk the remaining egg with the milk. Toss each fishcake lightly in flour, dusting off the excess, then dip in the egg–milk mixture, then turn in the breadcrumbs (on a plate or tray) until even coated. A pair of forks is useful in performing this slightly delicate operation.

The cakes should be deep- or shallow-fried (turning once) in hot oil for 5–6 minutes until golden-brown and crispy. You will have to do them in at least 2 batches, so put finished fishcakes in a warmed dish lined with greaseproof paper and keep in a low oven (150°C/300°F/Gas Mark 2) while the second batch is cooking.

Serve with a leaf salad, or fresh young peas and broad beans, and *salsa rossa* (page 118).

Chillied Fish with Sweet Potato
Serves 4

This is not dissimilar to the previous recipe, but quicker to make and a bit more rough and ready – a sort of stir-fry. Quantities and ingredients need not be precise, and you can invent your own variations as far as the spices are concerned.

I lb/450 g sweet potatoes
1½ lb/675 g white fish, filleted and skinned
I onion, thinly sliced
2 tbsp sunflower *or* other oil for frying
I small fresh red *or* green chilli, finely chopped
2 garlic cloves, finely chopped
2 tsp garam masala
5 fl oz/150 ml coconut milk (*optional*)
salt and black pepper

Peel the sweet potatoes and simmer in salted water until just tender. Drain, leave to cool, then cut into 1-in/2.5-cm cubes. Cut the fish fillets into bite-sized pieces.

Heat the oil in a large frying pan over a moderate heat and sweat the onion until softened. Add the chilli, garlic and garam masala, and cook for 2 further minutes. Add the cooked sweet potatoes and cook for a further few minutes, stirring frequently, until the ingredients are well mixed and just beginning to colour.

Stir in the fish, and cook for a further 5 minutes, shaking the pan and stirring, until all the pieces of fish are heated through and cooked. To make this a wet, rather than a dry dish, add the coconut milk and heat through before serving. Serve with a leaf salad or mixed stir-fried vegetables.

Baked Gurnard with Vegetables

Serves 4

The joy of this recipe is that it produces a complete dish in one pot: the vegetables, infused with the fishy, winy juices, are eaten with the fish, and nothing else is required.

A 3-lb/1.3-kg gurnard will serve 4 people. If you can only get small fish – of, say, 12 oz – 1 lb/350–450 g, then buy one per person. Small cod, haddock and other white fish can be similarly treated.

Clean and scale the fish, scraping from tail to head with a blunt knife, and cut off its spines and large pectorals with a stout pair of kitchen scissors. Massage a little of the oil over the fish and season with salt and pepper, both inside and outside the cavity.

Wash all the vegetables thoroughly. Peel the potatoes and carrots and cut into ½-in/1-cm dice. Slice the leeks and celery sticks into ½-in/1-cm lengths. Sweat all the vegetables in a little oil, together with the garlic, for about 5 minutes.

Place the fish belly down on a lightly greased baking dish, deep enough to hold the vegetables as well. Spread the vegetables evenly around the fish (they could reach 1 in/2.5 cm or more up the sides of the fish) and pour over the wine. Cover the dish loosely with foil and bake in a pre-heated fairly hot oven (200°C/400°F/Gas Mark 6) for 25–30 minutes, until the fish is just cooked through to the middle (use the knife or needle test described on page 138 to test for doneness).

To serve the fish, remove it from the dish and flake the flesh away from the bones in pieces as large as you can manage. Serve with the vegetables, making sure to spoon plenty of the juices over each helping.

I gurnard, about 3 lb/1.3 kg
olive oil
salt and black pepper
I lb/450 g potatoes
2 large carrots
4 celery sticks
2 small leeks
I garlic clove, crushed
I wine-glass white wine

Thai Hot and Sour Soup with Squid

FOX AND GOOSE

Serves 4

Lime leaves and galangal (a root that looks not unlike ginger) are widely available in specialist oriental supermarkets. Outside London they may be harder to find, in which case you can add the finely pared zest of ½ lime and a bay leaf, instead of the lime leaves, and double the quantity of ginger to compensate for the lack of galangal.

3 pts/1.75 litres good fresh chicken stock
8 kaffir lime leaves
1 tsp peeled and finely grated galangal
½ tsp peeled and finely grated ginger root
2 tbsp chopped lemon grass
1 tbsp Thai fish sauce
½ tsp harissa *or* chilli paste
1 small fresh red chilli, finely chopped
2 tbsp chopped spring onion
2 tbsp julienne of carrot
2 tbsp julienne of leek
3 oz/85 g squid, cleaned and finely sliced
juice of 2 small limes
1 tbsp chopped fresh coriander

In a large saucepan, heat the chicken stock with all the trimmings from preparing the vegetables and seasonings. Simmer for 30 minutes, then strain through a fine sieve or chinois, discarding all the vegetable trimmings.

Bring the stock back to the boil, add the lime leaves, galangal, ginger and lemon grass, and boil rapidly for 10 minutes.

Turn down the heat, add the fish sauce, harissa or chilli paste and the red chilli and simmer for a further 2 minutes. Add all the julienne vegetables and squid to the pan, and leave for 30 seconds. Add the lime juice, tasting as you go (all might not be needed, but the soup should be sour), and season with salt if necessary.

Divide the vegetables and squid pieces evenly among 4 large, warmed bowls, ladle the soup over and sprinkle with chopped coriander.

Variable Fish Soup
Serves 6

In fact all recipes for fish soup should be flexible: I named this dish in order to emphasize the spirit of compromise that you should adopt when you go in search of your ingredients at the fishmonger. The important thing is to include some shellfish for sweetness (shell-on prawns are likely to be the most economical buy, but you could use langoustines, or small shore crabs if you have time to scour a beach), some bony or gelatinous fish, such as dogfish, conger eel or a piece from a small shark, to give body to the stock, and some white fish whose flesh can bulk out the soup. All the fish should be on the bone and unskinned.

The final dish is not a *bouillabaisse* (which contains pieces of whole fish) but a smooth, provençal-style *soupe de poissons*, and a robust dish none the less. Eaten with plenty of crusty bread and butter, and the traditional accompaniments of grated Gruyère cheese and *rouille*, it can be considered a whole meal.

A thinner, less filling version of the soup can be made by using fish bones and heads only. This is, of course, much more economical, and very nearly as delicious.

Clean all the fish if this has not been done by the fishmonger, and cut into 2-in/5-cm cutlets. Leave skin and bones intact. Do not discard the heads. Any extra heads or skeletons you pick up from the fishmonger can also be included, but all should be scrupulously fresh.

Sweat all the vegetables and the garlic in the oil in a large saucepan until softened but not brown. Shell the prawns and add the shells (but not the prawns), the fish (including the extra heads and skeletons if you are using them) and the bay leaf to the vegetables and cook for a few more minutes. Add the water and bring to the boil. Allow to simmer, uncovered, for 15 minutes.

With a slotted spoon, remove the meaty pieces of fish (not heads or skeletons) which will by now be cooked. With a knife and fork, or your fingers when the fish is cool enough to handle, remove the flesh of the fish, putting all that is free of bones on one side. Return the bones, skin and other debris to the soup as you go along. When you have finished this operation, remove the two potato halves (they should now be cooked). Place the potatoes, the boneless fish and the shelled prawns in a liquidizer, add a ladleful of strained liquor from the soup and blend until completely smooth.

Allow the soup to simmer on gently until it has cooked for 45 minutes in all. Then strain through a robust wire sieve, or better still a chinois (see page 22), pressing down with the back of a ladle to extract as much rich juice as possible. You can even grind up the bones and vegetable debris in a food processor and sieve them again – anything that will pass through the sieve will add extra flavour and body to the soup. Do, however, remove fish skins before processing as they are liable to spoil the colour of the soup.

Reheat the strained soup, stirring in the puréed fish and potato until the consistency is smooth. Season to taste with salt and pepper. Heat through thoroughly, but do not allow to boil again for anything more than a moment.

1½ lb/675 g white fish, ideally a whole small haddock, hake, whiting or similar (a John Dory would be excellent if you are prepared to spend a little more)
1½ lb/675 g dogfish, conger eel, gurnard *or* a mixture of all three
2 onions, finely chopped
2 carrots, finely chopped
3 large ripe tomatoes, chopped
1 fennel bulb, finely chopped
1 medium potato, peeled and halved
4 garlic cloves, crushed
2 tbsp olive oil
8 oz/225 g shell-on prawns
1 bay leaf
4 pts/2.25 litres water
salt and black pepper

For the *rouille*
4 garlic cloves
½ tsp salt
1 small fresh red chilli
1 slice stale white bread
1 tsp tomato purée
4 tbsp olive oil

To accompany
olive oil
French bread
grated Gruyère cheese

To make the *rouille*, mash the garlic cloves and the salt with a fork until you get a paste (this is a bit like making a taramasalata, see below). Chop the chilli as finely as possible, almost to a purée, and mix with the garlic paste.

Soak the bread in a little water for a few minutes and then squeeze almost dry. Mix with the garlic and chilli paste, and the tomato purée, in a small bowl. With a small wire whisk, beat in the oil, a little at a time, to get a smooth, glossy paste.

Serve the soup with a trickle of oil in the top of each bowl. Pass around the *rouille*, a bowl of grated Gruyère and plenty of warm crusty French bread. The *rouille* can be stirred into the soup, or spread sparingly (it should be pretty fiery) on the bread which is then dunked. Ditto the cheese.

A chilled Provençal rosé is a fine accompaniment.

Taramasalata
Serves 6 generously

This recipe will prove a revelation to anybody who only knows this dish from the fluorescent pink version so ubiquitous these days in delicatessens and supermarkets. It can easily be made in a food processor, but preparing it by hand produces a nice grainy texture which I slightly prefer. If possible, buy a whole piece of cod's roe, still in its tough outer membrane. If it weighs more than 8 oz/225 g, you can adapt the quantities accordingly.

8 oz/225 g smoked cod's roe
1 garlic clove
8 slices white bread, crusts removed
5 fl oz/150 ml milk
10 fl oz/300 ml good olive oil
2 tbsp lemon juice
1 tbsp finely chopped fresh parsley
1 tbsp finely chopped fresh chives
black pepper

With a spoon scrape the cod's roe out of its skin and put into a mixing bowl. Mash the garlic clove with a fork and mix with the roe. Soak the bread in the milk for a couple of minutes, then squeeze to extract most of the milk. Add the squeezed bread to the cod's roe in the bowl.

Mix thoroughly, then beat in half the oil with a heavy wire whisk, 1 tbsp at a time. Then add the lemon juice, also a little at a time, alternating with the remaining oil. (This is heavy elbow-work, and you may prefer to use a food processor, in which case trickle the oil slowly into the bread and roe through the funnel of the working machine. Alternate oil and lemon juice when the first tbsp of the oil has been incorporated.)

Finally mix in the parsley, chives and a few twists of freshly ground pepper. Spoon into a pot and refrigerate until required. Serve with hot buttered toast, black olives (ideally calamata) and radishes.

Anchovy Dressing
THE BRACKENBURY

This recipe, which Adam Robinson has adapted from Roger Vergé, makes a large quantity (about 1 pt/575 ml), which will keep for 2 weeks in the fridge.

Blend all the ingredients in a liquidizer until completely smooth and decant into a jar. Whisk or shake thoroughly before each use. If you want to serve the dressing warm (which is a good idea if it is dressing something hot), heat it gently through, whisking in a little butter (about 2 oz/60 g for the quantities above) and 2 tbsp cold water as you go. This should help to emulsify the sauce, but do not worry if it separates a little – it will still taste delicious.

This dressing is delicious with steamed/boiled broccoli and curly kale – trickle it over the vegetables while they are hot and serve at once with a few shavings of fresh Parmesan cheese, as a first course. It also accompanies the Brackenbury's Skate Wings with Noodles (page 176).

5 oz/150 g canned anchovy fillets
15 fl oz/450 ml olive oil
4 garlic cloves
1 tsp fresh thyme *or* ½ tsp dried
1½ tbsp fresh basil leaves
1½ tbsp Dijon mustard
1 tbsp red wine vinegar
1 small dried chilli
½ tsp black pepper

Three Uses of a Bloater
THE BRACKENBURY

These three recipes illustrate Bon Marché cooking principles at their best: an inexpensive ingredient renders three different delicious dishes with absolutely no waste.

West African Fish Soup

Serves 6

4 bloaters, each 12–14 oz/
   350–400 g
6 oz/170 g dried white haricot
   or navy beans
1 bacon bone
1 bay leaf
1 tbsp olive *or* sunflower oil
1 onion, sliced
2 garlic cloves, chopped
½–1 small chilli, depending on
   strength
1 scant tbsp tomato purée
salt and black pepper

Fillet and skin the bloaters, remove the roes, soft or hard, and discard the guts – or ask your fishmonger to do this for you. The roe and fillets are set aside for the following recipes.

Bring the beans, bacon bone and bay leaf to the boil in plenty of unsalted water, boil fiercely for just 5 minutes, then cover and leave to simmer gently until the beans are completely tender (1½–2½ hours depending on the size and age of the beans).

Heat the oil in a large saucepan and sweat the onion, garlic and chilli for a few minutes without browning. Add the reserved bones, heads and skins from the bloaters, and the tomato purée, and cover with 2 pts/1.1 litres water. Bring to the boil, then simmer, covered, for 30 minutes.

Strain this stock through a sieve or, preferably, a chinois (see page 22), pressing hard with the back of a spoon or ladle to extract maximum juices.

Purée the beans in a liquidizer with a little of this stock, and return the purée to the rinsed-out saucepan. Over a low heat, stir the remaining stock into the purée. The soup should be thick, but not excessively so. Season well with black pepper, and salt if it needs it. Do not reboil the soup, but heat it right through.

If you want to make a meal of this soup, rather than trying out the following recipe, the fillets of bloater can be sliced and added to the soup just before it is heated through.

Bloater and Potato Salad

Serves 4

The secret of this deliciously simple dish is to dress and mix it while the potatoes are still hot. If they are very small, they can be boiled whole; otherwise cut into halves or quarters as appropriate.

Boil or steam the potatoes in their skins until tender, then drain well. Put at once into a bowl with the bloater fillets. Shake the ingredients for the dressing together in a jar, or else whisk with a fork, pour over the fish and potatoes and mix thoroughly. Serve warm or cold, but not chilled.

    If you are starting with cold cooked potatoes (perhaps you have some left over) then heat them through, either in a steamer or in a pan with a tiny amount of water, before you assemble the dish.

NOTE: a similar salad can be made using kipper fillets or pickled herrings. If you use pickled herrings, add a small carton of soured cream to the dressing.

1 lb/450 g small waxy new potatoes (ideally Pink Fir Apple)
4 bloaters, filleted, skinned and sliced into 1-in/2.5-cm strips

For the dressing
1 large or 2 small shallots, very finely chopped
1 tbsp finely chopped fresh parsley
3 tbsp best olive oil
salt and black pepper

Bloater Roe Paste

Pound the bloater roes with the butter until blended and smooth, or use a food processor. Season well with a good squeeze of lemon and black pepper.

    You can use olive oil instead of butter, beating it in by degrees, as if for a taramasalata (page 164). A lighter version can be made with fromage frais.

    This paste will keep for 2–3 days in the fridge. I like to serve it with the West African Fish Soup, spread on slices of grilled bread rubbed lightly with garlic.

bloater roes, soft and hard
an equal weight of unsalted butter, softened, or olive oil, or fromage frais
lemon juice
black pepper

Herb-crusted Sea Bream with Fresh Tomato Sauce

THE WHITELEAF AT CROYDE

Serves 4

David Wallington writes: 'The fish is cooked skin-side down which protects the flesh from drying out. The top (inside) of the fillet is then coated with a herb crust and finished under the grill. Cooked in this way the flesh itself is not exposed directly to the heat source. The fish should have a crisp and edible skin, moist flakes of white flesh, a savoury but complementarily flavoured crust and a robustly flavoured slightly chunky sauce. Served with a green vegetable (sugar snap peas, broccoli, green beans, etc.) on a plain background it is a stylish and colourful dinner-party main course. You can prepare the crust the day before you buy your fish.'

3–4 oz/85–115 g fresh breadcrumbs
1 small onion, finely chopped and sautéed until golden-brown
2 medium mushrooms, finely chopped
4 black and 4 green olives, stoned and finely chopped
a few good sprigs of coriander, dill, chives, tarragon, thyme, parsley, as available, finely chopped
salt and black pepper
olive *or* groundnut oil for frying
1 lb/450 g ripe flavourful tomatoes *or* a 14-oz/400-g can Italian peeled tomatoes
10 fl oz/300 ml *passata* (sieved tomatoes) *or* 2 tbsp tomato purée made up to 10 fl oz/300 ml with water
'sharpeners and sweeteners' (lemon juice, orange juice, sugar, vinegar, Worcester sauce, see recipe)
fresh parsley, basil *or* coriander, chopped
4 fillets of sea bream, each 6–8 oz/170–225 g

Twenty-four hours in advance, place the breadcrumbs in a bowl, add 2 heaped teaspoons sautéed onion (reserve the remainder), the mushrooms, olives and a good tablespoon finely chopped mixed herbs. Season robustly with salt and pepper, and mix in 2 tablespoons oil.

Peel, de-seed and chop the fresh tomatoes. Add to the remaining sautéed onions in a saucepan with the *passata* or tomato purée–water mixture. If using canned tomatoes, strain the juice over the saucepan, de-seed and chop the tomatoes and add to the pan. Bring to the boil, then simmer and reduce to a rich pulpy sauce. Season to taste. You are aiming for a rich, slightly sweet-sour tomato flavour, and could use any of the following to achieve this: lemon juice, wine vinegar, balsamic vinegar, brown sugar, orange juice, Worcester sauce. Add a sprinkling of chopped fresh herbs before serving.

To cook the bream, heat a frying pan over a moderate heat, brush the skin-side of the fish with oil and cook 1–2 fillets at a time, skin-side down, until the skin is lightly crisped and brown (about 5–6 minutes). The flesh on the upper side should start to look cooked around the edges with the raised centre still raw. Carefully remove the fillets from the pan and place skin-side down on a piece of oiled foil in a grill pan. Cover each fillet with a layer of the crumb mixture, pressing with your hand to ensure that it is even and remains in place. Cook under a moderate grill until golden-brown (4–5 minutes).

Serve as soon as possible with the tomato sauce.

Griddled Brill with Saffron Garlicky Mash

THE FOX AND GOOSE INN

Serves 4

The mash in this dish, flavoured with fish stock and garlic, is rich, creamy and quite sloppy – almost a sauce. Saffron is expensive, but adds a wonderful flavour and colour, and you only need a pinch. If you think it is too extravagant, use 1 tsp finely chopped fresh thyme.

Hake, halibut and cod can also be prepared in this way; choose whichever is freshest, and within your budget, on the day. If you prefer to get your fishmonger to prepare the fish, ask him for a few bones and heads to make the fish stock.

Lemon oil – olive oil infused with lemon zest – is available from the best Italian delicatessens. Or you can make your own, by putting the zest (thinly pared, with no white pith) of 2 lemons in 1 pt/575 ml good olive oil. Seal or cork and leave for at least a week before using.

Clean, trim and fillet the brill (ideally you should have 8 neat pieces of fish). Put the head, bones, skin and trimmings (but not the guts) into a saucepan with the onion, celery, carrot and bay leaf. Pour over the wine and water. Bring to the boil, then simmer gently, covered, for just 20 minutes. Strain this stock and set aside.

Rub the potatoes through a sieve or put through a potato ricer and set aside. In a medium saucepan gently heat 3 tbsp of the oil and cook the garlic without colouring. Add half the fish stock with the saffron, if used, and infuse for 5 minutes over a very low heat. Add the cream and the sieved potato and the remaining oil. Beat well together over a low heat until the mixture is hot (and, if you are using the saffron, coloured a beautiful gold). Add a little more stock if you feel the mixture should be thinner. (Any remaining stock can be frozen.) Season to taste with salt and pepper, and keep warm, covered.

Heat a heavy frying pan or griddle until very hot. Season the brill and very lightly flour the pieces, then brush with oil. Sear very quickly on both sides (no more than 3 minutes in all), so that the fish remains moist inside.

To make the *gremolata*, simply mix together the finely chopped parsley and garlic with the grated lemon rind. In this instance it is used dry; on other occasions 'wet' *gremolata* may be bound with a tablespoon or two of olive oil, and a squeeze of lemon juice.

Spoon generous pools of mashed potato on to 4 warmed plates. Overlap 2 fillets of fish on each plate, sprinkle with a good pinch or two of *gremolata* and add a little swirl of lemon oil. Serve at once.

1½–2 lb/675–900 g brill
1 small onion, roughly chopped
1 celery stick, roughly chopped
1 carrot, roughly chopped
1 bay leaf
½ wine-glass white wine
10 fl oz/300 ml water
1 lb/450 g floury potatoes, cooked
8 tbsp olive oil
3 garlic cloves, finely crushed
a good pinch of saffron threads (*optional*)
5 fl oz/150 ml double cream
salt and black pepper
flour and olive oil for coating
lemon oil, to finish (*optional*)

For the *gremolata*
3 tbsp chopped flat-leaf parsley
1 small garlic clove, very finely chopped
1 tsp very fine grated lemon rind

Salt Cod

To salt your own cod (also ling and haddock) choose only very fresh fish; buy large fillets or preferably a whole large fish, and fillet it yourself. The flesh of big fish has bigger flakes, which makes for a better texture when salted.

Lay the fillets skin-side up, touching but not overlapping, in a large shallow dish or tray. Cover generously with rough rock or sea salt (the cheaper the better – you will need about 1 lb (450 g) salt for every 3 lb/1.3 g fish). After 24 hours, the salt will have dissolved in the water drawn from the fish, to form a brine. The salt cod can now be used, and in this form will keep for up to a week. If you want to keep it longer, add half as much salt again and make sure that the brine completely covers the fish. Cod thus preserved can be kept for over a month. If you want to keep it even longer, then the fillets should be hung to dry in a cool, well-ventilated place. Once completely dry and hard, salt cod can be kept indefinitely.

'Wet' salt cod (i.e. preserved in a brine according to the first two methods described above) should be soaked in cold water for 24 hours before using, and the water changed at least three times. Dry salt cod will take about 48 hours, and several more changes of water. Always taste salt cod raw before you use it, and if it is unpalatably salty then soak for a little longer.

Marinated Salt Cod and Peppers

THE BRACKENBURY

Serves 6

In this dish the humble cod is elevated to new heights of luxury.

Prepare the salt cod for use by soaking and rinsing, as described above. Combine all the ingredients for the marinade. Cut the salt cod into thin strips, toss well with the marinade, and leave covered for at least 6 hours. Then mix well with the sliced tomatoes, strips of red pepper, and any juice saved from either. Season with pepper, refrigerate and leave to infuse the flavours for at least a further 6 hours or overnight. Serve with crusty bread or pitta, to mop up the juices.

8 oz/225 g salt cod

For the marinade
½ red onion *or* 2 shallots
1 tbsp white wine vinegar
5 tbsp good olive oil
1 large garlic clove, finely chopped

6 good flavourful tomatoes (preferably plum), peeled and sliced
3 large red peppers, roasted, skinned and cut into strips (see page 85)
black pepper

Cod with Tomato, Lemon and Fennel

JEMIMA'S

Serves 4

Salted lemons are a North African speciality, and can be found in jars in many Arab-run delicatessens and grocers. They are easy to make at home. Scrub the lemons under a warm tap to remove any wax or mineral oil, then cut a slit through the middle of the lemon, from top to bottom, but without cutting right through either end. Make another cut at right angles to the first, so the lemon is cut into quarters that are still held together by the ends. Squeeze the ends of the lemon to open the slits you have made, and rub a good tablespoon of rough salt into the middle. Pack as many lemons as you can fit into your chosen jar, add another tablespoon of salt for each lemon, and pour over boiling water to fill the jar. Leave to cool before sealing, and keep for at least 2 weeks before using.

1 lb/450 g salt cod (see page
  170)
1 tbsp olive oil
1 onion, chopped
1 garlic clove, chopped
1 lb/450 g tomatoes, peeled
  and chopped
1 salted lemon (see above)
salt and black pepper
  (*optional*)
1 tbsp fresh fennel leaves,
  chopped
12 black olives, stoned and
  roughly chopped

Soak the salt cod in cold water for at least 24 hours (see page 170), then cut into 4 equal pieces. Heat the oil in a saucepan and gently fry the onion and garlic until translucent. Add the tomatoes with any saved juice and bring to the boil. Leave to bubble gently, stirring occasionally, for about 20 minutes, until the sauce is thick and pulpy. Cut the lemon into quarters and discard the flesh, dicing the peel. Put the cod and lemon peel into the tomato sauce and continue cooking for 20–30 minutes, thinning the sauce with some dry white wine or water if it is in danger of burning. Check for seasoning; salt is not usually needed, but pepper may be. Sprinkle with the fennel and olives a minute before serving.

Marinated Mackerel
Serves 4 as a starter

This is a dish to be made only with the freshest possible mackerel – ideally fish you have caught yourself, or at least bought on the quayside. It is not as raw as *sashimi*, or as harsh as a *céviche*, but may lead the uninitiated to an appreciation of both these dishes. You can prepare a really fresh herring in the same way.

plenty of salt (rough crystals or
  sea salt are best)
1 lb/450 g mackerel fillets
1 medium onion (ideally red)
4 tbsp best olive oil
1 tbsp lemon juice
black pepper

Sprinkle a thin layer of salt over a plate or tray and lay the mackerel fillets on top of it, skin-side down. Sprinkle more salt thickly and evenly over the fillets, and place the dish in the fridge for 2 hours.

Thinly slice the onion and mix with the oil and lemon juice. Remove the fillets from the fridge after 2 hours and wipe off the salt with a clean damp cloth (rough crystals or sea salt will come off much more easily than fine table salt).

Peel the skin from the fillets and slice them diagonally into ½-in/1-cm pieces. Toss with the onion, oil and lemon juice, season with black pepper, and return this mixture, covered, to the fridge for at least 4 hours to marinate. Provided the fish is entirely covered with the marinade (you can make sure of this by cramming the mixture into a large jar) it will keep for 48 hours, but not longer. I prefer the fish after a light marinade, about 6 hours, when it is not too 'pickled' but still tastes beautifully of the sea.

Serve with brown bread and butter, to mop up all the marinade, and the little slivers of onion.

Grey Mullet Braised in the Greek Style
Serves 6

Grey mullet is a vastly under-rated fish (see page 147), but not in Greece, where it is prepared in this simple, garlicky braise.

Clean and scale the mullet, removing the fins and tails. Rinse well and pat dry. In a large braising pan into which all the fish will fit, heat the oil and gently soften the garlic and onion. Season with salt, pepper and oregano, add the wine and water and simmer for about 20 minutes until the liquid is reduced by about one-third. Add the sliced potatoes and simmer for a further 10–15 minutes. Move the potatoes to the sides of the pan and place the mullet in the centre. They should be half-covered by liquid, so add more water if necessary. Braise very gently, uncovered, for 15–20 minutes until the fish is cooked through (see page 138 for how to test). Add the squid and prawns, if used, a few minutes before the end of cooking, and pour the lemon juice over just before serving.

To serve the fish, remove from the pan and flake the flesh with a fork and palette knife, dividing it among 6 warmed plates. Spoon the potatoes, onions and juices from the pan generously on to each plate.

Recommended accompaniments are two simple salads, one of tomato and basil dressed with lemon and olive oil, another of green leaves, a thinly sliced onion, calamata olives and a few fresh orange segments tossed in olive oil.

2–3 grey mullet, about
  3½ lb/1.5 kg in all
4 fl oz/100 ml olive oil
1 small whole garlic bulb,
  peeled and chopped
1 onion, chopped
salt and black pepper
a sprig of fresh oregano
5 fl oz/150 ml dry white wine
1 pt/575 ml water
1 lb/450 g waxy potatoes,
  thickly sliced
2 small squid, cleaned and sliced
  (*optional*)
a few shell-on prawns
  (*optional*)
juice of 1 large lemon

Roast Plaice

1 whole small plaice per person
polenta meal
plain flour
finely chopped fresh parsley
salt and black pepper
sunflower *or* groundnut oil for
   frying

Adam Robinson writes: 'At the Brackenbury we use the term "roast" to describe fish which are cooked on the bone in the oven. In fact we usually start them in a pan on the top, then move them to the oven to finish cooking.

'Until recently it was thought too much to ask customers to bone their fish on the plate – hence the fashion for every piece of fish being at best a simple fillet, at worst stuffed with a mousseline or cut into strips and made into a plait.

'Personally, I am convinced that fish cooked on the bone produces a more succulent and savoury end-result. I also like to cook with unskinned fish – there is a layer of fat beneath the skin which helps to keep the flesh moistened during cooking. The challenge is to make the skin crispy. I like to do this by rolling the fish in a 50–50 mixture of polenta meal and wheat flour, well-seasoned, and start by frying the fish quickly on both sides before putting it in the oven in the same pan.

'This treatment can be given to whole small round-fish such as cod, haddock, whiting, and whole small flat-fish such as flounders. Larger specimens can also be cooked whole, or in portion-sized cutlets on the bone.

'Whole, small plaice given this treatment are delicious, and a bargain: add some finely chopped parsley to the polenta–flour mix, coat the plaice, then fry it in a little very hot oil for 1 minute on each side. Put straight into a pre-heated fairly hot oven (200°C/400°F/Gas Mark 6), or transfer to a warmed roasting dish if your frying pan is not ovenproof, and, in 7–10 minutes, depending on its size, your plaice will be cooked.'

NOTE: this is delicious served with the Fox and Goose's garlicky mash (page 169) and wilted spinach (see page 94).

Warm Salmon Salad Niçoise with Basil

THE FOX AND GOOSE INN

Serves 4

This is pretty served in individual Provençal painted or white bowls, but plates can be used. The potatoes and beans can be freshly used while still warm, or heated up gently from cold in either a microwave or a conventional oven.

First make the vinaigrette: shake the ingredients together in a jar. Toss the warm beans and potatoes in enough of the vinaigrette to coat, and divide among 4 bowls. Arrange the eggs and tomatoes on top of the beans and potatoes, around the sides of the bowls, and keep warm.

Season the salmon, and very lightly dust the pieces with flour seasoned with salt and pepper, then brush them, again lightly, with oil. Heat a frying pan or griddle to a very high heat and sear the salmon pieces very quickly on all sides, taking no more than a minute at the very most.

Pile the pieces of salmon on top of the bowls, and garnish with the olives and plenty of freshly torn basil leaves. Trickle over a little more olive oil and serve.

6 oz/170 g French beans, cooked lightly and drained
8 oz/225 g cooked small new potatoes (with or without skins on), cut into pieces the size of a 1/2 walnut shell
4 lightly hard-boiled eggs, quartered lengthways
4 tomatoes (preferably plum), quartered and de-seeded
8 oz/225 g fresh salmon fillet, cut into 1-in-thick fingers
a little plain flour and olive oil for coating
salt and black pepper

For the vinaigrette
1 tbsp wine vinegar
4 tbsp best olive oil
1 tsp mustard
2 tsp finely chopped fresh basil
salt and black pepper

To garnish
20 black olives, stoned
1/2 oz/15 g fresh basil leaves
a little top-quality olive oil

Skate Wing with Noodles and
Anchovy Dressing

THE BRACKENBURY

Serves 4

4 × skate wing portions,
  skinned but on the bone,
  each 8–10 oz/225–285 g
polenta meal
plain flour
salt and black pepper
olive oil for frying
8 oz/225 g tagliatelle
  preferably fresh and home-
  made
8 oz/225 g French beans
Anchovy dressing, prepared
  following instructions given
  on page 165

Wipe rather than wash the skate wings, then coat in a 50–50 mixture of polenta and flour, well seasoned with salt and pepper. Cook as for the plaice on page 174. The skate wings will take 8–12 minutes in a hot oven, depending on thickness. Test for doneness (see page 138) at the thick end of each portion.

While the fish is cooking, prepare the tagliatelle and beans: top, tail and slice the beans into 1-in/2.5-cm lengths and boil or steam until *al dente*. If the pasta is fresh, start the beans cooking first. If using dried tagliatelle, put the pasta on first, and start cooking the beans about 5 minutes before it is done.

Drain the tagliatelle and the beans and add enough of the Anchovy Dressing, warmed through, to coat lightly – about 4 tbsp should do it. Divide the pasta among 4 warmed plates and place a skate portion on top of each. Pour a little more of the Anchovy Dressing over each skate wing and serve.

Grilled Sprats with Mustard Sauce

THE WHITELEAF AT CROYDE

Serves 4 as a starter, 2 as a main course

Inexpensive, tasty and nutritious, sprats make an easily prepared starter or light meal. See page 154 for advice on choosing sprats. They are surprisingly substantial – 1 lb/450 g will serve 4 as a starter or make a good meal for 2. Serve with brown bread and butter and a lightly dressed mixed leaf salad.

1 lb/450 g fresh and shiny-
  bright sprats
olive oil
sea salt and black pepper
chopped fresh parsley

First make the sauce: in a small saucepan mix the crème fraîche with the mustard, add the butter, salt and a twist or two of black pepper. Place over a very low heat, stirring occasionally, and allow to thicken without boiling.

Prepare the sprats: place a piece of foil on the base of a grill pan, brush thoroughly with oil and sprinkle with pepper. Lay the sprats on the foil and cook under a very hot grill until the sprats start to brown and blister. Turn over and cook until the heads and tails are going crispy and the skin is golden-brown. Sprinkle with sea salt and chopped parsley. Place on a warmed circular plate like the spokes of a wheel, tails to the centre. Garnish the sauce with more chopped parsley and spoon on to the centre of the plate over the tails.

NOTE: for a less pungent sauce use Dijon mustard on its own or in combination with English. For more 'zing' add 1 tsp English mustard powder, first mixing it with a little of the sauce. Not for the squeamish, sprats should be eaten entire, heads and all.

For the sauce
4 tbsp crème fraîche
4 tsp made English mustard
½ oz/15 g butter
a pinch of salt and black pepper

Crab Ramekins
Serves 4 as a starter

You can buy ready-cooked crabs for this dish, provided you are confident they are quite fresh. Do not fail to include the brown meat from the crab – it has most of the flavour. To get 1 lb/450 g crab meat, you will need a crab of at least 2¼ lb/1 kg, or 2 crabs weighing 1½ lb/675 g each.

Pick over the crabs, cracking the claws and legs to extract as much meat as possible (a pair of tweezers is a useful aid). Scrape all the brown meat, including any coral (the red stuff), from inside the main shell. Season to taste with salt and pepper.

Mix the crab meat with the béchamel sauce, mustard, dill, vermouth and lemon juice. Divide the mixture among 4 ramekins lightly greased with a little of the butter. Mix the Gruyère with the breadcrumbs and sprinkle evenly over the ramekins. Dot the top of each with small pieces of butter. Bake in a pre-heated hot oven (220°C/425°F/Gas Mark 7) for 8–10 minutes until bubbling hot and crisp on the top.

1 lb/450 g cooked crab meat (white and brown)
salt and black pepper
scant 5 fl oz/150 ml thick béchamel sauce, made with half milk, half cream (see page 399)
1 tsp made English mustard
a few sprigs of dill, finely chopped
1 tbsp dry vermouth (Martini or Noilly Prat)
a squeeze of fresh lemon
1 oz/30 g butter
2 oz/60 g Gruyère cheese, grated
2 oz/60 g fresh breadcrumbs

VARIATION: for an unusual but delicious Thai-style variation on this dish, substitute coconut milk for the béchamel, and instead of mustard, vermouth and dill, add 2 finely chopped garlic cloves, a small chopped fresh chilli and a walnut-sized piece of fresh ginger root, grated or finely chopped. Omit the Gruyère cheese in the topping.

Crab and Orange Salad with Avocado Sauce

THE ARK

Serves 6 as a starter

3 medium (1½-lb/675-g) or 2 large (2-lb/900-g plus) freshly boiled crabs, or ready-dressed crabs to feed 6

3 large oranges, peeled and separated into segments

mixed salad leaves: radicchio, oak leaf, watercress, little gem and frisée

light vinaigrette (4 parts olive oil to 1 part vinegar, seasoned with salt and pepper)

fresh basil leaves, to garnish

For the sauce
2 ripe avocados
juice of 1 lemon
1 garlic clove, crushed
salt and pepper
10 fl oz/300 ml soured cream
3 spring onions, chopped
chopped fresh basil (optional)

Prepare the crabs in the usual way, cracking with hammer and nutcracker, and extracting as much meat as possible from the claws and legs with skewers and tweezers.

To make the sauce, mash the avocados with a fork or in a food processor with the lemon juice, garlic and salt and pepper. Beat in the soured cream and fold in the chopped spring onion and a little basil, if used.

Lightly toss the salad leaves in the vinaigrette and arrange in piles on 6 plates. Arrange the crab meat (white and brown) and orange segments over the leaves. Spoon some of the avocado sauce into the centre and garnish with basil leaves. Serve the rest of the sauce separately.

Spicy Mussel Broth

THE BRACKENBURY
Serves 8 as a starter, 4 as a feast

Dashi-no-moti, Japanese fish stock powder, available from Japanese grocers and some health food shops, is optional, but desirable in this recipe.

Heat the wine with the onion in a large saucepan. When boiling, add the mussels in batches, removing them as they open with a slotted spoon. When all the mussels have opened, strain the liquor through a clean cotton cloth into a jug and reserve. Shuck (shell) roughly two-thirds of the mussels, leaving the remaining third in their half-shells.

To make the broth, sweat all the diced vegetables in the oil in a large saucepan together with the lime leaves, lemon grass, chilli, garlic and ginger, for around 10 minutes until the vegetables are softened but not browned.

Add to the vegetables the reserved mussel liquor, the fish stock and, if used, the dashi made up with boiling water according to the instructions on the packet. Heat through. (If using the noodles, which turn the broth from a starter into a meal, add them now, a few minutes before serving and cook until tender.) Divide the mussels among warmed bowls, making sure everyone has a few unshucked mussels, and ladle the broth, including some of the vegetables in each portion, over the mussels. Garnish each bowl with a few whole coriander leaves.

2 wine-glasses white wine
½ onion, sliced
4½ lb/2 kg mussels (See page 149)

For the broth
½ onion, finely diced
2 carrots, finely diced
½ leek, finely diced
2 celery sticks, finely diced
I fennel bulb, finely diced
2 tbsp oil
2 lime leaves
I lemon grass stem, cut into short lengths
½ fresh red or green chilli, finely chopped
2 garlic cloves, finely chopped
I in/2.5 cm piece fresh ginger root, peeled and grated
I pt/575 ml fish stock
I sachet dashi-no-moti (*optional*)

To garnish
fresh coriander leaves
6 oz/170 g cellophane or buckwheat noodles (*optional*)

Szechuan Spiced Prawns

JEMIMA'S
Serves 4

Try to get large Mediterranean prawns for this dish – 6 per person makes a decent portion for a starter. If you can't find them (or if those you find do not look very fresh), use ordinary shell-on prawns (see page 151), allowing 3 oz/85 g per person. Dublin Bay prawns (langoustines) would be delicious, but extravagant. If you can find uncooked prawns, and are satisfied they are quite fresh, these can also be used, though the stir-frying will take a few minutes longer. Szechuan peppercorns can be found in Oriental grocers', but you could substitute the more widely available green peppercorns, pickled in brine.

24 large cooked prawns
6 tbsp sunflower oil
4 garlic cloves, crushed
½ tsp salt
I tsp Szechuan peppercorns
2 tsp sesame seeds
½ tsp ground cumin
I tsp ground coriander
¼ tsp chilli powder
I tsp peeled and grated ginger root
salad leaves, to garnish

Peel the prawns and pat dry. Combine half the oil with the garlic, ginger, salt and spices, and mix to a paste. Heat the remaining oil in a pan large enough to take all the prawns in one layer. Pour in the spice paste, stir for a few seconds, add the prawns and stir-fry for just a couple of minutes, until hot and sizzling. If the spices start to burn before the prawns are ready, splash in a little water. Serve without delay, garnished with a few salad leaves.

Squid and Prawn Salad with Walnuts

THE ARK
Serves 6

I lb/450 g squid, cleaned and cut into ½-in/I-cm slices
I½ lb/675 g cooked, shell-on prawns (see page 151)
3 fl oz/75 ml olive oil
I garlic clove, crushed
6 fl oz/175 ml vinaigrette (made from lemon Juice, Dijon mustard and olive oil)
3 oz/85 g walnuts, coarsely chopped
4 tbsp chopped fresh parsley
salt, cayenne and black pepper
lemon wedges, to serve

Dry the squid well. Peel the prawns and pat dry. Heat the oil with the garlic in a large frying pan. Add the squid before the garlic takes colour, then toss over a high heat for 1–2 minutes until opaque and still tender. Place in a bowl, mix with half the vinaigrette, and leave to cool. Stir the peeled prawns into the remaining vinaigrette. Combine the prawns and squid, and add the walnuts, parsley and salt, cayenne and black pepper to taste just before serving. Serve with lemon wedges to squeeze over the dish.

Grilled Butterflied Squid with Chilli and Garlic

Serves 4 as a generous starter or
light main course

For this recipe you should choose small squid, but not the really tiny ones which frazzle to nothing on a hot griddle or barbecue. Squid with bodies 5–7 in/12.5–17.5 cm long are perfect. You can also use cuttlefish. See page 155 for advice on buying squid and cuttlefish.

The preparation procedure described below sounds tortuous, but is not hard to master and becomes a speedy operation with practice. Once the squid is prepared, the rest of the recipe could hardly be simpler.

To prepare the squid, 1) pull the head and tentacles out of the body cavity. Squeezing the head just in front of the eyes, cut off the tentacles so they remain attached to a small ring of flesh at the front of the head. Discard the rest of the head and any insides attached to it. Rinse the tentacles well under cold running water.

2) Take the body cavity and feel inside for the quill-like bone – pull this out with your fingers. With a sharp knife, slit the squid from the opening of the cavity to the back, opening it out so you have a large triangular sheet of flesh. Scrape out any remaining intestines, sand, ink and general gunge.

3) Turn over the flesh so the outside of the body is uppermost, and peel away the pinkish membrane with your fingers. Pull off the 'wings', discarding them if they are very small, but keeping those from the larger squid, trimming off the slightly horny edges where they were attached to the body. Rinse the squid well and wipe dry.

4) Lay the flat piece of squid down on a board, inside uppermost. Once you have removed the membrane from the outside it becomes very difficult to distinguish between the inside and outside, so be careful to lay the squid inside-up as soon as you have performed this task. (If you lose track of which side is which, the inside is slightly softer.)

5) Using a blunt knife this time (I find an ordinary table knife with a serrated edge perfect for the job), lightly score the inside surface of the squid with parallel cuts about ½ in/1 cm apart. The

Preparation
2 lb/900 g squid *or*
1½ lb/675 g prepared squid

cuts should not go right through the squid – with the right pressure applied, the slight toughness of the outer skin will prevent this. Make another set of cuts at an angle of 45 degrees to the first, to get a criss-cross effect. Then cut each squid body into 2–3 pieces (perhaps 4 if you have only been able to buy large squid). You are aiming for pieces about the size of half a postcard, though geometrical precision is not required. Perform the same scoring operation on any wings you have saved.

If you can't face the first messy stages of the above procedure, ask your fishmonger to clean the squid for you. He should present you with the clean but intact body of the squid, and the tentacles. You simply have to cut open the body according to step 2) and then proceed from step 4) above.

For the marinade
2 tbsp olive oil
2 small fresh red or green
  chillis, finely chopped
3 garlic cloves, finely chopped
salt and black pepper

To marinate, take the pieces of butterflied squid and toss them in a bowl with the oil, chilli, garlic and a little salt and pepper, and leave in the fridge for at least 30 minutes or until you are ready to eat. The preparation can be done several hours in advance, but unless you know the squid is quite exceptionally fresh, do not leave overnight.

The squid thus prepared can be cooked in a number of ways. A barbecue is best of all, the cast-iron griddle pan a close second, but an ordinary frying pan will also produce excellent results.

The Cooking

If you use a barbecue or griddle pan (which should be thoroughly pre-heated and very hot), shake each piece of squid to remove any excess oil, then lay as many pieces as you can fit at a time on the barbecue or pan. Turn over with a pair of tongs after just 2 minutes. The squid will curl up, which is no problem, but pressing it back down from time to time ensures that both sides are seared by the bars of the barbecue or the ridges of the griddle – 3–4 minutes is all it takes (perhaps 5 if the squid is very thick).

If you use an ordinary frying pan, do not add any extra oil, but heat the pan dry until it is very hot, then flash-fry the squid for 3–4 minutes, turning frequently, until it is curling and slightly charred.

Serve as soon as it is ready, with a salad of interesting green leaves (a mixture of rocket and *pousse d'épinards* – see pages 74–6 – is ideal), and chips (see page 88) if you want to make a meal of it.

CHAPTER FOUR

Meat

We eat too much meat in this country. Too much for our health, too much for the welfare of our farmed animals, and far too much for the quality of the meat we eat to be consistently high.

Whether the post-war boom in factory farming of livestock was a response to demand, or whether, in tandem with intensive marketing campaigns and nutritional 'education', it was the cause of it, is a chicken–egg question, the investigation of which is of dubious value. The fact is that our butcher's shops and supermarkets are now filled to overflowing with cheap meat from intensively farmed animals who live painful and stressful lives, and are fed a diet that is scandalously inappropriate for their species – indeed often it *is* their own species. If you want the full horrors of factory farming spelled out for you, consult Audrey Eyton's excellent book, *The Kind Food Guide* (Penguin, 1991).

The important question facing the consumer today is not 'How did this happen?' but 'What are we going to do about it?'

You don't have to become a vegetarian to make a stand against intensive farming practices. If you happen to believe, as I do, that meat is a valid part of the human diet, and there is no moral imperative not to kill animals for food, you do not automatically align yourself with the factory farmers. And if you are particularly concerned, as I am, about the eating quality of the meat you buy, then you have even less reason to support their operations with your custom. (Poor flavour is perhaps the least of the evils of factory farming, but at least it is one the consumer can directly relate to.)

Those of us who wish to continue to eat meat can make our protest against factory farming, and its second-rate products, in a different way: by boycotting those products in favour of 'real' meat from animals that have been raised outdoors with the freedom to move and a diet to which they are by nature inclined.

So before we get on to the specifics of how to assess the quality of meat, and use it economically, I make this general plea: try very hard not to buy second-rate meat. Learn a little (or even a lot) about the origin of the meat at the outlets where you regularly shop. Eat more game which, if not entirely wild these days, is at least free-roaming, naturally-feeding, healthier and tastier. Support the initiatives of both butchers and supermarkets to offer meat and poultry that has been naturally fed and humanely reared.

Organic and near-organic meat

Organic farming is conducted without the use of chemical pesticides and fertilizers. In the case of organically reared livestock, the animals are reared on mixed farms, with stock and crops rotated to replenish the land in the traditional way. A natural diet is assured, animals are kept outside throughout the grazing season, and the use of antibiotics and growth promoters is not allowed. This is all good news, not just for the animals' welfare, but for the taste of the meat. Look out for a stamp of approval from the Soil Association. This organization can provide you with a comprehensive list of producers and suppliers of organic meat in this country. Contact the Soil Association, 86 Colston Street, Bristol BS1 5BB (0272 290661).

The conditions that have to be met for meat to qualify as organic are stringent. There are many stock farmers who do not farm organically, but who nevertheless raise their animals in non-intensive systems with a proper regard for their welfare, their diet and the high quality of their meat. Look out for informative labels at the butcher's and in the supermarket. A label stating that meat is produced to Conservation Grade standards means that, although production is not fully organic, animals are reared on a natural diet in accordance with the highest animal welfare standards, and by environmentally friendly practices. The terms 'Naturally fed' and 'Traditionally reared' are likely to be good indicators of quality for beef, pork and lamb; 'Free-range' and 'Outdoor-reared' are also used for pork. For chickens, turkeys, ducks and most other poultry, 'Free-range', and preferably 'Corn-fed' or 'Fed on an all natural diet' as well, should ensure tasty birds.

Equally, be wary of bogus labels designed to give the impression that factory-farmed products originate from some quaint rustic idyll: an oven-ready chicken labelled 'Farm-fresh' with a picture of a wheatsheaf on it is practically guaranteed to come from a factory, and to have been fed on high-protein pellets made from animal by-products. If it doesn't say 'Free-range' or 'Corn-fed', assume it isn't.

The best-quality meat will, for the time being at least, cost you a little more. Balance this extravagance by eating meat a little less often – this book will help you to be more adventurous in cooking fish, vegetables, pulses and fruit. If you are really loath to cut down on meat, try buying the cheaper cuts. You will get far more from your carnivorous diet if you learn to vary the cuts you buy and the techniques you use to cook them. The next three chapters are intended to help you with that too.

Butchers today

Just as the quality of meat has been in decline for decades now, so has the quality of butchering. Most housewives of my grandmother's generation would have had a local butcher whom they knew by name and visited several times a week. He in turn would have known them, remembered what they liked and, more crucially, what they didn't like. For they would have made no bones about telling him if a joint of beef had been tough, a chicken on the skinny side, or a piece of lamb's liver less than perfectly fresh. Equally, they would have taken the trouble to thank and congratulate him when his meticulously prepared crown roast of lamb had gone down a treat with their dinner guests.

That tradition of customer feedback and personal service is not quite dead, but it is in a poor state of health which is beginning to look terminal. The big chains of high street butchers, in competition with supermarkets to keep prices keen, have cut staff, cut costs and cut corners. The sharp practices of shoddy butchers go way beyond the traditional sin of putting bread in their sausages: they have been selling defrosted frozen meat as fresh; labelling imported meat as English or Scottish; and prolonging the life of tired meat with lurid pink preservatives unconvincingly called 'Chinese-style' marinades.

The traditional, independent, local butcher, offering a personal service and quality products, struggles to compete in this climate. Many have had to shut up shop, leaving fewer and fewer outposts to make a stand against the encroachment of mediocrity and mass-produced meat. Butchers brave enough to make this stand do still exist, however, and they deserve our support. It is well worth taking the trouble to find one.

How to find a good butcher

A superficial assessment of a butcher's operation can be made with a quick glance around the shop. How is the meat presented? Sloppily, with lamb chops thrown in a pile and lumps of liver sitting in a pool of blood? Or neatly, in a well-ordered and logical display that allows you to find easily whatever you are looking for? How well is the meat labelled? Are there tags with comprehensive information about the origin and character of the meat? Or are there simply the standard issue plastic spike labels saying 'Local Lamb' or 'Scottish Beef'? Is the shop well-staffed, with assistants busily preparing meat to the specification of waiting customers? Or is there one grumpy man in a bloody apron with a look that says 'I hope you're not about to ask me to *do* something'.

There are a number of pretty reliable indicators that a butcher is a man dedicated to his craft:

○ He has his own brine tub, and will salt any piece of meat for you on request.
○ He makes his own sausages (ideally without preservatives).
○ He makes his own black pudding.
○ He boils his own tongues and hams.
○ He stocks a range of game in season.
○ He has a good selection of offal.
○ Frozen and imported meat, if he sells it at all, is clearly labelled.

But there is one consideration that overrides all of these: ultimately the best butcher is the one who gives you what you want – *even if you have to ask.* Even a butcher who does not normally keep hares or tongues in stock or sell traditionally reared beef or free-range chickens probably knows perfectly well where he can get them. Even if he does not usually hang his meat for long, he can do so for you. Perhaps he usually stocks only frozen chicken livers, but he can put some fresh ones on one side if he knows you are coming to collect them. That is his job, and it is all good business for him.

The Q-Guild

There is a trade organization which was set up some years ago with the specific aim of reversing the declining standards of butchery in this country. It is called the Q-Guild ('Q' for Quality), and its members are subjected to rigorous quality controls over many aspects of their business, including product range, hygiene and customer service. Many (though not all) stock organic or traditionally reared meat. Those that don't may be able to find it for you. For further information and a list of Q-Guild butchers, call 0908 677577, or write to The Q-Guild, PO Box 44, Winterhill House, Snowdon Drive, Milton Keynes, MK6 1AX.

Buying meat in the supermarket

Buying good meat in the supermarket is an uphill struggle. Having said that, standards are improving, and at the time of writing a number of the major supermarkets, including Asda, Marks and Spencer, Tesco, Safeway, Sainsbury's and Waitrose, are making some concessions to real meat lovers, offering a few cuts of beef or lamb that are labelled 'Organic' or 'Traditionally reared', and 'Outdoor-reared' pork and bacon as well as free-range and corn-fed chickens, turkeys, geese and ducks.

There is clearly only one way that the range and quality of supermarket meat is going to continue to improve: customers must respond to these initiatives. At the moment organic meat is almost certainly a 'loss leader' for most supermarkets. Only a good public response can turn loss-leading products into real profit, at which point new loss-leaders, maybe blanched sweetbreads or pork from traditional breeds, will be introduced to the range.

The really limiting factors about buying meat in a supermarket are the narrow range of cuts on offer and, of course, the lack of a butcher. The first of these may be improving very slowly, but the second is a harder problem to crack. A supermarket cannot slice your liver to the thickness you request, give you a few veal bones to make stock, or throw in a couple of pig's ears at no extra charge. These are the valuable perks of having a good local butcher.

However, as write I am aware of an initiative in the larger Sainsbury's stores whereby customers can order specific cuts of meat by telephone which can be prepared to their specification by the store's resident butcher. If you are one of those unfortunates who, on account of a busy timetable, simply *has* to do all their shopping in the supermarket, then I urge you to test this service to its limits. Perhaps it will catch on.

Other ways of buying meat

Besides the butcher and the supermarket, there are a couple of other ways in which you can buy your meat. They are not the cheapest, and they may not be convenient for everyone, but they come with an unmatchable assurance of quality. Both involve buying direct from the producer.

Farm shops

Increasingly, producers of organic and traditionally reared meats are butchering their own meat and selling direct to local customers through their own farm shops. Try looking in Yellow Pages under 'Butchers', 'Farm Shops', 'Meat' and 'Organic', or contact the Soil Association (see page 186).

Home delivery

There are now a number of home-delivery firms around the country specializing in organic and/or traditionally reared meat. All the farms that supply them have to fulfil certain stringent conditions in the rearing and feeding of their animals. Among the best are the Pure Meat Company in Devon (0647 40321), Greenway Organic Farms in Edinburgh (031 557 8111), Ian Miller's Organic Meat in Fife, Scotland (0738 85498), and Swaddles Green in Somerset (0460 234387). The Soil Association (see above) can provide a more up-to-date list.

On choosing meat in general

There are two basic principles for the Bon Marché shopper to bear in mind, both of which are fairly obvious, yet remarkably often ignored by the careless customer. They are:

1. *The meat you choose should be suitable for its intended purpose.*

There is no point in stewing a fillet steak, or flash-frying a shin of beef and trying to serve it pink. If, therefore, you cannot get the cut of meat appropriate for your proposed recipe, you may be better off revising your cooking plans than trying to muddle through with an inappropriate cut. For example, you may want roast pigeons for supper, but discover that the only pigeons the butcher has are clearly old birds. But you've promised pigeons to a loved one, and you decide to buy them anyway. It's no use hoping that these old birds will by some lucky quirk of fate have led such leisurely lives that they evade the infallible rule that old pigeons are tough pigeons which are likely to test your dental strength if you decide to roast them. Casserole them instead (see page 286 for recipe).

2. *The importance of the quality of the meat you choose is approximately inversely proportional to the length of time you propose to cook it for.*

In other words, if I am going to make, for example, an oxtail stew (see page

231), in which the oxtail will be cooked for 3 hours in a rich liquor of beef stock, vegetables and wine until it is literally falling off the bone, then I am not going to worry unduly about whether or not my chosen tail comes from a prize-winning Aberdeen Angus that has grazed only on the lush organic meadows of a small Dorset farm, and been hung at 4°C/38°F for 3 weeks. The same applies to pig's trotters and ears, and other very tough cuts for slow cooking. Having said that, I think it is always worth choosing quality, well-hung meat when you have the choice, as it strengthens the real meat lobby against the factory farmers, and that must be a good thing. And in many slow-cooked dishes, such as *daubes* of beef and braises of pork or lamb, you will certainly notice the difference in both taste and texture.

When the meat is to be roasted, grilled or fried, or otherwise quickly cooked, the quality of the raw product is of paramount importance. This applies to all farmed meat – beef, pork, lamb, veal and domestic fowl – and most particularly to beef or lamb when they are to be served pink. In the case of game, only younger birds are suitable for roasting fast and serving pink.

The flavour of meat

It is worth knowing that the flavour of meat comes essentially from fat. This is not simply because fat is intrinsically tasty (though the dripping from good-quality meat does have plenty of flavour) but because its presence in the meat helps to lubricate, so that it retains its succulence, giving up its juices only when it is chewed, and not during cooking. A good marbling of fat is therefore a desirable quality in meat. Intensively farmed animals, which are grown at such a pace that they do not have time to develop their natural fat reserves, lack marbling, and have a tendency to dryness and a disappointing flavour.

The importance of fat to flavour is the reason why meat for stewing and slow-cooking should not be zealously trimmed of all fat, and why, if your meat for a stew is very lean, it is a good idea to include a quantity of fat-rich pork belly, salt pork or good-quality bacon. Lean joints of meat, and rabbits, hares and game birds, are often threaded with pork or bacon fat (this is called larding), or covered (barded) with a few strips of fat or bacon, in order to prevent them drying out during cooking.

'Sealing' meat

As far as retaining the moisture of meat is concerned, there is a conventional wisdom that advises cooks to 'seal' meat, usually by quickly browning it in hot oil, before subjecting it to further cooking in the stew pot, roasting tin, or whatever. In fact, it has been scientifically demonstrated that the searing or browning of meat does nothing to seal in its juices – for a detailed exposition see Harold McGee's *On Food and Cookery*, pages 112–115. This does not mean, however, that we should forsake the procedure. Its real benefit is in caramelizing some of the sugars of the meat – a very worthwhile practice which will add richness and depth of flavour to your meat, and the other ingredients with which it is cooked.

Storing fresh meat at home

If meat is to be used on the day of purchase, it need not be refrigerated, but can be kept covered in a cool larder – in fact, providing the larder is reliably cool, it can be so kept for up to 24 hours. Meat that is to be kept for longer than that should be refrigerated. Ideally, chilled meat should be removed from the fridge a few hours before cooking and brought to room temperature, otherwise it may contract on heating and turn out tougher than it need be.

Never store a joint of fresh meat for any length of time in airtight polythene wrapping – it should be allowed to breathe. If you have bought it wrapped in polythene, unwrap it, and rewrap it loosely in paper or muslin, or simply cover with a clean cotton cloth. Once meat has been butchered from a hung carcase it will not improve or mature any further by keeping. It is therefore unwise ever to keep fresh meat for more than 3 days before cooking it, and even then only when you are confident it has not been hanging around in the butcher's tray for long.

Frozen meat

As I explained, quoting Harold McGee, in Chapter 3, freezing of fish or meat damages the tissue by forming ice crystals, which 'leach' when the meat thaws, causing loss of proteins, salts and sugars and, naturally enough, flavour. This means that any meats which are cooked after they have been frozen are likely to be drier and less tasty than they would have been if cooked from fresh. To minimize these effects, frozen meat should be thoroughly defrosted (uncovered, at room temperature), before cooking.

The extent to which meat is affected by freezing will vary according to inherent texture characteristics of different kinds of meat. Open-textured meat, such as the cheaper stewing cuts of beef, veal and lamb, will form larger ice crystals and be more adversely affected. Freezing also facilitates the oxidation of unsaturated fats in meat: pork and poultry are particularly affected, and can develop a slightly rancid flavour if frozen for a long time.

If you accumulate a lot of game in the winter months, then freeze it you must. But I see very little reason to eat frozen beef, lamb, pork or chicken, when the fresh products are so readily available.

One more thing. The extent to which food is adversely affected by freezing also depends on the speed at which it is frozen: faster freezing means smaller ice crystals will form, and less damage will be done. Many domestic freezers have an adjustable temperature, or a fast-freeze button. Make sure the freezer is on the coldest possible setting when you put fresh food into it.

Meat products, charcuterie and the delicatessen

This book is primarily about shopping for and cooking with fresh produce, so I do not propose to fill too much space discussing ready-to-eat or ready-to-cook prepared meat products. Nevertheless it is worth pointing out that a number of the farmers who are taking the trouble to rear carefully bred animals according to traditional methods are also taking an interest in traditional ways of butchering, preparing and curing their animals. Many of them sell excellent hams, bacon, sausages, pâtés and pies that have been prepared on the premises, as well as stuffed, marinated, or otherwise oven-ready birds and joints. These are often available in the shops attached to the farms themselves or by home delivery (see page 190), or in the butchers and delicatessens through which these farmers sell.

At the same time a good local delicatessen can be an invaluable fund of high-quality ingredients, which may not be easily available at your local butcher or supermarket. Pancetta (Italian smoked belly of pork), for example, is an excellent lubricant and flavouring for many sauces and casseroles, and certainly preferable to second-rate, waterlogged bacon. It is called for in several recipes in this book. I have yet to find it in a supermarket, yet it is available in practically every good Italian or Portuguese-run deli in the country. Similarly salamis, chorizos and other specialist sausages, regional hams and other cured meats, are often found in the tiniest family-run delicatessens in a wider range and of a better quality than in the best and biggest butchers and supermarkets. Never disregard the small operator. They may have just what you are looking for.

Basic butchery

There is no doubt that some knowledge of how meat is butchered gives considerable extra power to the shopper. If you go to the butcher's shop, or even the supermarket, armed with even the most basic understanding of how different animals are divided up, and which pieces are suitable for what kind of cooking, then you already have the advantage over most other shoppers – and over one or two butchers as well.

The guide to butchers' cuts that follows covers the principal British cuts of beef, lamb and pork, with some of the better-known cuts mentioned in passing. Each cut is assessed for quality, value and suitable cooking methods. Cuts that are possibly unfamiliar, but particularly rewarding for the adventurous and cost-conscious cook, are marked with a +.

GUIDE TO BUTCHERS' CUTS

Beef

In her great book *French Provincial Cooking*, Elizabeth David pointed out one of the difficulties facing the English shopper when buying meat in general, and beef in particular: the laziness of our butchers. She cites a tendency crudely to dress up cheaper cuts of beef – rolled top rib or a piece of top rump or silverside, for example – as little packages suitable for roasting. When exposed to a hot oven the stretched membrane and sinews contract, the 'parcel' loses its shape, and consequently much of its moisture, and the result is a dry, tough roast that will spread doom and gloom on any Sunday lunchtime.

Sadly, little has changed since ED described this problem in 1960. One of the great barriers to good butchery in this country is the tolerance of the meat-shopper for second-rate beef. Another is the national obsession with Roast Beef (with or without Yorkshire pudding) as a dish that Every Good Englishman and True should enjoy as often as the family budget allows. Now, I don't want to knock good old roast beef – the right cut, lovingly prepared, is indeed a great treat. But if I have a mission in this short section on beef, it is to persuade readers to vary their technique for cooking this excellent meat, and in particular to encourage largely neglected and highly rewarding slow-cooking practices such as braising, salting and poaching, and the classic *pot-au-feu* (page 221). These techniques produce excellent results with even the cheapest cuts of beef.

Assessing the quality of beef

The supermarkets, and even some butchers, would have us believe that good beef is pink, bloody and 'fresh'-looking. In fact excessive moisture is a sign of poor-quality, under-matured beef. The best beef should be neither too dark nor too pale (though perhaps darker than is customarily seen in the supermarket), and shiny rather than wet. Generally speaking it should be firm and elastic, though very well-matured beef for fast cooking, such as fillet, sirloin, rump and forerib, may be darker, should give a little to the prod of a finger, and not spring back at once but retain a dent. Even the leanest cuts of beef should show marbling – a distribution through the flesh of small veinings of fat. Beef fat should be firm and cream or creamy-yellow in colour.

The cuts

Hindquarter cuts

+LEG OF BEEF: a cut from the top of the back leg. It is tough, but lean, and can yield plenty of meat for long, slow cooking. I prefer to cook it in the piece and on the bone, either with vegetables, as a kind of *pot-au-feu*, or to salt and then boil it. Trimmed and cut up, the meat can be used, along with shin, for well-flavoured stews. The leg is also known as the hock, or, in Scotland, the hough – the But 'n' Ben's excellent dish of Potted Hough with Stovies is described on page 221. Also good for making your own mince (see page 199).

+THICK FLANK: the cut immediately above the leg, which yields a greater amount of similarly tough meat. Still good value for slow-cooked *daubes* and *pot-au-feu*. Boned, it makes an excellent large piece for salting and boiling.

TOPSIDE/TOP RUMP: these are two muscles, of the inside leg and front thigh respectively, which overlap. The two muscles can be sold separately – top rump is marginally more tender than topside – but more usually a joint comprising a large piece of each muscle held together by connective tissue is sold for roasting. In the best quality of animal, and where the meat has been well hung and properly aged, roasting is rewarding and the meat can be served just pink. It should not be roasted fast, however, like a fillet, but slowly, with a little stock or water in the pan. Braising, on a bed of vegetables moistened with stock, is also appropriate. (Roasted or braised, a good piece is also excellent served cold – ideally uncut until completely cool.) Top rump is a classic cut for French *daubes*, particularly if kept whole or in large pieces (see the recipe from Jemima's for Slow-cooked Beef with Tomatoes on page 212). A slow-cooked *daube* is perhaps the best way of using a piece of topside or top rump that is of uncertain quality or inadequately hung. As salt beef both cuts would certainly be fine, but no great improvement on the cheaper silverside.

+SILVERSIDE: this is the back of the thigh, a large, lean muscle, whose wide-grained texture is a testament to the hard work it does in propelling its owner from one place to another; it is tough. It is often sold (to the above-mentioned patriots) as a cheap roasting joint. Such a treatment is, in my view, a complete waste of time. It is, however, fabulous for boiling, spicing and salting – in each case as one whole piece.

FILLET (aka UNDERCUT): in a 600–700-lb/300–350-kg beef carcase there is a scant 5–6-lb/2.3–2.7-kg of fillet, which is the least exercised muscle of a castrated young bull – no wonder it is so expensive. One of the reasons why beef bullocks are castrated is that, as you might imagine, it makes them less inclined to mate, or even practise mating, and so prevents a rigorous form of exercise that would strengthen (and toughen) a great number of muscles, the fillet in particular. Fillet is therefore supremely tender, especially from a well-hung carcase, and consequently much prized by chefs. But it has less flavour than other cuts – and an over-cooked fillet has practically no taste at all. Frying, grilling and quick roasting (of a whole or large piece) are all appropriate cooking methods. Tournedos (a chunky portion of fillet for one), châteaubriand (a chunky portion of fillet for two) and noisettes (ever so delicate neatly trimmed rounds of fillet, 3 of which usually make a portion) are all popular sub-cuts of fillet, especially in restaurants that are, or aspire to be, French.

RUMP STEAK: considerably cheaper than fillet, rump steak (not to be confused with top rump) is also tastier and chewier, though if it is not properly matured it can be less than tasty and too chewy by half. It is suitable for frying, grilling and barbecuing, in thickish slices. When you are really sure of the quality and maturity of a piece of rump, and if it has particularly good marbling, then a large piece of the 'eye' – a muscle which can be separated from the rest of the rump – makes a fabulous roast, which can be cooked fast and served rare. A 'string vest' of caul fat (see page 232) will help to baste it during cooking. The meat from the lower muscle of the rump is rather tougher. Good butchers will separate it from the piece from which they cut their rump steaks and sell it as braising steak.

SIRLOIN (incorporating *ENTRECÔTE, CONTREFILET,* T-BONE and PORTERHOUSE): there is some confusion as to what the sirloin is these days: the term is often used to refer to a small part of the whole sirloin, i.e. a trimmed, boneless piece of meat from which 'sirloin steaks' or *entrecôtes* are sliced to order by the butcher. In fact a whole sirloin is a large piece taken from the lower-middle of an animal's back, which includes the much-prized FILLET (see above). The sirloin on the hindquarter joins on to the foreribs on the forequarter. The muscle that is the fillet is attached to the underside of the sirloin (it is the 'undercut' of the sirloin) and in fact whole sirloins are usually hung with the fillet still attached. A T-bone steak is a cross section of the unfilleted sirloin. On one side of the T-bone is a piece of fillet, on the other the meat which, when taken off the bone, is the entrecôte or 'sirloin steak' of common butcher's-shop parlance.

When the *entrecôte* side of the sirloin is removed from the bone, trimmed of all gristle and excess (but, please, not all) fat, and neatly parcelled up, it is a fine joint for roasting. This is the eye of the sirloin, what the French call *contrefilet* (because it is on the opposite side of the bone from the fillet). A little cheaper and a little tastier than fillet, it is almost as tender, and should be roasted fast and served pink.

A great cut of beef for roasting on the bone is a large cross-section of sirloin, i.e. potential T-bone steaks as yet uncut, with the fillet on one side and the contrefilet on the other. You may have to request this specially as many butchers fillet sirloin as a matter of course. Ask for sirloin on the bone, and specify that you would like your joint to include the all-important undercut. The joy of this cut is that it retains and absorbs flavour from the bone, and you can offer your guests a choice of incredibly tender fillet, and especially tasty *contrefilet*.

Finally, and just for the record, a piece of lean meat cut from the thick (head) end of the sirloin, or the tail end of the foreribs, is traditionally known (especially in America) as a porterhouse steak. I have no idea how it got this name but it seems wonderfully appropriate for this gargantuan portion of meat.

+HINDQUARTER FLANK: this is the chunk immediately below the sirloin, and before the ribs begin. In other words, the belly. It is boneless, cheap, very fatty, but quite delicious if cooked very slowly in casseroles or a *pot-au-feu* (page 221).

Forequarter cuts

+FOREQUARTER FLANK: this is a similar cut (and bargain) to the hindquarter flank, with the principal difference being that it has ribs in it. Some may see this as an inconvenience, but flavourwise it is definitely a plus. They are fine in a *pot-au-feu* (page 221), and can also be salted. I have my own rather greedy way of doing them: tenderized by slow cooking, they are then crisped up briefly in a hot oven, and served rather like a rack of spare ribs, with a horseradish relish (page 414).

+BRISKET: a cut from further up the rib-cage, brisket is marginally leaner than flank, and still a bargain. It is often sold (and can certainly be ordered), as a rolled fillet, in which form it lends itself well to boiling, particularly if salted first (see page 212). On the bone, treat as forequarter flank above.

+FORERIB: the bovine equivalent of a rack of lamb is roast forerib of beef. There is plenty of lean meat in the eye of these 'chops', and a single rib 'cutlet' is often served roasted in restaurants as a two-person portion. Since the muscles at this end of the animal are in constant use as it raises and lowers its head while feeding, the meat can have a tendency to be tough. Forerib from a poor-quality, inadequately hung or (perish the thought) frozen animal is a complete waste of time. From a first-class beast and a first-class butcher it is quite superb, a real carnivore's cut, and can be roasted and served pink.

The trimmed fillet, or eye, of the forerib gives a cut which is particularly popular in America – the rib-eye steak.

BACKRIB: like the forerib, only less so. In other words there is less lean meat, and what there is will be a little tougher. A fine-quality joint of backrib can, however, still be roasted – slowly, with liquid (stock or water) in the pan to prevent drying.

+SHIN: this, the top of the foreleg of an animal, is a bargain cut which is quite delicious if cooked very slowly in a flavoursome liquor. On the bone, it can be braised with wine and vegetables; off the bone it makes excellent stew, and can be mixed with LEG OF BEEF (see above). Do not, however, mix with chuck steak, as this does not take as long to cook.

CHUCK STEAK: technically this is the meat taken from around the blade bone in the animal's shoulder. It is sold, usually ready-cut, for stews and casseroles. Sometimes chuck steak will include trimmings from other parts of the animal, but it should be less tough, and is likely to be more expensive, than other meat sold for stewing. Larger pieces of chuck steak are often sold as 'braising steak' – this is good for *daubes*.

STEWING STEAK: what's left of the carcase meat – mainly from around the neck and shoulder – is likely to find its way into the butcher's tray that is labelled 'Stewing Steak'. In the shop of a conscientious butcher this is not a bad buy, and suitable for long (upwards of 2 hours) very slow stewing. Personally I prefer to know exactly where my stewing meat is coming from, which is why I like to buy shin and leg for long slow cooking and top rump, topside or good chuck for *daubes* and casseroles where larger, even-sized pieces of meat are required. Where possible buy your meat for stews in the piece, so you can cut and trim it to the size you require – butcher's stewing steak can be very uneven and fatty.

MINCED BEEF: Butcher's mince is often very fatty, and likely to be made from the cheapest cuts of his poorest-quality animals. It is also usually too finely ground – the juices run out when it is cooked and it becomes insipid. It is a sound practice, therefore, to choose your own cut of fresh beef, and mince/process it yourself at home. This can be done with a food processor. Using the regular slicing blade, you can choose just how fine you want your mince to be.

If the mince is to be slow-cooked, for example in a bolognese or other pasta

For a steak tartare, rump steak or sirloin of the highest quality should be used – fillet steak does not have enough flavour to support the heavy spicing, and anyway it is prohibitively expensive. Trim the meat of all fat and sinew, then process or mince finely. Serve with chopped shallot, parsley and capers, Tabasco and Worcester sauce, salt and pepper, and a raw egg yolk, to be mixed with the meat to the personal taste of each guest.

sauce, a chilli con carne or a stuffing for vegetables, the best cuts to choose are those usually used for stewing – leg, shin, or neck. If you buy a leg or shin on the bone you can trim the meat off for mincing and use the bone to make a stock which will enrich whatever you are cooking. For hamburgers, meatloaf and any other dishes you might be inclined to cook quickly or serve pink, the leaner and marginally more tender silverside and chuck (blade) are recommended.

BEEF STOCK: A good beef stock requires some care, a little skill, and plenty of time in the making. The best method is to follow closely the procedure described on page 221 for *pot-au-feu*. If you simply want a stock, with no meat dish arising from it, then use only bones – but note that you will always get a better stock if you include *some* fresh meat.

Lamb and mutton

Generally speaking British sheep have not been subjected to the horrors of intensive farming – growth promoters, hormones, unnatural feeds – that have so threatened the quality of our beef and pork. But different breeds of stock, and the variable quality of the land on which they graze, mean there are still vast differences in flavour and texture from one piece of lamb to the next – and who would have it any other way? Life would be very dull if a Scottish sheep that grazed amongst the heather tasted the same as a Welsh animal that spent its days on the bracken-bearing chalky soils of the Welsh hill country.

Although the quality of British lamb is something to be proud of, it would be misleading to imply that a second-rate British product does not exist. It does, and I have tasted it many times – meat with an excess of gristle and fibre that is too tough when served pink and dreadfully dry and tasteless when overdone to compensate. Such meat is the product of farms, and there are many of them, where sheep are not a priority, but a seasonal stop-gap – a thrifty use of land that has been impoverished by intensive arable farming. In such situations the sheep do more for the land than the land does for the sheep.

Spotting poor-quality lamb at the butcher's is not always easy. Enquiring as to its origin is a start, though there is no guarantee that the response will be either honest or significant. But butchers who have proved their worth in other areas are unlikely to fail you when it comes to providing a good piece of lamb, and country butchers whose beef and pork is not always excellent may nevertheless have access to local lamb that is less disappointing.

The other great variability factor with lamb is, of course, age. Young Easter lambs will be tender, sweet and require little hanging to develop the meat. From midsummer onwards lambs will not only be larger and have a more developed flavour, they will be inclined to toughness. Older lambs need to be hung properly to counteract this; often they are not. Blood-spots and wet-looking meat are signs of under-hanging. If your butcher is friendly, it is well-worth specifying that you like your lamb well hung.

In fact, a whole leg of lamb is one of the few take-home cuts of meat that is still capable of being further matured at home, though you must have the necessary cool space to do this properly. A leg of lamb should be hung, preferably covered in muslin or a clean cotton cloth, from a butcher's hook, hip-down, knuckle-up, in a well-aired place where the temperature is reliably less than 8°C/44°F. In the summer months only a very cool cellar is likely to fulfil these requirements, though in autumn and winter a cold stone outhouse might just about fit the bill. Butchers hang meat in large fridges where the temperature is never more than 4°C/37°F. Since the temperature at home is likely to be much less reliable, it would be unwise to hang a leg of lamb for more than 3 days, and even then only if you are confident that it was under-hung in the first place.

A simpler solution for lamb that is on the tough side, especially for chops and lean cuts that are to be fried, grilled or barbecued, is a light marinade: toss the meat in good olive oil and a splash of red wine, then leave covered in the fridge for not more than 24 hours – the meat should be merely coated in the marinade, not drenched or submerged. Slivers of fresh garlic, sprigs of fresh rosemary and a few twists of black pepper are 'optional extras' – but in my view verging on the essential.

A large leg or shoulder of autumn lamb which you suspect of being insufficiently hung is a good excuse – not that one is needed – for preparing the slow-cooked dish that the French call *à la cuillère* – so named because the meat

'Mutton', as once appreciated by many hearty British appetites, is scarcely available these days – the carcases of breeding and wool-giving sheep go mainly for pet food. If you can get it, it is well worthwhile, as it has excellent flavour. It needs long slow cooking, until the meat is coming from the bones. The *à la cuillère* method (see bottom of page) and the recipe for neck of lamb on page 218 can both be adapted.

is so tender it can be cut with a spoon. This dish is similar to the Ark's 'Weeping' Lamb (page 214), only it is braised, with stock vegetables, potatoes, water and a splash of red wine, in a much slower oven (150°C/300°F/Gas Mark 2), in rather than above the pan, for upwards of 3 hours. I would recommend Sheila Kidd's recipe 'Weeping' Lamb for younger lamb of proven quality, and *à la cuillère* for older animals.

The cuts

LEG (including +SHANK): there is no doubt that a good leg of lamb makes a fabulous roast; and no doubt either that an overcooked roast, dry and grey, is a terrible disappointment. I do not belong to that foodie elite which tries to insist that those who do not like their lamb pink are gastronomic philistines, but I do think that those who like their lamb well done would enjoy it all the more if it was succulent and tender to boot. The solution to this is braising and pot-roasting, both of which are particularly satisfying if you are cooking the cheaper shank end of the leg (a half-leg) for a small number of people. Some butchers will sell you the shank itself – a generous one-person portion of on-the-bone meat which is excellent if slowly braised (or included in the Brackenbury's Hotch-Potch on page 219.

Boned leg is a popular roasting joint in many households, as it can be easily stuffed, and carving is a piece of cake. But unless you have a cunning stuffing, which will absorb and retain flavours and juices from the meat, then having your leg boned for roasting is both a waste of time, and a waste of the flavour and moisture that would be contributed and retained by the bone.

An economical use of a boned leg is to separate the leanest muscles and divide them into portion-sized (6–8-oz/170–225-g) pieces. You should get 5–7 of these, depending on the size of the leg. These can then be 'butterflied' – scored with a knife so they open out into rough-edged steaks – before marinating in olive oil with garlic and rosemary; they are then grilled, fried, barbecued or griddled, each steak being served as pink or as well done as the individual likes it. The smaller muscles and trimmings from the steak can be used to make a curry, included in a Scotch Broth (page 223), or minced for a shepherd's pie or the Spicy Lamb Cakes on page 218.

+CHUMP: this is the equivalent of the rump of beef, and is most often encountered in the form of lean and generous chump chops, which are slightly more expensive than loin chops or neck cutlets. In fact the chump can also yield a lean nugget of lamb fillet which is perfect for fast roasting, and makes a very generous meal for a greedy carnivore, or 2 more modest portions. A good and friendly butcher should be able to bone out a whole chump for you, but this French cut is not familiar to most English butchers and you will probably have to explain exactly what it is you're after. Alternatively, ask for a whole chump on the bone: it is not hard to see where the desirable muscle runs, nor to trim it out with a sharp knife. The bone and trimmings can go towards making a stock with which you can deglaze your frying pan to make a sauce.

SADDLE (aka LOIN): the saddle is the ovine equivalent of the sirloin of beef: it is where loin chops are taken from, but it is also, in its entirety, a prime roasting cut. With more lean meat than a single leg or shoulder, a whole roast saddle of a good-sized lamb should serve up to 10 people; it is therefore not always as uneconomical as its price per lb/450 g might suggest. Roast a saddle loosely covered in well-buttered foil in a moderate to hot oven (190°C/375°F/Gas Mark 5) for 1–1¼ hours. Then remove the foil, turn the oven down to 160°C/325°F/Gas Mark 3 and cook for a further 20–30 minutes. Baste the joint regularly during this last half-hour, if possible with a cup of good strong stock made from lamb bones and trimmings. The shorter cooking times are for smaller saddles and/or pinker meat.

+BREAST: an under-used and under-rated cut, the breast (which includes part of the belly) is also gratifyingly underpriced. It is certainly a fatty cut, not ideally suited to the Jack Sprats of this world. But rolled up round a dry stuffing (say of breadcrumbs, garlic and herbs) to absorb the fat, it makes an economical roast, with lots of tasty crispy bits on the outside and succulent, naturally basted meat on the inside. A more time–consuming, but ultimately very rewarding treatment, is the French method known as *Sainte-Ménéhould*: the Whiteleaf does an excellent version of this using offcuts from a rack of lamb (see page 215). Follow the same procedure with breast.

BEST END: the best end of the neck is that which is most remote from the head. A versatile cut, it is trimmed and subdivided in various different ways. It can be cut into tidy little chops which, when trimmed of excess fat and the chine bone to which they were attached, are known as cutlets. When the little nugget of meat from a single cutlet is removed and further trimmed, you have a noisette. If all 8 cutlets on a best-end joint remain attached you have a joint called 'rack of lamb'. The French *carré* is the same joint, but the bones are trimmed and the chine bone removed to make a lighter, prettier roast. It is on to the projecting bones of the *carré* that, at the end of cooking, those miniature frilly paper hats are traditionally placed, a decoration which I have always found just a little too quaint.

When 2 racks of lamb, one from either side of a carcase, are left joined together and deftly cut by the butcher to form a circle, then you have that great party piece known as the 'crown roast' – and more paper hats than I care to think about.

SHOULDER: wrongly thought of as the poor man's leg, the shoulder offers plenty of tender meat, albeit in a form that is not as easy to carve. One way round this problem is to ask the butcher to bone and roll it for you – it roasts particularly well in this shape, as some of the plentiful fat on the shoulder is rolled into the inside of the joint and bastes it from within. A great French classic for rolled shoulder is the method known as *boulangère* – so called because villagers who did not have an oven in their own home would take their shoulder of lamb to the local bakery when the morning batch of bread was baked and cook it slowly in the residual heat of the bread oven for at least 2½ hours. The lamb is placed in a casserole or covered braising pan, resting on a bed of whole new potatoes, garlic cloves, sliced onions and tomatoes, which cook in the fat and juices of the meat and make this simple dish into a complete meal. These days the dish is easily replicated in a domestic oven (at 150°C/300°F/Gas Mark 2). It can be cooked for a shorter time – say 1½ hours at 190°C/375°F/Gas Mark 5 – if you want the meat pink.

+MIDDLE NECK and SCRAG END: as the neck continues towards the head the meat becomes tougher and a little more sparse, but no less tasty. Filleted neck and scrag makes great stewing meat, but I think it is even better if cooked on the bone. Lancashire Hot Pot is perhaps the most celebrated use of scrag, and is properly made with cross sections of the scrag, about 1 in/2.5 cm thick, with bone still in. Cooked long and slow enough (for about 2½ hours at 150°C/300°F/Gas Mark 2), the bone will be tender enough for those so inclined to chew it up with everything else. A friend of mine showed me how to use neck of lamb to make another delicious dish, of Greek origin, which is flavoured with thyme and lemon juice. The recipe, which appears on page 218, should convert any doubters to the merits of scrag.

+SHIN (aka FORESHANK): the top part of a sheep's foreleg, which you will encounter on a roast shoulder as the thin, tapering bit which becomes very crispy, is barely recognized as a cut in its own right. However, when a shoulder is boned, this piece, the equivalent of a shin on beef cattle, is removed and, more often than not, discarded. Ask a butcher to save you some, so you can make a cheap and easy stew, or include it in the But 'n' Ben's recipe for Scotch Broth on page 223, or instead of the lamb shanks in Adam Robinson's Hotch Potch on page 219.

+MINCED LAMB: this is useful in all sorts of ways – for kebabs and rissoles, for making moussaka or shepherd's pie, and as an alternative to beef in many pasta dishes (such as lasagne, and even bolognese sauce). You are better off mincing your own lamb, as butcher's minced lamb tends to be very fatty and, for my taste, too finely minced. A food processor will allow you to control the texture of the mince; almost any cut can be used, including trimmings from a leg, rack or shoulder. If you are buying lamb especially for mincing, scrag end of neck or any meat sold as stewing will be fine, provided it comes from a good, fresh British lamb.

Pork

Pork is a rich, fatty, close-grained meat, which can have an excellent flavour. Unfortunately it is rarely sampled at its best in this country. There is such a huge market for this popular meat, and its wonderfully flexible cured by-products of bacon and ham, that many pig farmers will stop at nothing to pile the pounds on their piglets. Over the years this has involved ruthless selective breeding of fast-growing varieties, with little consideration for flavour or quality of meat. The bland but bulbous Euro-pig is then stuffed with highly unnatural processed high-protein feeds and hefty cocktails of growth-promoting drugs, before being rolled off to the slaughterhouse.

Unfortunately the maltreatment of the meat does not always end with the poor animals' death: men in white coats have devised fiendish ways of bulking out pork products, bacon and ham in particular. A popular trick is injecting large amounts of water into the meat: this explains the common but none the less disturbing phenomenon of rashers of bacon shrinking to a third of their original size and exuding an unpleasant cloudy liquid when subjected to a little light grilling or frying. It has long surprised me that consumers are prepared to put up with this; I fear that it has been going on for so long that many people think it is quite natural. Fortunately there is a small – but, I hope, growing – number of farmers who are prepared to do something about it. Perhaps in the nick of time, they have revived traditional English breeds of pig which, though they may not gain weight at the same alarming speed as their bingeing cousins on more intensive farms, gain plenty of flavour and character in their longer, more leisurely lives.

Among the breeds that are being championed are the Tamworth, Shropshire and the charmingly named Gloucestershire Old Spot. Such well-bred animals deserve the very best treatment in death as well as life. Such is the level of commitment among the farmers that many of them do their own butchering, curing and smoking, and sell their fresh pork, bacon and hams in their own farm shops. Others may supply direct to butchers who they know will honour and appreciate the quality of their product – many of the Q-Guild butchers (see page 188) stock traditionally farmed pork.

A general note on cooking fresh pork: as pork is never served pink, there is little virtue in roasting it purely for the sake of it. Of course roast pork, with crackling, good gravy and a sharp sauce (classically apple) is a great English treat which I would not wish to slight. But slower-cooking methods, such as braising or pot-roasting, even of the tenderest cuts, such as loin, can often bring out the best flavour of the meat.

Assessing the quality of pork

Good pork should be a uniform pale pink colour, and quite odourless. If there are any dark red tinges or irregular kernels of colour in the meat it should be avoided. The meat should show an even, close grain and not be flabby or wet-looking. The fat surrounding the meat should be a clean white untinged by yellow or grey – although small black spots in the fat are normal in pork from black or brown-skinned varieties of pig. The skin or rind on joints of pork should be thin, smooth and even. Young pork is always likely to be a little more tender than that taken from a mature animal; if you are roasting or grilling it is best to avoid huge joints taken from older pigs.

LEG: a classic joint for roasting, either on or off the bone, leg of pork is usually divided into sub-cuts. The fillet is the leaner top end of the leg, the knuckle a cut from the foot end. Knuckle of pork, as well as of ham and bacon, is extremely good value, and suitable for slow cooking, either on the bone or, if filleted and trimmed, as stew.

LOIN: pigs have a long back, and a whole loin on the bone is a bigger joint than you could ever get into an ordinary domestic oven, let alone a cooking pot. It is traditionally divided into two cuts and several loin chops. In times past the hind loin was often sold on the bone with the kidneys still attached, and some butchers still honour this tradition. Loin chops from the hind end can also be had with a cross-section of kidney included – an extra bonus for those who like the rather strong taste of this piece of pig offal. Sadly, an EC directive may soon put paid to both these traditions. The foreloin, taken from the neck end of the animal, is a narrower, shorter joint, but is good and lean, and roasts particularly well. The French sometimes call this cut *carré* of pork, reflecting the fact that it is the porcine equivalent of the best end of lamb.

The trimmed eye of the loin is known as the tenderloin, and is the most expensive cut of pork; it is, however, still cheaper per lb/450 g than the equivalent fillet of beef or lamb. It is an easy and rewarding piece of meat to stuff, then truss up like a large sausage, in which shape it can be roasted or braised. I have invented my own stuffing for loin of pork, which can also be enjoyed by vegetarians as a dish in itself – see page 320.

+BELLY: most pork bellies go towards making streaky bacon. In fact uncured belly is a cheap, interesting and under-used cut of meat which lends itself to a variety of cooking methods. Pre-salted, it can then be slow-cooked (either stewed or braised) with vegetables. Such dishes can take a lot of piquant spicing, and the meat responds particularly well to the 'sweet-and-sour' treatment. Thick rashers of belly can be marinated – try a mixture of sherry, fresh ginger root and a little brown sugar – then grilled or, better still, barbecued. Good belly can even be stuffed, rolled and roasted; the skin of the belly makes extra-good crackling. Pieces of pork belly, either salted or fresh, are a very handy addition to a stew or casserole, particularly one that contains pulses. The fat from the belly enriches or, as Elizabeth David puts it so feelingly, 'lubricates' such dishes, as well as adding good flavour. It is essential in a *cassoulet*.

⁺SPARE RIB: besides being divisible into plural spare ribs, this is a useful (and inexpensive) joint in its own right, being the approximate equivalent of the middle neck of lamb. It is not to be confused with a rack of ribs, a cut which is often encountered in American restaurants, but which does not include the generous neck meat that makes the traditional English spare-rib joint so worthwhile. From a good animal it is tender enough to roast whole on the bone, but can also be braised or casseroled in cutlet-like portions.

⁺BLADE BONE: this is another under-estimated and useful joint, taken from the upper shoulder above the spare rib. The blade bone can be removed, creating a cavity which begs to be stuffed: for this reason it is often used as a roasting joint. But there is no good reason why a stuffed joint of pork cannot be braised, and this is certainly the best way to ensure a blade-bone joint avoids toughness or dryness. Meat from around the blade bone can also be trimmed and used in stews.

⁺HAND: this is the foreleg of the pig, a joint which traditionally used to include the partially severed front foot (hence the name hand?). These days it is usually severed just below the knuckle (knee bone). Hand is a great bargain, and can be delicious if slowly braised, either on or off the bone, with plenty of vegetables and some alcohol (perhaps cider) to tenderize it. It is often sold as a cheap joint for roasting – not a treatment designed to show it to advantage.

NOTE ON CURED PORK PRODUCTS: there is not space in this book to discuss at length bacon, ham, gammon and other pork charcuterie. Suffice it to say: (a) that the cuts are named as for pork and (b) that cured pork from naturally reared, free-range pigs is considerably superior to that which is intensively farmed and factory produced. See also the note on page 206 about traditionally farmed pork.

Veal

Veal is a very expensive meat which has an inherent tendency to be dry and bland – hardly a flying start as far as the Bon Marché cook is concerned. To make matters worse, availability is severely limited in many places. Many butchers stock only a few of the most obvious cuts, such as escalopes, loin chops and perhaps the odd hunk of leg for roasting, so anything else may have to be ordered. Dutch veal is still regarded as the best; English veal is widely derided by chefs and butchers alike. I suppose the quality of the meat 'suffers' because the animals don't. (English veal calves are not as restricted in their movements as Dutch; their meat is therefore tougher. For veal escalopes, this is a problem; but if you are slow-cooking shin of veal in an *osso buco*, or braising a breast of veal, it really doesn't matter. As these are the only two veal cuts I cook with, I always buy the more humanely reared British veal.)

The controversy over veal production methods seems to have died down considerably in recent years, perhaps because those of us who were once young and full of conscience are now older, more cynical, and rather partial to a nice slice of calves' liver. I'm not about to reopen the debate, except to say that it would be foolish to believe that Dutch veal calves are having a significantly better time these days than they used to.

The problem of dryness is due to the veal's natural lack of fat – roasting joints are therefore often bound up with a large strip of pork fat around the outside, and lean pieces of meat for grilling or braising are traditionally larded with strips of fat bacon or pork belly (the fat is threaded through the surface of the meat with a larding needle). The more moisture that is retained, the more flavour the veal will have. But it is worth pointing out that its rather insipid taste, which could perhaps at best be described as 'delicate', is in fact the *whole point* of veal.

Personally I do not care greatly for the large lean cuts of the young calf – escalopes for frying, large leg fillets for roasting, or loin chops for grilling – and I certainly don't care for their prices. Even the classic *blanquette de veau* seems to me to be a rather pointless exercise – why serve a tasteless meat in a tasteless sauce? Veal fanatics, of whom I know a few, are inclined to explain rather patronizingly that 'It's a texture thing, you know.' I like to irritate them by replying, 'Well, it's certainly not a flavour thing.' It usually does the trick.

The cuts

Whilst no cut of veal comes into the 'bargain basement' category, some cuts are, shall we say, 'less extortionate' than others. I will mention only a couple of the cheaper cuts of veal. I happen to think that as well as costing less, they afford the most pleasure. Apart from that I would add only that veal is butchered, and all the cuts named, exactly as for lamb. Many of the cuts are also similarly prepared and cooked, though unlike lamb veal is quite unpalatable if underdone. I would refer vealophiles who feel short-changed by this section to Elizabeth David's *French Provincial Cooking* (pp. 425–44 in the Penguin paperback) or *The Constance Spry Cookery Book* (pp. 582–93 in my 1961 hardback). Between them they are fairly comprehensive.

SHIN: taken from either the front leg, or the lower part of the knuckle on the back leg, shin of veal is much more expensive than shin of beef but very worthwhile if nicely cooked. Naturally less beefy than the same cut from an adult, it invites the addition of other flavours into the liquor in which it must be very slowly cooked (preferably on the bone). Garlic, fresh herbs and wine are standard; orange, ginger, even cinnamon have been used by clever chefs to superb effect. The classic Italian *osso buco* is shin of very young veal, sawn into chunks 1 in/2.5 cm or so thick, and including a cross-section of bone with its delicious marrow. The *ossi* are stewed very slowly, in a single layer in a wide-bottomed pan barely covered with white wine, water, a *mirepoix* of carrots and onions, tomatoes and plenty of fresh herbs (which should include oregano). The dish can be served cold, in which case it will have set in its own tremendously flavoursome jelly. Hot or cold, it should be sprinkled with *gremolata* of oregano (see page 416) just before serving.

The gelatinous quality of shin and other veal bones make them a worthwhile addition to any stockpot.

BREAST: what little fat there is in veal is concentrated around the breast of the calf. Consequently it lubricates itself better when roasting or braising than other cuts of veal. It *should* cost less than any other cut you might be tempted to roast, but many butchers will have to order it, and may charge you heavily for it simply because it is veal. When boned and laid out flat it is a blissfully easy process to spread a stuffing over a 3–4-lb/1.3–1.8-kg piece of breast, roll it up like a big sausage, then tie it tightly. A good stuffing can be made by splitting a couple of herby butcher's sausages, discarding the skin, and mixing together with 12 chopped black olives, a bunch of chopped fresh parsley, a couple of handfuls of fresh white breadcrumbs, 2 crushed garlic cloves, an egg, if needed, to bind, plus salt and pepper. Simply braise the rolled breast on a bed of sweated onions and a few slices of tomato, moistened with 1 wine-glass of white wine and another of water. Include the breast bones in the pan for extra flavour. Three hours, in a slow oven (150°C/300°F/Gas Mark 2), covered in oiled foil, does the trick. This is an adaptation of an Elizabeth David recipe. She liked the dish cold, with the strained juices chilled to a jelly. I have only had leftovers like this. In fact there wasn't much left over, but what there was was very good.

Perhaps the only genuine bargain products of the veal calf are its feet and head, which will be covered in the next chapter, on offal.

Recipes

Beef Slow-cooked with Tomatoes and Red Wine

JEMIMA'S
Serves 4

The simplest of *daubes*, yet hard to improve on.

2 lb/900 g topside or thick flank of beef
I tbsp olive oil
I oz/30 g butter
2 small onions, chopped
4 garlic cloves, finely chopped
2 celery sticks, chopped
4 oz/115 g streaky bacon, diced
I oz/30 g plain flour
½ bottle good red wine
10 fl oz/300 ml beef stock or water
a faggot of fresh herbs e.g. bay leaf, thyme, parsley, oregano
a strip of orange zest
salt and black pepper
I lb/450 g good tomatoes, peeled, de-seeded and chopped
a few fresh basil leaves

Trim the meat and cut into 4 equal pieces. Heat the oil and butter in a heavy casserole, brown the meat quickly on all sides and remove from the casserole. In the same fat, over a lower heat, sweat the onions, garlic, celery and bacon for 10 minutes, then add the flour and stir to take up the fat in the pan. Return the meat to the casserole, bring the wine to the boil in a separate pan, and pour over the meat and vegetables. Add enough hot beef stock or water to just cover the meat, add the herbs and orange zest, and season with salt and pepper. Cook, covered, in a pre-heated low oven (150°C/300°F/Gas Mark 2) for about 1 hour, then add the tomatoes and return to the oven for another 30 minutes or until the meat is tender. Remove the herbs, taste for seasoning, and stir in the basil, torn up, at the last minute.

Salt Beef

THE BRACKENBURY

Adam Robinson writes: 'We are told – or at least I have been – that the only cuts for salt beef are silverside and brisket, the former being much superior. At the Brackenbury we have experimented with many different cuts and, as long as it's not too lean, any cheap tough piece of beef will do. Boned cuts, in reasonably sized pieces (minimum 1 lb/450 g) are ideal.'

If your piece of beef is a small one, say less than 4½ lb/2 kg, then half the quantities for the brine should be sufficient.

In a large saucepan, stir the brine ingredients well over a low heat until the sugar and salt are dissolved. Bring to the boil, allow to bubble for 1–2 minutes, then remove from the heat and leave to cool completely.

Cover your piece of beef completely with the cold brine, weighting it down if necessary. Leave the meat in the brine for 5–10 days (joints of less than 5 lb/2.3 kg should not be left for more than a week, or they will become too pickled).

Before cooking, soak the beef for 24 hours in fresh cold water, changing the water at least once. Then cover the beef in fresh water, and poach very gently, either on top of the stove or in a low oven (150°C/300°F/Gas mark 2) if you prefer, with the bouquet garni and the stock vegetables. A 5 lb/2.3 kg piece of beef will take 2½–3 hours.

Serve the salted beef carved into slices, with Puy lentils, boiled potatoes, and either creamed horseradish or the green herb sauce described on page 427.

Note:
Recently claims have been made that saltpetre may be carcinogenic. As its sole function is to keep the meat pink, it can be omitted.

Your chosen cuts of beef
For the brine
8¾ pts/5 litres water
1 lb 1½ oz/500 g demerara
  sugar
3½ lb/1.5 kg coarse sea salt
1 tsp black peppercorns
1 tsp juniper berries
5 cloves
2 bay leaves
a sprig of thyme
a bunch of parsley stalks
5½ oz/160 g saltpetre

Stock vegetables
1 carrot
1 onion
1 stick of celery
1 leek
½ garlic bulb
1 bouquet garni

Salt Beef Stovies

The Brackenbury makes stovies with the trimmings of salt beef.

Mix the ingredients well and form into cakes. Heat the oil or dripping in a heavy frying pan, add the potato cakes and fry, turning occasionally, until crispy and golden on both sides. Serve with wilted spinach (see page 94), and a fried egg on top.

8 oz/225 g salt beef trimmings,
  shredded
1 lb/450 g mashed potatoes
1 scant tbsp freshly grated
  horseradish root
black pepper
oil or dripping for frying

'Weeping' Lamb with Potato and Mushroom Gratin

THE ARK

Serves 6

In this dish the gratin is enriched and flavoured by the fat and juices dripping from the lamb, which roasts immediately above it.

1 well-hung leg of lamb
3 garlic gloves, cut into thin
  slivers
2 tbsp olive oil
salt and black pepper
1 tbsp each chopped fresh
  thyme and rosemary
3 oz/85 g butter, softened
2 lb/1 kg potatoes
1–2 onions
8 oz/225 g flat mushrooms
extra garlic (*optional*)
1 pt/575 ml lamb *or* veal stock

Trim the lamb. With a sharp, thin-pointed knife, make cuts all over the surface and insert a sliver of garlic into each. Massage olive oil all over the lamb. Place in a roasting tin and season with salt, pepper and the herbs. Massage again. Leave for an hour or so at room temperature. When ready to cook, spread the butter over the top. Start roasting in a pre-heated hot oven (220°C/425°F/Gas Mark 7). There will be a lot of sizzling! Baste after 15 minutes and return to the oven.

Meanwhile, thinly slice the potatoes, onions and mushrooms. Mix them in a bowl and season with salt, pepper and more garlic, if liked. Gently heat up the stock.

When the lamb has been roasting for about 30 minutes, remove from the oven and lift the leg out of the tin. Add the potatoes, mushrooms and onions to the tin, and mix well with the buttery juices. Pour over the stock. Put the leg of lamb on a large roasting rack which will fit in the tin above the vegetables, or place the leg directly on an oven shelf above the tin so that it 'weeps' on to them. Roast at a slightly reduced temperature (190°C/375°F/Gas Mark 5) for about 1 further hour, or 1¼ hours if it is a large leg. Remove the lamb and finish the gratin under a hot grill if you like a crisp topping.

Three Dishes from a Best End of Neck of Lamb

THE WHITELEAF AT CROYDE

Like Adam Robinson's trio of bloater recipes (pages 165–7), this economical way of dealing with an expensive cut of meat produces three distinct dishes where normally you would only get one. If you wish to attempt the Lamb Sainte-Menehould on its own sometime (it is very delicious), it can be made with one of the cheapest of lamb cuts, breast. Just follow David Wallington's instructions, substituting breast for the ribs.

The dishes are:

8–10 portions of Welsh Cawl Soup
4 portions of an unusual starter: Lamb Sainte-Ménéhould with split
  pea purée
4 portions of a luxury main course: Rack of Lamb with Burgundy
  Gravy

David Wallington writes: 'Fortunately no one has yet found a satisfactory substitute for fresh air and grass for producing one of this country's premium food products, British lamb. Natural methods produce natural food and the nature of lamb is to produce fat along with the succulent lean flesh. Only the earliest lambs can be eaten entire without considerable trimming and waste. The key ingredients for these recipes are a nice plump mid-season lamb and a butcher of helpful disposition. Ask for a double best end of neck and haggle over the price. Normally the butcher will sell only the eye fillet and a few bones attached as rack of lamb. You should ask specifically for an untrimmed rack, and expect to get a better price per lb/450 g. If you have a choice, look for a minimum ¼ in/5 mm of fatty meat on the rib-bones. If the butcher is still talking to you, ask him to split the double best end down the centre of the back-bone into two untrimmed racks of lamb, and chine the racks for you (remove the back-bone). Now ask him to remove, in one piece, the fatty meat on the ribs above the level of the eye-meat on each rack, then to chop off the ribs about 2 in/5 cm from the eye-meat, and then to trim the 2 racks of fat and meat between the bones. You will now have a nice heap of bones and trimmings, 2 rectangular slabs of fatty meat and 2 nicely trimmed, quite lean racks of lamb, and quite probably a demented butcher.'

For the stock and the Lamb Sainte-Ménéhould

Tie the slabs of fatty lamb together like a parcel.

Place the bones and trimmings, the vegetables and the shin of beef, smoked gammon and shoulder of lamb in a roasting tin with the

2 slabs of fatty lamb meat
lamb bones and trimmings
1 large onion
2 carrots
1 medium parsnip
3 celery sticks
2 leeks
6–8 oz/170–225 g each in the
  piece: shin of beef, smoked
  gammon, trimmed shoulder
  of lamb
3 tbsp olive oil
a few sprigs of parsley and
  thyme
a few bay leaves
a few black peppercorns
salt
10 fl oz/300 ml dry white wine
  or dry cider

olive oil. Brown quickly in a pre-heated hot oven (220°C/425°F/Gas Mark 7) for 20–30 minutes, turning twice. Lift from the tin into a large saucepan, placing a layer on the bottom, then the uncooked fatty lamb parcel, then the remainder from the roasting tin. Tip off the fat from the roasting tin and deglaze with a little of the wine or cider. Pour this 'gravy' into the saucepan. Add the wine and enough water to cover the contents of the pan by 3 in/7.5 cm and add the herbs and the peppercorns and salt. Bring to the boil, then reduce to a very gentle simmer and cook for about 3 hours, skimming assiduously and maintaining the liquid level. Remove from the heat and allow everything to cool in the pan, then refrigerate overnight.

Lift the fat off the top and carefully remove the meats including the parcel of fatty lamb. Put the other meats to one side. Warm the stock and strain through muslin or a clean cotton cloth. Discard the bones and vegetables, and pour the strained stock into a clean saucepan, with the parcel of fatty lamb. Reheat to boiling, then simmer for a few minutes. Remove the parcel and drain for a minute or so. When partly cool, wrap in cling-film and put between two plates, with a weight on the top plate. Refrigerate when quite cool. Check the seasoning of the stock and simmer on to reduce to a good strong flavour. Reserve 10 fl oz/300 ml of the stock for the rack of lamb gravy – the rest can go to the soup.

For the Welsh Cawl Soup

the strained stock (see above)
1 onion
1 carrot
2 celery sticks
2 whites of leek (green part
  reserved for the garnish)
the 3 meats (beef, gammon and
  lamb), cut into ½-in/1-cm
  square pieces
a few sprigs of parsley, thyme
  and chives, chopped

Heat the stock to a simmer. Chop the vegetables into pieces similar in size to the meats and add to the stock. Cook until just tender (8–10 minutes) then add the meats and cook for a further 5 minutes. Serve immediately or cool, refrigerate and reheat later. Garnish with the herbs and finely sliced green of the leeks.

To finish the Lamb Sainte-Ménéhould, and make the split pea purée

Abundantly season the breadcrumbs with salt, pepper and mace. Cut the lamb into ½-in/1-cm fingers, coat thoroughly in melted butter and roll in the seasoned breadcrumbs, pressing on for an even coating. Refrigerate until required.

Rinse the split peas and place in a saucepan with the onion, potatoes and garlic. Cover generously with water and cook until the onion and potatoes are soft and most of the water has been absorbed. Remove the cloves from the onion. Season the contents of the pan generously and pass through a sieve to make a smooth purée. (If these quantities produce more than is required for immediate use, the surplus can be frozen.)

Place 1 heaped tbsp of the purée per person in a saucepan, add the butter and cream and gently heat through, stirring. Allowing 4–5 fingers of lamb per person, brown under the grill or in a pre-heated fairly hot oven (200°C/400°F/Gas Mark 6) until crisp all over.

6 oz/170 g fresh white breadcrumbs
salt and black pepper
a pinch of ground mace
the fatty lamb meat, pressed in the fridge (see above)
melted butter for coating
18 oz/500 g green split peas
1 large onion, studded with 2 cloves
3 medium potatoes, peeled
2 large garlic cloves
1 oz/30 g butter
1 tbsp double cream

Rack of Lamb with Burgundy Gravy

Place all the ingredients except the lamb, salt, pepper and mace in an ovenproof dish large enough to catch the drippings from the lamb. Place in a pre-heated hot oven (220°C/425°F/Gas Mark 7).

Heat a non-stick pan or skillet and, without using any oil, thoroughly brown the lamb all over except on the backs. Season with salt, pepper and mace. Place in the oven on a rack above the dish. Cook for 14 minutes for a pink succulent finish, longer if you must!

Remove the lamb from the oven and cover loosely with foil. Strain the contents of the pan through a sieve into a saucepan and reduce over a moderate heat until the liquid starts to thicken. Then strain through a fine sieve or chinois, and you have your gravy.

The racks of lamb may go to the table on a large meat dish with a cutlet frill on each bone, if that appeals, and surrounded by potatoes and other vegetables, with the gravy in a jug. Alternatively, cut each rack through the middle, and stand each portion (½ rack) in a pool of gravy on a warmed plate.

the 2 racks of lamb
½ small onion, sliced
reserved 10 fl oz/300 ml stock (see above)
4 fl oz/100 ml Burgundy or other red wine
1 slice lemon
1 slice orange
1 heaped tsp redcurrant jelly
a shake of Worcester sauce
a shake of Angostura bitters
6 peppercorns
2 parsley stalks
2 bay leaves
a sprig of rosemary and/or thyme
1 tsp balsamic vinegar
ground mace
salt and black pepper

Spicy Lamb Cakes
Serves 4

This is a good way of using up trimmings from a boned leg or shoulder of lamb (if you only have a few trimmings, half the quantities for this recipe will give you a nice meal for 2). The recipe can also be made from cooked lamb (provided it was not overdone) or minced lamb from the butcher (in which case omit the first stage). Feel free to vary the spices, according to your tastes and what you have in store.

1½ lb/675 g lean lamb (see above)
2-in/5-cm piece fresh ginger root, peeled and grated
2 garlic cloves, finely chopped
2 tsp cumin seeds
1 tsp ground cardamom
1 tbsp chopped fresh coriander
1 small fresh green chilli, finely chopped
2 tbsp natural yoghurt
salt and black pepper

For frying
seasoned plain flour for coating
sunflower oil

Trim and roughly cut up the lamb, discarding any tough sinews. Mix well in a bowl with all the other ingredients, and leave to marinate for a couple of hours. Unless the lamb is already minced, put the mixture into a food processor and process until the meat is coarsely chopped – you do not want a smooth, paste-like consistency.

Form the mixture into 8 round, but slightly flattened, small patties. Toss them in the flour to coat. Heat the oil in a frying pan, add the patties and fry over a moderate heat for 6–7 minutes, turning occasionally. You can use a deep-fat fryer, if you have one, in which case the cooking time will be slightly less (4–5 minutes). Serve the lamb cakes with a simple salad of tomatoes, onions and olive oil, and perhaps some mango chutney.

Neck of Lamb with Lemon and Thyme
Serves 4

This recipe comes from a Russian friend of mine. Its origins, he tells me, are Greek. One of the joys of eating it is mopping up the juices with bread. The combination of lamb fat, olive oil and lemon juice, infused with thyme, is quite delicious. Scrag end is the cheapest cut to use: the bones and fat all add to the flavour, and the meat will emerge quite tender at the end of cooking. Ask the butcher to cut the scrag into slices 1 in/2.5 cm thick. Any really fatty bits may be trimmed away, but a certain amount of fat is crucial to the success of the dish.

Heat the oil in a heavy-based saucepan or deep-sided frying pan. Add the lamb to the pan and allow it to sizzle and spit for a few minutes, turning until it is lightly browned.

Add the lemon juice, thyme and water to the pan and turn down the heat, bringing the mixture to a gentle simmer. Leave to simmer, with the lid on, for 35–40 minutes, until the meat is tender.

Serve with plenty of good white bread, and perhaps a simple tomato salad.

4 tbsp olive oil
2 lb/900 g scrag end of neck of lamb, on the bone, or chops from the neck end, or a mixture of the two
juice of 1½ lemons
7–8 sprigs of thyme
1 wine-glass water
salt and black pepper

Duck and Lamb Hotch Potch

THE BRACKENBURY

Serves 4 if just the lamb shanks are used, 6–8 if the confit of duck is included

A variation on the *cassoulet* theme, this is a very hearty dish indeed. The duck can easily be left out, if you don't have a confit to hand, or the time to make one. Substitute a good sausage, if you like.

Finely chop the celery, onions and carrot to make a mirepoix, and sweat in the butter in a large saucepan or braising pan for a few minutes. Brown the lamb shanks briefly in a separate frying pan, then add them to the vegetables with 1 pt/575 ml water. Braise the lamb over a moderate heat, or in the oven pre-heated to 180°C/350°F/Gas Mark 4 for about 1½ hours, turning the meat occasionally, until it is tender and cooked through, but not yet falling apart. (If you are going to use the duck, and serve 6 or more guests, you can divide each cooked shank of lamb into 2 or more pieces at this point, removing and discarding the bone. That way everyone will get a piece of lamb. Otherwise leave the lamb, and serve each shank on the bone, one to each person.)

Strain and reserve the juices from the braising pan. Drain the soaked beans and place in a saucepan with the bacon bone and bay leaf. Cover with cold water and bring to the boil, then simmer until tender (see page 294 for general remarks on cooking pulses). Drain well. Wipe excess fat from the duck legs, and crisp them up in a pre-heated moderate to hot oven (190°C/375°F/Gas Mark 5) for 30 minutes.

2 celery sticks
1 large onion
2 carrots
1 oz/30 g butter
4 lamb shanks, each about 12–14 oz/350–400 g, on the bone (see page 202)
8 oz/225 g dried white haricot beans, rinsed and soaked for at least 5 hours
1 bacon bone
1 bay leaf
4 legs of confit of duck (see page 280)
8 oz/225 g French beans, topped, tailed and cut into 1-in/2.5-cm lengths (*optional*)
4 good butcher's sausages (*optional*)
salt and black pepper

Place the pieces of lamb in an earthenware pot or ovenproof casserole, together with the duck legs, if used, the cooked haricot beans, the juices from the braising pan, any fat from the duck pan and the French beans, if used.

Mix well, adding a little extra water if the ingredients look dry, and place, uncovered, in a pre-heated slow oven (160°C/325°F/Gas Mark 3) for 1 further hour. If you want to add a few sausages, brown them lightly and add to the pot about 30 minutes before the end of the cooking time. The Hotch Potch is ready when the beans are soft and creamy and the meat very tender. Season to taste with salt and pepper before serving.

Indonesian-style Pork

JEMIMA'S

Serves 4

1 lb/450 g lean spare rib or shoulder of pork
2 fresh green chillis, de-seeded and chopped
1 large onion, chopped
4 garlic cloves, chopped
1-in/2.5-cm piece fresh ginger root, peeled and finely chopped
1 tbsp sunflower *or* groundnut oil
2 tbsp soy sauce
1 tbsp lemon juice
2-in/5-cm stem lemon grass
2 kaffir lime leaves *or* bay leaves
salt and black pepper

Trim the pork and cut into strips ($2 \times \frac{1}{2}$ in/5 × 1 cm). Pound the chilli, onion, garlic and ginger together to a paste, in a pestle and mortar, or mash on a chopping board with a fork. Heat the oil in a saucepan and fry the spice paste for 1–2 minutes. Add the pork strips and stir-fry until they change colour. Add the soy sauce, lemon juice, lemon grass and lime or bay leaves, season to taste with salt and pepper, add a little water to make a sauce and simmer uncovered until the meat is tender (20–25 minutes). Add more water as required during the cooking, allowing the sauce to reduce a little towards the end.

Serve with Coconut Rice (see page 318).

Potted Hough with Stovies

THE BUT 'N' BEN

Serves 8–10

A traditional New Year dish served with garden beetroot and stovies, which are a staple in Scotland – the best Scottish butchers even sell special beef dripping for making them.

Put all the ingredients for the hough into a large pan and cover with cold water. Bring slowly to the boil, skimming off any scum that rises to the top of the pan, then simmer very gently for 3½–4 hours until the meat is completely tender. Strain and reserve the stock. Mince the hough with any meat from the pig's trotters and return to the strained stock. Bring to the boil, season to taste with salt and pepper, then pour into shallow dishes or terrine moulds and leave overnight in a cool place to set.

To make the stovies, peel the potatoes and cut into large, roasting-sized pieces. In a large, heavy saucepan, sweat the onions in the dripping, stirring constantly until transparent. Add the potatoes, season well with salt and pepper and keep stirring until they are well coated. Turn down the heat as low as possible, cover the pan with foil, then jam on the lid so that the seal is tight, and leave for about 1 hour. Never add water – the potatoes have their own moisture, and provided the heat stays low they should not burn.

Serve slices of the cold potted hough with hot stovies and slices of boiled beetroot.

For the hough
3 lb/1.3 kg hough (Scottish term for hock of beef, see page 195)
1 beef nap (knee) bone
2 pig's trotters
1 large onion, studded with 10–12 cloves
2 bay leaves
salt and black pepper

For the stovies
2 lb/900 g floury potatoes (Records are particularly good)
2 lb/900 g onions, chopped
4 oz/115 g fat (ideally beef dripping)
salt and black pepper

Pot-au-feu

Serves 6

Among the most eloquent of all Elizabeth David's writings are her pages in *French Provincial Cooking* demystifying the classic French stock-pot dish known as *pot-au-feu*. My recipe is little more than a distilled and simplified version of hers: follow the procedure and you will get good results every time. If you wish to learn more about the many possibilities for varying this intrinsically flexible dish, then consult a copy of the good book.

Like Elizabeth David's, this recipe provides you with two dishes: a fine beefy soup and a substantial meat course.

2 lb/900 g forequarter flank of beef (see page 198)
2 lb/900 g shin of beef, in 1–2 large pieces
2 lb/900 g knuckle of veal, on the bone
giblets from 1 or 2 chickens
3 leeks
3 large carrots
2 celery sticks
2 onions
1 small turnip
½ small parsnip
2 large tomatoes, halved and grilled
a bouquet garni of 2 bay leaves and a few sprigs of parsley or thyme
about 6 pts/3.35 litres water
salt and black pepper

To finish the soup
1 onion
3 leeks
3 celery sticks
3 large carrots
1 oz/30 g butter or olive oil
8 oz/225 g fine spaghetti or vermicelli
salt and black pepper

To finish the meat (hot version)
good red wine
creamed fresh horseradish
boiled potatoes

Into your biggest saucepan (capacity at least 10 pts/5 litres) put all the meat, giblets and vegetables and the bouquet garni. Pour over enough water to cover.

Over a low heat, bring very slowly to simmering point. As you do so, a brownish scum will start to rise to the surface. Skim this off as it appears, and continue to do so for the first 10 minutes or so of very gentle simmering. Once the scum is a clean white colour it can be left – it will eventually disperse. Season with salt (about ½ tbsp) and pepper at this point.

Put the lid on the pan, slightly to one side so that the steam can escape, leave to simmer very gently, with a few bubbles just rising in the centre of the surface, for 4 hours.

Remove from the heat and lift out the meat with a slotted spoon. If the *pot-au-feu* is to be served hot (see below), put the meat into a dish with a ladleful of the stock, cover and keep in a warm place (for example, a slow oven). Remove the vegetables, giblets and bouquet garni, and discard. Strain the stock through a sieve lined with muslin or a clean cotton cloth into a clean bowl. Skim as much fat as you can from the top of the pan: laying sheets of kitchen paper over the surface and removing them as soon as they are saturated is a particularly effective method.

To prepare the soup, thinly slice the onion and the leeks, and chop the celery and peeled carrots into small dice. In a medium saucepan, sweat these vegetables in the butter or oil until soft but not brown. Ladle over 3½ pts/2 litres of the stock, and bring to the boil. Add the pasta and simmer until it is cooked. Season to taste with salt and pepper. The soup should be prepared at the last moment, so that the pasta is not overcooked.

To serve the meat hot, add a splash of red wine to the stock that remains, pour into a pan and boil over a high heat to reduce to a rich gravy. Remove the ribs from the foreflank – the meat should be so tender that the bones slip out very easily, and pick any meat from the veal knuckle with a fork. Slice the shin meat into thick pieces. Serve everybody a mixture of the meats, with hot boiled potatoes, plenty of gravy and creamed horseradish. Or you can combine the horseradish and potato to make a creamy horseradish mash (see page 112).

To serve cold, separate the meat from the bones while it is still warm. Cover and leave to cool. Mix together the dressing. Serve thin slices of the meat with generous quantities of this mixture. Accompany with two simple salads, one of potatoes, one of tomatoes.

If you decide on the cold option (my personal favourite), the *pot-au-feu* can be made a day in advance. Put the strained stock to chill in the fridge, and the fat can be scraped from the top very easily before you make the soup.

To finish the meat (cold version)
Dressing
I tbsp very finely chopped
  shallot
4 tbsp finely chopped fresh
  parsley
I tbsp chopped gherkins
I tbsp chopped capers
I tbsp white wine vinegar
I generous tsp strong mustard
4 tbsp olive oil
salt and black pepper

Accompaniments
potato salad
tomato salad

Scotch Broth

THE BUT 'N' BEN
Serves 8

Margaret Horn writes: 'This was the traditional soup of my village when I was a child. It was made for Sunday lunch in a huge pot and lasted for a few more days. The beef was removed and placed in a large oval dish in the middle of the table, surrounded by whole potatoes, carrots, onions and lumps of neep – extra to the grated vegetables. The whole vegetables would be added about 40 minutes before the end of cooking time. My Granny would sometimes add a boiling fowl as well, and if I am feeding a lot of people I do the same.'

Put the beef and bones into a large stock-pot and cover with the water. Bring slowly to the boil, skimming off any brown scum that rises to the top. When the only scum rising is a clean white, add the barley and dried peas and simmer gently for about 3 hours. Skim and remove the bones and beef (which can be served as a separate meal, as suggested above). Add all the vegetables, season well with salt and pepper, bring back to the boil and continue simmering for at least 1 further hour. The soup can be served at once, or can be left to cool and reheated the next day when it tastes even better. ('My Dad always asked for second day broth' – MH.)

I lb/450 g boiling beef (shin or
  foreflank)
2–3 beef bones
about 4 pts/2.25 litres water
6 oz/170 g pearl barley
6 oz/170 g dried green peas
4 large leeks, finely sliced
2 large onions, grated
6 carrots, grated
I small or ½ large neep
  (turnip), grated
12 oz/340 g curly kale, roughly torn
salt and black pepper

Steak and Kidney Pudding

THE FOX AND GOOSE INN

Serves 4

At the Fox and Goose this pudding is made to serve 2 people, but they rarely finish it. It will certainly serve 3, and even 4 if appetites are modest.

For the filling
12 oz/350 g chuck steak *or* shin of beef
4 oz/115 g ox kidney
¾ tbsp plain flour
1 small onion, thinly sliced
3 oz/85 g mushrooms, sliced
a splash of mushroom ketchup
1 tsp chopped fresh thyme
1 tsp chopped fresh parsley
1 bay leaf
salt and black pepper
10 fl oz/300 ml beef stock *or* water

For the suet crust
8 oz/225 g self-raising flour
a pinch of baking powder
3 oz/85 g shredded beef suet
salt and black pepper
a pinch of dried thyme
cold water
a small nut of butter for greasing

Cut up the beef and kidney, toss with the flour to coat, and put into a bowl with the onion, mushrooms, mushroom ketchup, herbs, salt and pepper.

In another bowl prepare the suet crust by combining the self-raising flour, baking powder, suet, salt and pepper and thyme. Add a little cold water to bind and mix by hand until you have a well-mixed ball of dough. Grease a 2-pt/1.1-litre pudding basin with the butter. Roll out two-thirds of the suet dough and use to line the basin right to the top. Then fill with the meat mixture and pour in the stock or water. Roll out the remaining dough to make a pastry lid, and cover the pudding with it, crimping the lid to the lining with your fingers so that the pudding will not leak.

Make a double-layered foil lid for the basin, and tie securely with string. Put the basin into a large saucepan with a 2-in/5-cm depth of simmering water, cover and simmer for 3–3½ hours, topping up the water from a just-boiled kettle if the pan is in danger of boiling dry.

Remove the foil lid and turn the pudding out on to a warmed plate. Serve with buttered wilted greens (see page 95) or cabbage, and strong English mustard.

Whiteleaf Stock-pot Soup

When I asked David Wallington for the recipe for his stock-pot soup, the wise answer came back, 'But it's never the same twice'. Instead he provided me with a set of guidelines for 'good stockmanship', the economical use of trimmings by a conscientious and cost-conscious cook, with a strong emphasis on flexibility. I leave his words largely unedited.

David Wallington writes: 'This is not so much a recipe as a way of life! The final objective is a rich, thick, chunky bowl of soup which combines a variety of textures and flavours and makes a meal in itself. There are two stages: the making of the stock and the finishing of the soup.'

For the Stock

Poultry, lamb, game or beef bones (the latter cut into short lengths) may be used, together with onions, carrots, swedes, turnips, celery, leeks, celeriac, garlic, parsley stalks, herbs as available (thyme, marjoram, oregano, sage, rosemary, bay leaves, etc.), olive oil and wine.

Ingredients may be acquired specially, or better still be leftovers, such as poultry carcases, vegetable trimmings, herb stalks and peelings. Use as much or as little of anything as you like, but as a guide, equal-sized heaps of bones/meat and of vegetables (chopped) will work. The total should approximately half-fill the pan in which you intend to cook the stock.

In a roasting tin heat a little olive oil, add the bones and vegetables and turn to coat with oil. Place in a pre-heated moderate oven (180°C/350°F/Gas Mark 4) until brown and crusty (about 1 hour). Lift the bones and vegetables from the roasting tin into a saucepan. Tip off any fat left in the roasting tin and deglaze with a few tablespoons of wine (dregs will do). Add to the bones and vegetables. Cover with double their volume of water and for each quart/litre of water add 1 garlic clove (unpeeled), 2–3 parsley stalks, 6 peppercorns, 1 bay leaf and 2–3 sprigs of other herbs (see suggestions above). Bring to the boil, skim, then simmer gently for 4–5 hours until the bones break up. Cool as quickly as possible and strain off the liquid. Refrigerate overnight.

Remove the fat from the surface, reheat the stock and strain through muslin or a clean cotton cloth. Add wine according to taste and pocket, season to taste and reduce until you have a rich, unctuous stock. If you end up with more than you need, freeze the surplus.

For the Soup

Anything goes except fatty meat. Lean pieces of cooked poultry, ham, beef, pork or raw trimmings may be added to your stock, as may leftover cooked vegetables, provided they were not overcooked (and not cabbage or sprouts which will add a bitter flavour). Chopped raw vegetables (carrots, celery, leeks, parsnips, whatever is seasonal) can be added, sweated in a little oil first, then cooked through in the stock.

If you want to thicken the soup (which we usually do) you can do so with cooked floury potatoes, sieved and then stirred in, or a thick purée of some cooked pulse, such as beans (butter, haricot, cannellini, borlotti) or split peas (yellow or green). Whizz the cooked beans briefly in a food processor with a little of the stock, then blend into the soup.

When the soup is cooked (leave some crunch in the vegetables), season to taste and add a little cream or milk before serving if you like. Serve garnished with chopped fresh parsley and accompanied by some good crusty bread.

High-rise Yorkshire Pudding with Rich Onion Gravy
THE WHITELEAF AT CROYDE
Serves 4

In its home of Yorkshire, a batter pudding was traditionally served at the beginning of the meal – especially to children, so they wouldn't eat too much precious meat.

David Wallington writes: 'This is an impressive-looking start to a meal that will take the edge off the most majestic of appetites, allowing for a light main course. You will need 8 deep ramekins or miniature soufflé dishes approximately 3 in/7.5 cm in diameter and 2¼ in/5 cm deep. Straight-sided cups of similar dimensions can be used but the high oven temperature may not improve them. The puddings should be 3–4 in/7.5–10 cm high.'

Critical factors are the temperature of the oven, ramekins and oil, not opening the oven door for at least 17 minutes and cooking for long enough to produce thoroughly crisp puddings which can be handled without collapsing.

First make the onion gravy. Heat the oil in a heavy-based saucepan over a moderate heat, add the onion and cook slowly until soft and beginning to brown. Lift with a slotted spoon into a sieve and drain the oil back into the pan. Reserve the onion. Sieve the flour into the oil and cook over a moderate heat until nut-brown, stirring from time to time. Heat the stock and wine and add to the cooked flour off the heat. Return to the heat, whisking continuously, until boiling. Turn down the heat to low and whisk in the tomato purée and mustard. When smooth and velvety, season with salt, pepper and Worcester sauce and simmer, stirring occasionally, for 10 minutes. Strain through a conical sieve, return to the pan and stir in the onion. Cover the pan and keep the gravy warm until the puddings are ready.

Now make the Yorkshire puddings. A food processor will give excellent results. Add all the ingredients, pulse three or four times to amalgamate, then whizz for 15 seconds with the funnel plunger removed (this helps to aerate the batter). Alternatively, sieve the flour into a mixing bowl with the salt, make a well in the centre and put the eggs and egg yolk in it. Mix into the flour with a wooden spoon, gradually adding the milk and water until you have a smooth batter.

Set the oven to 230°C/450°F/Gas Mark 8, and allow 15 minutes to heat thoroughly. Place the ramekins on a heavy baking sheet and grease the base of each with a teaspoon of olive oil. Heat in the hot oven for 10 minutes. Select a measure which will hold a generous 2 fl oz (50 ml) or 3½ tbsp. Have the batter ready in a jug, give a quick whisk, remove the ramekins from the oven and tip a measureful into each. *If the mixture does not sizzle and start to cook around the edges, the ramekins/oven are not hot enough. Turn the oven up, wait 10 minutes and try again.*

Cook for at least 17 minutes, then turn the baking sheet around. If the puddings are yellowish, turn the oven up 10°C and cook for a further 10 minutes. If everything has worked the puddings will lift easily from the ramekins. If some stick, return them to the oven for a few minutes, placing the exhumed puds on a lower rack. Once they are all removed from the ramekins cook on a rack for a further 3–4 minutes. To serve, cover 4 warmed plates with the onion gravy and place 2 puddings on each.

For the Yorkshire puddings
4½ oz/125 g plain flour
½ tsp salt
2 medium eggs, plus 1 egg yolk
5 fl oz/150 ml milk
5 fl oz/150 ml water
8 tsp olive oil for greasing

For the onion gravy
4 tbsp olive oil
1 large onion, thinly sliced
¾ oz/20 g plain flour
8 fl oz/250 ml rich meat stock
  (see page 225)
2 fl oz/50 ml red wine
2 tsp tomato purée
1 tsp made mustard
salt and black pepper
a dash of Worcester sauce

NOTE: if you don't have enough suitable ramekins, one large, well-risen pudding with a crisp outside and slightly sticky centre will do just as well. You will need an 8 × 12-in/20 × 30-cm dish to cook this quantity of mixture.

CHAPTER FIVE

Offal

The old-fashioned English term for offal is 'variety meats', a phrase which always brings a smile to my lips as I involuntarily form a mental picture of an all-singing, all-dancing troupe of pigs' trotters, calves' tongues, sheep's sweetbreads and oxtails. In fact 'variety' is by no means an inappropriate word for offal. The difference between a fillet steak and a pork chop, in terms of flavour and texture, counts as nothing compared with the difference between sheep's brains and oxtail, calf's tongue and pig's liver.

Shopping for Offal

For the Bon Marché cook, offal should be the most exciting thing about going to the butcher's, especially since most offal cuts, with a few notable exceptions, are blissfully CHEAP. In general, when buying internal organs (sweetbreads, hearts, brains, fries), you should be satisfied that the offal in question is fresh. It should not be dried-out or crusty, but have a clean, wet look and be totally lacking in smell. With feet, trotters, cheek, ears, oxtail, which all require very long and slow cooking times, you should not worry unduly as to whether the selected piece came from a prize-winning animal or not: after hours of tenderizing and exchanging flavour with some well-chosen herbs and vegetables, I guarantee that nobody will be able to tell.

What follows is a brief alphabetical guide to offal shopping, with a few simple cooking suggestions. The list is categorized not according to the different species of animal, but according to their common anatomy. Differences in character and use between similar body parts of different animals are explained as we go along.

Brains

Brains are perhaps the most stigmatized of all offal cuts – no doubt because of the mystery surrounding this organ generally. People who have never tried brains somehow imagine that they *must* taste disgusting. Someone once told me that they thought brains would taste 'like the inside of a burnt-out fuse box . . . because of all those synapses firing and stuff'. Other charming speculations (none of which is based on experience) which I have canvassed include 'rotten scrambled eggs', 'acrid jelly' and 'fishy haggis'. In fact brains are quite delicious, tasting mild and slightly sweet, with a rich, creamy texture that bears some comparison with soft herring roes. Coated in flour, then fried so that they are crispy on the outside, with a sprinkling of sage leaves and capers thrown into the pan, they really are one of my very favourite foods. Few who try this dish fail to be instantly converted.

It is because brains are generally from Dutch veal calves that we can be reasonably confident that they will not be infected with BSE. I would personally refrain from using the brains of British cattle until the government has given greater and more convincing assurances that there is no danger.

The brains of calves, sheep and pigs can all be eaten, though few butchers will let you have a set of pig's brains separate from the head. If you are buying a pig's head for making brawn (see page 236), then the brains, which should be removed before you boil the head, can be incorporated later into the brawn, or fried up and claimed as 'chef's perks'. In my experience the three types of brains are practically indistinguishable in flavour. However, calf's, being bigger and less fiddly to prepare than sheep's, are in greater demand. Because of this, and because they are mostly imported (they come from the Dutch veal calves), they are more expensive. Sheep's brains, though they can be hard to find, should cost very little. Allow one set of sheep's brains per person; one set of calf's brains will serve 2.

Buying brains is not always easy. Few butchers keep them permanently in stock, though some London butchers, including several in Soho, usually have some. Some butchers keep a stock of sheep's brains in their freezer, but the frozen product is a great disappointment. Brains, either calf's or sheep's, will therefore generally have to be ordered in advance – 24 hours' notice should be enough.

The preparation of brains is simple, but takes a little time. They should first be picked over, and any little flakes of skull, or large clots of blood, removed. Then soak the brains in a bowl of cold water for 4–5 hours to leach out the rest of the blood. You should either change the water frequently or, better still, stand the basin under a trickling cold tap in the sink, allowing it to overflow gently.

If you want to be a perfectionist, you should then pick off the membrane that covers the outside of the brains and, holding the brains directly under a trickling cold tap, remove the last traces of blood by running a finger through the crevices. This is not strictly necessary, but it is a task which I find strangely therapeutic.

The brains should then be gently poached for about 15 minutes in water acidulated with ½ cup wine vinegar per 2 pt/1 litre of water and flavoured with ½ onion or 1 garlic clove and a few black peppercorns. Drain the brains – or they can be left in the cooled bouillon in the fridge for 24 hours. When it comes to cooking them, they should be patted dry, each lobe sliced into 2–3 pieces, rolled in seasoned flour, then fried in hot butter, olive oil or bacon fat until golden-brown. Throw in the aforementioned sage and capers halfway through cooking.

Caul fat

The caul is a thin membrane veined with fat that encases the stomach of animals. That most commonly used is taken from slaughtered pigs. It needs to be soaked in cold water for about 3 hours before use, to make it flexible, then gently wiped dry with kitchen paper.

Although there is no way of preparing the caul as a dish in its own right, this piece of offal serves a useful purpose as a 'jacket' for other dishes, which it protects and lubricates with its fat. It is particularly useful if wrapped around lean pieces of meat which are to be roasted or braised, for example a rump of beef or a chump of lamb. A caul fat 'jacket' does not need to be sewn up but will bind on itself if it is overlapping.

If you stuff a saddle of rabbit for roasting (see page 287), a piece of caul is particularly useful. Wrap it round the saddle and you will both bind in the stuffing and help to lubricate the rabbit while it roasts.

You can easily make your own *crépinettes* (the French for caul is *crépine*) by mixing sausage-meat (or pork trimmings minced in a food processor) with fresh herbs, a chopped chicken liver if you have one, some finely chopped sautéed mushrooms and a splash of brandy. Form into flat cakes and wrap each in a piece of caul fat. Dip in egg, coat in breadcrumbs, brush with melted butter and grill or griddle, turning occasionally, until very well browned and crispy.

Cheek

Cheek, the muscle which works the mouth and face, is really just another cut of meat, but because it comes from the head of an animal it has been stigmatized over time. It is a rich but tough and fibrous meat, which is extremely rewarding when slowly cooked. Recipes for pig's cheek can be found, but it is barely worth the trouble these days – though the cheek contributes some of the most succulent meat to a pig's-head brawn. The cheek of serious interest to the Bon Marché cook is that of the ox: most butchers should be able to track one down for you. Weighing over 2 lb/900 g, a good-sized cheek (actually the flesh from all around the muzzle) makes a substantial stew which can serve up to 8 people. The recipe on page 247, adapted from Mrs Beeton, should convert doubters. In France it is popular eaten cold with a herby vinaigrette – soak in salt water for 24 hours, rinse, then simmer with stock vegetables until tender and drain. When cold, break up the meat with a fork, discarding any tough bits or skin, then dress. Serve with chopped hard-boiled eggs and salads. Alastair Little swears that ox cheek makes the best chilli con carne.

Ear

A true Bon Marché cook's bonus, a pig's ear is something that a friendly butcher will give you for next to nothing, or throw in for free with the rest of your shopping. One per person is a snack, 2 a worthy main course. Adam

Robinson recommends the following treatment: thoroughly scrub each ear in warm water, removing any bristles or thick hairs with a knife or razor. Cover in boiling water (adding a few stock vegetables if you wish), then simmer for at least 2 hours until the ears are completely tender. Drain. When cool, pat dry and brush with good English mustard, slightly thinned if necessary. Coat thickly in seasoned breadcrumbs, then crisp up in a hot oven, or on a griddle, or by deep- or shallow-frying.

Feet
(and TROTTERS)

Most butchers throw away dozens of pigs' trotters every week; they should cost you only a few pence, if anything. Calves' feet will probably have to be ordered, but they are also very cheap. A pig's or calf's foot can happily be popped into any stock-pot, and will enrich the flavour, adding valuable gelatinous body. It is particularly sensible to do this if you want to make sure your stock will be set firm when cold.

Pigs' trotters enjoyed a great gastronomic revival in the 1980s, becoming the signature dish of one of London's greatest chefs, Pierre Koffman. Many disciples followed suit. But it is not necessary to stuff a pig's trotter with expensive wild mushrooms and luxurious forcemeats to make it a treat. Bon Marché cooks can get just as much pleasure from the simple recipe for grilled pigs' trotters on page 247. If you do use a calf's foot in a stock, and cook it for long enough to make the foot tender, then the meat that you can pick from it is delicious eaten cold, with creamed horseradish, or a vinaigrette made piquant with the addition of chopped capers and gherkins.

Sheep's trotters have so little to offer besides skin and bones that they are barely viable for the home cook, though Mrs Beeton, the grand mistress of good kitchen economy, has a recipe for them.

Fries

Fries are the testicles of cows, pigs or sheep. On the Continent all are used (in Spain bull's testicles are considered a great delicacy and an enhancer of masculinity). In this country you are only likely to encounter lamb's fries – any good butcher will get them for you, though only a few keep them permanently in stock. They do not appear very appetizing in the raw, but once prepared they lose their fearsome aspect and, like brains, I think most people would find them quite palatable if they didn't know what they were.

Preparing fries

Before cooking, fries must be blanched in boiling water for about 2 minutes, refreshed under cold water and skinned immediately. (Some butchers sell fries pre-blanched and skinned – make sure you know when you buy them whether or not they have had this treatment). After skinning, soak them in plenty of cold water for 8–10 hours, changing the water several times. Then drain them and press between 2 flat plates with a weight on top for 1–2 hours.

An alternative and quicker treatment is to marinate the blanched, skinned fries in a couple of tbsp each of olive oil and vinegar, a sliced onion and a few sprigs of thyme and parsley. Change this marinade after 1 hour, and leave them in the fresh marinade, supplemented with the juice of ½ lemon, for a further 2 hours. They are then ready to cook.

Fries prepared by either method should then be sliced, tossed in well-seasoned flour and fried in hot butter or oil until golden-brown (6–7 minutes). Serve with a mustardy vinaigrette into which you have stirred finely chopped shallots, capers and parsley.

Head

The head of either a pig or a calf is one of the great bargains to be had from a butcher's shop. Not everybody feels happy walking home with an animal's head in their shopping. But let's face it: pork chop, trotter, pig's head – deep down it's all the same, isn't it? Edible dead pig. Calf's head and pig's head can be cooked in exactly the same way, to produce *fromage de tête*, and brawn, respectively. Proceed as follows.

Get the butcher to split the skull in half, remove the brain intact and remove and discard the eyes. Unless you have a very large saucepan, it is probably also wise to ask the butcher to split the head again, crossways into quarters. The head should be thoroughly cleaned, then soaked in cold, well-salted water for an hour or so before cooking. Then rinse well, place in a pan with an onion studded with 2 cloves, a carrot, a celery stick, a bouquet garni and a few black peppercorns. A pair of pig's trotters or a calf's foot, as appropriate, will add both flavour and gelatine. Cover with water, bring to the boil, then simmer gently for 3 hours, until all parts are tender and the flesh can be easily separated from the bones of the skull (feel free to poke around with a knife or skewer to ascertain this point has been reached).

Drain the head, reserving the stock, which should be strained, preferably through muslin or a clean cotton cloth. While the head is cooling, remove all the bones and set aside. Chop all the meat into small strips or chunks (they need not be too perfect). If you added a foot to the stock, you can be confident that it will form a firm jelly, in which case all you need to do is check the stock for seasoning. When you are satisfied, place the chopped meat in a loaf tin, basin or other deep mould. You can at this stage add pieces of chopped, poached brain (see above) to the meat: I heartily recommend that you do. Pour over enough stock to cover the meat, then chill thoroughly until set. If you are in doubt as to the gelatinous properties of your stock, you can return it to the heat, with the bones added, and simmer for 1 further hour, letting it reduce gradually, before you pour it into your mould. Or you can cheat by adding gelatine – but this will be at the (unnecessary) expense of flavour. In France *traiteurs* like to decorate their 'house head-cheese', as we might call it, with strips of blanched carrot, leek and even French beans. And why not?

This *terrine* (for that is clearly what it is), whether of pig or calf, is excellent served cold with a very mustardy vinaigrette. Similarly dressed cold Puy lentils and a simple salad of sliced tomatoes are unbeatable accompaniments.

Heart

Sheep's hearts are found in most butchers' shops. If you never eat hearts you may be surprised to learn that, in the general population, they are really quite a popular item. The butchers I know sell a good number every week. There is little point in seeking out the more expensive, and barely superior, hearts of calves. Ox hearts can be found fairly easily, but are more difficult to prepare and, as they tend to be tough, they need to be soaked overnight in water acidulated with vinegar (1 tbsp per pt/575 ml). I wouldn't want to discourage you from trying, but first-timers are certainly better off with sheep's hearts. They should weigh 10–14 oz/300–400 g each.

Preparing hearts

To prepare a heart, cut away all veins and arteries back to the muscle itself, and rinse it in cold water. As the meat of hearts is very densely textured and naturally dry, it needs to be kept moist while cooking, and benefits from being braised (up to 2 hours for large hearts) in a strongly flavoured stock, ideally of beef or veal. Traditionally this is reduced at the end of cooking to a rich gravy, though there is really no need to thicken it with flour as many old recipes recommend. The heart's natural cavity lends itself to stuffing, and a good stuffing can help to baste the heart from the inside. Sage and onion is a classic, but make sure yours is a moist version, incorporating some butter or fat. More simply, a couple of prunes wrapped in good fat bacon will do the trick.

Kidneys

Calves' kidneys are excellent, expensive and usually Dutch; lambs' are almost as good, and a fair bit cheaper; pigs' are often bitter and of rather tainted flavour; ox kidney tends to toughness, but is very good if slowly cooked until tender (as in the Fox and Goose's Steak and Kidney Pudding, page 224).

As with liver, freshness is critical when choosing kidneys: as the function of the kidney is to filter the animal's urine, you can imagine that there are things in it that will make the best possible use of time spent hanging around waiting to be bought – and render the flavour less than delicate for the unlucky late buyer.

Uncut, whole kidneys are likely to be in better condition than ones that have been chopped up and left in a pool of their own blood in a butcher's tray. The best butchers keep kidneys in their natural surrounding of fat, breaking it open and preparing the kidney for customers on request. It used to be traditional to cook a whole calf's kidney by roasting it still sealed in this natural casing of suet, but it is no longer possible since the EC declared that the kidney fat must be at least partially broken open (so that the condition of the kidneys can be checked), before the product can be passed on to the consumer.

Preparing kidneys

If you buy whole kidneys, they must be 'skinned' – remove the outer membrane with a sharp knife; then slice to the size you require, trimming off the gristly central core (a small sharp vegetable knife is useful for this task).

Kidneys are very often chopped into bite-sized pieces, which is perfectly sensible if you are making a stew, ragoût or pie in which the kidneys are to be combined with mushrooms, vegetables or other meats. But if you are braising, grilling or frying kidneys more or less on their own, cutting them up small will merely allow all the natural juices to run out; the resulting morsels will have lost both succulence and flavour. Lambs' kidneys can be cooked whole, or else cut straight across the width of the kidney into 3 or 4 thick slices.

Cooking kidneys

As far as the 'doneness' of kidneys is concerned, they should ideally be presented in one of two ways: if cooked fast (fried, grilled or sautéed), they should be still just pink in the middle (or, if not pink, then only *just* not pink): 6–8 minutes is usually enough. If cooked more slowly (i.e. braised or stewed), then you should ensure they are thoroughly cooked and quite tender before serving – this is likely to take a good half-hour of slow braising, more like an hour in the case of ox kidney.

I always think kidneys are best served with a sauce that is slightly sweet or spicy: devilled kidneys are a classic. Simply grilled, kidneys are delicious with an anchovy and tomato butter; my own favourite recipe is with chilli and lentils (see page 245).

Liver

CALF'S LIVER became immensely popular on restaurant menus of the 1980s, and we all tried to have it pinker than the next man. The enthusiasm shows no signs of abating. I suspect that many non-veal eaters are not aware that almost all calf's liver in this country comes from Dutch veal calves. The conscientious should look for English calf's liver. You are more likely to find it in the supermarket than the butcher's – try Safeway and Sainsbury's. All calf's liver is expensive, so if your conscience permits, you may as well get the very best. Look for the palest possible colour, and avoid anything with a purplish or bluish tinge, or blotchy colouring. It should always be freshly sliced for you by the butcher from a whole liver (which you should feel entitled to inspect). It is hard to improve on the simplest of cooking methods: a thin slice simply fried or grilled, with mash, or perhaps polenta, and a sweet onion Confit (page 112).

CHICKEN LIVER: chicken-liver pâté has become hugely popular in recent years, and is pretty cheap in most supermarkets. This is understandable, given the huge number of chicken livers that are available from the intensive poultry industry. I rather shudder at the thought of the commercially produced pâté, though I have had some excellent home-made versions.

But I prefer chicken livers cooked whole, and served pink straight from the frying pan. Frozen chicken livers are available in almost all butchers and supermarkets – their flavour is much improved if they are soaked in milk for a couple of hours after defrosting. Fresh livers are infinitely preferable if you can get them. If you have found a butcher who deals in top-quality free-range poultry ask him, with a couple of days' warning, to put on one side for you the fresh livers of half a dozen birds. On the day you collect them, sauté in hot oil for just 2–3 minutes, adding a couple of garlic cloves, very finely chopped, and 1 tbsp finely chopped parsley, for the last minute of cooking. Serve up on a bed of green salad leaves with a good olive oil vinaigrette.

Whether you use fresh or frozen chicken livers, be sure to trim off any yellow parts (the gall) and the tough, fibrous membranes.

LAMB'S LIVER is a different prospect altogether from calf's and in many ways a better one for the Bon Marché cook. It is certainly less tender, and much stronger in flavour than calf's liver but if it isn't overcooked it doesn't have to be tough. Like all glands and internal organs, liver should be eaten as fresh as possible; frozen liver is perhaps marginally preferable to ageing liver, but neither is likely to bring a beaming smile to a liver-lover's face. The best lamb's liver deserves respectful treatment: like calf's liver, it can be sliced thinly, flash-fried or grilled, and served pink to those who like it so. I find bloody lamb's liver a bit much, but see no need to overcompensate with too severe a grilling: 5 minutes in all, turning once, is usually enough to cook a ½ in/1 cm thick piece of liver right through. If your bacon, mash and fried onions are also cooked with this much care, then you have a traditional liver platter on which it is hard to improve, though I can heartily recommend Jemima's unusual recipe for lamb's liver with Dubonnet (see page 245).

PIG'S LIVER is larger, tougher and stronger in taste than either calf's or lamb's liver. In my view it is also much harder to serve palatably. I mentioned in the previous chapter the extremely intensive way in which most pigs are raised for food, and I suspect that this takes a heavy toll on the animals' livers which, along with the kidneys, play a key role in assimilation and dispersal of toxins in the diet. The liver from more traditionally reared pigs is even harder to get hold of than their meat, but I did manage to procure some in order to test my theory: in a blind tasting of simply fried pig's liver, everyone agreed that the liver of a Gloucestershire Old Spot, obtained from a butcher specializing in traditionally reared rare breeds, was infinitely superior.

OX LIVER, taken from mature cattle, is the toughest (and cheapest) of the lot. It requires a long, slow braise, and even then is likely to be on the tough side, but the flavour can be good, especially if the liver has been taken from a top-quality animal.

For both pig's and lamb's liver, braising is a technique that can be very rewarding, but must be executed with some care if the liver is not to end up dry and tough. A very gentle braise, in good stock and a little white wine, with a mirepoix of vegetables (finely diced carrot, celery, onion and leek), for no more than 40 minutes, should give a good result. To make a gravy, strain the juice, boil to reduce, whisk in a little butter and spike with a pinch of paprika. Celeriac Gratin (page 106) is a perfect accompaniment.

Oxtail

A medium-sized oxtail weighs around 3 lb/1.3 kg, and will make a hearty stew to feed 4. There is little advice to give the shopper when buying an oxtail except choose fresh, rather than frozen, if you possibly can. This may mean ordering a day in advance. Most butchers sell it all ready and cut-up, the portions bound together with string – it is not sensible to buy it in a piece unless you have a butcher's block and a heavy meat cleaver.

All recipes for oxtail require the same basic preparation, and if this is not specified, it should be done anyway. Untie the bundle and soak the oxtail in plenty of well salted cold water for a few hours or overnight. Place in a pot in fresh cold water and bring slowly to the boil, skimming regularly as the scum rises to the surface. Simmer gently, continuing to skim, for about 10 minutes. Drain, cool and wipe dry with a clean cloth. This pre-blanching and skimming process will prevent your soup or stew from being scummy-brown in appearance and tainted in flavour.

There are many recipes for oxtail stew: my own, on page 249, is rich, robust and completely satisfying.

Sweetbreads

Sweetbreads, or sweatbeards as a dyslexic chef I know used to write on his menu, are one of the most highly prized of offal cuts, and rightly so. Tender and creamy, with a delicate flavour, they have long been popular with restaurant chefs, less so with home cooks. This is probably because of the elaborate, but necessary, preparation to which they must be subjected before they are ready to be transformed into a finished dish. But if this procedure is a little time-consuming, it is certainly not in the least difficult.

It is not known who first applied the term 'sweetbread', but it was undoubtedly a good marketing move: neither 'pancreas' nor 'thymus gland' – the heart sweetbread and throat sweetbread respectively – has quite the same appeal. No particular distinction is made between these two different kinds of sweetbread at the butcher's, and both are prepared in exactly the same way. For the record, the rounder and slightly larger ones are likely to be heart sweetbreads (pancreas).

Both calf's and lamb's sweetbreads are readily available. Being larger and less fiddly to prepare, and no doubt also because they come from veal cows, calf's sweetbreads are more expensive. Taste-wise, the cheaper lamb's 'breads are every bit as good.

Preparing and cooking sweetbreads

The basic preparation of sweetbreads is as follows: soak as for brains – for at least 3 hours in plenty of cold water which should be changed several times.

Then, in unsalted fresh water, or a light vegetable court bouillon, bring the sweetbreads to the boil and simmer gently for just 5 minutes. Drain and leave to cool. When cold, or at least cool enough to handle, take each sweetbread in your hand and pick over it, teasing out the fatty, gristly, sinewy or horny bits and discarding them as you go. Use a sharp knife where necessary. The trick, which is quickly learned, is to do this without peeling off the thin membrane that holds the smaller parts of each sweetbread together. If you do not always succeed in this it is not the end of the world, you will simply be dealing with bits of sweetbread that are slightly smaller than might be ideal.

Your sweetbreads are now ready for whatever recipe you have chosen. Many Italian and French chefs like to serve them in rich, creamy sauces – something I have always found a cloying disappointment. I recommend the same treatment as for brains, i.e. coat in seasoned flour, then fry in hot oil until crispy and golden. Best of all, serve with identically treated lamb's brains and small slices of liver, with sage leaves and capers, for a classic *fritto misto* of lamb's offal.

Tongue

The tongue is not a gland or an organ but a muscle, so strictly speaking it need not be classed separately from other meat cuts. It always is, however, and for many people remains the source of great gastronomic squeamishness. This has always surprised me, given that all of us have a tongue in our mouth all of the time. You'd think we'd get used to it sooner or later.

The tongues you are most likely to encounter in the butcher's will be those of either calves or oxen. Sheep's tongues crop up from time to time, and are very tasty and easy to cook (poach until tender – about 1 hour – in a well-flavoured stock, then skin and sauté or quick-braise). They are becoming 'trendy' in a number of restaurants, which perhaps explains why they are not always as cheap as they should be. There is nothing wrong with pig's tongue – you will find plenty of it in every good brawn – but it is rarely encountered as a separate item in the offal trays. This is almost certainly because most pigs' heads can be sold whole, either to pork processing plants for spam and pork pies, or to the occasional discerning Bon Marché cook who wants to make his own brawn (see page 237).

Ox tongue is undoubtedly better value than calf's but a whole one can weigh over 4 lb/1.8 kg, so if you are buying one you need either to be sure you are feeding an enthusiastic bunch of tongue-lovers, or be a tongue sandwich fan yourself (I am). Neither calves' nor ox tongues have to be salted, but both benefit from it in my view as the texture becomes more yielding and the flavour is enhanced. You can buy whole tongues 'ready-salted' by the butcher, or it can easily be done at home. Adam Robinson's brine for salt beef (see pages 212–13) is also perfect for tongue. After at least 2 days (preferably a week) in the brine, soak the tongue in cold, fresh water for 4 hours, changing the water once. Then place in a pan and cover with more cold water. Add a large carrot, halved, ditto an onion, a few peppercorns and a bouquet of dried herbs. The tongue should simmer gently and may take over 4 hours (calf's about 2½) to cook. Mrs Beeton has a lovely test for the readiness of boiled tongue: it should be so tender that it is possible to pierce the meat with a straw. Try serving it with salsa verde (see page 427) and lentils.

Tripe

Sheep's tripe is also a very viable offal. Few butchers stock it, but a helpful one will track it down. If you know a farmer who slaughters his own sheep, then you may be able to get tripe that is fresh and unblanched.

Ox tripe is available in most butchers. For some time now it has been the law in Britain that tripe cannot leave the abattoir unless it is first sterilized by blanching (actually quite severe boiling). Many chefs of my acquaintance are inclined to moan that tripe so treated has lost all the important qualities – strong, gutty taste and a firm, almost rubbery texture – that make French and Italian tripe dishes so delicious. For a long time I took these experts at their word, and simply never bothered to cook English tripe. Then I came across a packet of ox tripe in my local Sainsbury's. On a whim I decided to give it a go. I even decided to follow the recipe on the packet, with a few minor alterations, to wit: adding 1 tsp cayenne, using beef stock instead of just water, and a few sliced carrots to boot. This, my own humble *tripe à la mode*, was a resounding success. I have since tried cooking with tripe from the local butcher, with similarly satisfactory results. Maybe the full intestinal aroma of continental tripe is not quite all there, but there will be some who regard that as no bad thing. I certainly see no need to boycott the British product. The recipe on page 250 was recently gleaned on a trip to Argentina; it is a particularly lovely way of eating tripe.

Recipes

Lambs' Liver with Dubonnet and Orange

JEMIMA'S

Serves 4

An original combination, which may sound eccentric, but the aromatic flavours of the Dubonnet and orange complement the liver remarkably well. The sauce comes from deglazing the pan, so it takes only a few minutes to cook.

Trim the liver and cut into slices ½ in/1 cm thick. Cover with the milk and leave in the fridge for 30 minutes to 1 hour. Drain the liver and pat dry, season well with salt and pepper and coat lightly in the flour, shaking off any excess. Heat the oil and 1 oz/30 g of the butter in a frying pan, and add the liver, turning it over when blood rises to the surface (3–4 minutes) and cooking for just 2 further minutes on the other side. Remove from the pan and keep warm while you make the sauce.

Deglaze the pan with first the Dubonnet, then the orange juice, adding the orange rind. Bring to the boil, scraping up all the crusty bits in the pan, let it bubble for about 10 seconds, then strain into a clean pan. Bring back to the boil, let it bubble for a minute, and remove from the heat. Whisk in the remaining butter, in pieces, to thicken the sauce. Taste for seasoning, sharpen with a squeeze of lemon, and pour the sauce over the liver.

Serve at once with a salad of orange slices and watercress.

1½ lb/675 g lambs' liver
10 fl oz/300 ml milk
salt and black pepper
plain flour
1 scant tbsp olive oil
3 oz/85 g butter
3 fl oz/75 ml Dubonnet
2 fl oz/50 ml freshly squeezed
 orange juice
grated rind of 1 orange
a squeeze of lemon

Lambs' Kidneys with Chilli and Lentils

Serves 4

The recipe below produces a dish that is quite fiery. If you prefer a milder piquancy, substitute 2 tsp Dijon mustard for the chilli. The whole dish is done rather at the gallop, over a high heat, and should be ready in just a few minutes if the kidneys are not to be over-done. Always cook it at the last moment.

1 lb/450 g lambs' kidneys
2 tbsp olive oil
2 garlic cloves, finely chopped
1–2 small fresh red chillis,
 finely chopped
1 wine-glass red wine
5 fl oz/150 ml double cream
10 oz/300 g cooked lentils,
 green *or* Puy (see page 301)
salt and black pepper
1 tbsp finely chopped fresh
 parsley, to garnish

Rinse the kidneys in cold water. Pat dry and cut in half. Trim away any skin and gristly core.

Heat the oil in a large, heavy frying pan over a high heat. Throw in the garlic and, a few seconds later, the kidneys. Sauté for barely a minute, tossing them in the pan until they are nicely browned. Add the chilli and pour in the wine – it should bubble vigorously – and quickly reduce to about half its volume. Add the cream, a good pinch of salt and a few twists of pepper, and boil to reduce still further. When the sauce is glossy and nicely coating the kidneys (not much more than 5 minutes after the kidneys first went in) add the lentils, mix well and heat through for just 1 further minute. Serve at once, sprinkled with the parsley, with plain boiled rice and a salad of watercress dressed only with olive oil and a squeeze of lemon.

Devilled Lambs' Kidneys

THE WHITELEAF AT CROYDE

Serves 1

Not for the faint-hearted, this potently piquant dish is a real belly-warmer.

¾ oz/20 g butter
2 lambs' kidneys, skinned,
 cored (see page 239) and cut
 into quarters
3 fl oz/75 ml red wine
½ tsp made English mustard
1 tsp hot chilli sauce
1 tsp balsamic vinegar
a dash of Worcester sauce
black pepper
chopped fresh parsley, to
 garnish

Melt the butter in a small frying pan or saucepan just large enough to hold the kidneys. When it sizzles, add the kidneys and brown quickly all over. Pour in the wine, then add the mustard, chilli sauce, vinegar, Worcester sauce and pepper. Stir vigorously and continue to cook over a high heat until the liquid starts to bubble quite violently and reduces to a smooth, shiny, thickish sauce. (Do not cook for too long or the sauce will separate and the kidneys will toughen.)

Garnish with the parsley and serve with crisp toast, fried bread or a crunchy poppadom.

NOTE: this recipe must be cooked over a high heat to reduce the sauce quickly and to keep the kidneys soft and not rubbery. The proportion of wine/butter, etc. to kidneys may be reduced for a larger quantity: for 6–8 kidneys (to serve 3–4), you need only double the quantities.

Crispy Pigs' Trotters

This is a variation on the Sainte-Ménéhould theme (see the Whiteleaf recipe for best end of neck of lamb on page 214). You should allow 1 trotter per person as a starter, 2 for a main course – perhaps 3 for the super-greedy.

Scrub the pigs' trotters under a cold running tap and remove any hairs or bristles (I use a razor for this, alternatively you can singe them with a lighter or over a gas flame). Wipe the trotters dry, lay them on a plate and sprinkle generously with salt. Leave overnight in the fridge. This salting may be omitted if you want to cook the trotters on the day you buy them, but it does help to tenderize the meat.

Rinse the trotters, put them into a saucepan with the vegetables, herbs and peppercorns, and cover with cold water. Bring to the boil, then simmer gently, covered, for 4 hours, by which time the trotters should be completely tender, the skin and meat coming away from the bones. Drain the trotters, and leave until cool enough to handle, then remove the larger bones – the smaller ones in the 'toes' should be tender enough to eat.

To finish, melt the butter and turn the trotters in it so they are well coated. Then dredge them thoroughly in seasoned breadcrumbs, so they are coated thickly all over. Lay them on an ovenproof dish, trickle any remaining melted butter over each, and put them in a pre-heated fairly hot oven (200°C/400°F/Gas Mark 6), until they are nicely crisped up (10–15 minutes). Serve straight from the oven, with a mustardy mayonnaise, or the green vinaigrette recommended for the *pot-au-feu* on page 223.

6 pigs' trotters
plenty of coarse salt
1 large onion
2 celery sticks
2 large carrots
a bouquet garni
6 black peppercorns

To finish
4 oz/115 g butter
4 oz/115 g fresh breadcrumbs
salt and black pepper
a mustard mayonnaise *or* green vinaigrette (see page 223), to serve

Devilled Stew of Ox Cheek
Serves 6

Ox cheek is beginning to be fashionable again on the restaurant scene, often served in a similar fashion to my oxtail recipe (see page 249), with an intense reduction of beef stock and garnished with glazed root vegetables. But cheek is not quite as rich as tail, and I prefer this hearty, old-fashioned version, adapted from Mrs Beeton, which is pleasantly piquant.

2½-lb/1-kg piece boned ox
  cheek
salt and black pepper
1 large onion
2 celery sticks
1 small turnip
2 large carrots
a bouquet garni

For the sauce
1 small onion, finely chopped
4 oz/115 g mushrooms, sliced
1 oz/30 g butter
1 tsp cayenne pepper *or* chilli
  powder
1 rounded tbsp plain flour
2 tbsp port
2 tbsp Worcester sauce
1 tbsp tomato purée
1 tbsp red wine vinegar

Purists may wish to
make this sauce
without thickening
with flour – you can
use a well-reduced
beef stock made
separately, to which
you can add the other
ingredients for the
sauce minus the flour.

Soak the ox cheek overnight in enough salted water to cover it (1 tbsp salt per 2 pts/litre of water). Wipe the cheek dry with a clean, damp cloth, and place in a large pan with the vegetables and herbs. Season with a few twists of pepper.

Pour over fresh water just to cover the meat, place the pan over a low heat and bring to a gentle simmer. Skim off any scum that rises to the surface. Place the lid on the pan, leaving a gap for steam to escape, and simmer very gently for 3–3½ hrs, until the cheek is completely tender and a fork can be pushed through it with little resistance. Alternatively, the cooking can be done in a very low oven (120°C/250°F/Gas Mark ½), but bring the ox cheek to simmering point on top of the stove first.

Remove the meat and set aside. Discard the vegetables, strain the cooking liquid though a clean cotton cloth and reserve. Cut the meat into generous but manageable chunks (about matchbox size).

To make the sauce, sweat the onion and mushrooms in the butter in a saucepan until the onion is soft but not coloured. Add the cayenne or chilli and the flour, and mix well. Cook for 1–2 minutes. Add the remaining ingredients, mix well, then add the still-warm stock by degrees, stirring all the time. You may not need all the stock – about 1½ pts/850 ml should be enough to produce a smooth gravy that is not too thick and floury. The final thickness of the sauce will not be apparent until you have allowed it to bubble for a minute or two. When this point is reached, add more stock if you think necessary and season to taste with salt and pepper. Add the pieces of ox cheek and reheat in the bubbling sauce for 1–2 minutes. Serve with plenty of creamy mashed potato (see page 89).

Oxtail with Red Wine Gravy and
Marrow-bone Bonus

Serves 6–8, depending on appetites and the
size of the oxtails

The addition of a beef marrow-bone to the pot ensures a good strong stock, which is then reduced with red wine to give a super-rich gravy. If you've never tried marrow-bone, you should.

2 oxtails, cut up by the butcher
1 beef marrow-bone, sawed
  into short lengths
2 large carrots
1 onion
2 celery sticks
1 small turnip
thinly pared zest of ½ orange
a bouquet garni
salt and black pepper
½ bottle good red wine

The oxtail should be prepared by soaking in brine for a few hours (see page 241). Then scrub the pieces under a cold running tap, and places, with the marrow-bone, vegetables, orange zest and herbs in a large saucepan. Add enough cold water to cover and bring slowly to a simmer, skimming any brown scum as it rises to the surface. Cover the pan and simmer very gently (or in a slow oven, 140°C/275°F/Gas Mark 1, if you like) for at least 3 hours, until the meat is tender and coming away from the bone.

Remove the marrow-bones from the pot after about 40 minutes. Ease out the marrow with a teaspoon (in whole pieces if possible) and set aside in a dish. (Heated gently through in a frying pan, it can be served on toast as a starter – with bacon and fried mushrooms if you are very greedy.) Return the bones to the pot and return the pot to the hob or oven to finish cooking.

Remove the pieces of oxtail from the pot with a slotted spoon. Remove and discard the remaining bones and vegetables and strain the stock through muslin or a clean cotton cloth into a clean pan. Add the wine and boil fiercely over a high heat to reduce. Just how much you want to reduce the sauce is a matter of personal taste. I like it fairly intense and rich, but I stop short of those very sticky reductions that seem *de rigueur* in expensive restaurants.

When you have reached the level of reduction you require, season to taste (do not do so earlier – if you judge the saltiness to be right before you reduce, it will be far too salty afterwards). Add a few more drops of wine if liked, to refresh the flavour. Return the oxtail pieces to the sauce and heat through thoroughly, allowing it to bubble for a couple of minutes. If you prefer, separate the oxtail meat from the bone while the sauce is reducing – this is easily done with fingers and a fork. Then return only the meat to the pan. Serve with creamy mashed potato (see page 89) and roast vegetables (for example small onions or shallots, carrots and leeks, see page 43).

Tripe with Chick-peas and Chorizo
Serves 4

I discovered this dish in a restaurant in Buenos Aires, and improvised it when I got home. Argentinians love their beef, and they love the offal cuts from their cattle too. The spiciness of the chorizo means that the distinct flavour of the tripe is not too prominent. This is therefore a particularly good dish to serve to those who may be sceptical about this rather maligned piece of offal.

1½ lb/675 g blanched ox tripe (see page 244)
2 tbsp olive oil
2 garlic cloves, finely chopped
2 × 14-oz/400-g cans tomatoes
8 oz/225 g chorizo sausage, cut into ¼-in/5-mm slices
1 small onion, thinly sliced
1 large carrot, cut into thickish matchsticks
5 fl oz/150 ml white wine
10 fl oz/300 ml meat stock
2 tsp tomato purée
8 oz/225 g cooked chick-peas (see page 300)
a good pinch of cayenne pepper
salt and black pepper

Wash the tripe thoroughly and cut into ½-in/1-cm slices. Heat all but ½ tbsp of the oil in a pan and add the garlic. Just before the garlic takes colour, add the tomatoes, turn up the heat and allow to bubble until most of the liquid has evaporated and the tomatoes are reduced to a thick, pulpy sauce: stir the tomatoes frequently while they are cooking, breaking them up and preventing the sauce from catching on the bottom of the pan. When you think you cannot reduce them any further without risk of burning, remove from the heat and set aside.

In a separate saucepan, heat the remaining oil and fry the chorizo gently until lightly browned and some of the fat is released. Add the onion and carrot, and sweat for just a minute. Add the wine, the stock and the tomato purée, bring to the boil and allow to bubble vigorously until the liquid is reduced by one-third. Then add the tripe, the chick-peas, the cayenne and the tomato sauce, mixing well. Turn down the heat and simmer gently for 25 minutes, uncovered, until the tripe is tender. Season with a little black pepper, and salt if necessary. Serve in warmed soup bowls, so that everyone gets plenty of sauce.

CHAPTER SIX

Poultry
and
Game

Mrs Beeton lists dozens of species of domestic fowl, and has plenty to say about the habits, temperament and eating qualities of all of them. These days, if you walked into a butcher's shop and asked him if he had any Spangled Polands or Chitteprats, the most polite answer you could expect would be a blank stare. Sadder still, there is barely a market any longer for the traditional boiling fowl – larger, older birds or hens that have proved less than prolific layers. And many butchers probably haven't heard of a capon – the castrated cockerel, fattened at an unforced pace to make a magnificent and flavourful roast.

But even in 1860 the rot had begun to set in. Mrs Beeton herself complains of 'the cramming and dungeon policy practised by some . . . fowls being huddled together in a small coop . . . instead of enjoying that repose which alone can insure the wished for object'. Just as well she's not around to witness the insane practices that abound in the poultry industry today. The last straw for me was a 1992 television documentary which revealed how intensive farming methods have led to grossly deformed birds which could not walk even if they had the space to do so. Such are the stresses to which birds are subjected that many production units have a premature mortality rate of up to 40 per cent. As for their diet – processed high-protein pellets, often of animal origin, supplemented with cocktails of growth-promoting drugs – at least it's something I can choose not to ingest, even if the birds can't.

Most people must know that their chickens are produced by these advanced and unnatural methods. Perhaps fewer people realize that the other poultry birds, though not produced in quite such huge numbers, have also become the victims of farming technology. Few farmed ducks or geese have even seen an expanse of water larger than the filthy trough they drink from – inside a shed. Even guinea fowl and quail are packed tightly into cages, and fed on high-protein concentrates rather than their natural diet of grubs and grains. Marketed as exotic gourmet foods, they fetch a far higher price than the humble broiler chickens, but the chances are their meat is every bit as bland.

Buying poultry and game

When shopping for poultry of all kinds, therefore, if you want to find a tasty bird that has not been raised by intensive methods, you must look for two key words: 'FREE-RANGE'. This means the birds have spent at least some of the time outside where they can forage, move around and more properly develop their musculature. A further indication of quality is a label that indicates a bird has been reared on a natural, grain-based diet, without the aid of growth promoters. The more comprehensive the information on the label, the more reassured you should be. In the supermarket such information is increasingly well displayed on the packs in which chickens are wrapped. At the butcher's you may well have to ask to find out what you need to know. If you are not happy with the quality of your butcher's poultry, be brave and tell him so. He may well be able to get you something better.

Game, on the other hand, offers the Bon Marché cook meat that is healthy, tasty and pretty much guaranteed to have lived free and fed naturally. It is, of course, rather more expensive than poultry, though not by as much as those who rarely eat it might imagine. Pigeons and wild rabbits are not so dear, and pheasants are often a bargain – at the height of the shooting season country butchers are often practically giving them away. Also seasonal, hares can be a very economical buy.

Certainly there is a leap of the imagination, or more precisely the wallet, to be made where the other game birds are concerned. In season, grouse, wild duck and partridge can all be had from good butchers, though at a price. Teal, woodcock and snipe are harder to come by; if you are insistent, and a valued customer, a good butcher might turn detective and track some down. You are more likely to find yourself in possession of one of the above if you are either a keen shot or a poacher – or the lover, spouse or cook of either.

The rest of this chapter considers the different species of domestic fowl and game, with tips on choosing, preparing and cooking them.

Chicken

These days I rarely buy a chicken unless I can be reasonably satisfied that it is free-range and, preferably, had a natural, primarily grain-based, diet. The latter is, generally speaking, harder to ascertain than the former: butchers and supermarkets will tend to make a big song and dance about the fact that certain of their chickens are free-range (they have to in order to justify the higher price), but this is not always a guarantee that the birds have also been fed a high-quality diet. A good butcher should know something about the origin, lifestyle and diet of his chickens, as he should about all his meat. Don't be shy about asking. There is no reason why you should not also tackle the supermarket chains with the same kind of question if you feel that the information on their labels falls short of what you would like to know: call their head office and ask for Customer Relations.

If you really communicate with your butcher, and rate him, and are keen to lay your hands on the tastiest possible chicken, then you should specify that you want your bird to satisfy the following conditions, none of which is beyond the call of duty for a dedicated butcher.

1   It should be free-range.
2   It should be reared on an all-natural diet, free of hormones, growth promoters and recycled animal protein.
3   It should be hung, undrawn (i.e. ungutted), for 2–3 days.
4   It should be drawn and trussed for you, on the day of collection/purchase.
5   It should come with its giblets.

Cooking a chicken

For me cooking a chicken has become, if not exactly a rare treat, then at least something to plan, look forward to, and take some care over. It is not a food I use as an emergency stop-gap or an everyday staple; I never keep chicken in the freezer. I would rather pay more than twice the price of a frozen supermarket chicken for something really special, and have it less than half as often.

Whenever practical, you should try to buy a whole bird. In my experience it is rarely impractical: an entire bird gives you the total package – skin, bones, fat, flesh, giblets, the lot – all of which can be used in one of the two or more meals that you can expect to get from your chicken, and all of which make an important contribution to the mission to get the most flavour out of your bird. You should always think in terms of two or more meals, or at least two or more dishes, even if one of those is just a quick soup or simple risotto made from your chicken's stock.

For large casseroles, barbecues, buffets, etc., chicken 'portions' often seem to be the most economical options. And maybe they are, if, for example, you want to flame-grill a couple of dozen drumsticks or thighs in a hurry, to make handy finger-food for a sizeable group. But if you're cooking chicken because good chicken is what you like, and you want your guests to like it too, then pre-portioned pieces of chicken are unlikely to give you a result worth shouting about: they almost invariably come from intensively farmed birds, and in the worst cases from those which were not 'pretty' enough to make it uncut, i.e. the cripples and hunchbacks of the pack.

Before barbecuing your chicken pieces, pound garlic and a few fresh tarragon or parsley leaves with some soft butter, and spread a little of this mixture under the skin of each chicken joint, and you will help to keep the meat lubricated, as well as introducing two flavours that never fail to add excitement to chicken.

Better to start with a whole bird of proven quality, then joint it yourself, or ask your butcher to joint it for you, as necessary. In my view you need a very good reason to joint a bird in the first place: remember that a bird in pieces, with cut flesh, will lose more of its precious juices in the cooking process than a bird which is kept whole. In a casserole, of course, of which the liquid is an intrinsic part, the flavour of the juices will not be lost.

The only other time I think it is really worthwhile to joint a bird is when it is to be cooked over wood or charcoal. Generally the temperature is likely to be too high for cooking a whole bird: the skin would be frazzled before the inside is cooked. And though moisture will be lost when smaller portions are cooked, it may be decided that this is not such a high price to pay for the unique and seductive taste of chicken cooked over a real outdoor barbecue.

Some cooking methods

Roasting

A whole bird, competently roasted, and served with its own juices, can barely be improved on. The following technique is pretty foolproof.

Into the cavity of a plump 3–3½-lb/1.3–1.5-kg bird place a generous knob of butter seasoned well with salt and pepper and mixed, if you like, with a crushed garlic clove and a good few leaves of tarragon or parsley. Rub more butter, or olive oil if you prefer, over the skin. Roast the bird in a pre-heated fairly hot oven (200°C/400°F/Gas Mark 6) for 20 minutes on each side, then for 20 minutes breast-side up. (For birds of 4 lb/1.8 kg plus, add 4–5 minutes on each side to the cooking time.) Every time you turn the bird, baste well with the juices in the pan. After about 1 hour your bird should be golden-brown, the skin crispy, and the roasting tin swimming in buttery juice: this is all you need by way of sauce, though it can be supplemented with a little stock made from the chicken giblets, 1 carrot, 1 onion, and a scant 10 fl oz/300 ml water, simmered together gently for 30 minutes. If you do add such a stock to the juices in the pan, then reduce the liquor a little over heat, and strain before serving.

If you think this sounds a bit boring (taste-wise, I promise it isn't), or appears just a bit too effortless to your guests, then extrovert hosts (and lovers of creamy sauces) can finish the sauce with half a ladle of flaming brandy, and a couple of spoons of double cream or crème faîche. Do this in the roasting tin, reduce over a gentle heat until lightly thickened, then strain, throw in a little extra chopped tarragon if you have it, season to taste with salt and pepper and serve in a sauce-boat.

Braising/roasting

A variation on the previous method, popular in France, adds the 10 fl oz/ 300 ml giblet stock at the beginning of cooking. The bird, which is turned frequently and basted with the juice, is guaranteed to remain moist and tender. The skin can still be crisped, if the chicken spends the last 20 minutes of cooking time breast-side up, is well seasoned with salt at the beginning of this time, and is regularly basted with the fat from the top of the pan juices, or brushed with a little extra melted butter. The pan juices left at the end will make an excellent gravy: treat as above.

Poaching

Traditionally the treatment for an old laying hen or larger bird that may be too tough for roasting, poaching is today a sadly under-used technique. It is still very worthwhile with larger birds; a first-class butcher might even lay his hands on a proper boiling fowl for you.

There is a two-fold benefit to boiling a fowl: first, the slow simmer is guaranteed to tenderize even the toughest bird; second, the process produces an excellent bouillon (stock), which can (indeed must) be enhanced by the addition of a few well-chosen vegetables. Traditionally this bouillon is either served on its own, as a first course, or goes towards making the sauce to serve with the chicken.

A tough old hen (5–6 lb/2.3–2.7 kg plus) will take about 2½ hours to cook, but an ordinary chicken, however large, should never need more than 1½ hours; always simmer very gently. If you remove the vegetables and replace them with fresh samples about 30 minutes before the end of cooking time, they can be served with the chicken. A sliced leek, some pieces of good fat carrot, celery sticks and a few small turnips are appropriate. One classic sauce is a velouté: the stock is reduced to intensify the flavour, thickened with a roux, enriched with a little cream, sharpened with a squeeze of lemon, and spiked, ideally, with chopped fresh tarragon.

A well-made vinaigrette, with fragrant olive oil, finely chopped parsley and shallots, is also delicious with hot poached chicken, and an ideal alternative to stock-based sauce, if you like to drink the bouillon as soup. But always keep a little of the bouillon back, to moisten the meat on the plate. There are numerous variations on this theme in the works of our more venerable cookery writers, especially Mrs Beeton, Constance Spry and Elizabeth David.

Poaching chicken is also often the best method of preparing a bird that is to be served cold. When the meat has been taken from the chicken, the stock can be further cooked with the bones, then reduced to a flavoursome consommé. Jellied when cold, and too tasty to be described as a mere garnish, it will nicely complement whatever sauce or mayonnaise is served with the chicken.

Frying

It will no doubt surprise many to learn that cold poached chicken is also the starting point for all the best recipes for fried chicken. The moist, lean pieces of chicken can be dipped in a light batter and fried in very hot oil for barely a minute and will neither lose their moisture, nor become saturated in fat, as will a piece of chicken that has to cook right through in the hot oil. If you have some leftover roast chicken, then provided you cooked it with care initially and it has not dried out, it can also be used for frying. The following batter – which, incidentally, is suitable for deep-frying anything from courgette flowers to prime cod fillets – is adapted from Mrs Beeton, is simple to make and gives excellent results:

4 oz/115 g plain flour   2 fl oz/50 ml melted butter or oil
8 fl oz/250 ml water   2 egg whites

In a mixing bowl, mix the flour to a smooth paste with the water and whisk in the melted butter or oil. Whisk the egg whites until frothy but not stiff, and beat into the batter. Leave to stand for 30 minutes before using.

The chicken, so battered, should be fried – deep-fried if possible – in very hot fat (190°C/375°F), drained on kitchen paper and served with a nice piquant sauce, such as the *salsa rossa* on page 118. Colonel Sanders, eat your heart out.

Casseroling

A jointed chicken, cooked with vegetables and herbs in a liquor that will take on the flavour of its principal ingredients and perhaps be further enriched by the addition of some alcohol, usually wine, is a fine idea in principle. Indeed, it has given us two classic chicken dishes – chicken *chasseur* and *coq au vin*. But for my part I find it hard to get excited by any dishes in which a thigh of chicken, or part of a breast, is hoiked out of a liquor, a ladle of which is then poured over the chicken piece, leaving me to wrest the meat from the bone and chase the elusive flavour around my plate. The aftermath of such a dish always seems to be a pile of debris consisting of pieces of bone, with tattered flesh still clinging, and flaps of flabby skin. So I include no such recipes, but if ever you should require one, Elizabeth David's Coq au Vin de Bourgogne (page 461, my Penguin paperback of *French Provincial Cooking*) should see you right.

OTHER DOMESTIC FOWL

Turkey

Turkeys are like chickens, only bigger. Let me elaborate on this rather facile-sounding remark. Like chickens, turkeys are intensively farmed in this country on a huge scale. Like most chickens, most turkeys are fed a cocktail of high-protein feeds laced with hormones and growth-promoting drugs for maximum rapid weight gain; they are inadequately hung and inappropriately butchered. With a high proportion of meat to fat, turkeys are always likely to be dry.

Having said that, good turkeys, like good chickens, can be found; ask your butcher for a free-range bird, preferably not too huge, that has been properly hung. It is always a good idea to order such a bird well in advance.

Roasting a turkey

Since you probably do not cook turkey very often, and since when you do it is likely to be intended for a large number of mouths, and possibly on a very special day of the year, and since you have also gone to some trouble to find a quality bird, it would be a shame to spoil it. I therefore offer the following basic tips for successful roasting:

1   10–14 lb/4.5–6.3 kg is a good weight and would serve 14–20 people. A really huge turkey is almost impossible to cook well.

2   The legs of a turkey take much longer to cook than the breast, because the meat is naturally tougher. Therefore remove the legs, and put them on to cook before the rest of the bird. The leg meat can be made particularly tender and delicious if the legs are braised in a dish on a bed of sliced onions, carrots and celery, moistened with a ladle of giblet stock and a glass of white wine. For the last 20 minutes, place on a clean dry baking tray, and finish cooking, basting with melted butter to crisp up the skin. The braising juices, strained, can then be an invaluable addition to your gravy.

3   Do not stuff your turkey. Most stuffings will absorb the juices from the meat, and even those that don't (i.e. fatty ones) will not help the bird retain moisture. By the time the heat has penetrated to the centre of the stuffing, the outer breast meat is likely to be dry and dismal. If, on the other hand, the cavity of the bird is left open, hot air can circulate in it, cooking the bird from inside as well as out. This allows a fairly fast cook in a moderate to hot oven (190°C/375°F/Gas Mark 5). A 12-lb/5.4-kg bird should cook through in about 2 hours at this temperature without the meat becoming dry, if the bird is covered with buttered foil for the first $1\frac{1}{2}$ hours' cooking. Stuffing can easily be cooked separately. Test the bird for doneness with a skewer in the thickest part of the breast – when the juice runs clear, not bloody, it is ready.

Duck and goose

Although ducks and geese are not quite as intensively farmed as chickens and turkeys they have nonetheless been subjected to the menace of factory farming. Nearly all those sold in Britain have been reared in their thousands inside huge sheds.

Young ducks pile on the fat at an impressive rate, and even a 4–5-lb/1.8–2.3-kg bird (dressed weight) is unlikely to be more than 10 weeks old, and sold, quite legitimately, as a duckling. Such birds are on the bland side, and it is well worth seeking out free-range alternatives. If you do get hold of an even bigger and more mature bird (perhaps you know someone who keeps ducks), then it is well worth tracking down some traditional recipes for duck pâtés, rillettes, etc.

I love duck, and most often have it simply roasted, with a gravy sharpened by fresh citrus. Orange is, of course, classic, but chef Stephen Bull once served me a roast duck with a sharp lime syrup. It is an excellent combination, which I have tried since in many variations.

Goose is a rarer treat, but an equally welcome one. Again, try to find a free-range bird. If your butcher can't help you, try the supermarkets – many of them stock geese at Christmas. The copious amounts of flavoursome fat which run off a goose make for days of delicious fried bread or, better still, a huge plate of roast winter vegetables (see recipe on page 122): duck fat can be used in the same way.

Roasting a duck or goose

Getting a roast duck exactly right is by no means hard, but requires some attention to detail. The aim is that by the time the meat is cooked (still just pink by the bone), most of the fat should have run out and the skin should be nice and crispy. The most common problem is that by the time the breast meat is cooked, a) the legs are still unpalatably underdone, and b) there is still too much fat under the skin. There are two simple solutions: before you roast the bird, a) cut the legs off the duck and use them later to make the confit described on page 280, and b) prick the skin with a trussing needle or sharp skewer, to help the fat to run out. This last operation should be executed with some care: prick only those areas where you can see the fat is thick under the skin, and be careful not to pierce through the fat into the flesh itself, otherwise you will release valuable meat juices as well.

The same technique can be used when roasting a goose. In both cases, remember to save all the fat that runs out of the birds – you will need it to make a confit of the legs. The running off of fat can be facilitated by starting the roasting with the bird on its side.

Of course you may think that saving the legs to make a confit is a rather tiresome business that you have no time for; and perhaps you would prefer to eat the legs with the rest of the bird. In which case, when the breast meat of your duck or goose is cooked (for a 4-lb/1.8-kg duck, after about 45 minutes in a hot oven (220°C/425°F/Gas Mark 7), for a goose of 8–9 lb/3.5–4 kg, 1¼–1½ hours at the same temperature*, take the bird out of the oven, remove the legs and return them, well-basted, to the top of the oven. Leave the rest of the bird to stand for at least 20 minutes* in a warm part of the kitchen. Then start to carve. By the time you have served everybody with some breast meat and crispy skin, the legs will have had an extra 30 minutes, and everybody can have a little of that rich, dark meat as well.

Both birds, but geese in particular, are delicious cold, served with piquant relishés, chutneys, or a simple confit of onions (page 112).

* Letting poultry and game rest before carving is one of the secrets of a tender bird. In the case of a large goose, upwards of half an hour would not be excessive.

Guinea fowl

Although some farmers keep a few guinea fowl on their shooting estates (their loud cackling wards off predators), few of these free-ranging birds end up on sale to the public. Those you find in butchers and supermarkets are likely to be factory-farmed. Since they have less meat, less taste, and are more expensive than a good free-range chicken, they are not worth bothering with. The situation is not hopeless, however, and free-range guinea fowl can be found. Birds imported from France (where they are called *pintades*) are often the best bet. Look out for a red label and the word *fermier* – this indicates that a bird is free-range and fed on a natural diet. There are a few small farms rearing free-range guinea fowl in this country too. You may encounter their product at some specialist butchers, and at farm shops on the premises where they are reared. Both French and English free-range birds will be expensive, but at least you will know what guinea fowl is meant to taste like.

Younger birds, also available free-range, are called *pintadeaux* in French. They are tender, and can be roasted or barbecued, though they are not much stronger in taste than a good free-range chicken. Pot-roasting, braising or casseroling (for example with bacon, shallots, chestnuts and red wine) are more suitable treatments for older birds, which are tougher, but have a good flavour, somewhere between pheasant and chicken. The bones of leftover guinea fowl make a fine stock.

Quail

Most quail in this country are intensively farmed in conditions that would hardly be envied by a battery hen. Some are farmed more conscientiously, mainly for restaurant chefs who are looking for birds with real flavour. Unfortunately, in the case of quail there is no statutory labelling legislation as far as the term 'free-range' is concerned. Most quail in the supermarkets will be factory-farmed (yet many supermarkets have the nerve to include them alongside pigeons and pheasants in a section of the chilling cabinet labelled 'Fresh Game'). If you want to buy quail that are free-range and grain-fed (the only worthwhile birds in my view), you will have to do a little homework. Ask a chef whose quail you have tasted and liked where he gets his from, or ring around a few Q-Guild butchers (see page 188).

Wild quail are native to the flat plains of Eastern Europe. No doubt they are delicious, but I have never seen them on sale in this country.

Cooking quail

Quails are usually roasted whole, or split across the breast and opened out, then fried or grilled. Even the best farmed quail are improved by a light marinade – for 4 birds, 1 tbsp red wine or raspberry vinegar, 4 tbsp olive oil, a small sliced onion and a good sprig of thyme. After marinating for 6 hours, or overnight, in this mixture, split quails are good griddled or barbecued until nicely charred and crispy.

One quail per person makes a starter, two a main course.

Giblets

Always make sure you get the giblets with your bird. They can be used to make a stock for deglazing your roasting tin, and rendering up a fine gravy. But hold back the liver from this procedure. If it is to be included in the gravy, it should be added, very finely chopped, at the end. The livers of duck and geese are such tasty morsels that I am inclined to claim them as chef's perks, and fry them to have on toast.

The giblets of a goose are substantial enough on their own to make a rather tasty stew: thinly slice 2 onions, and soften in a little oil (or goose fat). Add 4 oz/115 g thick streaky bacon or pancetta in chunky pieces, 2 large carrots, thickly sliced, 2 crushed garlic cloves, and sweat for a few minutes more. Add all the giblets (except the liver), including the neck of the goose, cut into 1-in/2.5-cm slices. Cover with 10 fl oz/300 ml water or, better still, light veal or chicken stock, add a bouquet garni (dried if you don't have fresh herbs), and simmer very gently, covered, in a slow oven (150°C/300°F/Gas Mark 2) for 2½ hours. To make this into a hearty meal for 4, the giblets should be supplemented, about 15 minutes before the end of cooking time, with a couple of spicy sausages and/or a few ounces of cooked goose meat, preferably from the leg, roughly chopped. Serve the stew with a purée of yellow split peas, or cabbage and mash.

GAME BIRDS

The problem of farming practices barely applies to game birds; they are wild, and therefore privileged to fly above the shoddy treatment that is dished out to their coop-bound distant cousins. Having said that, it is of course true that most pheasants, and some partridges, are reared birds, fed in pens, then released some time before the beginning of the shooting season. But at least we can say they are freer of range than any chicken, and enjoy the diet of a natural forager, supplemented only by grain. All in all, it makes for pretty tasty meat.

In selecting game, the only real factors to consider, apart from the hefty prices some butchers are likely to charge for certain species, are the age of your chosen bird, and the length of time for which it has been hung.

I will begin with pheasants, detailing basic principles of the buying, hanging, cooking and serving of them, and go on to discuss other game birds only in so far as they differ from the pheasant template.

Pheasant

For the last few years pheasant has been extremely cheap, especially in country butchers. Many large-scale shooting syndicates have been unable to sell all the birds they kill, and consequently many thousands of birds have been buried and left to rot. This is a terrible waste of excellent meat. But it does mean there is plenty of room for an increase in demand for pheasants, without provoking a corresponding increase in price. In the winter months pheasants will be easier to find than at other times, and at prices per lb/450 g that are just about comparable to those charged for free-range chicken.

Choosing a bird

Young pheasants can be quickly roasted, and provided they are well basted, or lubricated during cooking by barding with strips of streaky bacon, will retain their juices and can be served a little underdone. Older birds (i.e. of more than 1 year) given the same treatment, are likely to be tough and chewy if you try to serve them pink, but dry and bland if you roast them for too long. You will get a much better result if you braise or casserole them.

So if it is a roasting bird you are after, make sure you get a young one. If you are buying an oven-ready bird from the butcher, it is not at all easy to age it, though if it is unusually large it is probably past its prime. Apart from this rather unreliable guide, you can only ask your butcher, and hope he is an honest man (perhaps you have some idea about that already).

With a little pre-planning, however, it should be possible to order your game in advance (for the more recherché game birds, such as woodcock and snipe, this will probably be necessary anyway). This has the two-fold advantage that you can specify exactly what sort of birds you would like (young or old, cock or hen – hens are generally a little more tender) and also how long you would like your birds hung.

Age of birds

If you are regularly on the receiving end of game that is unplucked and undrawn, or if you like to buy it that way, then it is handy to be able to distinguish old birds from young. Young pheasants will tend to have a pliable beak, and short blunt spurs (the talons on its feet); both beak and spurs are harder, longer and sharper in birds of more than a year old. Even if they are large, young birds are likely to be rather more streamlined in shape than birds of the previous season. A particularly fat hen, or large cock, with a really magnificent tail, is bound to be an older bird.

Hanging of birds

There is much discussion among game aficionados as to how long game birds should be hung for. Those who tell you they should be hung until the body finally parts company from the head are not only spouting bravado, they are likely to be left waiting a very long time. I once forgot about a brace of pheasants that hung for over a month. They were none too pleasant-smelling when I rediscovered them, and I would not have dreamed of eating them; but they were still firmly in touch with their heads.

Nevertheless, there is no doubt that hanging of game makes a considerable difference to its eating quality. A pheasant that is hung for only a day or two, or not at all, will come up drier than a run-of-the-mill chicken, with barely any more flavour. The meat of a bird that has been hung for 10 days, on the other hand, will be moist, tender and full of gamy flavour. If you don't like your birds too gamy, a week will suffice; if you are sure you like your pheasants good and gamy, then 2 weeks will not be too long. But unless you are a 'specialist' and can rely on your nose to tell you exactly when your bird is in the state of decomposition which you personally favour, I would say 2 weeks is an absolute maximum.

These recommended times assume that the air temperature in which the birds are hung is reliably cool (below 10°C/50°F); in warm weather a pheasant may go bad well within a week. Birds should be checked daily, and taken down for plucking and drawing at the first whiff of decay.

According to purists, a cock pheasant will require about 2 more days' hanging than a hen. This makes sense – the cock is larger and generally tougher than the hen – but it is often impractical to follow this advice, as you may well want to cook a brace together. You can always serve the hen to the guests who like gamier meat.

No meat is unaffected by freezing, but it is safe to say that game, which is generally close-textured and low in fat, survives the ordeal rather better than farmed meat. A marinade (see page 279) will help to restore dignity to game birds, hares, rabbits and venison that have been thawed from frozen. Casseroling or braising is usually the best treatment for thawed-out game, though I have roasted young pheasants, ducks and grouse after defrosting and found them to be almost as good as fresh (though a shade drier and tougher), even when served pink.

Cooking pheasants

ROASTING: young pheasants should be barded with streaky bacon and roasted in a very hot oven (230°C/450°F/Gas Mark 8) for 45 minutes at most (35 is sufficient for a small hen which is to be served pink). The bacon should be removed and the breast allowed to brown during the last 10 minutes of cooking. Regular basting with the juices that run out of the bird is a good idea. Another useful tip is to pour a glass of good red wine over the pheasant halfway through cooking; by the time the bird is done the wine will have practically boiled dry, but when you deglaze the roasting tin (preferably with stock made from the pheasant's giblets) the wisdom of this move will be fragrantly revealed.

I'm a sucker for the classic English accompaniment to roast pheasant: real bread sauce, game chips, braised celery (see page 63) and the bird's copious juices. But every now and again I like to try a simple variation, inspired by Elizabeth David, that owes its origins to the Norman love of apples and cream.

Before you roast the pheasant, brown it in a hot frying pan, and flambé it with a glass of Calvados. Then proceed as above, omitting the wine treatment. Remove the bird when it is done, then deglaze the tin first with another slosh of Calvados then, when that has reduced by half, 10 fl oz/300 ml giblet stock. Reduce by half again, then add 2 generous tbsp double cream or crème faîche, a scant tsp redcurrant jelly, a pinch of salt and a twist of black pepper. Allow to bubble and thicken momentarily – your sauce is ready. The final touch is a few slices of tart eating apple sweated gently in butter for a couple of minutes, and served separately.

CASSEROLING: unlike chicken, pheasant rarely disappoints me when it arrives in a casserole, though I do prefer dishes in which the birds remain whole until carving time. There are scores of variations on the casserole theme; what seems to be common to most of them is a good choice of compatible vegetables, a light stock, some alcohol (often wine), perhaps a little bacon, a slow to moderate oven (160°C/325°F/Gas Mark 3), a tightly fitting casserole lid, and about 1½ hours' cooking. If you want an excellent recipe spelled out in more detail, see page 285.

FROTHING: this is a traditional English method of browning and crisping the skins of game birds (and other fowl) when they are roasted. The procedure is as follows: when the bird is about 10 minutes from its ETA on the carving dish (which may be about the same time as you decide to remove the bacon with which it has been barded) it should be well basted (with its own fat, or with butter) and lightly dredged with a sprinkling of seasoned flour. Then continue to cook the bird, basting occasionally, until it is browned and done.

NOTE: pheasant, especially casseroled pheasant, is delicious cold. Pheasant stock is a valuable commodity, and is the best possible base for the creamy parsnip soup described on page 117.

Pigeon

Perhaps the hardest-exercising of all birds that are commonly killed for food, the wild pigeon is a little powerhouse of a bird, which means its breast muscles are firm and close-textured, but inclined to be on the tough side. It is worth getting to grips with this problem, because pigeons are cheap, readily available throughout the year, and can be very delicious.

Choosing a pigeon

Young pigeons are more tender and can be roasted. It is not easy to be sure of a pigeon's age, and therefore suitability for roasting, unless you encounter the bird before it is plucked and drawn. In this state you should look for a flexible beak, a thick neck and a supple, pliable breast-bone. You may also perceive the 'flush of youth' in the fine colour of its feathers.

If the bird is 'oven-ready', you still have a bit to go on: try pressing gently to see if the breast-bone is supple. Does the skin look slightly rosy, as if it is stretched from beneath by a plump and youthful breast? Or is it a whitish-grey, slightly wrinkled, contracting over a hard, prominent breast-bone and tough, dark meat? Experience will sharpen your response to these factors, and in time you will be able to tell a youngster even through the clinging cellophane of its supermarket wrapping.

Cooking pigeon

When you have identified a young pigeon, it can be roasted or, if you like the meat very rare, griddled whole on a cast-iron griddle. If you have plenty of pigeons, and you don't feel you have paid too painful a sum for them, you may find serving up the birds is easiest if you just carve the breasts off each one, in whole pieces, and don't worry about fiddling with the rest of the carcase. This meat is dense and rich; I think it is particularly delicious when served on top of a simple salad, perhaps dressed with hazelnut oil, balsamic or raspberry vinegar, and sprinkled with a few *lardons* of pancetta or bacon. One breast, still just a little pink and bloody, cut into 4–5 slices, is a decent first-course portion per person, though it would take two to make a really satisfying main course.

Older pigeons, and indeed birds whose age is in doubt, should be braised or casseroled. The meat is so rich it can be thought of almost as beef, and recipes for stews and *daubes* adapted accordingly. Pigeons can be casseroled whole, then cut in half to make two portions, though very hungry pigeon fans might want a whole one. Cooking for 1½–2 hours, in a slow to moderate oven (160°C/325°F/Gas Mark 3), with wine, vegetables, stock, and with a closely fitting lid, etc., will do the trick. For lovers of details, there is a sound recipe on page 286, adapted from Constance Spry, which has the exciting addition of cherries.

Partridge

Most of what was said of the pheasant applies to the partridge, with suitable allowances made for the fact that the average weight is about half that of a pheasant. The basic parameters then come out as follows:

AGEING: hard and scaly feet indicate an old bird. Like pigeons, young birds should have a pliable breast-bone.

HANGING: about 10 days maximum.

PORTIONS: 1 per person is generous, ½ may be adequate.

ROASTING (young birds): about 30 minutes; bard with bacon, baste well, can be served pink (see PHEASANTS above).

SLOW-COOKING (old birds): casserole or braise, 1½ hours maximum.

ACCOMPANIMENTS: roast partridge is never better than when served with the outer green leaves of a Savoy cabbage. These should be briefly blanched, then heated through in olive oil, in which diced pancetta or bacon, and a few slivers of garlic, have already been nicely browned. A very hot plate is covered with the cabbage, garlic and bacon, and the whole roast partridge goes on top.

Wild duck
(chiefly mallard and teal)

Can be delicious, but can also be very tough and taste slightly fishy. There is always an element of pot luck, dependent on the largely unknown lifestyle of the bird you procure.

HANGING: 3–4 days is normal; maximum a week (a duck, being semi-aquatic in cold waters, contains some bacteria that thrive at low temperatures. It will therefore decompose at a marginally faster rate than other game birds).

PORTIONS: the meat on a wild duck is often scant, and if it is the main feature of a meal I would reckon on ½ a bird per person; teal are smaller, and hearty appetites could manage a whole one.

ROASTING: is appropriate. In a hot oven (220°F/425°F/Gas Mark 7), 40 minutes should be long enough (25 for teal) to serve the birds pink. Bard and baste aplenty and, if you want the skin crispy, froth well. Deglaze the roasting tin with wine and giblet stock to make gravy.

BRAISING: as it is nigh on impossible to age a mallard, unless it is early September and your bird is still clinging to its juvenile plumage, braising may be a better bet.

COOKING TIP: try braising on a bed of sliced celery, flavoured with the juice and grated rind of 1 orange, plus a little extra giblet stock. Braise slowly for 1½ hours, then press all the juices through a sieve, boil to reduce, and whisk in a little butter to thicken. Revitalize with a squeeze of fresh orange, and serve this sauce with the duck.

Grouse

The usual distinction betwteen young and old birds is particularly important with grouse. Any attempt to do battle with an old bird that has been roasted could result in substantial dental bills.

BUYING: prices in August are barmy, but grouse do tend to get a little cheaper as the novelty of the new season wears off. It's worth waiting until mid-October, and then shopping around – though grouse will never be cheap.

AGEING: young grouse have pliable beaks, and their skulls, when pressed firmly with the thumb, will give way – gruesome but telling. Oven-ready grouse cannot be subjected to such tests, but most butchers who stock them should be able to offer you a choice between young and old birds.

HANGING: one week. Young grouse are traditionally parachuted into top restaurants on the Glorious Twelfth, without taking time off to be strung up. Wait a while and you will taste the difference.

PORTIONS: ½–1 per person, depending on greed.

ROASTING (young birds only): 25 minutes, bard, baste and froth. Classically served with fried breadcrumbs, bread sauce and game chips.

CASSEROLE (old birds): casseroled grouse is quite delicious. I like to cook them for upwards of 2 hours in a slow oven (140°C/275°F/Gas Mark 1), so that the meat is really very tender and comes away from the bone. Pick off the lean meat, then strain the liquor, further reduce it, and heat the meat through in this rich gravy. This gives you an approximation of a *salmis*, which is very good accompanied by buttery mashed potatoes and cabbage or celery.

Woodcock and snipe

Highly prized game birds, held to be the most difficult to shoot, woodcock and snipe are barely available on the open market. When procured they should be hung for no more than a week, then roasted with the guts in, traditionally with the head still on and tucked under one wing. Cooking for 10 minutes in a very hot oven (250°C/475°F/Gas Mark 9) is sufficient for the tiny snipe, 15 minutes for the woodcock. Froth if you like. The guts of the cooked bird should be scooped out of its cavity and spread on a piece of fried bread on which the bird is then placed. Two woodcock make a portion; a hearty appetite could probably despatch four snipe. Either bird should be honoured with your best claret.

GROUND GAME

Rabbit

Both farmed and wild rabbits are widely available in butchers and occasionally in supermarkets. There is a notable difference in flavour and texture between the two. As you might expect, farmed rabbits are bred for size rather than flavour. They can weigh as much as 6 lb/2.7 kg (as opposed to a top weight of about 3lb/1.3 kg for a plump wild rabbit). There is plenty of meat on them, which is pale, almost white, and could most politely be described as 'delicate'. I think it is terribly bland, and generally less interesting than a well-chosen chicken. Wild rabbits are a better prospect. They are very cheap, and their close-textured flesh offers interesting and potentially delicious possibilities to the Bon Marché cook.

Choosing a rabbit

Ask your butcher if his rabbits are farmed or wild: if they are farmed, he will undoubtedly tell you that farmed are better – by all means take his word against mine. (But don't say I didn't warn you.) In the supermarket rabbit is sometimes available whole but more often cut into portions; it should be labelled as either wild or farmed. If it isn't, and the label contains no warning that 'this produce may contain lead shot', then assume it is farmed.

The most common way to buy rabbits is whole, but headless, and skinned. All too often the rabbit's liver is not available, having been thrown away when the animal was skinned. This a great shame, as the liver is quite delicious. If you are ordering rabbits in advance it is well worth requesting that the liver be kept for you – and the heart and kidneys, come to that. This little trio of rabbit offal makes a fine salad, if quickly fried, then tossed with some *frisée* and bits of streaky bacon or pancetta.

It is also worth asking for the (skinned) head. Along with the forelegs (on which there is very little meat), the neck and the skinny little flaps that can be trimmed from the lower ends of the rib section, it can be used to make a stock. This can then become the medium for your casserole, or a baste if you are roasting the animal.

The advantage of buying an unskinned rabbit is that you can tell its age. This is important if you are planning to roast it, which requires a young animal. Ragged, blunt claws, worn and broken teeth and tough, leathery ears are signs of an old rabbit, fit only for a long, slow simmer. Smooth, sharp claws are the surest indicators of youth and roastability.

The disadvantage of buying an unskinned rabbit is that you will have to skin it; although you can always ask to inspect your butcher's skin-on rabbit and, having ascertained its age, ask him to skin it for you.

If you shoot a rabbit for the pot yourself, or are given a freshly killed specimen, it should be gutted as soon as possible, then hung for no more than 4 days before skinning. In warm, humid weather 24 hours is enough.

Cooking rabbit

Many old recipes call for wild rabbits to be soaked overnight in acidulated salt water before any cooking is begun. The idea of this is to bleach the flesh and remove any 'gamy' flavour – a crazy notion, in my view, as rabbit is not a strong-tasting meat at the best of times. The idea that the meat is made more attractive by being bleached white, or more palatable by being robbed of its natural taste, is an outdated piece of dainty nonsense, and should be disregarded.

ROASTING: there is very little fat on a rabbit (slightly more in autumn and early winter), which means that any attempt to roast it will be a battle to preserve some juiciness in the meat. If this battle is won, then a roast rabbit is a very fine dish indeed. Constant basting in a moderate to hot oven (190°C/375°F/Gas Mark 5) is the key factor. It is sensible to remove the front legs and roast only the saddle and rather chunkier thighs.

A detailed and delicious recipe for roast rabbit, in which a well-basted beast is finished with a mustard glaze, appears on page 287.

CASSEROLES: long and very gentle cooking, until the meat is flaking off the bone, is a fine way to deal with all except the youngest, tenderest rabbit. The meat should be simply jointed: the legs cut off and the saddle divided cross-wise into 3–4 portions. The front legs may be included in the casserole, or used for stock as I suggested above.

The lack of natural fat means that bacon or pieces of fatty pork belly are a near essential component of most successful rabbit recipes. Wine (red or white) is always appropriate when slow-cooking rabbit; dark beer, such as brown ale or strong bitter, is a traditional English alternative which can produce excellent results. Whenever possible a good stock is infinitely preferable to plain water for covering the meat. If you don't have enough trimmings to make a rabbit stock, then chicken or light veal stock, or even ham stock, will do. The meat should be tightly packed in your cooking pot, and never more than *just* covered by the liquid.

Some recipes stipulate a cooking time of 1–1½ hours for rabbit casseroles, in a moderate oven (180°C/350°F/Gas Mark 4), i.e. at a fairly lively simmer. In my experience rabbit meat cooked in this way, though perfectly pleasant and undoubtedly 'done', tends to be still a bit chewy and clinging to the bone. I prefer a super-tender, flaking consistency which practically falls off the bone and could be eaten with a spoon. This is achieved by bringing the casserole just to boiling point on the hob, then moving it to a slow oven (140°C/275°F/Gas Mark 1), with the lid on the casserole, for 2½–3 hours.

BARBECUING: Whilst grilling is really too dehydrating to be a viable treatment, a dab hand at the barbie, who can keep the meat well basted and the flames low, can do wonderful things to a rabbit. Either a whole rabbit (ideal if your barbecue has a spit attachment), or pieces, can be used. Whatever you decide, the meat should be marinated first, for 3–4 hours, in olive oil with a few crushed garlic cloves and fresh parsley or thyme. Do not use the marinade for basting, though – the oil will drip on to the fire and encourage flames which will burn, rather than grill the meat. A better basting liquid is a strong, well-reduced stock (if not rabbit, then veal or chicken), with a splash of wine and a good dollop of mustard stirred into it. Make sure your grilling rack is a reasonable height above the hot charcoal; the rabbit must cook right through without being scorched on the outside.

Hare

There are two kinds of hare to be found in the British Isles. The brown hare, the larger of the two, is widespread throughout the country. The blue or mountain hare is common only in Scotland, where it greatly outnumbers the brown hare. The blue hare is rather skinny, and though it can be eaten it tends to be tough. The brown hare, on the other hand, is quite one of the most delicious wild creatures you could ever hope to eat. Most butchers in the south deal only in brown hares, though in Scotland and the north of England you might occasionally be offered a choice: go for the brown every time.

Buying a hare

The price of hare may vary considerably according to local availability, but they are rarely expensive. At the time of writing, my local London butcher is selling them for £8·50 a piece – not bad when you consider that a large specimen will feed 8 greedy people.

Many butchers keep hare in the freezer. Like most game, whose meat is always close-textured, it freezes reasonably well, and a defrosted hare would make an okay casserole if very slowly cooked. But fresh is preferable, and essential if you are roasting.

Cooking a hare is a special occasion, and it is worth going to some trouble to get a good specimen. Order it well in advance; be very firm that you want a fresh animal, not a frozen one; request that it should have been hung, undrawn, for at least 10 days, then drawn and skinned on the day you collect; and ask that any blood from the hare should be saved, and given to you along with its liver and kidneys. A lengthy hanging is essential for hare, serving both to tenderize the meat and develop its unique gamy flavour.

If you are given a hare you should hang it head downwards, with a plastic bag over its head, secured around the neck with a rubber band or string, to collect the blood that drips while it is hanging. (The blood is used either to enrich the gravy if you are roasting a hare, or to thicken the liquor in that most brilliant of English dishes, Jugged Hare, see below.) The hare should then be drawn and skinned the day before you want to cook it. Drawing a hare is a smelly business, and skinning it an acquired skill: you may want to take your hare to a butcher to have this done.

Cooking a hare

ROASTING: it is customary to roast only the saddle (i.e. body) of a hare, removing the legs and casseroling them separately (or you can use them in the But'n'Ben's game pie recipe on page 281.) However, if you have many mouths to feed, the back legs (which have plenty of meat on) can be left on for roasting. The saddle alone will serve only 4 at most. Keep the back legs on and it should serve 6–7.

Providing they have been well hung, all but the most ancient of hares can be roasted. However, like rabbits, they must be well protected from drying out. Besides basting during cooking, 24 hours in the general-purpose game marinade (see page 279) beforehand will help to ensure the meat is tender and moist. The hare should be thoroughly wiped free of the marinade, then lightly rubbed with olive oil before roasting. Another trick is to line the inside of the hare with a few rashers of streaky bacon, and have it upside down for the first half of the cooking. Remove the bacon halfway through the cooking, then deglaze the pan with the strained marinade and a little stock or water, and use these juices to baste the hare, now right side up, for the rest of the cooking. Roast hare can be served just a tiny bit pink, which it should be after 35–40 minutes in a fairly hot oven (200°C/400°F/Gas Mark 6).

GRAVY: it is easiest to make the blood gravy in a separate pan. The juices in the roasting tin – thinned with water or stock if they have boiled very dry – should be added slowly and by degrees to the blood, which you have warmed just a little in a small saucepan. Stir constantly, over a low heat, to emulsify this sauce. Add also a little of the excellent red wine that you are proposing to drink with the hare, and 1 tsp redcurrant jelly. Heat this right through, but do not allow to boil. Taste, and season if necessary with salt and pepper, then pour into a warmed sauce-boat and serve.

The Purée of Split Peas and Green Peppercorns on page 323 is an excellent companion to roast hare.

SLOW COOKING: see the recipe on page 283 for Jugged Hare, one of the finest of all English game dishes.

Venison

In this country venison is a generic term for meat that comes from any of our native deer species. Until the early 1980s the supply was limited and seasonal, and venison was pretty certain to come from the annual cull of red deer on Britain's sporting estates, mainly in Scotland. It was expensive and in short supply. Now that venison is widely farmed, it is both affordable and available.

In fact much of the venison sold in this country is still from wild animals, shot as part of a cull. There has been something of a boom in the Scottish deer population in recent years, and the channels that have opened up for the processing and distribution of farmed venison have helped facilitate the marketing of wild deer too. The result is that you may not always know whether your venison is farmed or wild – though if you buy it at the supermarket it is almost sure to be farmed.

The difference between the two is discernible but not huge: both farmed and wild deer graze naturally, and though farmed deer may get supplementary feeds they are not reared at a forced pace – yet. As farmed deer will lead less active lives, and will be slaughtered at a relatively young age, their meat is therefore likely to be slightly more tender. Wild deer, on the other hand, will range more widely and enjoy a mixed diet, so they will have a closer-grained meat, and will perhaps have the edge in flavour.

The cuts of venison are described as for lamb, except for leg and shoulder, which are both described as 'haunch'. Many butchers, and some supermarkets, are now selling venison chops, which are excellent, especially on the barbecue.

The great challenge when cooking venison is to keep the meat tender and moist. Twenty-four hours in the general-purpose game marinade (see page 279) will certainly help. Note that venison will form a natural crust when exposed to the air. This is impermeable and should be trimmed away before the meat is put in the marinade. After that a haunch or loin from a young, farmed deer can be fast-roasted and served just pink, but should be regularly basted with the leftover marinade. Older, wild meat, or any you suspect of being tough, should be slow-braised or casseroled. An excellent 'civet of venison' can

There is an alternative view to this conventional wisdom, one of whose champions is the cookery writer and highlandophile Adrian Gill. He maintains that the best meat for roasting comes from an old stag – provided it is properly hung (for anything up to a month). It should then be well barded with fat, roast fast, and served pink. It should rest for at least half an hour before carving. I have had such a roast cooked by Adrian, and it was indeed fine. The problem is finding venison that has been this well hung. Adrian, of course, hangs his own.

be made by following the recipe on page 283 for Jugged Hare. Use 3½ lb/1.5 kg venison in large dice, instead of the jointed hare, and simply omit the liaison with the blood – the gravy can be thickened with a little *beurre manié* (1 oz/30 g plain flour blended to a paste with 1 oz/30 g soft butter) crumbled and stirred into the liquid towards the end of cooking.

Although venison, being close-textured, freezes reasonably well, roasting is not recommended for a defrosted joint, as the battle to retain moisture is one you are unlikely to win. Braise, or use the meat in a casserole or pie instead.

Roe deer

Besides red deer, farmed or wild, a great number of our smaller native deer, the roe, are shot every year. Unlike the red deer, roe deer are prolific in the south as well as the north of the country – you might find it in farm shops or small butchers around Surrey, Sussex, Hampshire and the New Forest, especially in late summer and autumn.

Roe is a great treat if you can get hold of it – the meat is more tender and less inclined to be dry. From a young animal, it does not need to be marinated, and a shoulder or leg can be roasted fast and served pink, like lamb (you could follow the recipe for 'Weeping' Lamb on page 214). A piece from an older animal should be larded with fat bacon, and gently braised for about 3 hours until completely tender, like lamb *à la cuillère* (see page 201).

Recipes

All-purpose Game Marinade

There is no need to be particularly strict with these proportions, or with the precise combination of herbs, but something along the following lines will 'refresh' defrosted game birds and tenderize and lubricate meat you suspect is in danger of being dry and tough.

Mix the ingredients well and pour over the meat, in a bowl, and cover. Every few hours, turn the meat in the marinade.

5 fl oz/150 ml olive oil
½ bottle good red wine
1 medium onion, sliced
2 garlic cloves, crushed
a few sprigs of thyme
a few twists of black pepper
1 tsp juniper berries (especially for hare and pigeon)

Grilled Chicken with Ginger, Coriander, Chilli, Honey and Roasted Cashews

THE ARK

Serves 8

Joint the chickens into neat pieces, removing excess bones and fat but leaving each joint on its bone with the skin attached. Make a few small incisions in the chicken pieces to help absorb the marinade. Mix all the marinade ingredients together in a large, deep dish, add the chicken pieces and leave them in the marinade for a minimum of 8 hours, or up to 48 hours in the fridge.

The chicken pieces thus marinated can then be cooked on a barbecue, griddle or under a conventional grill. Cook for 20–25 minutes, basting with any leftover marinade and turning frequently until the skin is crisp and golden-brown and the juices run clear when the chicken is pierced with a skewer.

Toast the cashews in a dry frying pan and serve the chicken scattered with the cashews and herbs. Any juices left in the grill pan can be strained and served with the chicken.

2 small fresh free-range chickens

For the marinade
6 fl oz/175 ml olive oil
4 fl oz/100 ml grape-seed oil
4 garlic cloves, crushed
zest and juice of 1 lemon and 1 orange
1 fresh green chilli, de-seeded and finely chopped
1½-in/3.5-cm piece ginger root, peeled and finely grated
1 tbsp coriander seeds, crushed
2 tbsp chopped fresh coriander
1 tbsp runny honey
3 fl oz/75 ml dry sherry
1 fl oz/30 ml sherry vinegar
3 fl oz/75 ml tamari (optional – available from Chinese supermarkets and some delicatessens)

To garnish
3 oz/85 g cashew nuts
1 tbsp chopped fresh parsley
1 tbsp chopped fresh coriander

Confit of Duck with Purée of Split Peas and Green Peppercorns

THE FOX AND GOOSE INN

Serves 4

This dish is most easily made if you buy 2 large ducks, remove the legs, and roast the birds as suggested on page 261. The roasting should give you enough fat to make this confit. The fat, strained through muslin or a clean cotton cloth when hot, can be kept in sealed jars in the fridge for several months.

4 large Barbary duck legs, each about 12 oz/350 g
1 oz/30 g rock salt
1 tsp black pepper
2–3 sprigs of thyme *or* marjoram
2–3 bay leaves, broken
6 garlic cloves, crushed
2 tbsp olive oil
about 2 lb/900 g duck fat, or enough to cover
Purée of Split Peas and Green Peppercorns (page 323), to accompany

Rub the duck legs with the salt, pepper, thyme or marjoram, bay leaves and garlic, and leave for 2 days in a tray or dish in the fridge. Take out and scrape off all these seasonings and reserve.

Heat the olive oil in a heavy pan over a moderate heat, and brown the duck legs thoroughly, skin-side down first and then all over. Put the legs into an ovenproof dish in which they fit as closely as possible, with the seasoning scrapings and enough fat to cover, or almost cover, the meat. Then cook for about 2 hours in a pre-heated slow oven (150°C/300°F/Gas Mark 2) until the meat is nearly falling from the bone.

Remove from the oven and leave to cool. Put the duck legs into a larger kilner jar, or similar, or into a plastic tub with a lid, with enough fat to cover completely and seal the meat from the air. Thus preserved, the confit will keep for several weeks in a cool larder, or up to 3 months in the fridge.

When the confit is to be served, remove the duck legs from the container and scrape off most (not all) of the fat (rendered and filtered it can be used again). Place the legs skin-side down in a roasting tray. Put into a pre-heated hot oven (230°C/450°F/Gas Mark 8) for 4 minutes, drain off the melted fat, then return to the oven for a further 4 minutes, skin-side up, until piping hot and crispy.

Serve with Purée of Split Peas and Green Peppercorns (page 323).

Game Pie

The quantity below makes two 10-in/30-cm pies, each of which will serve 6. Margaret Horn writes: 'I use deep-pan pizza tins to get the right depth.'

First make the pastry. Toss the fat in the flour with the salt until coated, then mix with just enough water to get a medium-firm dough, with large pieces of the fat still intact in it. On a floured board, shape the dough by hand into a rectangle, and roll out with a well-floured rolling pin to about ½ in/1 cm, keeping the dough as near rectangular as possible. Turn one-third over from the top, fold the bottom third over that, turn the whole block a half-turn to the right and roll away from you into another rectangle. Repeat this procedure, folding and turning, at least four times, preferably six to eight. Fold up for a final time and chill for 1 hour before rolling out and using.

To prepare the pie filling, joint and trim the rabbits and pheasant, and cut the pigeons in half. Toss these pieces in the seasoned flour, shaking off any excess. Heat the dripping or oil in a large saucepan, add the game, and turn until all the pieces are well browned. Add the vegetables and the herbs and pour over enough cold water to cover. Bring to the boil, skim, and simmer gently for about 1 hour. Remove all the pieces of game and cut off all the meat in reasonable-sized chunks. Set the meat aside, and return the bones to the still-simmering pot.

Roll out the pastry and line two 10-in/30-cm pie dishes right to the edges. Fill to the top with the meat, and pour over each 2–3 ladles of stock from the pot. Brush the edges of the pastry with beaten egg yolk and cover the pies with pastry lids cut to shape, crimping the edges with your fingers to seal. Brush the top of the pies with the remaining egg yolk, and bake in a pre-heated moderate to hot oven (190°C/375°F/Gas Mark 5) for 45–50 minutes.

While the pies are baking, strain the remaining stock, transfer to a clean pan, and boil to reduce for a gravy to serve with the pies.

The But'n'Ben's
Ruff Puff Pastry
1 lb/450 g butter or lard, cut into small pieces
2 lb/900 g plain flour
a pinch of salt
iced water
1 egg yolk, beaten, to glaze

For the filling
2 oven-ready young wild rabbits
1 oven-ready large pheasant
3 oven-ready wood pigeons (Cushie Doos)
2 oz/60 g plain flour
salt and black pepper
2 tbsp dripping or oil
3 carrots, cut into large pieces
¼ large neep (turnip), cut into 2–3 pieces
1 large onion, quartered
2 celery sticks, cut into short lengths
a bouquet garni of mixed fresh herbs, including bay, parsley, sage, thyme

Hot Game Pie with a Suet Crust

THE WHITELEAF AT CROYDE

Serves 4-6

David Wallington writes: 'Wild game in fur or feather is one of nature's gifts and something we cook at the Whiteleaf as often as our customers will bear and our budget can afford. Game pies, both hot and cold, are always a Christmas project both for the menu and family presents. Accumulation of the ingredients starts on "Glorious 12th" halfway through August. A badly shot grouse, the legs of wild ducks and pheasants when the breasts are served separately, the forends of rabbits and hares and the occasional marked-down bargain off a supermarket shelf: any combination of meats can be used but a good basic mixture would be equal parts of pheasant, rabbit and venison. Allow 6–8 oz/170–225 g raw trimmed meat per person. If buying whole birds calculate half of the weight as meat. Once all the ingredients are acquired allow several days to make the pie and fit in with other jobs in the kitchen.'

2 lb/900 g mixed game meat, well trimmed and cut into bite-sized chunks

For the marinade
½ small onion, sliced
2 slices orange
2 slices lemon
2–3 parsley stalks
3–4 small sprigs of thyme
2 bay leaves
2 juniper berries, crushed
6 black peppercorns
5 fl oz/150 ml red wine

Place all the ingredients for the marinade in a pan and simmer for 10 minutes. Allow to cool, then pour over the meat in a dish and leave in a cool place for 24 hours, turning once or twice.

To make the stock, place the bones, meat and vegetables in a roasting tin with the oil. Roast in a pre-heated moderate oven (180°C/350°F/Gas Mark 4), turning occasionally until well browned (about 45 minutes). Lift the bones, meat and vegetables from the roasting tin into a saucepan, tip off the fat and reserve. Deglaze the tin with a few tbsp red wine and tip into the saucepan. Cover the contents with approx 2 pts (1.1 litres) water and simmer very gently for about 3 hours until the meat and bones are disintegrating. Strain off the liquid, cool and refrigerate overnight. Remove any accumulated surface fat, lift the meat from the marinade and set aside, and tip the vegetables and liquids into the stock. Simmer gently until reduced by half to a rich gravy stock, adjust the seasoning and strain through a sieve.

To prepare the pie filling, dry the marinated meat very thoroughly with kitchen paper and brown all over, quickly, in the oil.

Strain off any fat and reserve. Deglaze the pan with a little red wine and pour over the meat in a saucepan. Cover with the strained stock, bring to the boil and simmer, covered, for about 1½ hours. Test the meat for doneness and if necessary continue cooking until tender but still firm. Lift out the meat and strain the stock through muslin or a clean cotton cloth.

Place approximately ¾ oz/20 g of the reserved fat in a saucepan, melt and cook gently for a few minutes to drive off any moisture. Add the plain flour and cook to a mahogany-brown, stirring occasionally. Reheat the stock and off the heat add, with a splash of wine, to the cooked flour mixture. Stir thoroughly, scraping round the edges of the pan to remove all the flour, and bring to the boil, whisking all the time, then simmer for 10 minutes. Strain through a sieve over the meat, return to the pan and leave over a low heat for 10 minutes. Allow to cool, then refrigerate if you are not going to assemble the pie straightaway.

Place the meat filling in a medium pie dish around a support for the pastry (e.g. an egg-cup), if necessary.

To make the suet crust, rub the butter into the flour with the salt, mix in the suet, add 6 tbsp water and mix to a soft dough, adding more water if required. Roll out and cut to the shape of the pie dish and refrigerate for 20 minutes. Brush the edge of the pie dish with beaten egg and line it with pastry trimmings. Brush the pastry rim with beaten egg, and carefully place on the pastry lid, sealing the edges. Trim, flute and decorate, but do not make an air hole. Brush the pie with beaten egg and bake in a pre-heated hot oven (200°C/400°F/Gas Mark 6) for 30 minutes or until risen and golden-brown.

For the game stock
1–1½ lb/450-675 g game
    bones and/or trimmings or
    8 oz/225 g game meat, plus
    poultry bones and/or a pork
    hock
I onion, sliced
I carrot, sliced
2 celery sticks, sliced
the vegetables and liquid from
    the marinade
I tbsp olive oil
red wine
salt and black pepper

To finish the filling
2 tbsp olive oil
a little red wine
¾ oz/20 g plain flour

For the suet crust
2 oz/60 g butter
8 oz/225 g self-raising flour
I tsp salt
4 oz/115 g shredded beef suet
6–8 tbsp cold water
beaten egg, to glaze

Jugged Hare
Serves 8-10

This is one of the most magnificent of all game dishes, and one which deserves to be made with, and accompanied by, a top-quality red wine, ideally a Médoc. You will probably have to order a hare from your butcher. When you do so, mention that you intend to jug it, and ask him to save the blood and the liver. It is also worth specifying that you want an animal that has been well hung, and definitely not frozen.

1 large brown hare, skinned, plus its blood and liver
4 oz/115 g smoked streaky bacon
2 tbsp olive oil
1 rounded tbsp plain flour
6 oz/170 g mushrooms, sliced
1 oz/30 g butter
2 squares bitter chocolate
salt and black pepper

For the marinade
27-fl-oz/75-cl bottle good red wine
4 fl oz/100 ml brandy
3 garlic cloves, crushed
5–6 shallots, sliced
a few sprigs of thyme
a few sprigs of parsley
2 bay leaves
8 black peppercorns

Joint the hare with a heavy knife or meat cleaver, cutting off its legs and dividing the saddle into 5–6 pieces (or you can ask your butcher to do this). Put these pieces in a deep dish. Combine all the marinade ingredients and pour over the hare: cover, and leave in a cool place overnight.

Start to prepare the dish about 3 hours before you intend to eat it. Chop the bacon into ½-in/1-cm pieces and sweat for a few minutes in the oil in a large pan. Remove the pieces of hare from the marinade and wipe dry with a clean cloth. Add the hare to the bacon and cook gently for a few minutes, turning the pieces until they are nicely browned.

Sprinkle over the flour, cook for a further few minutes, then pour over the marinade, adding a little water if this is needed to cover the meat. Season with salt and pepper, and bring the pan to a gentle simmer. Cover and cook over a gentle heat, or in a slow oven (150°C/300°F/Gas Mark 2), for 1½–2 hours. In a separate pan, gently fry the mushrooms in the butter for a few minutes, and add them to the hare for the last 30 minutes of cooking. The hare is cooked when the meat is quite tender and begins to come away from the bone.

The final stage is to make a liaison of the blood, the liver and the cooking liquid. This has to be done carefully if the sauce is not to separate, but even if it does it is only the appearance, not the flavour, that is affected. I find this stage is most easily accomplished if you remove the pieces of hare from the pot to a warmed dish. Chop the liver very finely (use a mezzaluna if you have one). Spoon a little of the cooking liquid into the blood to both warm and thin it, and stir well. Off the heat add the chopped liver and chocolate to the pot. Then ladle in the warmed blood, a little at a time, stirring as you go. When the liaison is smooth and well blended, return to the heat and bring back to the boil. Return the pieces of hare and allow to bubble merrily for just 1–2 minutes before serving.

The dish is so substantial that I don't like to serve vegetables with it, but pieces of fried white bread are traditional, and excellent for mopping up the sauce.

Pheasant Casseroled with Bacon
Serves 3-4

This is an excellent way to cook a big old bird, or one which has been defrosted. A big bird will just about serve 4, but 2 smaller birds will easily be consumed by 6 hungry mouths. If you use 2 pheasants, do not double the quantities of the other ingredients, but increase by one-third to a half. It's best to over- rather than under-estimate how much pheasant you need as, cooked in this way, it is delicious cold.

Choose a pot into which your pheasant or pheasants fit neatly without too much room to spare.

Cut the bacon into 1-in/2.5-cm pieces. Heat the oil in a frying pan and fry the bacon or pancetta gently for a few minutes. After it has released plenty of its fat, but before it gets crispy, remove with a slotted spoon and transfer to the pot. Brown the pheasant on all sides in the sizzling fat, then place breast-side up in the pot. Add the carrots and onion to the frying pan and fry until they begin to take a little colour. Spoon these into the pot around the sides of the pheasant. Add the wine, stock, herbs and garlic to the pot, with 1 tsp salt and a few twists of pepper. The liquid need not cover the pheasant completely, but should come about two-thirds up the sides of the bird – add a little more stock or water if you need to. Bring to a gentle simmer, cover and cook for 1¼ hours. Remove the bird, pouring any juice from the cavity back into the pot. Remove and discard the parsley and bay leaf.

Carve the bird into good-sized portions rather than thin slices – half a breast and a good piece of leg or a whole wing per person. Spoon the bacon and vegetables, and plenty of juice from the pot, over each portion. Serve with mashed potatoes and either braised celery (see page 63) or Savoy cabbage or winter greens braised for just a few minutes in a ladleful of the juices from the pot.

1 large oven-ready pheasant
8 oz/225 g streaky bacon *or* pancetta, cut into thick slices
1 tbsp dripping *or* olive oil
2 carrots, sliced
1 large onion, sliced
1 wine-glass white wine
10 fl oz/300 ml stock (made with the pheasant's giblets)
1 bay leaf
a small bunch of parsley
1 garlic clove
salt and black pepper

Slow-cooked Pigeons Finished with Cherries
Serves 4

This is a good dish for any pigeon, but particularly those which may be on the old side, or have been frozen. I like the garnish of cherries (a suggestion from Constance Spry) but they are by no means essential. A good alternative is to serve the pigeons with Sweet Onion Confit (page 112). I like a whole pigeon to myself, but half a bird may satisfy more meagre appetites.

2 tbsp bacon fat *or* olive oil
4 oven-ready pigeons
4 shallots *or* 1 medium onion, thinly sliced
1 rounded tbsp plain flour
a bouquet garni
2 pts/1.1 litres chicken *or* veal stock
2 tsp red *or* white wine vinegar
1 tsp redcurrant jelly
salt and black pepper
8 oz/225 g stoned red cherries
1 oz/30 g butter

Heat the fat or oil in a large casserole and brown the pigeons well on all sides. Remove the pigeons and split in half down the breast-bone with a heavy knife. From each half trim the wings and the back-bone.

Add the shallots or onion to the fat in the casserole and fry until soft and lightly coloured. Sprinkle in the flour, stir well, and cook for 1–2 minutes. Return the pigeons to the casserole, packing them in closely, add the bouquet garni and pour over enough stock to cover them completely. Cover the casserole and simmer gently over a low heat, or in a slow to moderate oven (150°C/300°F/Gas Mark 2) for 1½ hours. Test with a skewer that the meat is tender (very old birds may need a further 30 minutes). Remove the birds from the casserole and place in a covered dish to keep warm.

Strain the cooking juices through a sieve into a clean pan, and add the vinegar and redcurrant jelly. Boil over a high heat to reduce to a light, syrupy consistency. Season with salt and black pepper.

While the sauce is reducing, sweat the cherries gently in the butter in a small saucepan until the juices start to run – this takes just a few minutes. Serve the pigeons on well-warmed plates, pouring plenty of sauce over them, and spooning the cherries on top. I like to serve this dish with fresh peas or beans and potato crisps.

Roast Rabbit with a Mustard Glaze

Serves 6

A roast rabbit that is not tough or dry is quite an achievement. Constant basting is the secret in this recipe – the vigilance is well worthwhile.

Cut the front legs off the rabbits, and the heads if they are still attached (if not, make sure the butcher gives them to you anyway). Put the heads, front legs and any giblets or trimmings into a large saucepan with the carrot, onion and bay leaf and barely cover with water. Simmer gently for 1 hour, then strain this stock through muslin or a clean cotton cloth, and reduce by boiling to a scant 10 fl oz/300 ml.

Meanwhile mix the glass of wine, oil, sugar and thyme with 2 tbsp of the mustard, and pour this marinade over the rabbits in a dish. Turn them in the marinade to make sure they are well coated, and leave for 4–6 hours.

Remove the rabbits from the marinade, wipe dry, and spread the remaining mustard evenly over them. Add 2 tbsp of the stock to the marinade and mix well – this gives you your basting liquid. Place the rabbits in a roasting tin and spoon the basting liquid over them. Roast in a pre-heated fairly hot oven (200°C/400°F/Gas Mark 6) for 30–35 minutes, basting regularly with the liquid in the tin – every 5 minutes is not excessive. Season the rabbits with salt and pepper about halfway through cooking.

After 30 minutes the rabbits should be well browned and glistening. Pierce the meat with a skewer. If the juices run clear, it is ready. If they are still pink it needs a few minutes more.

Transfer the rabbits to a carving dish and place the roasting tin over a low heat. Make a gravy by deglazing the tin first with a little red wine, then the remaining stock. Scrape the tin well with a palette knife to remove any tasty morsels of browned meat. I prefer a thin gravy, but you can thicken it with flour if you like. Season to taste with salt and pepper, then strain into a warmed sauce-boat.

Carve the rabbits and bring the gravy to the table. Celeriac Gratin (page 106) goes particularly well with this dish.

2 young oven-ready rabbits
I carrot, roughly chopped
I small onion, roughly chopped
I bay leaf
I wine-glass red wine, plus extra for deglazing the roasting tin
2 tbsp olive oil
2 tsp brown sugar
a few sprigs of fresh thyme
3 tbsp strong mustard (English or Dijon)
salt and black pepper
I oz/30 g plain flour (*optional*)

CHAPTER SEVEN

Pulses, Grains, Pasta and Nuts

The foods described in this chapter are all seeds or their derivatives, one of the oldest forms of food for man, and indeed many other animals. It is hardly a surprise that they are such a popular food for so many species: providing nutrition, albeit for the plants they are meant to germinate, is exactly what seeds are designed to do. To this end they are, uniquely among vegetables, high in protein as well as carbohydrates.

One of the great virtues of seeds is that they can be stored for very long periods of time – in some cases, and under the right conditions, almost indefinitely. This means that, from the shoppers' point of view, they are a dream.

Another quality of seeds, and one which is inclined to get lost in a celebration of their remarkable biological properties, is the huge range of tastes and textures they offer the cook, often at remarkably little cost. Meat-eaters have tended to be very lazy about exploring the full range of culinary possibilities offered by seeds, and have much to learn from vegetarians and those cultures for whom meat has always been a scarce and expensive luxury.

Pulses

Pulses, or 'legumes' as the Americans like to call them, are the edible seeds of leguminous plants that include beans, peas and lentils. Some, as we saw in the Vegetable chapter, are most commonly eaten fresh – peas and broad beans, for example. But a far greater number of species are dried, in which form they have been a staple food in many parts of the world for thousands of years. Today they still feature strongly in the cooking of Asia, the Middle East, the Caribbean, Central and South America.

Pulses are a relatively recent addition to the European diet: the broad bean and the pea were the only varieties known before the discovery of the New

World. Even now, despite the wide availability of many kinds of pulse, we lag behind the rest of the world in appreciation and application of these ingredients in our gastronomy. Perhaps this is because we are so spoiled by the ready availability of fresh meats and vegetables – in quantity if not in quality. But it seems we are just beginning to catch up, largely thanks to the influence of the ethnic communities in our major cities.

It is the very healthiness of high-protein pulses and roughage-rich grains that has, in some quarters, given them a bad name. For non-meat-eaters they are staples. Hence over-enthusiastic carnivores disparagingly refer to them as 'hippie food'. Such pulse detractors apparently believe that all pulses have the same taste and texture – bland and mealy – an absurdly narrow view which would easily be corrected by a comparative tasting of a few varieties, simply boiled, for example aduki beans, green split peas and Puy lentils. And of course simply boiled pulses are just the tip of the iceberg: they can be used in casseroles and salads, made into purées and soups, fritters and cakes, even pastries.

Add to their inherent qualities the effects that can be achieved by the addition of other ingredients – meat, vegetables, herbs and spices, whose flavours are absorbed very readily by most varieties of pulse – and it soon becomes clear just how exciting this group of foods can be, not just as the focal point of vegetarian dishes but also as an adjunct to meat and fish.

Choosing pulses

Pulses are not hard to come by; even the 'speciality' pulses associated with Asian, Oriental and South American cookery are easily found in ethnic grocers, often in supermarkets and health food shops too. Selection presents few problems for the Bon Marché cook: many recipes can be adapted to whatever beans are available, or appeal to the whim of the shopper on the spur of the moment. As a general rule, if you are cooking pulses in a spicy or aromatic liquid, as in a casserole, it is a good idea to choose mild-flavoured beans which cook to a soft, mealy texture – they will absorb the cooking juices and become impregnated with flavour. Good examples of such pulses would be chick-peas, yellow split peas, green or brown lentils, and beans such as the red kidney, white kidney (cannellini), butter bean (lima), black-eye, white haricot, navy bean, mung bean and black bean.

Dried pulses are a nigh-on indestructible product with a very long shelf-life. They therefore present few pitfalls for the shopper. It is always worth checking that the sell-by-date has at least a few months left to run, as even dried pulses do not last absolutely for ever, and very old specimens take an age to cook. Apart from that, I have only one tip: packets of mixed pulses and those which bear a label saying 'Product of more than one country' are perhaps best avoided, unless you anticipate a very long cooking time. Pulses of varying origin are likely to vary in age, and, like pulses in a mixed batch, will have varying cooking times. Some may still be tough by the time others are tender.

Storing pulses

Airtight jars are the best way of storing pulses, and have the added bonus of making a kitchen shelf look attractive and full of promise. Make sure your jars are scrupulously clean and dry before you add your pulses. Do not leave open packets of pulses around for too long, especially in damp weather, or they will soon start to soften and become vulnerable to moulds and weevils.

Basic preparation of pulses

Bits of grit and small stones can occasionally find their way into packets of imported pulses. They should always be thoroughly rinsed, even if soaking is not required, and picked over for potential tooth-breakers.

There are numerous ways of serving pulses but the same basic preparation is common to nearly all of them. Being dried, they must be reconstituted. In all except a few cases this involves soaking the pulses in cold water for several hours prior to cooking. 'Soak overnight' is the instruction most commonly given, but if you put your pulses to soak first thing in the morning, they will be ready for cooking 8 or so hours later, by early evening. If you want to accelerate the process, pour boiling water over them and leave covered for only 3 hours.

Pulses must always be thoroughly cooked, or they can be very indigestible and, in some cases, slightly toxic. The safest way to reduce such risks is to bring them to the boil and let them bubble pretty fiercely for 10 minutes, before cooking for an hour or longer at a more gentle simmer, until they are completely tender. If the beans are to be slowly cooked in a casserole or soup, then it is advisable to give them this 10-minute rapid boil before combining them with the other ingredients.

Some beans will give off a pale scum while simmering; this is harmless if white but should be skimmed off if it looks at all grubby.

Cooking times

It is almost impossible to give precise cooking times for dried pulses – variety, age and the conditions under which they have been stored will all have an effect. Only lentils can be cooked in much less than an hour. Older, tougher beans may take 2–3 hours. Generally, split pulses without their skins will cook more quickly, and are easier to cook to a purée. You will have to test your pulses at intervals while they cook – cool them with water or your own breath and bite to test for tenderness. If they are still very hard you should spit them out – even a single underdone kidney bean can cause stomach aches.

The chemistry of cooking pulses

Salt in the cooking water can make the skins of pulses very tough and prevent them from becoming quite tender. It is therefore best not to add salt until about 10 minutes before the end of cooking time. Similarly, highly acidic ingredients such as chillis, vinegar and lemon juice should not be added to a pulse dish until the pulses are already tender: acid inhibits the breakdown of materials in the cell walls, and no amount of boiling will further soften your beans once the cooking liquid has been made acidic.

It is also inadvisable to boil your pulses in huge amounts of water: the amount of protein and carbohydrate, and no doubt taste too, lost to the water will increase as the volume of water increases. Add enough water to be fairly confident that the pulses are in no danger of boiling dry, say about four times the volume of your beans, and no more. Be vigilant and you can always top up the water if it gets dangerously low.

Ways to serve pulses

As a vegetable

Many pulses have a distinctive enough taste or texture to be served whole, hot and unadulterated, except perhaps for a knob of butter or a light dressing of oil or herbs, as a vegetable to accompany a dish of meat or fish. There are various proven combinations popular in certain regional dishes: from the south of France, flageolet beans with roast lamb; from Tuscany, cannellini beans with cotechino sausage; and from the north of England, pease pudding with boiled bacon. Puy lentils dressed with olive oil and parsley are particularly good with fish, especially salmon and bass. Other suggestions are given in the alphabetical guide below.

Salads

Many types of cooked pulse are very good cold, particularly those that keep their shape when tender. A sharp dressing or combination with salty meats or fish can contrast beautifully with their mild flavour and creamy texture. See below for suggestions.

Casseroles

With meat or simply with other vegetables, pulses added to casseroles dramatically increase both their nutritional value and their ability to fill hungry stomachs, so that any pulse-laden casserole is likely to be, to coin a popular kitchen phrase, 'a meal in itself'. Classic pulse-based casseroles are the Mexican chilli-con-carne, made with red kidney beans; North American Boston Baked Beans, classically made with a variety of white haricot bean called the pearl haricot or navy bean (see page 298); and the *cassoulets* of south-west France, made with the larger white haricots (for the definitive wisdom on *cassoulets*, see Elizabeth David's *French Provincial Cooking*).

But there is no need to restrict yourself to the classics, or even to existing recipes. Pulses are highly adaptable and lend themselves well to experimentation. Spicy sausages, salted and smoked meats combine particularly well with rich creamy beans; garlic, olive oil and herbs make fine basic flavourings for a simple vegetable-based casserole; and once you are in the realm of cooking pulses with Asian spices the possibilities are endless.

Purées

Some pulses, such as yellow and green split peas, red and brown lentils, and skinless mung beans, disintegrate naturally to a purée when cooked. It is important not to cook them in too much water, or the purée will be thin and watery. Other pulses can be cooked until completely tender, then drained and mashed or puréed in a food processor. Thick purées, enriched with a little oil, butter or meat juices, make a good accompaniment to meat, particularly game: the absorbent properties of the pulses are especially good for mopping up the flavoursome juices.

Soups, fritters and dips

Purées can be thinned with stock and supplemented with other ingredients to make robust soups; thickened with egg and perhaps flour and fried to make fritters and croquettes (see page 322); or beaten with oil, herbs and other flavourings to make dips and spreads, such as hummus (page 300), or the garlic and broad bean paste described below (page 297).

Sprouting pulses

Bean sprouts, usually sprouted from soy beans, can be bought from almost every greengrocer, but they always seem to me to be over-sprouted and watery, sometimes tasting faintly of chlorine. They are nothing like as good as home-sprouted beans, fresh, crispy and still sporting a nutty-tasting piece of bean husk.

Mung beans are my favourites, but most small beans, and even lentils and chick-peas, can be sprouted at home. Some take a little longer than others, and require more watering, but the basic procedure is the same.

Soak 8 oz/225 g dried mung beans overnight in cold water and then rinse in clean water. Spread a wet cotton tea-towel, or a double thickness of clean wet J-cloths, on a tray. Scatter the mung beans over it; they can be touching but should not be more than one layer thick. Place the tray in a warm dark place, such as an airing cupboard, for 3–4 days, re-wetting the cloth with lukewarm water morning and evening. Before each watering give the tray a good shake, or gently rub the sprouts with your fingers, to make sure they do not take root in the cloth. In 3–4 days the beans should have good 1-in/2.5-cm sprouts, while still retaining a little of the nutty kernal. This is when I like to harvest them, though they can be left for a few days more until completely sprouted.

They should be rinsed again briefly before use. Then stir-fry, or use raw in salads (see page 104 for my favourite bean sprout recipe).

ALPHABETICAL GUIDE TO PULSES

The following is not comprehensive – there are literally hundreds of different pulses in culinary use throughout the world – but it is, I hope, a reasonably up-to-date reflection of what is currently available in this country.

Beans

ADUKI BEAN (aka ADZUKI): small, shiny and dark red, these beans have a distinctive, slightly sweet taste and are tender and creamy when cooked. This is the bean from which the Chinese make a paste for use in confectionery. It is also excellent in savoury dishes – try it in a clear soup made with chicken stock and a mirepoix of onion, celery and carrot.

BLACK BEAN: a black variety of the kidney bean, with similar character. Slightly sweet, it helps to thicken the liquid it cooks in. It cooks to a rich chocolate-brown, giving the characteristic colour to *fejoida*, the national dish of Brazil, a stew of black beans and mixed meats (among them, traditionally, a pig's ear and tail). Not as easily found in this country as the red kidney bean, it is *the* bean of Central and South America.

BLACK-EYED BEAN (aka COW PEA): small, grey-white beans with a distinctive black mark around the hilum (where the bean attached to its pod), these have come to be identified with 'soul food' dishes of the American Deep South, classically cooked with salt pork and Tabasco. They have a mild flavour and a good floury texture which absorbs other flavours well. A fine all-rounder.

BORLOTTI BEAN: another variation on the kidney bean, this pretty bean is creamy white to pale pink with dark purple-brown speckles. Popular in Italy, where it is widely grown, this bean is marginally less floury than the white cannellini, and is often used in soups and salads.

BROAD BEAN (aka FAVA): old fat broad beans are often dried, in which form they vary in colour from white to beige to dark brown. They will never regain the glory of their lost youth, but they make a very nice purée if cooked until completely soft, skinned, then puréed with plenty of garlic, lemon juice, black pepper and the very best olive oil. Serve cold as a dip with crudités, warm crusty bread and parma ham.

CANNELLINI: a white type of kidney bean, of good flavour, these are the most popular bean of Italy, usually cooked until creamy soft with plenty of garlic, olive oil and chopped fresh flat-leaf parsely. The simplest of bean soups is made by preparing just such a mixture, mashing some of the beans to a purée, then thinning with a little water or stock. It should be very garlicky, very oily and very thick.

FLAGEOLET: this pale green bean is one of the aristocrats of the dried pulses. It has a fine fresh taste and delicate texture even when reconstituted from dried. It is therefore a good bean for serving as a vegetable accompaniment.

Cooked flageolets are especially good served with lamb: heat through in a little of the cooking juice from the lamb, with an extra sprig of rosemary and a crushed garlic clove. Flageolets can also be served cold in salads, with a simple vinaigrette and slices of raw sweet onion, or better still, Sweet Onion Confit (page 112).

FUL MEDAMES: often spelled foul medames, which is hardly a good marketing ploy, these small, round, nut-brown beans are widely grown in Egypt and eaten all over the Middle East. Puréed and mixed with eggs, garlic and cumin, they are made into little cakes, which are either baked or deep-fried like felafel (see page 300). They can also be used like kidney beans in casseroles and soups, or cooked in tomato sauce. In ethnic grocers they are widely available, and not at all bad canned as well as dried.

HARICOT BEAN (aka WHITE BEAN): grown widely in France, but also in America, this is the principal ingredient of the French *cassoulet*, ideal because it is mild and creamy and absorbs plenty of fat and flavour from the meat and other ingredients. A smaller, rounder type of haricot, also known as the NAVY BEAN because of its one-time importance in provisions in the American navy, is the bean most widely used for canning in tomato sauce. It also goes to make a superb dish which is a forerunner of the canned baked bean, called Boston Baked Beans (see page 319).

LAB LAB BEAN: a member of the hyacinth family, this is another versatile bean eaten widely in Asia and Arab countries. It has a tough skin and requires long soaking and cooking to become completely tender. Alternatively, but laboriously, the beans can be shelled before cooking. It is a good all-rounder, particularly for including in casseroles with meat which requires long, slow cooking.

LIMA BEAN (aka BUTTER BEAN): pale green or cream-coloured, this is among the largest of the beans, being similar in shape and size, though slightly more regular, than the broad bean. Like flageolets, lima beans have a distinctive and pleasant taste which justifies serving them as a vegetable on their own. They are very good in salads, with canned tuna, onions, and a lemon and olive oil dressing, and also combine well with tomatoes – either cold in salads or hot in tomato sauce. Cooked lima beans are very good reheated in the tomato sauce described on page 100.

MUNG BEAN (aka MOONG DAL): these little olive green beans are one of my favourites. They are available split and skinless, in which form they can be cooked to a purée fairly quickly. I prefer them whole, either cooked with onions and a few curry spices, or just plain and buttered, when their mild creamy taste can be appreciated in isolation. In India they are often added to vegetable curries. They are also the best pulses for sprouting (see page 296, and recipe on page 104).

PIGEON PEA (aka GUNGA PEA): falsely called a pea, because of their shape, these pretty cream and pink beans are a staple in the Caribbean, where they are often cooked with rice and onions, and in speciality soups, such as jug jug, a Caribbean version of Scotch broth.

PINTO BEAN: another type of kidney bean, prettier than the ordinary red one because of their dappled beige and purple-brown colouring. They look lovely in the jar, but lose their variegated pattern in cooking, becoming as indistinguishable in colour as in taste from the regular red kidney bean.

RED KIDNEY BEAN: perhaps the most successful of the imported dried beans, red kidney beans vary in colour from pinkish-brown to dark maroon. They have a mild, slightly sweet taste and a good floury texture which will absorb plenty of liquid and flavours from the other ingredients with which they are cooked. They are commonly used in such highly spiced dishes as chilli con carne, but stand up for themselves in milder combinations, such as Noel Asbourne's Aztec Soup (page 319).

SOY BEAN: soy beans are the most widely grown of all the pulses, and are now the USA's single biggest cash crop. This, as you can probably guess from the relative scarcity of the dried bean product on our shop shelves, has little to do with the eating qualities of the bean in its natural state, and everything to do with the other uses to which it is put. Soy beans are used to make tofu (bean curd), soy sauce and innumerable texturized meat substitutes; they are processed into cooking oil, a milk substitute, and even used in industrial processes such as the manufacture of plastics. As far as the home cook is concerned, soy sauce and tofu are of more interest than the unprocessed dried bean, which is mild and bland, though perfectly pleasant and palatable if added to a well-flavoured casserole.

URD BEAN: small black-skinned beans, often sold split and skinless, in which form they cook to a creamy white purée. They are much used in curries and rice dishes in India and the Far East.

Lentils and Peas

Lentils are the only pulse which do not require soaking before cooking. They should, however, be thoroughly rinsed.

BROWN LENTIL: the whole red lentil with the seed coat still intact. Brown lentils take longer to cook but keep their shape better and have a pleasant nutty taste. Also good for curries.

CHICK-PEAS: one of the most versatile of all pulses, the chick-pea is also, after the soy bean, the most widely cultivated: in India almost as much land is devoted to growing chick-peas as to growing wheat. The two recipes most familiar to the English both come from the Eastern Mediterranean. Hummus is easily made by blending 8 oz/225 g cooked chick-peas with 2 crushed garlic cloves, the juice of 1 lemon, 2 tbsp tahina (sesame seed paste, see page 317), a good pinch of cayenne pepper and enough olive oil to make a smooth paste. This is the classic recipe, but it can be infinitely varied – I like it without tahina and with plenty of chopped fresh coriander. Curry spices can also be added.

Felafel is the classic Arab preparation of chick-peas: a thick purée of ground, part-cooked chick-peas mixed with garlic, onion, plenty of finely chopped parsley, ground cumin and coriander, a good pinch of cayenne pepper and baking powder (1 tsp per lb/450 g chick-peas). The mixture is formed into small cakes and deep-fried until golden and crisp, classically served stuffed into pitta bread with tomatoes and peppers, cucumber and yoghurt raita, and a dollop of tahina. It seems to be catching on as a takeaway food in London, which is no surprise as it is completely delicious.

Chick-peas are also ground to produce the versatile flour known as gram flour. This is used in numerous savoury cakes and pasties in the Middle East and India, and in particular to make the pastry for samosas, which are then deep-fried.

GREEN LENTIL: varying in colour from grey-green to brownish-yellow, this is the largest and flattest of the lentils. Green lentils can be cooked for a long time until soft and mushy, when they can be beaten to a purée; but they are also very good if cooked in stock or with vegetables in the water until just tender, so keeping their shape. In this way they can be served warm as a vegetable with roast meat and game.

GREEN PEA: peas grown for drying are a slightly different variety from those grown in the garden for eating fresh. Nevertheless if you have a surfeit of peas, on the overgrown side, they can easily be dried – just leave them on a tray in the airing cupboard or some other warm, dry place, until completely hard. Dried peas are available whole or split without the seed covering. Whole will require a long soak; for split peas it is not essential to soak them, but they will cook much quicker if you do.

Split peas cook to a purée from which warming soups and the traditional English dish of pease pudding can be made. To make pease pudding, simmer 1 lb/450 g split peas, with a ham hock or small gammon joint, for an hour or until the peas are tender. Drain and reserve the liquor, and set the ham hock aside. Mash or process the peas to a purée, and beat in 2 eggs, 2 oz/60 g butter and a splash of top of the milk or cream. Pile the mixture into a greased basin, cover it with foil, and bake, preferably in a tray of water, for 1 hour in a pre-heated moderate oven (180°C/350°F/Gas Mark 4). Meanwhile, finish cooking the ham in the liquor, or it can be glazed and finished in the oven if you prefer. Serve the pudding with the ham – any left over can be fried up for breakfast (excellent with bacon and black pudding).

A purée of green peas is in itself a good dish to accompany meat, especially good if prepared, as suggested by the Fox and Goose, with green peppercorns (see page 323).

PUY LENTIL: a speciality of Le Puy in the Auvergne region of France, also known as grey or blue lentil. These dark, mottled lentils, varying in colour from slate grey to blue-green, are the most highly prized, the prettiest and the most expensive. They have a pleasant, nutty taste, and should not be over-cooked but simmered for 15–25 minutes until just tender. Dressed with the best extra virgin olive oil, a squeeze of fresh lemon and a twist of black pepper, they are good enough to eat cold as a salad on their own. They can also be served in a mustardy dressing with cold cooked meats, such as tongue and ham, and warm with *bollito misto* – mixed boiled meats. They are a natural companion to *salsa verde* (see page 427), which is served with the *bollito*, but also with fish, especially sea bass and salmon. If you've never tried them, these are the pulse to have your finger on.

RED LENTIL: the commonest lentil is the small orange-red split variety, which disintegrates to a pale, nutty yellow purée when cooked. It is the lentil from which Indian daal is often made and, though not as fashionable in European cooking these days as green or Puy lentils, it is still the best bet for making a delicious purée, enriched with butter and perhaps spiked with a few drops of lemon juice for serving with game. It also makes a fine creamy soup – cook the lentils with ham stock or with a bacon bone in the pot and a few stock vegetables.

YELLOW LENTIL: flatter and a brighter yellow than yellow split peas which they resemble, this lentil is used almost exclusively in Indian cooking for making the very yellow daal that you see in some restaurants. There is no reason so to restrict their use, and they can easily be used as a substitute for red lentils, for a change. They are very good spiced with garlic, cardamom and cumin and mixed with spinach.

YELLOW SPLIT PEA: also cooks to a purée, and can always be substituted for green, although the flavour is milder, somewhere between peas and lentils. This pulse takes spices particularly well. See the recipe for Split Pea Fritters on page 322.

Grains and Cereals

It is a staggering thought that most of the carbohydrate intake of the entire world's population is provided by just two seeds of the grass family: wheat and rice. The prophet Isaiah was clearly on the mark when he said 'All flesh is grass'.

Carbohydrates are our basic sustenance which provide us with energy to live. In Britain, bread and potatoes are the most common carbohydrate elements in a meal, with rice and pasta trailing some way behind (though both have become considerably more popular in the last thirty years, and are gaining a bigger market share all the time).

Leaving aside the potato, for which I hope I have provided some useful cooking suggestions in Chapter 2, it seems that wheat, in the form of bread and pasta, and rice, are unlikely to be supplanted as primary carbohydrates in our culture by any of the other grains to which they are related. Yet although this is a genus of ingredients which few choose to explore, a more detailed knowledge of rice types in particular, and some understanding of the other grains and their uses, can add diversity and interest, at no great cost in time or money, to the culinary repertoire of the adventurous cook.

ALPHABETICAL GUIDE TO GRAINS, CEREALS AND ASSOCIATED PRODUCTS

Barley

The principal use of barley is in the brewing industry and as an animal feed, though in some countries barley flour is still used to make porridge and bread. The husked, polished grains are readily available as 'pearl barley', which can be added to soups and stews to give extra body. It is an essential ingredient in Scotch Broth (page 223). Barley malt, a sweet sticky substance the consistency of honey, can be bought in jars in health food shops and is used as a binder and sweetener in 'healthy' cakes and biscuits.

Buckwheat

Not strictly a cereal (its kernels are in fact analogous to the seeds of a strawberry), buckwheat is nevertheless made into a versatile flour, which is particularly favoured for making pancakes and blinis to be served with caviar, salmon eggs and soured cream. In Thailand and Malaysia it is also used in making a popular type of noodle, soba, which can now be found in many oriental grocers. Buckwheat 'groats' (the hulled grains) can be added to soup like pearl barley. Buckwheat groats and flour are both available in good delicatessens and health food shops.

Bulgar
(aka CRACKED WHEAT)

A product of wheat which is obtained by boiling and drying the grains, then roughly grinding them. A staple carbohydrate and accompaniment to meat in the Middle East, the best-known dish in which it features is the cold salad *tabbouleh*. This is delicious, and easily made: pour 1 scant pt/575 ml boiling water over 10 oz/300 g bulgar in a large dish or salad bowl, and leave to stand for 10 minutes to reconstitute. Add 4 large tomatoes, skinned and diced, with any juice you have saved, 1 medium onion, finely chopped, 2 tbsp chopped fresh mint and the same amount of chopped fresh parsley, season well with salt and black pepper, and dress generously with 5 fl oz/150 ml good olive oil and the juice of 3 lemons. Mix well and leave to stand for at least 2 hours before serving. Give it another stir, and garnish with more fresh mint and chopped spring onions.

In Lebanese cooking, bulgar is pounded with minced lamb, spices and a little egg, made into small rissoles shaped like rugby balls and deep-fried to give *kibbi*.

Corn
(aka MAIZE)

Whole kernels of corn are something I always keep to hand – I am inordinately fond of making my own popcorn. This is done by heating just enough oil (sunflower or olive) to cover the bottom of a saucepan, until it starts to smoke. Then add 2 handfuls of corn and put a lid on the pan immediately. When you hear the first grains start to pop, give the saucepan a good shake, replace on the heat, and keep shaking from time to time until all the kernels are popped. Toss the popped corn with melted butter, or even good olive oil, and salt and pepper. Eat while still warm.

Maize kernels are also ground to make POLENTA: see entry below.

Couscous

Couscous is a product of semolina, and therefore of wheat, so effectively it is a kind of granulated pasta. In Algeria, Morocco and Tunisia, couscous is the national dish, and it is served variously with a rich lamb stew containing vegetables and chick-peas, with fish stew and fish balls, and even in sweet dishes cooked with milk, nuts and dried fruit. The bona fide preparation of couscous is elaborate: it must be steamed several times and worked with the fingers and a little oil between each steaming to break up the lumps. Traditionally it is steamed in a special couscous pan, over the liquid in which the meat and vegetables are stewing. These days it is possible to buy coucous that can be simply boiled and drained in a sieve. It would no doubt offend a purist, but it seems fine to me. The great virtue of couscous is as a mopper-up of juices; it can therefore be served with any rich stew as an alternative to rice, noodles or potatoes.

Millet

Millet is a useful grain for anyone who is allergic to gluten, as it contains none. This also means that a dough made from its flour cannot rise (gluten is what gives wheat-flour dough its elasticity), but it can be turned into tasty flat breads and griddle cakes. Millet grains, whole or flaked, can be made into a polenta-like porridge that is quite palatable: it should be simmered in twice its volume of water, and regularly stirred, for about 20 minutes. Serve well seasoned with a knob of butter. Cooked the same way with milk instead of water, it can be eaten sweet, with butter, syrup or jam.

Oats

The great versatility of oats, and oatmeal which is ground from oats, is better known to the Scots than to the English. Besides their national dish of porridge, the Scots use oats to thicken soups and stews, in haggis, sausages, black puddings and meat stuffings, and also to make oatcakes. I am practically addicted to oatcakes, which I eat with marmalade for breakfast, with cheese at all times, and often with soups and salads in preference to bread. The Swiss use oats as the basis for muesli, but I prefer a delicious breakfast recipe I picked up in Brazil: put 1 large ripe banana, 8 fl oz/250 ml ice-cold milk and 1 tbsp of rolled oats into a blender, and whizz until smooth. Pour into a glass and drink like a milk shake. A recipe for the classic Scottish pudding, cranachan, made with toasted oatflakes, fresh fruit and whisky, appears on page 370.

Oatmeal, from which oatcakes are made, is available in several 'grades' according to the fineness of the grains. Rougher oatmeal makes a good alternative to breadcrumbs for coating fish before frying – particularly rich, oily fish such as mackerel, herring or even salmon fillets.

Pinhead oats, the roughest grade of all, make the best porridge, but must be soaked overnight in water first.

Polenta

A granular form of maize meal, the porridge that is made from it is a traditional winter staple of northern Italy, particularly Tuscany. It is either served wet, i.e. freshly made and hot from the pot, or turned out on to a dish and left to set in a cake shape, after which it is cut into slices and griddled or fried in olive oil. It can be an accompaniment to stews, but it is also often served on its own, or with a few stewed mushrooms, and always with melted butter or olive oil and plenty of freshly grated Parmesan cheese. To make polenta, bring 2 pts/1.1 litres well-salted water to the boil, and thoroughly stir in 10 oz/300 g polenta. Simmer the mixture gently (it should bubble like a geyser, but not too fiercely) for 25–35 minutes, stirring all the time with a wooden spoon. It is done when it has thickened to a smooth porridge, which drops a little reluctantly from the spoon. It is now possible to buy 'instant' polenta in many Italian delicatessens, which is very simple to cook, but doesn't have quite the texture of the real thing.

Rice

There are over 6000 varieties of rice, which is daunting, but the versatile cook need only concern him or herself with half a dozen or so.

ARBORIO (aka RISOTTO RICE): risotto is one of my favourite dishes, so this is the rice I probably use more than any other. A short, starchy grain, arborio absorbs a great deal of water and becomes pleasantly creamy when cooked. When making risotto the liquid, usually stock and perhaps a little wine, should be added a bit at a time, until the rice is *al dente*, and the risotto smooth and creamy. You should reckon to need at least four times the volume of your rice in liquid.

BASMATI: this excellent rice is grown, as its marketers are fond of telling us, in the foothills of the Himalayas. It is a long-grain rice – one of the longest and thinnest – and remains relatively dry (i.e. does not become sticky) when cooked. It is the rice that is traditionally eaten with Indian food, especially wet curries. It can be slowly cooked in a covered pan with a measured amount of water (1 pt/575 ml per 8 oz/225 g rice, or a volume ratio of 3 parts water to 2 parts rice), but I have always achieved satisfactory results by boiling the rice in plenty of salted water in an open pan, for 10–12 minutes until tender, then draining it in a sieve. Give it several good shakes in the sieve to evaporate as much of the excess moisture as possible, then stir in a knob of butter or a little oil. Basmati is also the rice to use for kedgeree – ideally it should be cooked in the milk in which your smoked haddock was poached, in which case the covered pan method is to be favoured. Brown basmati is also very good, but takes twice as long to cook. It is more tender if soaked in cold water for 30 minutes before cooking, and then rinsed.

BROWN RICE: brown rice has had the outer husk only removed – the bran remains. It has a higher vitamin and roughage content than white rice, takes longer to cook and has a slightly chewy texture. There are many different varieties, including brown ARBORIO, which can be used in risottos but does not have quite the same creamy results, and brown BASMATI, which is good. A mixture of brown and wild rice (see below) has a good nutty texture which goes well with fish and shellfish, particularly dishes that are finished with a *beurre blanc* or other creamy sauce.

CONVERTED RICE: not to be confused with special 'quick-cook' or 'easy-cook' or 'pre-fluffed' products, which are simple to cook but often bland, this is rice that has been par-boiled before milling and drying. It is not a modern technique; it has been practised in India and Pakistan for over 2000 years. Contrary to what one might expect, it actually improves the nutritional qualities of the rice (the B-vitamins in the bran and germ of the rice diffuse into the rice grain during the treatment, whereas with normal milling they would be hulled away), but increases the cooking time. Ordinary white rice on sale in this country, that is not otherwise labelled, is usually converted.

PUDDING RICE (aka SHORT-GRAIN or ROUND GRAIN): a plump, absorbent, short-grain rice not unlike ARBORIO, for which it can be substituted in emergencies, though it is mainly reserved for cream puddings (see recipe for Afghan Rice Pudding, from the Fox and Goose, on page 318).

SUSHI RICE: if you are making *sushi* it is essential that you should use the correct Japanese rice, which is available in specialist Japanese food shops and some health food shops. When cool it is slightly sticky and can be moulded with the fingers into the correct shapes for presenting raw fish. The preparation of vinegar rice for *sushi* is an elaborate procedure, which should be followed to the letter to ensure success – consult a Japanese cookbook.

WILD RICE: not strictly a rice at all, these long dark grains are in fact the seeds of a type of water-grass, native not to the rice-growing regions of Asia, but to the lakes of North America. Before drying it is first fermented, which gives it its delicious nutty, slightly sweet flavour – and helps to make it expensive too. It is very tasty, however, and a little goes a long way. It can be mixed with white or brown rice, though it is probably best to cook it separately, as it takes longer to become tender than either. It is good with fish dishes, and can even be added to kedgeree. I also like a few grains sprinkled on salads, or with hot buttered cabbage.

Semolina

This is a coarse flour made from the endosperm of hard durum wheat and is what all the best pasta is made from. If you are making your own pasta, it is best to use a combination of ordinary plain flour and semolina. I do not have the space to give detailed pasta-making instructions in this book, but would highly recomend the chapter on the subject in Marcella Hazan's *The Essentials of Classic Italian Cooking* – quite apart from its wisdom on the subject of pasta, it is one of the best Italian cookbooks there is.

The cooking of semolina in a porridgy English pudding, beloved of school dinners, is not something I care to celebrate, or even remember, but in the Lebanon and throughout the Middle East it is more winningly deployed in cakes, puddings and sweet pastries.

Wheat

Wheat is what gives us the flour to make our daily bread as well as pasta and most of our cakes, pastries and biscuits. There are many different grades of wheatflour, with their different roles in baking and bread-making. In this book the appropriate kinds of flour are stated in recipes where necessary. I would refer those who wish to expand their knowledge of the art of home bread-making and baking to a comprehensive and very readable work by Martha Rose Shulman called simply *The Bread Book*.

Pasta

Dried pasta

Pasta, the staple diet of Italy, is now popular all over the world, and especially in this country and America. There are so many brands of dried pasta available, in so many shapes, and now colours, that choosing from a well-stocked shelf can be quite bewildering. To try to list and define all the varieties here would only confuse you even before you got to the shops. At the end of the day quality is more important than shape, always providing the shape is more or less suitable for the use – I wouldn't recommend lasagne sheets to be tossed lightly in pesto.

As for quality, it is a reasonable supposition, though not an infallible one, that pasta made in Italy will be of a high standard. The best pasta is also likely to state on the label that it is made from '100 per cent durum wheat semolina'. Once you have got it home and opened the packet, you can test the quality by running your finger along the surface – it should be silky-smooth. Apart from that, it is a question of trying what you like the look of and then remembering what tasted good.

Cooking dried pasta

The length of cooking time depends on the thickness and shape of the pasta; most packets of dried pasta have cooking guidelines. Always err on the underside of done, testing the pasta a minute or two before you expect it will be ready, so you can catch it when it is just *al dente* and not a moment later. Once drained, if it is not to be mixed together at once with a sauce, you should toss it with a dribble of olive oil, which will prevent it from becoming glued together.

It is possible to cook pasta in advance, and then reheat it later in your sauce. Do not frown on this – even the best restaurants do it, and you would never know the difference. Pasta that is to be heated through should be slightly underdone, tossed in a little oil as described above, and kept covered with a damp (not wet) cloth.

Fresh pasta

Fresh pasta is always made with eggs (dried is often not), which is what gives it its soft texture and slightly rich taste. I am not a great fan of the brands of fresh

pasta that now seem to be ubiquitous in the chilling cabinets of supermarkets –
I find it a little too chewy, and prefer to stick to dried pasta. But fresh pasta that
is made on the premises in the best Italian delicatessens can be very good
indeed. The best pasta of all, of course, is the pasta you make yourself (as I
mentioned above, see Marcella Hazan's *The Essentials of Classic Italian Cooking*).
Cook it within hours of making it, and you can taste the freshness of the eggs. It
is best with the simplest sauces of all – pesto (page 105), a light tomato sauce, or
even just good olive oil, freshly grated Parmesan and black pepper.

Wholemeal pasta

The invention of a British manufacturer, wholemeal pasta is now being sold in
large quantities to the Italians, in one of the grandest cases of coals to
Newcastle ever known. The flavour is distinctive, and whether or not you like
it is a matter of personal taste. I find it a little heavy to serve with a rich, creamy
sauce, but I like it very much broken up and served in a clear soup with meat or
vegetables.

Nuts and other edible seeds

Nuts are little powerhouses of energy, and also often of taste. Broken or ground
to various degrees of fineness, they have numerous culinary applications, but
are rarely better, in my view, than when eaten whole in their natural state.

Buying nuts

As a general principle, buy nuts at a stage of refinement one or two levels above
that in which you intend to use them. By which I mean, if you want to eat raw
whole almonds, buy them in their shell, and they will taste fresher. If you want
to use ground almonds, buy whole blanched almonds, toast them very lightly
(they should not even brown, merely take on a tinge of gold), and grind them
yourself in a food processor – your dish will have a far nuttier flavour.

ALPHABETICAL GUIDE TO NUTS

Here is a brief run-down of the most common and useful kinds:

Almond

Available whole, shelled, blanched, flaked and ground, the almond is one of the most versatile and widely-used nuts. Ground and flaked almonds are particularly important in confectionery and baking – one of the simplest and most rewarding of such dishes is a fruit and almond tart (see page 360 for recipe).

Brazil nut

A deliciously rich and fatty nut with a similar flavour to coconut. Apart from being dipped in chocolate to make a sweetmeat for which I must confess a weakness, and turning up in the classier type of fruit cake, it is almost exclusively eaten *au naturel*.

Cashew

A good cocktail nut, which can also be used in Chinese cooking, classically in chicken dishes. Cashew butter makes a luxurious alternative to peanut butter.

Chestnut

Even more versatile, perhaps, than the almond, but under-explored in this country. The chestnut has sweet and savoury applications: it makes a fine stuffing for poultry, particularly turkey and goose – the Chestnut and Celery

Stuffing on page 320 is so good that it can be eaten as a dish in its own right. Being starchy and not too oily, the chestnut can also be treated as a vegetable – a purée of chestnuts cooked in stock goes very well with game, and pieces of broken cooked chestnut make a good addition to creamed brussels sprouts (see page 57). Elizabeth David, in *French Provincial Cooking*, gives a fine recipe for chestnut soup.

Preparing chestnuts

Fresh chestnuts can be roasted, in an oven or the embers of a fire, and eaten hot. If they are to be used in a recipe, fresh chestnuts should first be shelled and skinned. This can be done by scoring their skin on the rounded side and either roasting them (for 15 minutes at 180°C/350°F/Gas Mark 4) or boiling them for 8–10 minutes. As soon as they are cool enough to handle, and before they get cold again, the chestnuts should be squeezed from the outer shell, and the inner skin peeled away with a sharp knife. The peeled chestnuts will then need considerably more cooking to become tender.

Outside the chestnut season (late autumn and winter), dried and canned chestnuts can be used. Dried are best, and easy to deal with: like a pulse, they must be soaked for 8 hours or overnight in cold water, then simmered for at least an hour, often longer, until tender. Dried chestnuts are available from good delicatessens and health food shops.

Chestnut purée and chestnut flour are also available, the former widely, the latter in a few specialist health food shops. Both have many applications in baking and confectionery. A sweetened purée of chestnuts makes a delicious sauce for vanilla ice cream.

Coconut

Most people are pretty bewildered when presented with a coconut; it is a sad thought that of the thousands of coconuts won at fairs all over the country every year most probably get thrown away uneaten. I think coconuts are delicious, though I like them so much in their raw state that I rarely use their meat to cook with. Their milk, on the other hand, is a delightful addition to many Oriental soups and curries. Ideally, fresh coconut milk should be used: it is easily extracted by making two holes with a screwdriver or boring tool in the little soft patches – small black circles – at the top of the coconut. The milk can then be poured out. Canned coconut milk is also available, and quite worthwhile, though a little on the sweet side. Another very useful product is creamed coconut, available in blocks like pats of butter. This dissolves when heated and can be used as an alternative to coconut milk, though bear in mind that it is richer and you will need less.

When buying a coconut always give it a good shake close to your ear, to check that it does contain its milk. If you are not planning to cook with the milk, chill the coconut in the fridge when you get home, and then drink the milk through a straw. Put on your swimming trunks and stand by the radiator, close your eyes and think of the Caribbean.

Hazelnut
(aka FILBERT)

A particularly nutty nut, which is very good on its own as a dessert nut. Its aromatic oil is excellent for salad dressings; otherwise its applications are mainly in sweet dishes, the most famous confection made from it being praline. This is not difficult to make, though some experience of sugar's behaviour when melted is a help. The basic procedure is to toast 8 oz/225 g whole skinned hazelnuts until golden-brown – for about 10 minutes in a fairly hot oven (200°C/400°F/Gas Mark 6). Then heat 8 oz/225 g caster sugar with a spoonful of water in a heavy-based pan. When the sugar has melted and turned a golden-brown, add the still warm hazelnuts, stir very briskly to coat the nuts in the caramel, then pour the mixture on to a greased baking tray or sheet of foil. When completely cold, the praline can be broken up, ground to various degrees of fineness, and used in other recipes. Praline ice cream can be made by adding rough granules of praline to a basic vanilla custard before the freezing stage.

Hazelnuts have a great affinity with chocolate, and hazelnut praline ground to a fine powder can be mixed with a good dark chocolate, melted, and a little cream, to make luxurious praline truffles. Praline is also made with almonds using exactly the same procedure as above.

Macadamia

Imported from Australia and Hawaii, this is an expensive nut with a rich, buttery taste. It is hard to find except ready-roasted and salted as a cocktail nut, but if you can get unsalted macadamias they make a superb praline (follow procedure for hazelnuts above).

Peanut

(aka GROUNDNUT; MONKEY NUT)

The peanut is strictly a pulse: as the name suggests it is a member of the pea family; its 'shell' is in fact the dried pod. Everybody knows what a peanut tastes like. I have not found many culinary uses for it, except that I occasionally improvise a Thai-style dipping sauce by mixing peanut butter with crushed garlic, a little chilli sauce, fresh coriander and a splash of wine vinegar. It is rather good with chicken and lamb leftovers. Groundnut oil is good for deep-frying – all the best chip shops swear by it.

Pecan

A good all-rounder, delicious in the raw state, otherwise with mainly sweet applications. It can be used to make a praline (see HAZELNUTS above), which goes well in ice cream. It is also, of course, the star attraction of the famous American dessert, pecan pie.

Pinenut

The kernel of a type of pine cone, the pinenut or pine kernel has risen to popularity in the last few years, mainly by its association with the excellent Italian basil sauce, pesto (see page 105 for two versions). Pinenuts have other uses too: toasted until golden-brown, they can be sprinkled on salads –

especially good when olives and Parmesan or goat's cheese are also involved. In the Middle East the pinenut is used in many types of confectionery. It also adds considerable character to the Ricotta Tart described on page 402.

Pistachio

At its best, this is one of the finest cocktail nuts. Unfortunately pistachios have now become so popular that the market has been flooded with brands, most of which are oversalted, and many of which contain other unpleasant-tasting sulphur-based preservatives. Be on the look-out for these, and remember the best brands when you find them. Unsalted pistachios are harder to come by, but when found can be used in savoury stuffings and sauces, as well as in confectionery, baking and ice creams.

Pumpkin seeds

Often added to bread, pumpkin seeds have a nutty taste which also makes them an irresistible snacking food. Toasted to bring out their flavour, they can also be added to salads as an alternative to pinenuts. They are available both in and out of their shells; unless you are going to keep them a long time, it is better to buy them out of their shells, as shelling them is a very fiddly business.

Sesame seeds

One of the oldest seed crops, grown mainly for its highly aromatic oil, which is used particularly in Chinese and Japanese cooking, and also in Mexico. The seeds, lightly toasted, can be sprinkled on salads, and are rather good with sweetish shellfish: that great favourite of Chinese and Thai restaurants, sesame prawn toast, is the best example of that conjunction, but dressed crab, and cold prawns and langoustines, can all be served with a sprinkling of toasted sesame seeds.

Tahina is a paste made from sesame seeds. It has a strong taste, and though in the Middle East it is often eaten on its own with pitta bread, it is perhaps better mixed with a purée of cooked aubergines or chick-peas, to make a milder dip. The latter, of course, is hummus (see page 300).

In the Middle East, and also in America, sesame seeds are used widely in making sweet cakes and biscuits.

Sunflower seeds

Another good seed for nibbling, and adding to breads, the sunflower's seed is slightly smaller than the pumpkin's. Its real value is for the high-quality oil it yields. Sunflower oil is one of the lightest and healthiest of cooking oils, and imparts almost no flavour of its own. Along with olive oil, it is the one I use most in my kitchen.

Walnut

One of the most distinctive of all nuts, its rich, sweet taste, tempered by a slight bitterness, is unmistakable. Young green nuts, still in the fruit body that surrounds their shell, are available pickled in vinegar or brine. Green walnuts have a strong, bitter taste, which I have never much cared for, but some regard them as a great delicacy. The mature nut, shelled but usually unskinned (the skin contributes the bitterness to the taste) has many uses in sweet recipes, but has also long been valued, particularly by vegetarians, for its versatility in savoury dishes. In particular it makes a fine pasta sauce with cream, garlic and Parmesan cheese, and makes an excellent substitute for pinenuts in pesto. Its aromatic oil is one of the finest for salad dressings, especially good with bitter-tasting leaves such as chicory and radicchio. Walnut oil also has an affinity with Brussels sprouts, which are delicious shredded and stir-fried in it, with a hint of garlic.

Recipes

Afghan Rice Pudding

THE FOX AND GOOSE INN

Serves 4

Rosewater is available in good delicatessens, herbalists and some chemists. Along with the cardamom and pistachios it adds a delightful Eastern flavour to this rice pudding, a recipe which Ruth Watson attributes to the late Jeremy Round.

4 oz/115 g pudding rice
1 pt/575 ml milk
8 fl oz/250 ml Channel Islands
  (gold-top) milk
8 fl oz/250 ml double cream
2½ oz/75 g caster sugar
2 tsp rosewater
a good pinch of ground
  cardamom
1 oz/25 g unsalted, shelled
  pistachio nuts, finely chopped

Wash the rice and bring to the boil in a heavy pan in the pint of milk. Turn down the heat and simmer very gently until the rice is tender and nearly all the milk has evaporated.

Add the second lot of milk and the cream and bring back to the boil. Cook gently, stirring occasionally, until the mixture thickens slightly, then add the sugar. Continue cooking for about 5 minutes. (The rice has more or less been cooked in the first process, now you are thickening up the milk and cream.) Add the rosewater and cardamom, then immediately remove from the heat.

Serve at once if required hot, or chill and serve cold, either way with the chopped pistachio nuts sprinkled on top.

Coconut Rice

JEMIMA'S

Serves 4

8 oz/225 g basmati rice
2 tbsp sunflower oil
1 onion, chopped
1 tsp turmeric
1 tsp ground coriander
1 tbsp dessicated coconut
salt

A good accompaniment to dry, spicy dishes, such as Chillied Fish with Sweet Potatoes (page 160).

Soak the rice in cold water for at least 1 hour, then drain and rinse, and spread out on a clean cotton cloth to dry. Heat the oil in a saucepan and fry the onion gently, but do not brown. Add the rice, spices and coconut, stir-fry for 1–2 minutes, then add hot water to 1 in/2.5 cm above the level of the rice and a good pinch of salt. Cook for 8–10 minutes until the rice is tender and all the liquid absorbed.

Aztec Soup

A robust and nourishing dish which proves that you don't need meat stock to make a delicious soup.

Soak the kidney beans overnight in plenty of cold water, then rinse thoroughly. Bring to the boil in the water or stock, and cook at a merry simmer for 45 minutes.

Add the onion, garlic, thyme and cumin, and simmer gently until the beans are almost tender (this could take anything up to an hour). Then add the coconut milk or cream, spring onion and hot pepper or chilli. (If you have managed to find a West Indian hot pepper, make sure it does not break open. A chilli, on the other hand, can be chopped.) Season to taste with salt and pepper. Cook gently for a further 20 minutes.

Remove the pepper, if used, and purée the soup in a blender. Dilute with a little more water or stock if necessary.

Add the sweetcorn niblets, heat the soup through, and serve.

8 oz/225 g dried red kidney beans
2 pts/1.1 litres water or vegetable stock
2 small onions, finely chopped
2 garlic cloves, crushed
a sprig of fresh thyme
2 tsp ground cumin
10 fl oz/300 ml coconut milk, (or 5 fl oz/150 ml canned coconut cream)
4 spring onions, sliced
1 West Indian hot pepper, or 1 small fresh red chilli
salt and black pepper
6 oz/170 g cooked sweetcorn niblets

Boston Baked Beans

One of the great pulse dishes, the forerunner of canned baked beans, but infinitely superior.

Put the beans with the water and bacon bone into a large saucepan and bring to the boil. Boil rapidly for a few minutes, then turn down to a simmer, and cook with the lid partially covering the pan for 1 hour. Remove the bacon bone and drain the beans, reserving the cooking liquor.

Brown the salt pork gently in a little oil in a large casserole. Add the onion and sweat for a few minutes. In a separate bowl, mix the mustard, sugar and treacle with a little of the warm cooking liquor from the beans. Add this to the pork and onions in the casserole. Add also the beans and 1 pt/575 ml of the reserved cooking liquor, and

1 lb/450 g dried haricot or navy beans, soaked overnight
3 pts/1.75 litres water
1 bacon bone (optional)
1 lb/450 g salt pork (belly or loin), cut into ½-in/1-cm pieces
groundnut or sun flower oil
1 large onion, sliced
2 tsp strong made English mustard
2 oz/60 g dark brown sugar
4 good tbsp dark treacle
salt and black pepper

season well with salt and pepper. Bring to simmering point, put the lid on the casserole, then transfer to a slow oven (140°C/275°F/Gas Mark 1) for at least 3 hours, until the beans and pork are very tender. Take a look every hour, and add a little more of the cooking liquid if the beans seem to be dry.

There's not much I can suggest to accompany this dish – except a very hearty appetite.

Chestnut and Celery Stuffing

I call this a stuffing because I often use it to stuff a loin of pork (see page 207) and we always serve it at home with turkey for Christmas. In fact it is a dish in its own right, worthy of being the focal point of a meal. It's a good dish for vegetarians, if you omit the liver, though I must admit I like it with herby butcher's sausages.

1 lb/450 g chestnuts
1 celery head, washed and chopped
1 small onion, finely chopped
1 oz/30 g butter
12 plump ready-to-eat prunes, stoned and roughly chopped
1 tbsp chopped fresh parsley
salt and black pepper
1 egg, beaten
turkey liver (*optional*)
2 oz/60 g fresh breadcrumbs (*optional*)

Blanch or roast the chestnuts to ease peeling (see page 313), then simmer the peeled chestnuts in unsalted water for 35–40 minutes until tender. Drain the chestnuts and break them up with a fork – they should be roughly broken, not puréed. Sweat the celery and onion in the butter in a pan for a few minutes, then add the prunes, chestnuts and parsley. Season with salt and pepper, mix well and cook for a further few minutes. Remove the pan from the heat.

When the mixture has cooled a little, mix in the egg. If you are serving the stuffing with turkey you can at this stage add the chopped liver of the bird. Without the liver, this mixture can now be used to stuff a loin of pork (see page 207).

Pile the mixture into a suitably sized ovenproof dish and top with a sprinkling of breadcrumbs, if used. Bake for 30 minutes in a pre-heated moderate to hot oven (190°C/375°F/Gas Mark 5).

Spicy Aromatic Chick-peas

JEMIMA'S

Serves 4

This dish goes nicely with the following recipe for Coriander Rice.

Drain the chick-peas, put into a saucepan and cover by at least 1 in/2.5 cm fresh water. Bring to the boil and simmer for 30 minutes, or until soft when squeezed between thumb and finger. In a flameproof casserole, fry the onion and garlic in the oil until soft but not brown, then add the coriander, cumin and turmeric and stir-fry for a few seconds. Add the tomatoes and cook, stirring, until everything is amalgamated. Add the chick-peas and sufficient of their cooking liquid to just cover and leave to simmer for a further 30 minutes. Meanwhile, dry-roast the paprika and garam masala in a frying pan. Stir these spices into the chick-peas and cook for a further 10 minutes. Taste, and season with salt, the lemon juice and ginger.

This dish improves upon re-heating, and will freeze, but will require extra spices after defrosting.

8 oz/225 g dried chick-peas, soaked overnight
1 large onion, chopped
4 garlic cloves, finely chopped
4 tbsp sunflower oil
1 tbsp ground coriander
2 tsp ground cumin
1 tsp turmeric
8 oz/225 g peeled and chopped tomatoes
2 tsp paprika
1 tsp garam masala
salt
a squeeze of lemon juice
½ tsp peeled and grated ginger root

Coriander Rice

JEMIMA'S

Serves 4

Soak the rice in cold water for at least 1 hour, drain and rinse, and spread out on a clean cotton cloth to dry. Heat the oil in a saucepan and fry the onion and garlic gently until translucent, then add the rice and stir until coated with oil. Add hot water to 1 in/2.5 cm above the level of rice, stir in the salt, bring to the boil, cover tightly and leave over a very low heat for 20 minutes. Stir in the coriander and extra seasoning if required just before serving.

8 oz/225 g basmati rice
4 tbsp sunflower oil
1 onion, chopped
2 garlic cloves, finely chopped
1 tsp salt
4 tbsp chopped fresh coriander

Courgette and Tomato Daal

BRASSERIE DU MARCHE AUX PUCES

Serves 5-6

8 oz/225 g yellow split peas
1 pt/575 ml vegetable stock
1 onion, finely chopped
2 tbsp sunflower oil
2 garlic cloves, finely chopped
1 fresh green chilli, finely chopped
½ in/1-cm piece ginger root, peeled and grated
2 medium courgettes, diced
1 tsp made English mustard
1 tsp turmeric
1 tsp garam masala
1 tsp black poppy seeds
3 large tomatoes, skinned, de-seeded and chopped

Simmer the split peas in the stock with half the onion for about 25 minutes until completely tender. Pour off some of the liquid, leaving about 1 in/2.5 cm in the bottom of the pan, then beat the mixture to a rough purée.

Heat the oil in a pan, add the remaining onion, the garlic, chilli, ginger, courgettes and mustard and cook gently for 5–6 minutes without browning.

Add all the other spices and the tomatoes and mix well. Cook for a further few minutes until the vegetables are tender and the spices well amalgamated.

Over a low heat, stir the vegetables gently into the split pea purée and heat through. Serve with pitta bread and a green salad.

Split Pea Fritters with Tomato Sauce

BRASSERIE DU MARCHE AUX PUCES

Serves 4 as a starter

4 oz/115 g split peas
1 small onion, finely chopped
1 medium carrot, finely chopped
1 celery stick, finely chopped
¼ tsp dried mixed herbs
2 tbsp plain flour
1 egg, beaten
salt and black pepper
groundnut or sunflower oil for frying
tomato sauce (page 100), to serve

Rinse the peas and place with the vegetables and herbs in a saucepan. Add water to 1 in/2.5 cm above the peas. Bring to the boil and simmer, covered, for 40 minutes or until the peas are tender.

Add the flour and blend to a purée with a potato masher or in a food processor. If the resulting purée is on the thin side return to the heat to cook some of the water out of it. Beat in the egg and season to taste with salt and pepper.

Fry heaped tablespoons of the mixture in ½ in/1 cm hot oil in a frying pan, turning once, until golden-brown.

Serve with the tomato sauce.

Purée of Split Peas and
Green Peppercorns

THE FOX AND GOOSE INN

Serves 4

This is particularly recommended as an accompaniment to the confit of duck legs (page 280). The whole peppercorns make little punchy explosions in contrast to the smooth, slightly sweetish purée and the rich, fatty duck. The purée also goes very nicely with slow-cooked lamb (see page 202) or game casserole.

Soak the peas overnight in plenty of cold water. Drain, rinse and put into a saucepan with the vegetables and herbs, and enough water to cover. Bring to the boil, simmer and cook until tender. Drain off the water, remove the bay leaf and thyme, and put the peas and vegetables, with the butter, through a mouli-légumes, sieve or food processor (although the latter makes a less interesting texture). Now season to taste with salt and the sugar, add the peppercorns and mix well. Heat through before serving, thinning with a little hot water if the purée is very stiff.

12 oz/350 g split green peas
1 onion, finely chopped
1 carrot, finely chopped
½ celery stick, finely chopped
½ small leek, chopped
a sprig of thyme
1 bay leaf
2 oz/60 g butter
salt
a pinch of caster sugar
1 tbsp pickled green
  peppercorns (preserved in
  brine in a can or jar, not
  dried)

Split Pea and Bacon Soup

Serves 4

A robust winter warmer – more of a meal than a starter. The same soup can be made without bacon, using a chicken or vegetable stock.

Put the bacon knuckle into a saucepan with one each of the onions, carrots and celery sticks. Cover with the water, bring to the boil and simmer gently for 2 hours. Remove the bacon knuckle and set aside. Remove and discard the vegetables, reserving the stock.

Peel the remaining carrot and onion, wash the celery stick, and chop all three finely. In a saucepan, sweat these vegetables in the butter for a few minutes. Then add the split peas and pour over 1½ pts/850 ml of the reserved stock. Bring to the boil and simmer

a knuckle of bacon
2 small onions
2 large carrots
2 celery sticks
2 pts/1.1 litres water
1 oz/30 g butter
8 oz/225 g green split peas
salt and black pepper

gently, with the pan partially covered, for about 50 minutes. By now the peas should be tender and beginning to break up. Beat the peas with a wooden spoon to get a rough purée, or blend in a liquidizer if you want them to be completely smooth. Thin the soup with a little more stock if you want a thinner soup.

While the peas are cooking, cut the meat off the bacon knuckle, chop it into small pieces and add these to the soup just before serving.

CHAPTER EIGHT

Fruit

Fruits are among the most emotive and life-enhancing of foods, as reflected in the wealth of fruit imagery, not just in the world's literature, but also in our everyday language. Associations are almost always positive: 'fruitful', 'fruity', 'the fruits of one's labours', 'the apple of my eye', 'a peach of a goal', 'plum position' – even 'Strawberry Fields Forever'. Of course there are 'bad apples' and 'sour grapes', but these phrases only take on negative connotations in contrast to the beauty, perfection and lusciousness of the fruits of which they are tainted versions. Even the word fruit is etymologically a winner; it comes from the Latin root *frui*, meaning to enjoy or delight in.

Our own ancestors, the forest-dwelling primates, enjoyed a privileged symbiosis with fruits of their habitat. Their intelligence and adaptability enabled them to feast on a wider range of fruits than any other species. When ape became man, he quickly discovered that fruit could be cultivated. And when man became civilized it was not long before he was applying himself scientifically not merely to the propagation of fruit in quantity, but also, by means of hybridizing and grafting, to the improvement of his fruits' succulence, sweetness and flavour.

The result is that a wealth of fruity tastes, textures and aromas have for many centuries now enriched the lives of men and women all over the world. In the past, few who wrote of the joys of foreign travel failed to include among the happiest of their discoveries the peculiar fruits of the distant lands they visited. Today many of the exotics of which they wrote are readily available to all. Those who shun them, whose experience of fruit is restricted to the occasional apple or orange, a few tangerines at Christmas, and a splash of Jif lemon on their Shrove Tuesday pancakes, are practising a form of self-denial that verges on the perverse.

Getting the best from fruit

Even those who need no converting to the pleasures of fruit still have a number of obstacles to contend with if they are going to enjoy the maximum satisfaction this food can provide. The general principles of shopping for fruit are the same as those for vegetables, and are covered on pages 29–34. Indications of quality and ripeness for particular fruits are covered in the alphabetical guide to fruits below. But there are a few salient points which are worth discussing in general terms first.

Varieties within a species

The overriding concern for the consumer must be that shops continue to offer a wide range of different fruits, of a consistently high quality. That aside, one of the great achievements of cultivating fruits, historically, has been the development of numerous different varieties, with different eating and cooking qualities, within a single species.

This mission continues among fruit-growers today, though it has seen some undesirable diversions of late: fruit grown not for flavour but for looks, regularity of shape and shelf-life. The apple, the table grape, the plum and the tomato (see page 98) are perhaps the worst victims of this trend. Just recently I have been delighted to observe in some quarters a renewed effort to offer consumers a wider choice of more interesting varieties of these and other fruits.

It is essential that, as consumers, we do what we can to ensure that the modest diversification we are currently witnessing is no mere flash in the pan. It is not enough that I and other food writers should praise this policy in print; we, our readers, and anyone else who cares, must vote with our shopping baskets for greater choice.

In terms of a practical shopping strategy, this requires no great effort of will – just a keen and roving eye. Be aware that what is in stock will vary according to the season. Look out, in particular, for native varieties of fruit that may have short seasons. Our own greengages, which ripen in the late summer, are as good to eat raw as any imported plum. William pears in October and November, picked golden and ripe in this country, are far better than the hard green versions imported from the Americas. And varieties of late summer apple, such as Beauty of Bath or Worcester Pearmain, may not keep well but are superb when not long off the tree – you are more likely to find them in a small country greengrocer who buys locally, although the major supermarkets are also now making a point of stocking more unusual varieties of apple.

But it is not really necessary to go shopping armed with a list of names of my, or anybody else's, recommendations. A willingness to experiment will serve you in better stead, and a communicative greengrocer who knows his produce is a great bonus.

Cooking with fruit

The best ripe specimens of so many kinds of fruit are such unimprovable foods that cooking them is something to be done only rarely, and after careful thought. There are of course many recipes for fruit puddings which do not involve cooking fruit at all. The incorporation of fresh fruit into cakes, meringues, mousses, ices, etc. is often just a luxurious variant of the basic combination of fresh fruit and cream – a marriage whose sanctity few would question. Such classic dishes as peach melba, strawberry shortcake and summer pudding are cases in point – they are to the greater glory of the raw fruit. By the same token I would rather have fresh raspberries with a good vanilla ice cream than an ice cream made from crushed raspberries, though I am by no means averse to the latter.

What I am getting at is that elaborate and decorative fruit desserts composed of many elements, beautiful though they may be, are not a necessary part of the repertoire of the cook who simply wants to get the best out of fruit. The 'keep it simple' maxim applies equally to the various fruits whose flavour is improved by cooking. Generally speaking, these are the sour berries and currants, the more acidic of the pitted fruits, and a few types of apple and pear which do not have sufficient succulence or sugar content to be palatable in the raw state, as well as good eating varieties which are simply unripe. In these cases the cooking process is really no more than a kind of artificial ripening: the addition of sugar sweetens, and the application of heat releases the aromatic molecules of the fruit. In some cases, a gentle simmering may be appropriate to reduce the water content and thus intensify the flavours of the fruit. In others the fruit may be enhanced by the addition of flavourings such as cinnamon with apples and pears; vanilla with apricots; elderflower with gooseberries.

A rough purée of beautiful stewed fruit, like the best raw fruit, requires little further enhancement: a contrasting topping of crumble, pastry or toasted nuts, perhaps; a little cream, ice cream, or egg custard, and maybe a few nice biscuits. I love fruit puddings, but my favourite recipes rarely stray outside these simple parameters. In my own kitchen, a Fruit and Almond Tart (page 360) and a very simple Apricot Soufflé (page 366) are about as elaborate as I ever get.

Freezing fruit

As with vegetables, the ready availability of the fresh product means that it is rarely necessary to buy frozen fruit. However, for those who grow their own fruits, freezing the excess of the harvest is a useful home economy, and many types do freeze well. Only a few, however, come close to retaining the structure of their fresh incarnation after they have been frozen. These are the single-berry fruits such as blueberries, bilberries and gooseberries; the cluster berries such as blackberries, loganberries and raspberries; and the currants, red, white and black. If they are frozen carefully, they can, at a pinch, be thawed out and used as if fresh. Damage to the fruit can be minimized by selecting whole, unblemished berries, and open-freezing them in a single layer spread on a large tray. As soon as they are frozen quite solid, and before they become encrusted with frozen condensed water, they should be carefully transferred to a suitable polythene box with a lid. Again, spread out in a single layer for defrosting.

It is not worth the trouble of freezing large amounts of fruit in this way unless you really intend to use them in recipes which require the whole raw fruit. It is more economical of time and space to freeze purées of fruit or, better still, home-made fruit sorbets and ice creams. For those whose gardens produce a regular glut of soft fruits, an ice cream-making machine, far from being an extravagant luxury, will turn out to be a very economical item of kitchen hardware. (For basic procedures for sorbets and ice creams, see pages 363–4).

Cooking apples, quinces, plums, greengages and other fruits that are likely to end up being cooked anyway should be lightly stewed with a little sugar before freezing. You should err on the side of under-cooking and under-sweetening if you know the fruit is ultimately destined for pies, crumbles and the like: the fruit will undergo further cooking once thawed, and you can always add more sugar.

More tips on freezing particular fruits will be included in individual entries in the guide below.

Even if you do not grow your own fruit, you can avoid the often punitive expense of buying small punnets of summer soft fruits by visiting one of the pick-your-own farms which now seem ubiquitous in the fruit-growing regions of the country. Strawberries and raspberries are likely to top the shopping list, but many farms also grow black-, red- and white-currants, and gooseberries as well. Jam-makers and freezer-owners can enjoy the fruits of the P-Y-O farm all the year round.

ALPHABETICAL GUIDE TO FRUITS

Apple

In general terms, the traditional division of apples into eating and cooking varieties is a misleading one. Certainly some apples are too sour to be eaten raw. The most common of all British 'cooking' apples, the Bramley, is a case in point. But of the so-called 'eating' or dessert apples, many have culinary applications that belie this pedantic pigeon-holing. A more useful distinction for the kitchen is between varieties which keep their shape when cooked, and those which, with little encouragement, disintegrate into a purée. Bramleys come into the latter category and are therefore suitable for sauces, pies, charlottes and crumbles, also fools, ices and 'apple snow'. They are no good at all if you want to make a stylish *tarte aux pommes*, with layers of thin apple slices overlapping in concentric circles. For this, and for baking whole or making fritters, you should choose a firm-textured eating apple, tart enough not to lose its flavour in the heat of the oven. The French would use Reinettes for such a dish. These are rarely encountered here, but early season's Cox's Orange Pippins, still sharp and crisp, are as good a bet. They are, however, produced on a massive scale, and not always of best quality. The best-textured ones are small and hard; their skins should show no tendency to wrinkle when pressed with the finger. An emerald-green Granny Smith, if of good quality, can be a workable alternative. Golden Delicious do keep their shape well, but are over-sweet and somewhat bland: they may be partially salvaged by a generous sprinkling of lemon juice. Good local varieties which fulfil the criteria of sharpness and firm texture are well worth experimenting with. Some may give the best results of all.

Apple purée

The Bramley is much maligned by cookery writers, but it is a great bargain, and can make as good a purée as any apple if it is prepared carefully. Having peeled the apples, slice them thinly, and exclude any of the tough fibres close to the core. Gently heated in a heavy-based pan, with a little sugar, the slices will soon disintegrate to a foamy purée. This should be allowed to bubble gently and reduce to a thicker, darker purée, but you will have to watch the pan and stir regularly to prevent the apples from catching on the bottom. If the purée does burn, it may be rescued by transferring at once to a clean pan, without scraping any of the burnt matter from the bottom of the first pan. The flavour can be enhanced by the addition of the grated zest of orange – one orange for every 2 lb/900 g apples – near the end of cooking.

The result is a simple, tart apple sauce, delicious with pork and even better with black pudding. But served warm with egg custard, or chilled with whipped cream, toasted almond flakes, and a sprinkling of brown sugar, it is also a delightful pudding.

Apricot

In this country the choice is not between different types of apricot but between whatever is available fresh, and the dried product. As a fruit for eating raw, the fresh apricots we get here have a sad tendency to cotton-woolliness, and a disappointingly insipid flavour. Any exceptions seem to be a matter of good luck, being in the right shop at the right time, rather than any cunning strategy of selection. If you are hoping to find a sweet, ripe apricot for eating, you should choose fruits that have a warm, rosy-orange glow, and are slightly soft to touch. You may still be disappointed, but the alternative – hard, yellowish fruits – are certainly good only for cooking.

Even the most insipid fruit can be remarkably transformed, however, by a simple trick suggested by Elizabeth David in *French Provincial Cooking*. The apricots should be cut in half at right angles to the line between the stem end and the base of the fruit, and the stone removed. Arrange the apricot halves on a baking tray, cut side uppermost, and in the pit of each put a small piece (¼ in/.5 mm) of vanilla pod and a little heap of caster sugar (alternatively omit the pod and use vanilla sugar, made by filling a jam jar with caster sugar and a split vanilla pod and leaving it for at least a week). Then bake the apricots in a moderate oven (180°C/350°F/Gas Mark 4) for 15–20 minutes, until they are slightly tenderized but not completely mushy. Remove the vanilla pods when the apricots are cool.

This is far better than stewing the apricots as they retain their shape, at least partially. These par-baked apricots are now ready for all sorts of recipes – pies, crumbles and in particular in the Fruit and Almond Tart described on page 360. You can also eat them as they are, still warm from the oven. If you want to do this, be a little more generous with the sugar before you put the apricots into the oven, and bake them until they are quite soft, say 20–30 minutes. Should you find that their syrupy juices have trickled on to the baking tray, and caramelized with the heat, then deglaze with a little water and, if possible, a splash of kirsch or brandy. Pour the resulting syrup over the apricots, and serve.

Halved fresh apricots, tossed in a little kirsch, dipped in batter and deep-fried, make delicious fritters. Provided they are reasonably ripe they do not require pre-baking.

Dried apricots

For ice creams, sorbets, mousses, and the soufflé on page 366, I prefer to use dried apricots. The flavour is more intense, and they can be made into a thick, sticky purée that is more versatile than the slightly watery one that comes from stewing fresh apricots.

The simplest way to reconstitute dried apricots is to put them into a pan or ovenproof dish, and pour over just enough boiling water to cover them. The water should be sweetened – with about 2 oz/60 g caster sugar per pint/50 ml water. This will prevent natural sugars in the apricots osmosing into the water. Then transfer, uncovered, to a slow oven (150°C/300°F/Gas Mark 2), for at least 1 hour, until completely tender. The sweetness of dried apricots varies considerably, and so, correspondingly, will the amount of sugar required in any recipe. Rely on your own taste in this matter; you may or may not have to adjust the sweetness after baking. A squeeze of lemon juice will also help to sharpen the flavour.

Most of the bright orange dried apricots are processed using sulphur dioxide: this produces a distinctive, sherbety tang which rather masks the true flavour of the fruit. If possible buy 'unsulphured' or 'preservative-free' apricots. They are a dark golden-brown, and have a far better flavour. You can also buy a small, whole, sun-dried variety from Afghanistan called Hunza apricots. Hard and wrinkled, like little walnuts, they do not look appealing, but once reconstituted are quite delicious. They should be soaked overnight (again, in sweetened water) before being reconstituted as described above.

Banana

I once saw this little rhyme written on the back of a brown paper bag that a small local grocer wrapped my bananas in:

> A green banana's for cooking and keeping
> A speckled banana's for immediate eating.

It's not going to win any literary prizes, but it does encapsulate the basic wisdom of buying and keeping bananas. One might add that very ripe bananas, their skins thinned and almost black, are the sweetest and most intensely flavoured of all. Indeed they are so sweet, soft and strongly flavoured in this state that I find them rather hard to eat *au naturel*, but they are wonderful for making ices, mousses and fools. Blackened bananas can often be had at knock-down prices from grocers and market stalls.

The ripening of bananas is a process of converting starch into sugar. In a week or so, even the greenest of bananas will ripen if kept uncovered at room temperature. Never put bananas into the fridge; it not only halts the ripening process but sends the fruit into a quick decline. In the winter, beware also of keeping bananas in a very cold larder, and do not buy bananas which already show signs of chilling damage: their skins are a dusky grey-brown colour; they can be distinguished from bananas which are simply ripe by their firmness, their still unshrivelled stalk, and the fact that they are flushed all over, rather than simply speckled, with brown.

Rum is the classic alcoholic friend of the banana, though Jane Grigson in her *Fruit Book* says kirsch and gin are even better. I am not entirely convinced about the gin, but it is certainly worth a try. For a simple dish of boozy baked bananas, put one large banana per person into a moderate oven (180°C/350°F/Gas Mark 4) for 15–20 minutes (a little longer if they are unripe), until blackened and soft. Each person splits their own banana, pouring on a good slosh of the chosen alcohol. Serve with them double, whipped or clotted cream. A more sophisticated sauce can be made from sieved apricot jam heated with a slosh of rum, brandy or kirsch.

Good companions to ripe, raw bananas are thick Greek yoghurt, soft cheese or fromage frais and, of course, cream. Add to any of these a dribble of runny honey or a sprinkling of dark brown sugar, or even a blob of jam, and a few toasted almond flakes, or better still toasted slivers of coconut, and a modest banana is transformed into a wicked pudding. Even more wicked is a banana split: my recipe is simply a split banana, a scoop of vanilla ice cream, a good chocolate sauce and a few toasted almonds. (See also Banana and Lemon Ice Cream, page 365.)

Bilberry

(aka BLAEBERRY)

Not grown commercially, these dark little berries are very close cousins of the cultivated blueberry. Native to Britain, they can often be found on the high heaths and heather moors of the north of England, Scotland, Wales and Ireland in late summer and early autumn. Nibbled straight from their low, scrubby bushes, they have made a refreshing snack for many a tired hiker. If you take the trouble to gather a significant quantity, one of the best uses of them is in the traditional Scottish recipe of cranachan (page 370). They are also good in pies, tarts, jams, ices and bottled in alcohol, and can be used in any recipe which specifies blueberries; indeed the extra sharpness of their flavour mean that many such recipes will be improved. The French, who take them more seriously than we do, call the bilberry *myrtille*, and make a fine liqueur of the same name.

Blackberry

Blackberries are one of the best fruit freebies to be had in this country. In a good season, and where brambles proliferate, even a leisurely picker can fill a basket in less than an hour. I love blackberry and apple pie, but it is not as easy to make a good one as you might think, and Bramleys are certainly not the best apples to use. The recipe on page 367 gives a reliable procedure. Besides this perennial favourite, blackberries can also be used in cranachan (page 370), summer puddings, fools, ices and mousses and of course bramble jam. Blackberries cooked with a little sugar, then sieved and enriched with a splash of port, make a wonderful sauce for vanilla ice cream, or a light Genoese sponge to be served as a pudding with cream. The same sauce, sharpened with the juice of ½ lemon and sweetened with extra sugar, freezes to a superb sorbet. Wild blackberries come into season from August, but there are a number of cultivated strains that ripen earlier.

Blackcurrant

The half-dozen blackcurrant bushes in my parents' garden are so prolific that, even after half the crop has been given away, it is a struggle to find uses for what is left. Delicious though it is (preferable, I think, to a sorbet) we even tire of the blackcurrant ice cream that seems to half-fill the freezer after the glut, and every year it seems that what has not been eaten is rather guiltily thrown out of the freezer when the new crop is all too imminent. One of the problems is the currants' powerful flavour, so strong that just a few spoonfuls of a rich sieved purée are enough to flavour the basic ice cream mousse (see page 363). Bear this strength in mind also when making summer puddings – blackcurrants should never, I feel, make up more than a quarter of the overall fruit content. A preserve would be the obvious solution, but unfortunately none of my family is very partial to the strident flavour and sickly richness of blackcurrant jam. We keep pledging, so far in vain, that we will make vast quantities of crème de cassis. Jane Grigson's *Fruit Book* has a recipe, so who knows, maybe this year.

I don't expect you will believe this until you try it, but I have discovered that the flavour of blackcurrants goes remarkably well with coffee. A mild coffee ice cream, served with a purée of sieved, cooked blackcurrants, sweetened but still tart, is as delicious as it is unlikely.

Blackcurrant leaves, in late spring and summer, have fine aromatic qualities, imparting a muscaty flavour to a hot sugar syrup in which they are steeped for a few minutes. Sharpened with the juice and zest of a few lemons, such a syrup makes one of the finest sorbets.

Blueberry

The commercially grown version of the bilberry, the fatter blueberry is sweeter but can be a little bland. To buy fresh they are also expensive, as they are only grown in this country on a small scale, and most are imported from the USA. Their price has not encouraged me to experiment with them much. While working as a pastry chef at the River Café, in London, I did once use blueberries to make an almond tart (see pages 360–1). The results were excellent.

Boysenberry
see LOGANBERRY

Cherry

From the point of view of the shopper and cook, cherries can be divided into three classes. Sweet dessert cherries are grown for eating raw; sour cherries for cooking and canning; sour-sweet cherries, often known as dukes, cover both uses. There is no particularly strong reason for not using sweet cherries in your cooking, but the sharp flavour of a sour or sour-sweet variety will generally produce more interesting results.

The season for our native cherries is a short one: beginning in June, it is often over by late July. Even extended by early imports from southern Europe and later ones from the USA and elsewhere, it often seems that the cherries are gone before they have arrived. Be on guard, and make sure you get your share.

There are many interesting varieties of cherry which vary considerably in sweetness, flavour and succulence. The pale yellow Merton Glory, tinted with rose, is an excellent sweet English cherry; Black Tartarians are another good variety, dark, sweet and juicy. The dark red Montmorency and the black Morello (essential for black cherry jam and hence in Black Forest gâteau) are the best known of the sour cooking cherries.

Unfortunately the labelling of cherries is woefully inadequate in many of our shops; few tell you more than whether to expect the fruit in question to be sour or sweet. Even the juiciest dark red cherries, especially imported varieties, can turn out to be insipid and tasteless. Consequently the Right to Taste Before You Buy is to be championed where cherries are concerned. Any surly grocer who does not oblige your request does not deserve your custom. I even taste cherries in supermarkets, and I haven't been arrested yet.

Stoning cherries

Unless you enjoy a rather extended game of 'Rich Man, Poor Man', and are prepared to run the risk of broken teeth, it is advisable to stone cherries for use in many recipes. (The clafoutis on page 368 is an exception – the juices would turn the batter an unappetizing grey/purple when cooked.) I have a rather handy gadget which is incorporated into the handle of my garlic crusher. It is intended for stoning olives, but it works just as well on cherries (see page 11).

Cooking with cherries

Sour cherries go well with many types of meat, particularly strong game and duck. An excellent if rather elaborate procedure for Duck Montmorency (with cherry sauce) is described by Jane Grigson in her *Fruit Book*. A simpler version which can also be used for game is to deglaze the roasting tin with giblet stock and a lightly sweetened syrup in which you have already cooked some stoned sour cherries (these you have set aside). Then strain this gravy into another pan, reduce a little more, adjust the seasoning to taste, and whisk in a little butter so the sauce is smooth and glossy. Garnish each serving of the birds in question with the cherries, and serve with the sauce.

My favourite cherry pudding is the clafoutis recipe described on page 368. A sauce made from sour cherries cooked in a sugar syrup is excellent with pancakes, or ice cream, or both. Cherries and kirsch, the alcohol which is distilled from them, are both ingredients in the fruit salad that appears on page 372.

Cranberry

The English have never shared the American and Scandinavian enthusiasm for this berry, and neither, until recently, had I. They always seemed to turn out bitter however much sugar I cooked them with, until an American friend gave me a tip: cook them with just enough water to not quite cover them, or better still with freshly squeezed orange juice, and do not sweeten them until after they have softened (about 4–5 minutes). Then they can be sweetened with less sugar than you would think necessary (and less, in fact, than most recipes specify) – 8 oz/225 g per lb/450 g cranberries is usually enough. This gives you a basic cranberry sauce, which will keep for a couple of weeks in a jar in the fridge. It is good with venison and hare as well as turkey.

Because of their hard, waxy skins, cranberries keep extremely well – for several weeks in fact. The first cranberries are imported from early autumn, and remain available fresh in our shops until Christmas and beyond.

I have not experimented widely with cranberries in tarts and cakes, but I have used leftover cranberry sauce made according to the method above to make a cranberry and almond tart. Simply spread the sauce over the base of a blind-baked tart shell, and spoon over the almond batter, according to the recipe on page 360. The results are excellent.

Damson

see PLUM

Dates

Fresh dates

Having once been found only dried or packed in blocks, fresh dates are now available in this country – most readily in the autumn. Though the skin is a little crunchier than that on the familiar dried version, they have a very pleasant taste. They can be stir-fried in clarified butter for no more than half a minute, sprinkled with toasted almonds and served with cream (a good preparation suggested by Madhur Jaffrey). Simmered in a light sugar syrup until disintegrated, then sieved and enlivened with a tot of whisky or brandy, they make a fabulous sauce for vanilla ice cream. The same can be done with block or dried dates, but the results are not quite as delicious.

Dried dates

Dried dates are very variable in quality. Often coated in glycerine, to give them that supposedly desirable sticky coating, they become too sweet for my palate. The best dried dates of all are the giant Medjool variety from California. Deliciously dark, they are fat and chewy with a wonderful caramel flavour.

Fig

For several years now the fig tree in my parents' garden has not had enough autumn sunshine to ripen its fruit. A pity, as the figs we import from overseas, picked prematurely, are not a patch on the ones that are allowed to ripen on the tree. When buying fresh figs in this country (available from late August almost until Christmas), avoid those which look too green and firm. Examine the base of the fruit: a good sign of ripeness is if the skin has cracked here, seeping a little of its sticky juice. Whether or not you peel figs is a matter of personal taste. In my view the thin-skinned varieties, dark purple or purple-brown, certainly don't need it.

Unripe figs, and the bland flavour of the rather watery fruit that is sometimes encountered, can be greatly improved by grilling – put the figs on a griddle pan for a few minutes, turning occasionally, until the skins are lightly blistered. Figs grilled in this way are delicious with salty dry-cured ham, ideally from Parma, of course.

Dried figs vary considerably in quality; the rather hard kind, often dusted with white preservative powder containing sulphur compounds, are the least good. I prefer the moist, 'ready-to-eat' kind, either straight out of their plastic bag or simmered gently in fresh orange juice to make a compote – lovely with Greek yoghurt and toasted almond flakes.

Gooseberry

Would that wild gooseberries were as easy to find as blackberries. Unless you are privy to the well-guarded secret of a bush's location, your best bet for a decent price on large quantities of gooseberries is a pick-your-own farm. At the height of the season (which lasts from late June to September) they can sometimes be had for a good price in country greengrocers, though they seem to be unfairly expensive in supermarkets.

The fine tart flavour of fresh gooseberries, redolent, as Elizabeth David noted, of sorrel, has versatile applications, sweet and savoury. Only unusually sweet berries are good to eat raw. Most gooseberries are best lightly stewed, in only enough water to prevent them burning in their initial contact with heat. Once all the fruit has broken, and bubbled for just a few moments, it is cooked enough. The resulting fruit pulp, sweetened with icing or caster sugar, can be sieved (in which case it's unneccessary to top and tail the berries) for sauces, ice creams and sorbets; they need not be sieved (but must be topped and tailed) if you are making a fool, in which the seeds and skins contribute to the flavour as well as the character of the dish. When the gooseberries are cold, simply sweeten to taste, mash them with a fork, and stir into them thick double cream. Whisked egg whites and whipped cream are a heinous distraction. A fool was always meant to be rough and ready.

A tart purée of gooseberries goes well with oily fish: cold with smoked mackerel, or hot with fresh grilled mackerel, herring fried in oatmeal, or bloaters poached in milk. As hot puddings go, a gooseberry crumble (page 370), takes a lot of beating.

Grape

More acreage world-wide is given over to the growing of grapes than any other fruit. Only a tiny fraction, of course, are for eating. The rest go for wine.

Like cherries, table grapes are poorly labelled in the shops. Their country of origin, and whether or not you can expect pips, are all you are likely to be told. Well-known varieties such as Thompson seedless and Muscatel may be labelled. Otherwise the shopper should expect, on polite enquiry, to be allowed to taste what is available, and buy what he or she prefers.

Grapes should be gently but thoroughly rinsed in cold water before you put them into the fruit bowl. Apart from fruit salads, in which they are nicer if peeled and de-pipped, I rarely use grapes in any recipe.

The various forms of dried grapes, on the other hand, are a versatile ingredient essential to many fine dishes.

Currants, raisins and sultanas

These are all different types of dried grape. Currants come from small black grapes; the best are from Greece. Raisins should be prepared from varieties of Muscatel grape – preferably from Spain or California; Malaga raisins are the greatest delicacy. The best sultanas, made from white grapes, come from Turkey and Greece. According to purists, sultanas made from seedless grapes have an inferior taste; in my view, the gritty pips are a high price to pay for a difference in flavour that is probably marginal. The eagle-eyed shopper may have reason for self-congratulation if he or she finds sultanas that are described on the packet as seeded (i.e. the pips have been removed) rather than seedless (which never had any).

Grapefruit

The grapefruit is in fact one of the citrus hybrids, a cross between an orange and a pomelo – the latter is a good fruit, sweeter than an ordinary grapefruit, and is now widely available in our shops. The large, green-yellow ugli fruit is an interesting but expensive cousin of the grapefruit, well worth an occasional outing.

It is important to bear in mind when buying any citrus fruits that they will not sweeten any further, however long you keep them for, so you must choose well. The rose-flushed pink or ruby grapefruits from Cyprus and Florida are the best, though even these can be sour if they have been prematurely picked. Shiny, tight-skinned fruit with a good pink flush may look the most tempting, but in fact the duller fruit, slightly soft with a thicker, looser skin, are usually sweeter. Grapefruits will keep a little longer in the fridge, and are anyway more delicious served chilled.

Few elaborate preparations for grapefruit are really worthwhile. The only recipe I regularly prepare is a salad of fresh grapefruit segments and sliced avocado – the flavours combine beautifully, and the only dressing required is good olive oil, salt and black pepper, though a light mayonnaise can be used. Grapefruit also goes well with soft cheese – fromage frais or the branded Quark cheese.

Candied peel

Cost-conscious cooks with a little time on their hands can get a delightful bonus from citrus fruits if they save and candy the peel. It is full of goodness, containing more vitamin C than the flesh or juice. Strips of peel, ½ in/1 cm thick, including the white pith, should be simmered in plenty of boiling water for 20 minutes. Discard the water, bring a pan of fresh water to the boil, and repeat the procedure. Then make a light sugar syrup by dissolving 10 oz/300 g sugar in 5 fl oz/150 ml water (enough syrup for the peel of 2 grapefruits). Bring this to a rapid boil and add the twice-blanched peel. Remove the peel when the syrup is in danger of boiling dry, or shows the first signs of caramelizing (turning brown). Leave the peel on a rack in an airing cupboard for 48 hours, to dry off any stickiness, then toss the pieces generously in caster sugar and store in a jar.

Peel candied like this makes a delicious sweet, which can be coated in dark chocolate for extra luxury. It is also far better for use in cakes and puddings than any 'mixed peel' you can buy in the shops, though you should rinse off some of the excess sugar before using.

Greengage
see PLUM

Kiwi
(aka CHINESE GOOSEBERRY)

This versatile fruit, so pretty in cross-section, boomed in the 1980s and is so widely cultivated now, in Australasia and South America, that it is no longer expensive and is available all year round. A bad kiwi is a rarity, though you should avoid soft fruit and any whose skins are slightly loose.

The hairy brown peel is edible in theory, but the fruit is usually peeled and sliced. Championed by *nouvelle cuisine*, the kiwi has been over-used as a largely decorative element in savoury dishes. It is at its best simply on its own, or in a fruit salad. It certainly combines pleasantly with strawberries, and a strawberry and kiwi pavlova – a meringue base, heaped with whipped cream and decorated with slices of the two fruits – is a fine dessert. Kiwis make a good sorbet, a less good ice cream.

Lemon and lime

Buying lemons and limes is not hard; you merely have to avoid fruit that is damaged or looks old and a little wrinkled. With lemons it can be frustrating to slice the fruit in half only to find that the pith to flesh ratio has left you a little short-changed. It is usually the larger fruits that exhibit this syndrome, particularly those with extended pointy bits at either end (forgive the unscientific description, but you will know what I mean). I would not claim it is a hard and fast rule, but the smaller, rounder lemons seem to me to be more reliably fleshy and juicy.

Whole books could, and probably have, been written about the lemon. The culinary uses for it are practically without limit, and it is called for in many recipes in this and every chapter. I have no great wisdom to add to what is already appreciated, through experience, by most cooks. But I would urge cooks to be less wasteful of the skin of this and other citrus fruits. It contains the aromatic essential oils of the fruit which add scent as well as flavour to dishes. Most lemons in our shops have been waxed to prevent contamination. They should therefore be well washed in hot water before the zest or peel is used. Alternatively, buy unwaxed or organically grown lemons, increasingly available in supermarkets.

There is one important caveat: the pith of both lemon and lime will, when cooked for any length of time, impart a bitterness to the cooking liquid. When poaching or braising a fish, for example, or baking it in foil, it is advisable to use only the zest (i.e. the thinly pared rind, free of white pith) and the juice of lemons or limes.

Pith-free zest can be stripped from the fruit with a potato peeler, but a zester, designed specifically to do the job, is better, and not expensive. The same applies when you are preparing a sugar syrup for a sorbet, ice cream, mousse or sauce. On the other hand the pith should be included when you are making candied peel (see GRAPEFRUIT above). Most of the bitterness is removed by the blanching process, and what little is left is an important part of the flavour of the sweetmeat.

'Preserved' lemons, salted rather than candied, are much used in North African cookery – see page 171 for technique and recipe.

The more distinctive taste of the lime is less often called for in recipes than the lemon, but it is essential in many foreign dishes, such as Thai thom yum and Mexican ceviche. It can usually be substituted, for a change from lemon. The results will certainly be different, but rarely inferior.

Loganberry and other soft fruit hybrids

The loganberry was claimed by its inventor, a Judge Logan of Santa Cruz, to be a cross between a raspberry and a blackberry. Other botanists have since suggested it is simply a cultivar (i.e. variant strain) of the Pacific blackberry. Either way, it has good qualities, being sweet, sharp and aromatic. Popular in the USA, it is also grown on a small scale in Britain, and can be used in summer puddings, or to make fools, ices and jams. Other cluster-berry strains which make an occasional appearance in our shops are the boysenberry and tayberry, both good, but usually expensive. They can be found in some pick-your-own farms, however, in which case you can expect to get them for a better price.

Lychee

Once available only canned, and something of a joke as the only dessert available on the menus of some Chinese restaurants, the lychee is now imported fresh, and we can appreciate its considerable qualities. The tough, knobbly, red-brown skin is easily peeled away to reveal a juicy whitish pulp enclosed by a thin membrane. In the centre of the pulp is a large brown seed. This is inedible and should be discarded. I have never cooked with lychees, though I have eaten a delicious dish of hot lychee fritters coated in a crunchy caramel in Chinese restaurants.

A relative of the fruit, which looks like a lychee with a hairy skin, is the rambutan. The rambutan's rough skin should be cut away with a sharp knife, and the pulp eaten in the same way, except that the seed, which has a nutty almond taste, can also be eaten.

Mango

Several sizes and varieties of mango are available. This skin of all types is green when unripe, but turns yellow, orange or red, or a combination of all of these, as the fruit ripens. A ripe mango should yield to pressure from fingertips, but too much softness suggests bruising, and very squishy fruit should be avoided unless you want it for a fool, ice cream or sorbet. Very hard green mangoes will spoil before they ripen, but those showing the first flush of ripeness can be left to sweeten in a warm room or, better still, on a sunny windowsill. The smaller, orange mangoes, which are more often found in ethnic markets than supermarkets, are often the best.

Mangoes have a powerful aromatic flavour all their own, so I rarely combine them with other fruits, oranges excepted – Jemima's restaurant makes a particularly fine sorbet of Mango and Blood oranges (page 373). Mixed with cream, mashed mango flesh makes a delicious fool.

Mangosteen

One of the best of all fruits, and one of the most difficult to cultivate, I have encountered the mangosteen only rarely but live in hope that it may become more widely available in this country. The size of a small apple, it has a thick, smooth, aubergine-coloured rind, buffed with streaks of brown. The rind is peeled away to reveal five plump segments covered with a delicate pink fibrous membrane. This is gently scraped away, and the juicy, ivory-coloured segments eaten whole. Texture and flavour are superb. If ever you travel to the Far East – Thailand, Malaysia, Sri Lanka, the Philippines or Vietnam – do not miss the chance to taste this fruit. You may never want to come home. In March and April you will sometimes find mangosteens in the grocers of Soho's Chinatown.

Melon

The growing English taste for this fruit has encouraged our greengrocers and supermarkets to increase the varieties on offer. As they are grown in both hemispheres, melons are available all the year round. Those that arrive from southern Europe in September, the Cantaloupe and Charentais in particular, are among the best. I like all melons, provided they are ripe and in good condition. They do not sweeten much after picking, so it is important to find a ripe specimen. The way to test is the same for all types: press your thumbs gently into the base, which should give a little. The rest of the melon should be firm and unbruised. The best types of melon are fragrant when ripe, even before being cut. Another good sign is a clean break where the melon has been detached from the stem. A cut stem still attached to the fruit suggests it was picked prematurely. It is a myth that you can ripen a melon on a sunny windowsill; the flesh will soften after a day or two, but you cannot expect any significant improvement in flavour.

A good ripe melon should be refrigerated when you get home and then kept only for a few days. Melons are at their best when freshly cut, but half a melon or a slice can be kept wrapped in clingfilm in a refrigerator for 24 hours. Apart from keeping the melon fresh, clingfilm is essential to prevent the flavour from permeating other foods in the fridge.

A pinch of ground ginger sprinkled over the fruit is a traditional complement to melon, but I prefer the fruit unadulterated unless it is slightly unripe or disappointingly bland (as some Honeydews can be). A half-melon with the seeds scooped out makes a good receptacle for a salad of other fruits, but there is no need to get too elaborate: the sliced flesh of a sweet ripe pear and a few fresh raspberries with melon is a simple combination which is hard to improve on.

Melon sorbet can be superb, but requires a very sweet, ripe and aromatic fruit, such as the best Charentais or Cantaloupe. Damaged or overripe fruit bought cheaply can be used in this way. Purée the flesh in a blender, add a squeeze of lemon juice, and a little sugar syrup only if you feel it needs extra sweetening. It often doesn't.

The combination of melon and Parma ham may be a cliché, but for good reason: it is delicious.

The distinctive watermelon gets a separate entry on page 359.

Mulberry

So delicate and soft is the ripe fruit of the mulberry tree that harvesting and transporting it is completely impractical. Only if you own, or know of, a tree, will you be able to enjoy this delightful, finger-staining fruit. Mulberries can be added to (late) summer puddings, and used to make jams, sorbets and ices, or simply eaten gluttonously with cream. They are best gathered when fully ripe and fallen from the tree – those in the know spread sheets, called drop cloths, around the tree to prevent the delicate fruit from becoming dirty. Mulberries are so delicate that washing will damage them, though a very gentle rinse is perhaps advisable if you doubt their cleanness. Lightly cooked with a little caster sugar, just until the juices run, a compote of mulberries is delicious served with fresh ripe pears and cream.

Orange, Tangerine, Mandarin, Clementine and other citrus hybrids

The many types of orange available in our shops chop and change throughout the year. Many look so similar that it is hard to get a grip on particular sub-types. Better to go with the flow, always avoiding dry, damaged or wrinkled-looking fruit, and simply appreciate the differences in acidity and sweetness as a seasonal variation. If you use oranges every day, as I do, the occasional insipid fruit, or one with a disappointing yield of juice, is an occupational hazard that one has to accept philosophically. Having said that, Navel oranges always seem to be reliably juicy and flavourful – I probably buy them more often than any other kind.

For marmalade, and also for many recipes in which oranges are cooked, bitter Seville oranges are unmatchable. They are available for a few weeks only, from late January to February, but as they freeze well (whole but wrapped in clingfilm) the season can be extended.

Blood oranges, apart from their dramatic colouring, definitely have a distinctive flavour, redolent, I think, of blackberries. They are the most beautiful fruit to present on their own in a salad, ideally in a caramelized syrup, with julienne strips of peel.

As with all citrus fruits, it is a shame to waste the aromatic flavour of orange skin. The peel can be candied (see GRAPEFRUIT above for instructions), and the zest, thinly pared with a zester, added to any dish in which the juice is being added as a flavouring. Thin julienne strips of pithless peel do not require the elaborate candying process: they can be simmered in a sugar syrup for 5 minutes, then added to fruit salads, used as a garnish, etc. A large piece of orange rind, thinly pared with a sharp knife or potato peeler, gives good flavour to a beef stew or *daube* and also to fish soup. It should be removed at the end of cooking.

Mandarin is the general name for small members of the orange family with a loose skin which peels easily. The family includes the tangerine, grown in the Mediterranean; the satsuma, specially developed in Japan to be seedless and keep well; and the clementine, a spontaneous hybrid of the orange and mandarin.

Citrus fruits hybridize well, and some recent products of growers' ingenuity are now widely available in supermarkets. The minneola, with its distinctive knob at the stem end, is a cross between a mandarin and a grapefruit. Sharp and very juicy, as well as easy to peel, it is a welcome addition to the range. The mapo has the yellow-green colour of a pomelo, is slightly larger than a tangerine, and has a hint of grapefruit bitterness. No doubt other variations will appear in the future.

Papaya

The papaya is fragile, and usually carefully packed in tissue to prevent damage. Despite this precaution, papayas in this country are all too often bruised before they are ripe, and no good to anybody. A careless purchase is a sad waste of too much money. You are very lucky if you find a fully ripe and quite unblemished fruit. Your best bet is to choose a clean fruit that is still on the green side and take good care of it at home. On a sunny windowsill, or close to a warm lamp, green fruit will soon ripen to yellow. The ripe papaya should be soft to the touch but not mushy. Chill before serving, then cut the papaya in half, scrape out the seeds, and scoop out the flesh with a teaspoon. A squeeze of lime is, I would suggest, essential; lemon definitely second-best. I always eat papayas on their own in this way, my favourite breakfast treat. The subtle taste is lost if it is swamped in a fruit salad.

Unripe green papayas are used a lot in Indian and Far Eastern cooking. They are a pleasant but unexciting addition to a curry; as they are expensive this may be regarded as something of a waste.

Passion fruit
and Grenadilla

The skin of the passion fruit hardens to a dark, dimpled shell, from which the seeds and powerfully flavoured pulp can be scooped with a spoon, and greedily eaten with little ceremony and, if you like, a lot of cream. The intense aroma of the fruit means that it makes a good ingredient as well as a great indulgence when eaten raw. Ambitious chefs will want to experiment with soufflés (there is an excellent recipe in Jane Grigson's *Fruit Book*), bavarois, mousses and the like. I am content to restrict my repertoire to sorbets and ice cream. For the former, add an equal quantity of light sugar syrup to the sieved juice and pulp of your passion fruits, and freeze in your machine, or in the old-fashioned way in the freezer (see page 365). For ice cream, blend enough of the fruit pulp (you can keep the pips in if you like) with the basic custard and cream (see page 363) to give a sharp but not overpowering passion fruit flavour.

The grenadilla is a larger, yellow-orange fruit of the same family. The flavour is similar but less intense, and it can be eaten and used in the same way. The grenadilla is sometimes called the yellow passion fruit, and the passion fruit sometimes called the purple grenadilla.

Peach
and Nectarine

No distinction is necessary between these two fruits: the nectarine is simply a smooth-skinned variety of peach, usually a little smaller than the fuzzy kind. A more valid distinction is between the freestone and clingstone varieties of both fruits: the terms describe how easily the fruit can be separated from its stone. The more robust clingstones, which travel better, now predominate in the market-place, but the large, white-fleshed peach, one of the finest varieties, is a freestone.

The dry, cotton-woolly texture of some peaches is caused by premature picking and a long stay in cold storage. Peaches will ripen at home to an extent, especially if exposed to sunlight on a windowsill. But do not expect miracles: a rock-hard, sour-fleshed peach will never come good. It is best to choose those that are at least approaching ripeness, and give a little when pressed with the fingertips. The skin of a ripe peach should peel away fairly easily, without taking any of its flesh with it. Fruit with a slightly wrinkled skin, that seems soft on the surface but harder underneath, is also to be avoided; it has probably had the cold-storage treatment.

Peaches that have not had to travel too far – for example, those from Spain and Italy – are likely to be the best bet. Those that arrive towards the end of our summer have not been forced or grown under glass, and are particularly worth seeking out.

When you do get a perfect peach, it seems a shame to do anything other than eat it without further ado. Peaches that are not quite ripe can be peeled, cut into quarters or eighths, and poached gently for just a few minutes in a light syrup. Alternatively, layer thin slices overlapping on the bottom of a flame-proof dish, sprinkle with soft brown sugar and place under a grill until the juices run and the sugar bubbles (2–3 minutes). Serve either preparation with vanilla ice cream (or better still, crème brûlée), and a purée of raspberries.

Pear

A pear is ripe when the stalk end starts to soften a little. It is right that pears should be picked before they are fully ripe; they become mealy if left too long on the tree. On the other hand, like peaches, if they are picked too early they will never become sweet. If a pear is so hard and green that you cannot believe it will ripen, then it probably never will. English pears in season (August–November) are usually picked with care: buy them while still firm and allow them to mellow in a warm room at home for a day or two. Out of the native season, the imported variety I have least difficulty with is the elongated, slightly russeted Conference pear. Buy those with a little 'give' around the stalk and they will soon ripen. A good ripe pear is delicious with a salty blue cheese: Stilton, Roquefort and, my favourite, Gorgonzola.

Happily, even unripe pears can be transformed by poaching in wine, though this is not as easy as some cooks seem to think. It requires a well-thought-out recipe, such as the one I have adapted from Alan Davidson's *Fruit* (see page 372). It goes back to medieval times, and has certainly stood the test of time.

Of all the variations I suggest for the Fruit and Almond Tart on page 360, pear is the best.

Physalis
(aka CAPE GOOSEBERRY)

The physalis is unmistakable on account of the papery brown husks in which the little fruit is hidden. They keep and travel well and have a fine sour-sharp taste. To eat them you pull back the papery husk and, holding on to it, bite away the pink-orange berry, skin, seeds and all. Apart from this the only way I have ever had the fruit is dipped in fondant icing or white chocolate, at the end of meals in smart restaurants. These dainty petits fours are very good indeed, and could easily be made at home.

Pineapple

A good pineapple is worth every ounce of labour in its preparation. However, you don't want to be landed with a sour, unripe fruit, so choose carefully. The first guide is the size of the leafy plume on top of the pineapple. Contrary to what you might expect, this should be as small as possible relative to the fruit. Besides having a large plume, an unripe pineapple is hard and has a greenish tinge. Softer, orange-brown skin indicates a sweet and juicy fruit. A good pineapple ready for eating will also smell fragrant and tempting.

It may be a personal blind-spot, connected with unhappy memories of school food and motorway service stations, but I have yet to be converted to the use of pineapple in savoury recipes. I fear the ubiquitous pressed gammon steak topped with a slice of canned pineapple has put me off for life.

With other fruits, however, pineapple is very versatile. There is no need to overcrowd fruit salads: try a simple four-fruit combination of pineapple with a good orange-fleshed melon (ideally Cantaloupe), fresh strawberries and bananas.

Plum, Damson, Greengage

The many varieties of plum and greengage all have their good points, but only a few are really delicious eaten raw. A workable rule, though it has exceptions, is that yellow and green varieties are the sweetest and best to serve *au naturel*, whereas red, purple and black kinds generally require cooking. This gives us, for eating: our own greengages and a good golden plum called, rather charmingly, the Warwickshire Dropper (both seasonal for a couple of months from late August or September); imported golden plums from the southern hemisphere (which arrive over here in early spring); and best of all, if you can track them down, the small yellow Mirabelles from France and the Continent.

Red, purple and black plums, for example the Santa Rosa and very dark, round Friar from California, and our own native Victorias and damsons, have a less pleasing texture and tend to be on the sour side. Cooking, and the addition of a little sugar, transforms them. Unless you intend to make a smooth purée it is better to cook plums whole and with the skins still on: the tannins in the skin add a slightly bitter note to the flavour which, in most dishes, is a bonus. A small slit in each plum – traditionally a cross in the bottom – will help the juices run. Only a little water is needed in the pan, to prevent the plums from burning; they will stew in their own juice. As with all fruit, fierce cooking is inadvisable: a gentle simmer will soften the fruit nicely without entirely destroying its shape. Add sugar towards the end of the cooking, allowing your taste to tell you how much is required: it will vary greatly according to the natural sweetness of the fruit. The stones can, if you wish, be removed after stewing.

Hot stewed plums with custard made from fresh eggs is a great treat on a chilly autumn day; cold, they are delicious with thick cream. For pies and crumbles (see page 370) it is advisable to use part-stewed fruit, drained, if it is very runny, of some of the excess liquid. This will prevent the dish from becoming too sloppy.

For ice creams and sorbets, it is probably a good idea to peel the plums, as the tannic flavour is less desirable in such dishes. If they do not peel easily, scald them with boiling water and leave for 30 seconds. After peeling, stew with sugar, then reduce to a fairly concentrated purée, and pass through a sieve. The purée can then be stirred into your basic ice cream custard, or thinned with a little sugar syrup if you want to make a sorbet (see pages 363–5 for detailed techniques). Damson ice cream is excellent, which is worth knowing as English damsons are very cheap in a good season (early autumn).

Prune

The prune is one of the greatest of all dried fruits, delicious on its own, and a versatile ingredient too. The finest, and also the most expensive, are the *pruneaux d'Agen*, from the Armagnac region in France. No great surprise, then, that the prune has been brought together with that region's most celebrated product: prunes soaked in Armagnac are one of the great gustatory experiences. It is not really necessary to use either Agen prunes or an expensive Armagnac to re-create this wonderful concoction (though an Armagnacien would, I am certain, fervently disagree). Simply cram a jar full of good prunes (ideally not the very moist varieties, as being moist already they will absorb less of the alcohol) and pour in enough brandy (a decent brand, even if it is not Armagnac) to fill the gaps. Put a lid on the jar and leave the prunes to plumpen and infuse in the alcohol for at least a week. A sealed jar will keep for months, but it will require more self-control than I possess to leave them on the shelf for long. I like Armagnac prunes with vanilla ice cream.

California is now easily the largest producer of prunes, and the Agen plum is widely used there too – another reason why one should not feel obliged to buy expensive French prunes. The best prunes are naturally sun-dried and contain no preservatives – check the packets when you are buying. Some varieties of pitted prunes are very hard and dry; to make them palatable you will have to soak them in tepid water or tea for a few hours (say 3–4). Whichever you use, sweeten it with a little caster or icing sugar: otherwise the natural sugars of the prunes will osmose into the liquid.

To make a good compote of prunes, poach them gently in tea (Lapsang Souchong is best), or fresh orange juice, red wine or water, according to your preference. Serve warm or cold, with egg custard or cream, or plain for a healthy breakfast.

The savoury applications of prunes are numerous: in stuffings (see page 320); in stews and casseroles, particularly of pork or rabbit; and to make a well-known canapé or savoury of which I never tire – prunes wrapped in streaky bacon, and baked in a fairly hot oven (200°C/400°F/Gas Mark 6), charmingly known as Devils on Horseback.

Pomegranate

A tasty and beautiful but problematic fruit. It is the seeds that are eaten, coated as they are in an aromatic, sour-sweet pulp. The membrane in which they are embedded is bitter, and will taint the juice if the fruit is crushed. The raw fruit is most easily eaten if cut in half, across either axis; the pips can then be scooped out with a spoon, but carefully, so as not to scrape away with them any of the membrane. If you want to make a sorbet, ice cream or long drink from fresh pomegranates, you will have to remove all the seeds carefully in this way, then rub them through a nylon sieve to get the juice. Choose ripe pomegranates, of a dark rusty-red, with a hard, slightly crinkled skin.

Pomelo

(*see* GRAPEFRUIT)

Quince

The luxury of a whole quince, baked in the oven, is something to treasure. Wipe any patches of soft grey down from the fruit, peel it, and hollow out the core from the top with a sharp knife (or use an apple corer). Fill the cavity with unsalted butter creamed with an equal quantity of sugar. Bake in a moderate oven (180°C/350°F/Gas Mark 4) for 30 minutes, until the quinces are tender. Serve with cream and more sugar if needed.

Unless you happen to own or know of a quince tree, you may have trouble acquiring this fruit and, when you do find it, it is unlikely to be a bargain. Add to this the fact that quinces are rarely sweet enough to eat raw, and it begins to seem as if this fruit is hardly worth the trouble. But those who know it and use it will tell you otherwise. It has fine aromatic qualities, like an apple blessed with the scent of the finest melon. And it is not necessary to buy huge quantities to get the full benefit of its flavour. One or even half a quince added to a dish of stewed apples, or sliced and added to an apple crumble or pie, will transform the dish, adding a delicate pinkness as well as a fine musky flavour when cooked.

Quince jam or jelly keeps well, and will add the flavour of quinces to pies and crumbles in concentrated form when the autumn season is over. For those who are not enthusiastic about making their own preserves, Wilkin and Sons, under the Tiptree label, make a fine quince jelly. Alternatively, a purée of cooked quince kept in the freezer can be deployed in the same way.

Raspberry

Buying raspberries in small punnets in the shops is an expensive business, nor is the fruit likely to compare with raspberries you pick yourself, for a fraction of the price, at one of the many fruit farms that now operate on a pick-your-own basis. July is the best month for raspberry picking, though some farms have late-cropping varieties that come good in September and October. The sign of a ripe fruit is that it comes easily away from the tough central core, leaving you with a clean fruit that is conveniently ready to eat. Raspberries should not be washed, as they become waterlogged and quickly lose their charm. Instead, simply pick over the fruit and discard any bits of stalk, leaf matter, etc. If you have picked a large quantity of fruit it may be worth setting aside any damaged fruit to purée for a coulis, sorbet or ice cream, or to add to a Summer Pudding (page 377).

At every stage of making a raspberry purée, avoid the use of wire sieves and other metal utensils, as they will taint the colour and to some extent the flavour of the fruit. If you crush raspberries in a food processor, use the plastic rather than the metal blade. I simply mash them in a bowl with my fingers – a gleefully messy task – and then rub them through a nylon sieve with a wooden spoon.

Fresh raspberries make the best of all sorbets. (See page 365 for basic principles of sorbet-making.)

Unless you are making jam it is rarely appropriate to cook raspberries, though raspberry and almond tart is a rather wonderful pudding – see page 362 for instructions.

Whole raspberries freeze better than most soft fruits – see guidelines on page 330.

Rhubarb

Rhubarb is coming into the shops as I write, in early spring. I have come through the unpleasant childhood experience of over-stewed rhubarb with custard made from powder, and learnt to enjoy this peculiar vegetable that masquerades as a fruit. Honey, ginger and orange (one, two or all three of them together) greatly enhance its slightly astringent taste, turning a plebeian dish into an aristocratic one.

Choose the thinnest, pinkest stems of rhubarb, ideally ones that are stiff, not bendy. Cut off the leaves and also the flat, brown part from the root end, and slice the stems into 2-in/5-cm lengths. For good stewed rhubarb, put the pieces into a heavy-based saucepan, adding, per 1 lb/450 g of fruit, the juice and zest of 1 orange, 2 generous tablespoons of honey or sugar, and a nut-sized piece of fresh ginger root, peeled and grated. Put over a moderate heat and once the juices start to bubble put the lid on and simmer for just 7–8 minutes, until the rhubarb is completely tender but not absolutely falling apart. Eat hot with real egg custard, cold with cream (mixed in, if you like, then chilled and served as a fool). The mixture can also be sieved or liquidized, and mixed with 10 fl oz/300 ml basic custard (see page 363) and 5 fl oz/150 ml double cream to make a fine ice cream.

A rather more tart purée of rhubarb, made with half the sugar specified above, makes a surprisingly good sauce for smoked or grilled mackerel.

Strawberry

The enormous pleasure given by this favourite of the English summer soft fruits is, I feel, being diminished by attempts to make it available all year round by importing from all over the world. Red these foreign impostors may be, but ripe and juicy they usually are not. The summer season of the English strawberry, its association with picnics, Ascot and Wimbledon, are a part of its charm. I for one am not inclined to meddle with it.

As with raspberries, the pick-your-own system means that large quantities of fine English strawberries can be had at a good price, with the assurance of absolute freshness. If this does not suit you, the caravans that set up in lay-bys and sell strawberries through the window may offer a keener price than your local greengrocer or supermarket. A wizened or bruised strawberry is not an appealing prospect for immediate eating, but provided it is not actually going bad, imperfect fruit can be crushed for sauces, ices, jams and the rather fine Strawberry and Mint Soup described on page 376.

As with raspberries, there are few good recipes, apart from jam, in which the strawberry benefits from cooking. Unlike raspberries, whole strawberries do not recover well from freezing; if you have a glut on your hands it is better to freeze them as a purée or make them into ice cream or sorbet. Even then the flavour fades faster than it does from other fruits, and strawberry ices should be eaten within a month.

Tangerine
(*see* ORANGE)

Ugli fruit
(*see* GRAPEFRUIT)

Watermelon

The increasing availability of watermelons in this country is something to celebrate: they are not expensive, and unbeatably refreshing when chilled.

If possible, buy whole watermelons rather than cut pieces, unless the piece has been cut for you and will not have to wait to be eaten. From midsummer to October a small and manageable variety called Sugar Baby, imported from Israel, is widely available. But even a full-sized watermelon can be swiftly despatched by a few enthusiasts.

Choose firm watermelons that feel as heavy as possible for their size. The pale yellowish patch from where the melon has been lying on the ground is quite normal.

Cut pieces of watermelon should be wrapped in clingfilm, kept in the fridge and eaten as soon as possible. Apart from being delicious *au naturel*, watermelon can be made into a fine sorbet: to 2 pts/1.1 litres of the sieved flesh add a light syrup made from 6 oz/170 g caster sugar and a little water and the juice of 1 large lemon. Freeze in the normal way (see page 365).

Recipes

Fruit and Almond Tart

Serves 8-10

Makes one 10 in/25 cm pastry case

This dish lends itself to all kinds of variations. The basic almond cream filling is simple to make and all manner of fruits combine well with it. The fruits are arranged in a pre-baked pastry shell, the almond cream spread over them, and the tart baked in a moderate oven. After the basic recipe for the pastry case and the almond cream I give a few suggestions for fruits you might like to use, with simple notes on how the recipe may be varied for each one.

My pastry recipe gives a crisp, biscuity result which I particularly like, but if you have your own preferred recipe for sweet pastry then feel free to use it. I always use a loose-bottomed, metal tart tin, as the tart can then be pushed out and transferred to a large plate on which it is attractively presented and easily served.

For the pastry shell (Basic Sweet Pastry recipe)
6 oz/170 g plain flour
a pinch of salt
3½ oz/100 g cool unsalted butter, diced
scant 2 oz/50 g caster sugar
2 egg yolks
1 scant tbsp cold water
a little extra flour for rolling

Sieve the flour into a mixing bowl with the salt. Add the butter, which should be cool but not too hard, and rub in with your fingers until the mixture is like breadcrumbs. Sieve in the sugar and mix in lightly with a fork. Make a well in the centre and add the egg yolks. Mix from the centre, gradually drawing in the flour. As the pastry stiffens and takes shape, work it with your fingers, adding the cold water only if it seems too dry. Do not overwork the pastry, but knead just long enough so that everything is well mixed and the texture even. Then wrap the pastry in clingfilm, foil or greaseproof paper and chill in the fridge for 1 hour.

Alternatively, you can make the pastry in a food processor, processing first the flour and butter, then the other ingredients, except the water. It is best not to over-process, and to finish the kneading by hand, adding the water at this stage, and only if it is needed.

Roll out the pastry on a clean, cool surface, using a light sprinkling of flour to make sure it doesn't stick. Line the tart tin, pressing the pastry into the edges and filling any cracks or holes with little strips of leftover pastry. Chill the pastry case in the fridge for 30 minutes, then prick the surface all over with a fork (these holes will allow air to escape and prevent the pastry from bubbling). Cover the pastry with tin foil or greaseproof paper and a layer of clay baking beads, or use dried kidney beans or similar. These will weigh down the pastry while it is cooking and also help to prevent blistering.

Bake the pastry case in a pre-heated moderate to hot oven (190°C/375°F/Gas Mark 5) for about 15 minutes. Then remove the foil/paper and beads/beans and leave the pastry in the oven for a further 2 minutes. At the end of this operation, known as 'baking blind', the pastry should be pale and lightly cooked, not browned, except perhaps at the very edges where it has not had the protection of the paper or foil.

The tart shell can be filled when still warm, and re-baked straight away, or covered when cool and left for a few hours, but certainly not more than 24.

For the almond cream
6 oz/170 g unsalted butter, softened
3 oz/85 g caster sugar
3 large eggs
6 oz/170 g ground almonds
1 tbsp rum

Cream the butter with the sugar until the mixture is pale and light. Beat in the eggs, one at a time, then the ground almonds, and finally the rum. The mixture should be a smooth cream, not too stiff, and almost pourable. If it is very stiff, perhaps your eggs were not very large – add another one, and beat in well. This can all be done in a food processor, but you will get a lighter result if you do it by hand.

Assembling the tart

Arrange the fruit in the bottom of the tart shell – the quantity should be generous, but not crammed so tight that there is no room for the almond cream to spread between the fruit.

Spread the almond cream evenly and carefully over the fruit, so the fruit is not dislodged but remains evenly distributed. If you like, you can sprinkle a few flaked almonds over the top.

Bake in a pre-heated moderate to hot oven (180°C/350°F/Gas Mark 4) for 30–35 minutes until golden-brown on top. Serve warm or at room temperature, but do not refrigerate or leave in a cold place before serving. Almond and fruit tarts can be served with cream, but crème fraîche is even better.

APRICOTS: choose 10–12 fresh apricots that are not too ripe or squashy. Prepare and bake as described on page 333; then arrange the apricot halves cut side down in concentric circles in the pre-baked tart shell. Spread over the almond cream and proceed as above.

BLUEBERRIES: you will need about 1 lb/450 g to make an even layer, one berry deep, in the bottom of the tart shell. Rinse the blueberries and toss them dry in a clean cloth. Put into the tart shell, spread over the almond cream and bake as above.

CHERRIES: you will need about 1 lb/450 g. Spread the almond cream into the tart shell, then press in the stoned cherries at equal intervals. Bake as above.

DATES AND PRUNES: dates and prunes work excellently with this tart, but both are very sweet, so withhold 1 oz/30 g of the sugar from the almond cream mixture. Mix about 12 oz/350 g roughly chopped, stoned prunes or dates with the finished almond cream, spread over the tart shell and bake as above. If you use prunes they can, for extra luxury, be soaked in brandy or Armagnac first.

PEACHES: choose fruit that is on the firm side of ripe. Four large peaches, peeled and halved, should be enough: you can fit 5–6 halves, cut side down, around the edge, and 2–3 in the middle. But if your peaches are small, you may need 6–7. Spread over the almond cream and bake as above.

PEARS: 5–6 large pears, ripe but not squashy (Conference are recommended), peeled, quartered and trimmed of any core. If the pears are very hard, peel them, and gently poach whole in a light syrup for 20 minutes, then cut into quarters. Arrange the quarters in a ring around the edge of the tart shell, almost touching. Fill any space left in the centre with one or two more pieces (trimmed to fit if necessary). Spread over the almond cream and bake as above.

PLUMS: as for apricots, except that it is not necessary to pre-bake the plums.

STRAWBERRIES AND RASPBERRIES: both are delicious with an almond tart, but should not be cooked in it as they become soft and mushy and tend to waterlog the tart. Better to cook a plain almond tart, leave it to cool, then arrange a layer of whole fresh raspberries, or sliced strawberries, on top, and glaze with a little warmed, sieved jam (raspberry or strawberry as appropriate).

Home-made ice creams and sorbets

For anyone who is as fond of these desserts as I am, an ice cream-making machine will save a great deal of time and trouble. The exhausting wrist action of beating a partially frozen ice-cream mixture is a strong disincentive to making ices at home, and even if you are prepared to perform this labour of love, the results will never be as creamy-smooth as those produced by a machine. Once you have a machine you can experiment and indulge your chilly fantasies to your heart's content.

Once made, fruit ices can be kept almost indefinitely in a freezer. The intensity of flavour will, however, gradually lessen over time. To enjoy them at their absolute best, eat fruit ices within 4 months of making them. Deep-frozen ices should be transferred to the fridge to soften about 2 hours before you plan to eat them.

Raspberry ice cream made with basic mousse custard
Makes 1³⁄₄ pts/1 litre

Many people make fruit ices by simply mixing a purée of fruit with double cream and sugar. I find the head-on clash between cream and the acids of the fruits means that ice creams made in this way do not always emulsify as well as they might, and they are either too acidic, or lacking in real fruit flavour. I prefer to use an egg custard as the basis for my fruit ices, particularly as the following technique, adopted from Constance Spry, means you can avoid both the time and risks normally associated with making custard.

Dissolve the sugar in the water in a small saucepan over a low heat. Turn up the heat, bring to the boil, and boil rapidly for about 5 minutes to get a light syrup (make sure you remove the pan from the heat before the syrup takes any colour and begins to caramelize). Whisk the egg yolks in a bowl and, as you do so, pour in the hot syrup in a thin trickle. Continue to whisk, allowing the heat of the syrup to cook the egg yolks, until you have a light, mousse-like cream. Lightly

4 oz/115 g caster sugar
5 fl oz/150 ml water
3 egg yolks
15 fl oz/450 ml double cream
1 lb/450 g raspberries

whip the double cream and fold the egg and sugar mousse into it. Rub the raspberries through a nylon sieve (not metal – see page 23), then stir this purée into the cream and eggs. Pour this mixture into your machine and freeze.

Alternatively, place in a mixing bowl in the deep-freeze, beating the partially frozen mixture every hour or so to break down the crystals. After the third or fourth beating, by which time the mixture should be thick and smooth, transfer to a suitable container and leave to freeze solid.

Variations

Into a custard made in exactly the same way, you can stir any number of fruit purées. For loganberry or blackberry ice cream, substitute the same amount of either of these fruits for the raspberries and proceed exactly as above. For strawberries, peaches, mangoes, melons and other less acidic fruits, add the juice of ½ lemon to the puréed fruit before incorporating with the custard. Some fruits, such as plums, damsons, cherries, gooseberries and blackcurrants, will have to be cooked first. When the cooked fruit is cold, rub it through a sieve and proceed as above. If the fruit has been cooked with a little sugar, use a little less (say 2 oz/60 g instead of 4 oz/115 g) when making the syrup for the mousse. You can also use a mixture of fruits: apricot and orange; papaya and kiwi, sharpened with lime; or a compote of blackberry and apple, rubbed through a sieve. In the alphabetical guide to fruits (pages 331–59), I have mentioned when a particular fruit is suitable for making ice cream, but the only real limits are your own imagination.

Besides cream and the custard base described above, there are other dairy items which can be used as 'emulsifiers' in fruit ices. Yoghurt, besides having a health advantage over cholesterol-rich cream, gives a zesty tang to such desserts. Below is an excellent recipe for a banana and lemon ice made with crème fraîche. Fromage frais, and even cream cheese, can also be used. Don't be shy of experimenting with such products – you might easily create something fabulous.

Banana and Lemon Ice Cream
Serves 6-8

The acidity of the lemons, and the freezing temperature at which this dish is served, seem to counteract the normally overpowering flavour of very ripe bananas. The result is an ice that is sharp, fruity and refreshing – one of my favourites. If the bananas are really very ripe and sweet, you can dispense with the sugar.

Combine all the ingredients in a blender or food processor and process until completely smooth. Pour into your ice-cream machine and blend until frozen according to the instructions. Alternatively, place in a mixing bowl in the freezer, beating the partially frozen mixture every hour or so to break down the crystals. After the third or fourth beating, transfer to a suitable freezing container and leave to freeze solid.

4 large, ripe bananas
grated rind and juice of 3 lemons
2 oz/60 g caster sugar
8 fl oz/250 ml crème fraîche

Sorbets

Sorbets are even easier to make than ice creams. Instead of custard, a light sugar syrup is your base. As a general rule, sorbets should be sharp and sweet. Before you freeze the mixture it should, if anything, be too sharp and too sweet. Your taste-buds are less stimulated by frozen foods, and what seems a little sickly and acidic when at room temperature should, when frozen, be refreshing and tangy. For 2 lb/900 g raspberries, sieved, I would make a syrup of 10 fl oz/300 ml water and 8 oz/225 g caster sugar. Dissolve the sugar in the water over a low heat, then boil the syrup rapidly for 5 minutes. Leave the syrup to cool before adding the fruit purée.

As with ice creams, some fruits, such as strawberries, peaches and apricots, will benefit from the addition of a little lemon juice. Very sweet fruits will require only a minimum of syrup – maybe even none. I once made a sorbet from a couple of very ripe, almost over-ripe, Cantaloupe melons. All that went into it was a purée of the flesh sharpened with a squeeze of lemon; the result was delicious.

Once you have experimented a little with the wealth of possibilities afforded by frozen fruit ices, you will quickly learn to rely on your own taste-buds to judge the sweetness, sharpness and flavour of your unfrozen mixes. When this point is reached it is time to branch out into the unknown, and invent recipes of your own.

Apricot Soufflé

Serves 3–4

The natural stickiness of dried apricots means that no flour-based mix is required for this soufflé. The result is particularly clean and fruity.

8 oz/225 g unsulphured dried apricots – ideally Hunza (see page 334)
2 oz/60 g caster sugar
2 whole large eggs, separated, plus 3 egg whites
4 fl oz/100 ml double cream

Unless they are the 'ready-to-eat' variety, soak the apricots in sweetened water for at least 3 hours or overnight (see page 333). Drain and place in an ovenproof dish with just enough fresh water to cover them. Cook uncovered in a slow oven (150°C/300°F/Gas Mark 2) for 1 hour, until the apricots are completely tender. Drain off all the water and sieve the apricots into a mixing basin, or purée them in a food processor until they are completely smooth.

Stir the sugar and cream into the apricot purée and beat in the 2 egg yolks. In a clean bowl whisk the 5 egg whites to soft peaks. Fold gently but thoroughly into the apricot mixture and turn into a smallish (not more than 2-pt/1-litre capacity) soufflé dish. Bake in a pre-heated moderate to hot oven (190°C/375°F/Gas Mark 5) for about 20–25 minutes, until well risen and lightly browned on top. Serve without delay, with cream.

Banana Fritters with Lime Syrup

THE FOX AND GOOSE INN

Serves 4

Pineau des Charentes, a fortified wine, adds a fine flavour to the batter for this greedy pudding. It is available in good off-licences and some supermarkets, but if you don't have it you could try a more traditional companion to bananas and add a tablespoon of rum.

First make the lime syrup. Blanch the zest by pouring boiling water on to it and then discarding the water. Repeat three times more. Dissolve the sugar in the 10 fl oz/300 ml water over a low heat, bring to the boil and simmer fairly rapidly for about 10 minutes to get a light syrup. Add the blanched lime zest and boil for 1 further minute. Remove from the heat and leave to cool, then add the lime juice and orange or lime blossom water to taste. Store in a bottle or container in the fridge until required.

To prepare the fritters, make up a smooth batter with the flour, water, sugar and wine, either whisking them together or using a food processor. There is no need to let the mixture stand.

Cut the bananas in half lengthways. Coat evenly with the batter, then deep-fry 2 or 3 at a time (more if you are a dab hand) in the oil at 190°C/375°F for about 3 minutes or until lightly golden in colour. (Shallow frying is possible, but not ideal.)

Place 2 half-banana fritters on each plate and pour over a generous splosh of lime syrup.

4 largish bananas
groundnut or sun flower oil for frying

For the batter
6 oz/170 g self-raising flour
10 fl oz/300 ml water
1 tbsp caster sugar
1 fl oz/30 ml Pineau des Charentes

For the lime syrup
juice and zest of 1 lime, zest cut into fine strips, all pith removed
8 oz/225 g caster sugar
10 fl oz/300 ml water
1 tsp orange blossom *or* lime blossom water

Blackberry and Apple Pie
Serves 8

This is more a covered tart than a pie – a sort of blackberry and apple shortcrust sandwich. It can easily be adapted for other fruits – gooseberries or rhubarb are both particularly good. The important thing is that the fruit filling should be cooked first, then drained of any excess thin juice. Thus the pastry does not become too waterlogged.

Roll out about two-thirds of the pastry to a thickness of about ¼ in/5 mm. (Knead any leftover scraps back into the remaining pastry, which you will use to make the cover of the tart.) Line a 10-in/25-cm tart tin with the rolled-out pastry and bake blind according to the instructions given on page 360.

Meanwhile, peel, core and slice the apples, wash the blackberries, and put into a saucepan with the lemon juice and sugar. Heat very gently until the juices begin to run. Cook the fruit, stirring occasionally, at a very gentle simmer for 10–15 minutes, until you have a juicy compote. Strain off most of the juice, and reserve.

1 lb/450 g sweet shortcrust pastry (made according to the recipe on page 360 using double quantities)
1½ lb/675 g good tart eating apples such as Cox's Orange Pippins
1½ lb/675 g blackberries
juice of ½ lemon
6 oz/170 g sugar

Roll out the remaining pastry, rather thinner this time, so it is wide enough to cover the top of the tart with a bit to spare. Fill the tart case with the cooked fruit, mounding it up slightly in the middle. Lay the pastry lid over the fruit. Normally the blind-baked shell will have shrunk a little during cooking. If so, this allows you to tuck the edges of the pastry lid between the edge of the baked case and the sides of the tin, and will be helpful in preventing leakages when you bake the tart. If there is no such space, try to make sure the lid goes right to the edge of the tin, and press it around the sharp edge so the tart is completely covered. Cut a small cross in the centre of the pastry to allow air to escape. Bake in a pre-heated fairly hot oven (200°C/400°F/Gas Mark 6) for about 30 minutes, until the top is nicely browned.

While the pie is baking, boil the strained juices, adding a little extra sugar if required, to reduce and make a sauce. Serve the pie warm with the sauce, and vanilla ice cream or cream.

Cherry Clafoutis
Serves 8

The simplest of dishes, a clafoutis is really just 'fruit in the hole'. The classic recipe, from the Limoges region of France, uses black cherries, but it works well with all kinds of fruit – try blueberries, small greengages, Mirabelles or apricots (the blueberries whole, the other three in halves, cut side down in the dish).

butter for greasing
1 lb/450 g black *or* red cherries
3 oz/85 g caster sugar
4½ oz/125 g plain flour
a pinch of salt
3 eggs, lightly beaten
10 fl oz/300 ml milk
1 oz/30 g icing sugar

Lightly grease a 10-in/25-cm round, or 10 × 8-in/25 × 20-cm rectangular, ceramic or tin baking dish. De-stalk the cherries but do not stone them (see page 338). Toss with 1 oz/30 g of the sugar. Spread the cherries in the bottom of the dish.

Sieve the flour, salt and the remaining sugar into a mixing bowl. Make a well in the middle and pour in the eggs. Mix well, drawing in the flour from the sides. Beat in the milk, a little at a time, until you have a smooth batter. Pour the batter into the dish over the cherries, and bake in a pre-heated moderate oven (180°C/350°F/Gas Mark 4) for about 35 minutes, until lightly browned and puffed up like a Yorkshire pudding.

Clafoutis should be eaten lukewarm. Dust with the icing sugar just before serving, and serve plain or with cream.

Cherry and Walnut Chocolate Pots

THE WHITELEAF AT CROYDE

Makes 8

Melt the chocolate and the butter in a microwave or a heat-proof bowl over a pan of simmering water. Warm the milk or cream sufficiently to dissolve the instant coffee. Combine all the ingredients except the cherries, walnuts and cherry brandy in a food processor and whizz briefly.

Carefully split the cherries in half, remove the stones and place 2 halves in the base of each of 8 small ramekins. Fill the halved cherries with cherry brandy. Pour over the chocolate mixture to within 1/8 in/2 mm of the top of the ramekins. Refrigerate. To serve, place a walnut half on each. The pots will keep covered for several days in the refrigerator.

6 oz/170 g dark chocolate
  (minimum 55% cocoa solids)
1 tbsp unsalted butter
5 fl oz/150 ml milk *or* double
  cream
1 heaped tsp instant coffee
1 large egg
2 tbsp brandy *or* other liqueur
  (*optional*)
8 very large, very ripe cherries
a little cherry brandy
8 walnut halves

Clootie Dumpling

THE BUT'N'BEN

Serves 6–8

Margaret Horn writes: 'This is my mum's recipe which I had to translate as a young bride from her 'a wee puckle of this, a wee drappie o' that or a knifful (fist) o' yon'.'

Mix the dry ingredients, apple and carrot together in a large bowl. Warm the treacle and add to the bowl, mix well, and add enough milk by degrees to get a dough that is well bound and soft but not too wet.

Line a small mixing bowl with a clean square of cotton cloth (in Scotland such a dumpling cloth is called a 'cloot', hence the name of this dish. A piece of cotton sheet or tea-towel, about 12 in/30 cm square, will do nicely). Dust the inside of the cloth with flour and spoon the dough into the cloth, gather the edges together in pleats, and tie up securely 1–2 in/2.5–5 cm above the dough to leave room

1 lb/450 g self-raising flour
8 oz/225 g shredded beef suet
8 oz/225 g sugar
1½ lb/675 g mixed dried fruit
2 cooking apples, grated
2 carrots, grated
2 tsp ground mixed spice
4 oz/115 g black treacle
up to 10 fl oz/300 ml milk, to
  mix

for expansion. Lift the dumpling in its cloth out of the basin, and pat it to a nice round shape with the flat of your hands.

Bring a large saucepan of water to the boil with an old china saucer on the bottom. Lower the dumpling into the boiling water on top of the saucer – it should be completely covered. Boil at a brisk simmer for at least 3 hours, keeping a kettle of water on the boil to top up the pan from time to time.

Carefully remove the cloth from the dumpling to preserve the skin which will have formed. Place in a slow oven (150°C/300°F/Gas Mark 2) for about 10–15 minutes to firm up this skin. Serve warm, cut into wedges, with pouring cream or custard, or cold for tea.

Cranachan

THE BUT'N'BEN

Serves 6

This, the Scottish answer to summer pudding, can be made with all kinds of soft fruit, either a single fruit or a mixture. Try in particular strawberries, raspberries, blackberries, blueberries or redcurrants. Wild strawberries are particularly delicious.

1½ lb/675 g soft fruit (see suggestions above)
1 pt/575 ml double cream
4 tbsp Drambuie *or* whisky
4 oz/115 g coarse oatmeal, toasted in the oven until crisp
4 oz/115 g mixed chopped nuts, toasted
4 oz/115 g dark chocolate, grated

Pick over and prepare the fruit (large strawberries, for instance, should be sliced), and divide among 6 large wine glasses (each should be half full of fruit). Whip the cream, and stir in the alcohol (sweeten with a little sugar if you use whisky).

Mix together the oatmeal, nuts and grated chocolate, and sprinkle a layer of this mixture over the fruit, then add a layer of cream, then the oatmeal mixture, then more cream, and a final sprinkling of the oatmeal mixture on top. Do not wait long before serving or the oatmeal will lose its crispness.

Gooseberry and Other Crumbles

Serves 6-8

Crumbles are easy to make; the only secret to their success is in the crumble mixture itself – always make it by hand, for extra lightness. I find the following mixture infallible (quantities are sufficient to cover about 1½ lb/675 g fruit in a medium-sized pie dish). If you prefer, you can omit the breadcrumbs and add an extra 1 oz/30 g each of flour and ground almonds. You may also want to try adding more exotic things such as caraway or sesame seeds.

First make the crumble topping. Sieve the flour and salt into a mixture bowl and add the butter. Rub in the butter with your fingers and, when it is well incorporated, add the remaining ingredients, rubbing them in and sifting them through your fingers.

Gooseberry, plum and rhubarb are my favourite crumbles. In all three cases I like to par-cook the fruit first, with a little sugar, just until the juices run. This means you can pile the crumble on top of the soft fruit in an even layer, without it falling between the cracks in the fruit. In each case stew 1½ lb/675 g fruit gently with 4 oz/115 g sugar. A scant tbsp water will be enough to stop the fruit burning until its own juices run; if you are very careful, you may not need any. When the fruit is lightly stewed (4–5 minutes with rhubarb, 8–10 for gooseberries, perhaps 15 for plums), pile it into your dish with a slotted spoon, then pour over the juices from the pan, withholding some if you feel there is too much (most likely in the case of plums).

Sprinkle the crumble evenly over the fruit (do not pack it down as this will prevent it from being light) and bake in a pre-heated moderate oven (190°C/375°F/Gas Mark 5) for about 30 minutes, until the top is golden-brown. Serve with cream, ice cream or home-made custard.

APPLE CRUMBLE: for an apple crumble it is not necessary to pre-cook the fruit. Peel, core and slice 2 lb/900 g Bramley apples, putting the slices in a bowl with 1 tbsp lemon juice as you go. Layer the apple slices in a dish, sprinkling each layer with 1 tbsp caster or light brown sugar (3 tbsp in all). Scatter the crumble evenly over the top and bake in a slightly cooler oven than the above crumbles, and for slightly longer, say 40 minutes in a pre-heated moderate oven (180°C/350°F/ Gas Mark 4).

1½ lb/675 g fruit of your choice (see recipe)
4 oz/115 g sugar

For the crumble topping
3 oz/85 g plain flour
a pinch of salt
4 oz/115 g cool unsalted butter, diced
3 oz/85 g ground almonds
5 oz/140 g light brown or caster sugar
½ tsp ground cinnamon
2 oz/60 g fresh white breadcrumbs

Gooseberry and Elderflower Fool

THE ARK

Serves 6

Sheila Kidd writes: 'An old favourite, good when the first very sharp green gooseberries are ready. But, depending on the season, you may have to wait for the elderflowers! Useful for gooseberries you have topped, tailed and frozen.'

1¼ lb/550 g gooseberries, topped and tailed, defrosted if frozen
2 oz/60 g unsalted butter
2–3 elderflower heads
2–4 oz/60–115 g caster sugar to taste
15 fl oz/450 ml double cream, whipped

Stew the gooseberries with the butter and the elderflowers (quickly rinsed and tied in a little piece of muslin or cotton cloth) in a covered pan until soft. Squeeze the muslin against the side of the pan and remove. Crush the gooseberries with a fork and sweeten to taste with sugar. This gives a rough purée – the gooseberries can be sieved if you prefer. Cool and mix with the cream. Pile into glasses or custard cups, then chill. Serve garnished with small sprays of elderflowers and accompany with shortbread or almond biscuits.

Italian Fruit Salad

Serves 10

10 fl oz/300 ml freshly squeezed orange juice
grated zest and juice of ½ lemon
4 tbsp kirsch or maraschino liqueur
1 tbsp caster sugar
flesh of 1 small or ½ large melon
6 oz/175 g cherries
6 oz/175 g seedless white grapes
2 Cox's Orange Pippin apples
2 ripe pears (Conference recommended)
2 ripe peaches or nectarines
2 small bananas

This is an excellent all-round fruit salad. The recipe is adapted from one in Alan Davidson's *Fruit*. He in turn credits Marcella Hazan, so my version is third-hand, but none the worse for that, I hope. Don't worry about precise quantities of the fruit, and if you can't get something that is specified, just leave it out. It's a variable feast, but always a good one.

Put the orange and lemon juice, liqueur and sugar into a bowl and mix well. Add the fruit to this liquid as you prepare it. Cut the melon into 1-in/2.5-cm dice, or balls if you have a melon-baller, wash and stone the cherries, wash the grapes. Peel and core the apples and pears, and cut into ½-in/1-cm dice. Peel, stone and cut the peaches or nectarines into slices, then halve the slices. Peel and slice the bananas. Mix all the fruit well in the juices, cover the dish with clingfilm and refrigerate for at least 3 hours. Mix again before serving.

Mango and Ruby Orange Sorbet

JEMIMA'S

Serves 6

This sorbet is a beautiful colour, and has an equally beautiful taste.

Dissolve the sugar in the water over a low heat, then turn up the heat and bring to the boil. Boil rapidly for 5 minutes to form a syrup, and set aside to cool. Squeeze the juice from the oranges and liquidize with the flesh from the mango and 5 fl oz/150 ml of the syrup. Sieve and taste for sweetness (see advice on page 365), adding the remaining syrup if required. Freeze in an ice-cream machine/ sorbetière if you have one, otherwise in the freezer, stirring vigorously every 2 hours to prevent the formation of ice crystals.

This is delicious served either slightly slushy as a granita, or as a firmer sorbet.

8 oz/225 g sugar
1 pt/575 ml water
4 blood oranges
1 large ripe mango

Deep-fried Mince Pies

THE WHITELEAF AT CROYDE

It's pushing it a bit to call this a fruit recipe – but I include it by virtue of its deliciousness.

Pour the oil into a deep-fryer or saucepan to a minimum depth of 2 in/5 cm. Roll out the pastry to the thickness of a 5p piece. Using a 2½-in/6-cm round pastry cutter, cut into circles. Pile the pastry trimmings on top of each other, re-roll and cut out more circles. Place 1 heaped tsp mincemeat in the centre of each of half the pastry circles. Brush the edge of each circle with beaten egg, place another circle on top and press together tightly. Allow to rest in the fridge for 30 minutes or until required.

Heat the oil to 170–180°C/330–350°F and lower in the pies a few at a time. Turn occasionally and cook for 5–6 minutes or until risen and browned. Place on kitchen paper, and keep in a warm oven until all are cooked. Dust with icing sugar and serve with clotted cream mixed with Drambuie.

good-quality light cooking oil
  (i.e. sunflower)
chilled puff pastry or trimmings
good-quality mincemeat
beaten egg
icing sugar
clotted cream
Drambuie

Peaches with Cardamom and Sabayon Cream

THE ARK

Serves 6

This luxurious dish is a variation on the peach melba theme, with the sabayon making an interesting and delicious change from ice cream. Preparation of a sabayon requires a strong arm, unless you happen to have an electric whisk – then it becomes a doddle.

6 ripe but firm peaches
zest and juice of 1 orange
8 oz/225 g stoned Mirabelle
  plums or cherries (*optional*)
4 cardamom pods, split
4 oz/115 g raspberries

For the sabayon cream
4 egg yolks
4 tbsp caster sugar
6 fl oz/175 ml marsala *or other*
  sweet wine
6 fl oz/175 ml double cream

Skin the peaches by plunging them into boiling water for a few seconds. Refresh in cold water and slip off the skins. Slice to the stone in ½-in/1-cm pieces. Place these in a pan with the orange juice, the plums or cherries, if used, and the cardamom pods. Poach very gently for 3–4 minutes. Remove from the heat, add the raspberries and leave to cool. Remove the cardamom pods and chill the fruit in the fridge.

Meanwhile, prepare the sabayon: place the egg yolks, sugar and wine in a large bowl over a pan of just-simmering water. Whisk vigorously until thick, fluffy and doubled in bulk. Remove from the heat and continue whisking off the heat until the mixture is cold. Whip the cream (not too stiffly) and fold gently into the sabayon.

Divide the fruit among 6 individual glasses, reserving a few raspberries and cherries, if used, and pour the sabayon cream on top. Decorate with the reserved raspberries or cherries. Return to the fridge, but do not allow to stand around for more than an hour or two before serving.

Pears in Red Wine

Serves 4

An excellent way to transform slightly unripe pears; indeed, ripe pears are not suitable for this treatment.

Carefully peel the pears, leaving the stalks on. Put the wine into a saucepan with the sugar and all the spices except the ginger. Stir until the sugar is dissolved, then turn up the heat and bring to the boil. Allow to simmer merrily for 4–5 minutes, until you have a light syrup which has reduced slightly. Add the pears and bring back to a more gentle simmer this time. Poach the pears gently for about 20 minutes, until they are tender (test with a fine skewer).

Remove the pears and set aside to cool. Strain the syrup into a clean sauce-boat or jug. When it has cooled a little, add the ground ginger, a little more sugar if you feel it is required, and perhaps another pinch of ground cinnamon. Pour the syrup back over the pears and chill before serving.

4 unblemished, firm pears
27-fl-oz/75-cl bottle red wine
2 oz/60 g sugar
2 cinnamon sticks or 2 tsp
  ground cinnamon
2 cloves
1/2 tsp ground mace
1/2 tsp ground anise or 1 tsp
  fennel seeds
1/2 tsp ground ginger

Raspberry, Hazelnut and Cinnamon Torte

THE ARK
Serves 8

Butter an 8-in/20-cm spring-release cake tin and line the base with greaseproof paper. Toast the hazelnuts in a fairly hot oven (200°C/400°F/Gas Mark 6) for 10 minutes. Leave to cool a little, then rub off the skins with your hands. Grind the nuts finely in a food processor.

Add the butter, sugar, flour and egg to the food processor, and process until smooth. (Or cream the butter and sugar by hand, and beat in the egg, then the flour and ground hazelnuts). Spread half the mixture in the tin and smooth out. Sprinkle the raspberries on top and dot the remaining mixture over them, spreading it out as evenly as possible. Bake in a pre-heated moderate oven (180°C/350°F/Gas Mark 4) for 40–45 minutes until golden-brown. Cool a little in the tin before releasing and carefully turning out. Sieve the icing sugar with cinnamon and dust the top of the torte with this mixture.

5 oz/150 g unsalted butter,
  softened
5 oz/140 g shelled hazelnuts
5 oz/140 g caster sugar
5 oz/140 g self-raising flour
1 egg
10 oz/300 g raspberries
1 tbsp icing sugar
1 tsp ground cinnamon

For the sauce
12 oz/350 g raspberries
1 tbsp lemon juice
icing sugar to taste

To make the sauce, sieve the raspberries, sharpen with the lemon juice and sweeten with icing sugar to taste. Serve the torte still warm if possible, with the sauce and crème fraîche, double cream or Greek yoghurt.

Iced Strawberry and Mint Soup
Serves 6

This is definitely a dessert, not a first course. It is a good dish for using slightly bruised strawberries, as all except a few are to be puréed. It can be taken to picnics, chilled in a Thermos flask.

1 ½ lb/675 g strawberries
2 oz/60 g caster sugar
juice of ½ lemon
2 tbsp kirsch (*optional*)
1 generous tbsp chopped fresh mint leaves
a few sprigs of mint, to garnish

Hull the strawberries and, as you are doing so, set aside the best dozen or so. Crush the remainder with your hands, or a plastic potato masher or other suitable implement, then rub them through a nylon sieve (not metal – see page 23). Into the purée stir the sugar, lemon juice, kirsch and chopped mint. Chill for at least 2 hours.

Slice the reserved strawberries into quarters, and float these, with a sprig of fresh mint, on the top of each bowl when you serve the soup. Cream is not appropriate, but *cantuccini* biscuits, or *langues de chat*, are a nice accompaniment.

Smoothies

For breakfast I subsist largely on fruit, and I have devised a number of recipes for delicious drinks made by puréeing fruit in a blender with a little crushed ice (or, if I have them, a few frozen raspberries). In fact it is hardly the same recipe twice: whatever fruit is to hand goes in the blender. I must admit I feel rather evangelistic about these drinks. In Thailand, Brazil and many other countries where fruit is plentiful and cheap, they are widely available, freshly made in cafés and street-corner restaurants. Here Harrods juice bar, and a few other places, charge punitive prices for similar products. But they are incredibly easy to make at home. Here are a few proven combinations:

Melon, raspberries and banana
Orange juice and fresh apricots
Pineapple, watermelon and banana
Blackberries and freshly pressed apple juice
Grapefruit, pineapple and mint
Papaya, raspberries, banana and lime juice
Strawberries, orange and banana
Mango and freshly pressed apple juice
Banana, milk and 1 tbsp oats

A splash of water, or better still another fruit juice, may be necessary to help liquefy some combinations. Extra sugar is not usually necessary, but you can add a teaspoon if you have a sweet tooth.

Summer Pudding
Serves 8

The important thing about a summer pudding, which some recipes I have tried fail to deliver, is that it should contain enough juice to ensure that the bread becomes completely soaked. For this reason I cook the blackcurrants with a little sugar, and sieve them to get a purée. They contribute their flavour and juices to the dish; their skins and seeds, I feel, one can do without.

Wash and remove the stalks of the blackcurrants and redcurrants. Put the blackcurrants into a saucepan with the sugar and water, bring to a gentle simmer and cook for about 10 minutes, stirring frequently, until you have a rich, syrupy pulp. Rub this through a sieve into a clean bowl. While the purée is still hot, stir in the redcurrants and raspberries – the heat will help their juices to run a little too.

Lightly butter a 2-pt/1-litre pudding basin, and line it with the slices of bread, cutting smaller slices to fill any gaps. The bread should fit neatly and not overlap too much. Trim the bread so it is flush with the top of the basin. Pour in the fruit mixture so the basin is completely full but not overflowing. Cover with more slices of bread, cut to fit, and place a plate on top of the basin, with a weight on it to

1 lb/450 g blackcurrants
10 oz/300 g redcurrants
1 lb/450 g raspberries
6 oz/170 g caster sugar
1 tbsp water
a small piece of butter for greasing
6–7 slices stale white bread

compress the pudding. Leave for at least 5 hours, or overnight, in the fridge.

To serve the pudding, remove the weight and plate, cover the bowl with a serving plate, and invert to turn out the pudding. Serve with thick cream or crème fraîche.

CHAPTER NINE

Cheese

Different cheeses are like different cuts of meat. They are all made of the same basic stuff: just as meat is all made from bonded proteinous muscle fibres, so (almost) all cheese derives from the coagulated curds of milk. But when it comes to character, cheeses are by no means all the same. A Cheddar is no more like a Brie than a steak is like a piece of liver. Like meats, the character of different cheeses can be defined in terms of different tastes and textures. Some are robust, some delicate, some hard, some soft, some sweet, some sour, some creamy-smooth, some lumpy and granular. And just as some meat is mass-produced, under-matured, and shoddily prepared for the customer, so are all too many cheeses.

Shopping for cheese is therefore an acquired skill, and one which in this country very few people have mastered. To be a real expert on cheese requires great dedication, and even years of study will never furnish you with a complete knowledge of the subject. Indeed, those who are involved in the production of the world's great cheeses, such as Parmesan, Cheddar or Brie, will probably tell you that it takes a lifetime of hard work to unravel the mysteries of a single cheese.

But do not despair. For those of us who simply wish to enjoy the pleasure of a few good cheeses in optimum condition, a little care in the way we buy, store and serve cheese will help us to avoid the major pitfalls.

Buying cheese

Ninety per cent of the battle is won if you can find a good cheese shop. Unfortunately a first-rate cheese shop is an even rarer find than a top-quality fishmonger or butcher. If you are lucky enough to find one, which is staffed by people who genuinely understand and care about their product, then you may learn more from a few trips to such a place than you will from this chapter.

An enormous selection is not the only clue to a good cheesemonger. A few well-chosen cheeses, nicely displayed and carefully labelled with regard to their origins and individual characteristics, are far more useful than a vast and confusing array of mysterious wheels, rolls and squares. Apart from anything else, a heavily stocked shop, unless it has a reliably high turnover, is unlikely to be able to keep all its cheeses in prime condition.

A reliable indicator of quality is a shop that allows – better still, encourages – its customers to taste cheeses before they buy. If this policy is accompanied by an enthusiasm for the subject and a willingness to communicate on the part of the shopkeeper, then you know you are on to a good thing. Even if you place yourself entirely in the hands of your cheesemonger, the chances are you will do well.

Such a happy state of affairs is likely to be the exception rather than the rule, and most shoppers will be buying their cheeses in supermarkets or delicatessens where the staff, however well-intentioned, are not experts on the subject of cheese. Under these circumstances, the shopper will need to be a little more self-reliant. To this end, information about the desirable and undesirable features of certain popular cheeses are given in the guide below. Labels are a particularly salient indicator. Many fine cheeses have their imitators, most of which are a pretty poor representation of the real thing. But strict laws about labelling in the countries of origin mean that the impostors can usually be identified and avoided: again see notes on individual cheeses below.

When experimenting with less well-known cheeses, at home and abroad, pay particular regard to those which are locally produced, or whose labels indicate that they are farmhouse- rather than factory-made. They are likely to be the products of enthusiasts dedicated to the art of cheese-making rather than the art of making money. Unpasteurized cheese are always likely to be interesting, but they do present a small risk to pregnant women and breast-feeding mothers.

Bear in mind that it is usually preferable to buy pieces cut from a whole cheese than pre-packaged portions. Once a cheese has been cut, its character is unlikely to develop further, particularly if it has been vacuum-packed in plastic. Lastly, be particularly wary of cheeses whose labels indicate that they contain artificial colours or preservatives (though vegetable and other natual dyes are traditionally added to some cheeses, such as Cheshire and Leicester).

Storing cheese

Any lengthy storage, except of whole, uncut cheeses, is generally inadvisable. Whole hard or semi-hard cheeses, such as Cheddars or Stiltons, can be stored for a few weeks in a cellar or reliably cool larder, provided the temperature (which should be between 4° and 8°C) does not fluctuate, and the air is not too damp. Any attempt to store cheeses for longer, or mature them at home, requires a greater understanding of technicalities than there is space to expound here.

Refrigeration

Generally it is best to buy cheeses that are ripe and ready for eating, in quantities that will be consumed within a few days. Very fresh cheeses, such as cream cheese, ricotta and fresh goat's cheese, should be treated as dairy products and refrigerated. Soft cheeses such as Brie and Camembert may be refrigerated if they are very ripe, to prevent further development. But they should be removed from the fridge an hour or two before serving, and kept at room temperature, so they can develop their full flavour. Hard and semi-hard cheeses do not need to be refrigerated, but should be kept in a cool cupboard or larder. Again, they should be transferred to room temperature a couple of hours before serving. Cut cheeses should always be well wrapped, separately so that the flavours do not mix, and in most cases foil or greaseproof paper is suitable, but preferably not clingfilm. A few, such as *grana* cheeses (e.g. Parmesan, see page 395), are better off wrapped in a damp cloth, and others, such as feta, ricotta and mozzarella, have special requirements peculiar to their type (see guide below).

Serving cheeses

When cheeses are served, and what they are served with, is a matter of tradition that varies hugely from country to country. Cheese is variously eaten at breakfast, as an aperitif with drinks, or as a course of a meal, either before the dessert (as in France) or after it (as in this country). It may be served with bread and biscuits, with raw vegetables such as celery or fennel, or with fruit. How you decide to pick and choose from these traditions is entirely a matter for you.

More important than when and with what you eat cheese is the temperature at which you serve it. All cheeses, even fresh ones, should be brought to room temperature before serving if their best qualities are to be appreciated. On the other hand there is a danger that cheeses kept in a warm room for too long, or left sitting in direct sunlight, will start to deteriorate. Soft fresh cheeses may start to liquefy, and hard cheeses will become harder and may start to sweat. Once they have started to break down in this way, cheeses will not make much of a recovery. When compiling a cheeseboard it therefore makes sense to put on it only as much cheese as you feel is likely to be eaten at that sitting. If you are serving cheese out of doors on a hot day it may also be advisable to have a wooden or ceramic cover for your cheeseboard, or at least cover it with a damp cloth, to protect it from the worst effects of heat and sunlight, not to mention marauding insects. Best of all, serve on a slab of marble that you have pre-chilled in the fridge.

Cooking with cheese

The great variations in character between the different cheeses mean that they respond to heat in very different ways. From a simple snack of good Cheddar melted under the grill on a piece of toast, to the wonderful creamy taste of spinach gnocchi made with fresh ricotta, cheese proves itself to be one of the most delightful and versatile of all cooking ingredients.

It is a fallacy that if cheese is to be used for cooking, then the quality of the raw ingredient can be neglected. You only have to taste the difference between a pasta dish on to which a piece of fresh Parmesan has been grated, and one which has been sprinkled with dried Parmesan powder from a plastic dispenser, to know how much difference a quality cheese can make to your cooking. The above guidelines should therefore be borne in mind when choosing cheeses for the kitchen as well as the cheeseboard.

The cooking qualities of particular cheeses, and suggestions for their use, are discussed in the guide below.

British cheeses

A note on English Farmhouse Cheeses

Since 1954 the Milk Marketing Board has run the Farmhouse Cheesemakers Scheme to help independent farmers market their cheese. The scheme has its own rigorous quality control which ensures that all cheeses which sport the Farmhouse English Cheese symbol are guaranteed to have been made on English or Welsh farms according to traditional methods. They are of the highest quality. Unfortunately at present the scheme is only applied to a restricted group of the better-known English hard cheeses – Caerphilly, Cheddar, Cheshire, Double Gloucester, Lancashire, Leicester and Wensleydale – and the symbol may only be used by producers who market their cheese through the Milk Marketing Board. This means that many small farms making excellent traditional English cheeses, some with unpasteurized milk, are not allowed to use the symbol. Most of them, justifiably, have found other ways to communicate on their packaging that their cheeses are a genuine farmhouse product, produced on a small scale. Such cheeses deserve the attention of the consumer, and repay the trouble taken to seek them out. You may wish to look out for the following farmhouse cheeses in particular (the list includes local cheeses from Scotland and Ireland, as well as England and Wales):

ACORN: a fine, crumbly sheep's-milk cheese from Wales, occasionally with a natural streak of blue.

BEENLEIGH BLUE: a semi-hard cheese made in Devon from unpasteurized milk.

CASHEL BLUE: a famous Irish blue cheese, smooth and creamy.

DESMOND: a Swiss-style, piquant-flavoured hard cheese made in Ireland.

CORNISH YARG: moist, crumbly and coated in nettle leaves.

LANARK BLUE: one of the best British blue cheeses, from Scotland.

LLANBOIDY: like a good Cheddar, but creamier, made from the unpasteurized milk of Red Poll cows.

LOCHABER: a very interesting Scottish smoked cream cheese, rolled in oats.

SPENWOOD: a pale hard cheese from Berkshire, nutty and sweet.

TEIFI: a semi-hard Gouda-style cheese from Dyfed in Wales.

Literally thousands of different cheeses are produced worldwide, and the scale of their production varies from the multi-million-pound industry to the tiny farmhouse that may produce only enough cheese for one family and a few close friends. Enthusiasts who want to explore the subject further should invest in Sandy Carr's compact but remarkably comprehensive *Pocket Cheese Book*, published by Mitchell Beazley, or Patrick Rance's more leisurely volumes, *The French Cheese Book* and *The Great British Cheese Book* published by Pan Macmillan.

Brie

The big wheel of Brie is perhaps the most celebrated of all French cheeses, and when a good specimen is encountered the reasons for its fame are clear. Bries that are made outside France are usually of dubious quality – and some that are made inside France can also be disappointing. The best of all is Brie de Meaux, unpasteurized and made in the *département* of Seine-et-Marne where Brie originated. The cheese should be soft, glossy and straw-coloured, oozing slightly but not (contrary to popular belief) completely runny. The rind should be a dusky white, rather than the snow-white that is characteristic of some commercial Bries. Avoid Bries that have a hard, chalky middle, and any very liquid cheeses that smell of ammonia.

Cooking with Brie

Brie is not usually used for cooking, but it does turn to a rather delicious goo when heated. In little puff pastry parcels, baked golden-brown, Brie makes fine canapés, or an equally good starter, served with a salad of bitter leaves such as radicchio, *frisée* or chicory. A waste of a really good Brie, perhaps, but certainly a useful way to improve the second-rate commercial product.

Camembert

The best Camembert comes from the Pays d'Auge region of Normandy, but like Brie the cheese is widely, and generally poorly, imitated all over the world. To make sure you get the genuine article, look at the label. It should have the words *fromage fermier*, and *lait cru* or *non pasteurisé* on it, and the initials *VCN – Véritable Camembert de Normandie*. A good Camembert has a creamy-white rind (which may be flecked with reddish-brown), and looks plump, not sunken in the middle. The paste should be smooth and glossy all the way through, with no chalky patches. Most good Camemberts come wrapped in waxed paper and packed in wooden boxes. If you can't examine the cheese, at least give the box a good shake – there should be no 'rattle', as the plump cheese should fill the box.

Cooking with Camembert

As with Brie, cooking Camembert is best seen as a way of rescuing a bland, inferior product. Cooking with a good Camembert will, of course, produce better results, but it is likely to offend a Frenchman – and simply appal a Normand. However, I am rather partial to deep-fried cubes of Camembert. Dipped in milk, then flour, then beaten egg, and finally breadcrumbs, they should be fried in hot oil until golden-brown. A tart sauce made with sorrel, gooseberries, or even rhubarb, is a good accompaniment.

Cheddar

The most famous cheese in the world, and the most widely made, Cheddar is, alas, also the most variable in quality. As Sandy Carr points out in his *Pocket Cheese Book*: 'There are fewer than 20 farms in the West Country of England still producing Cheddar by traditional methods, and only a handful use unpasteurized milk, notably the Montgomerys, the Keens and the Times Past Dairy.' Find one of these unpasteurized cheeses, and you have a terrific treat in store.

Failing that, a good farmhouse Cheddar is not so hard to find, and a slice with rind on it is likely to be a good bet. Cheddars are sold as both 'mild' and 'mature'. Mature Cheddar should be at least 9 months old, and some good farmhouse cheeses are kept for over a year. It has a more powerful, nutty flavour. Mild Cheddars, particularly the commercial variety, can be very bland, almost tasteless. The best Cheddar is hard and smooth and, if cut with a cheese-wire or stiff-bladed knife, should not crumble.

Cooking with Cheddar

Cheddar is one of the best all-round cooking cheeses, and a good mature farmhouse cheese should be used whenever a strong cheesy flavour is required – in sauces and tarts, for topping gratins, or simply grated on to a baked potato. It melts beautifully, but should not be over-heated under a grill as it becomes bitter when burnt. Strong English mustard is a natural companion, and a vital ingredient in a good Welsh Rarebit (see page 403).

Cheshire

The milk from cows grazed on the salty pastures of Cheshire, Shropshire and Clwyd give this fine, white, semi-hard cheese its distinctive tang. It is usually sold young, when it has a pleasant, fresh taste despite its saltiness. More mature Cheshires have a stronger flavour – one of the best is Appleby's. The quality is reliable, even from cheeses which are creamery- rather than farmhouse-made. But if at all possible buy Cheshire cut from a whole round, rather than a lump in a vacuum pack. Avoid cheeses which are dry-looking or starting to crack. 'Coloured' Cheshire (actually a deep peachy orange) has been dyed with annato (an extract from a South American tree), but the flavour is exactly the same. A Blue Cheshire, with thin veins of mould, is made in Leicestershire by Long Claudon Dairy, who also produce Stilton; it is excellent, if you can find it.

Cooking with Cheshire

Cheshire makes an interesting change from Cheddar in the kitchen, and it can be substituted in most recipes. Its saltiness makes it a good addition to a salad of crunchy fresh leaves. If you use it in sauces or tarts they may not need extra salting – let your taste be the judge.

Chèvre

Chèvre is just the French generic name for goat's-milk cheeses, but in this country the name tends to denote fairly fresh, soft cheeses, usually round or in a trapezoid block, either with a light natural rind or coated in ash or herbs. By law, any cheese that goes by the name of 'Chèvre' or 'pur Chèvre' must be made entirely of goat's milk and contain at least 45 per cent fat. Some are lighter than others, but all have the distinctive, goaty tang. British-made goat's-milk cheeses are on the increase, and many compare favourably with those imported from France.

Cooking with chèvre

The very light, soft chèvres are wonderful mixed with fresh herbs, and served either on the cheeseboard or as a course on its own with salad and warm crusty bread. They can also be incorporated into soufflés and mousses. Slightly firmer, denser cheeses, such as the commonly encountered log of chèvre, from which round slices are cut and packaged for sale, are delicious grilled: toast or fry a few thin slices of French bread, rub them with garlic, and place a slice of chèvre on each. Put these slices under the grill until lightly browned (not blackened), then serve at once, ideally with a salad of bitter leaves. A couple of slivers of sun-dried tomato on top of each cheesy croûton (before they are grilled) is a nice touch.

Cottage cheese

I am not a great fan of cottage cheese, so beloved of slimmers, in its natural state. Low in fat it may be, but it is also low in taste. I do not find its granular, curdled texture very appealing either. However, I include it because it is a useful cooking cheese – its lightness and freshness are appropriate for making cheesecakes, for example. In emergencies it can be substituted for ricotta in any recipe, but it should be sieved first, as the granular texture of ricotta is far finer.

Cream cheese

Cream cheese is the unripened curd of single or double cream. Cream cheese made from the latter is usually described as 'full-fat' – it has a creamy-yellow colour and is very rich indeed. Dull on its own, cream cheese can be made interesting by the addition of garlic and fresh herbs: far better to do this with your own fresh herbs than to buy a commercially produced herby cream cheese. Cream cheese mixed with chopped dill or fennel leaves is very good with smoked salmon in sandwiches, or better still, bagels. A 50–50 mixture of cream cheese and lightly cooked chicken livers, with plenty of chopped fresh parsley, can be mixed to a smooth paste in a food processor and used to top biscuits for canapés – not the apex of sophistication but tasty none the less. Provided it is completely unsalted, cream cheese can also be sweetened with sugar or honey and served with fruit.

The packaged Philadelphia, a medium-fat cream cheese, seems to me to be as good as any more rustically presented cream cheese. I often use it, with good results, for making cheesecakes.

Emmental

The classic holey Swiss cheese, real Emmental comes only from Switzerland, though it is widely imitated. Those who think it dull may never have had the genuine article, which is made from rich, unpasteurized milk. Authentic Emmental has the word 'Switzerland' stamped all over the rind (NOT the word 'Emmental'). The taste is mild, nutty and slightly sweet. It is said that in the best Emmental the size and distribution of the hole should be such that you can get your three largest fingers in them at a comfortable stretch.

Cooking with Emmental

Emmental melts beautifully, producing long, stringy elastic strands that characterize the classic fondue, of which it is an essential ingredient. It can also be used for tarts, soufflés, sauces and for topping gratins, and in general 'melts' when you fancy a slab of creamy bubbling cheese on top of just about anything. Little cubes of raw Emmental are very good in salads, with a mustardy vinaigrette.

Fetta

The best-known cheese from Greece, fetta should be made from 100 per cent ewe's milk, though cow's milk is used in many foreign imitations of the cheese. Varying in texture from quite soft to hard and crumbly, blocks of fetta get their salty taste from being matured in brine. The longer they spend in the brine, the harder they become. It is best to buy fetta taken straight from the brine. Many Greek and Turkish delicatessens store it in this way, and if you intend to keep it for more than a few days it can be put in a sealed tub with enough brine to cover it – otherwise it can simply be wrapped in foil. If it turns out to be unpalatably salty, it can be mellowed slightly by soaking in cold milk or water for an hour or two.

Cooking with Fetta

The classic Greek salad is a crude combination of strong flavours, made or marred by the quality of the ingredients. With ripe aromatic tomatoes, rich black olives, cool fresh cucumber, good fetta, dressed with the best possible olive oil and a squeeze of lemon juice, and sprinkled with a little chopped fresh mint, there is no salad to beat it. The cheese is also delicious crumbled over baked or grilled aubergines.

Fromage frais

Fromage frais is a generic term describing unripened fresh soft curd cheese. The thickness and fat content vary. Those described as *maigre* (or in this country 'low-fat') can be used as a light and slightly tangy alternative to cream, either poured straight on to fresh fruit and other desserts, or incorporated into fools and ice creams. Fromage frais also has many savoury applications: it can be mixed with fresh herbs and used as the basis for dips and light creamy salad dressings. Usually sold in plastic tubs, there are a great variety of brands, the best-known being Jockey, from France, and Quark, from Germany. Many supermarkets in this country have their 'own-label' brands of fromage frais. A little watery liquid separated from the curds may rise to the top of the tub; this is normal and it can be poured off or stirred back into the cheese.

Gorgonzola

Italy's most famous blue cheese is creamy, mild and mellow, with a sharp tang provided by its rich blue veins. Its rind, which is entirely natural, should, on a good specimen, be rough and reddish-grey, with whitish powdery patches, and is quite edible. The rind may not always be visible as the cheese is often sold wrapped in foil. Gorgonzola that has a brownish tinge, is turning hard, or has a bitter ammoniac smell, should be avoided.

Dolcelatte is the brand-name of a factory-produced version of Gorgonzola; not quite up there with the best of the genuine article (from Lombardy), it is none the less consistent and very pleasant. A *torta di gorgonzola*, or *torta dolcelatte*, is made by layering the cheese with mascarpone (see below) and pressing it in a mould. It is rich but quite delicious.

Cooking with Gorgonzola

A fresh ripe pear is perhaps the best companion to Gorgonzola, as it is for several blue cheeses, including Roquefort. I am wary of cooking with blue cheeses, as the flavour is powerful and all-pervasive, and few blue-cheese concoctions improve on the flavour and texture of the raw product. However, there is one very simple dish made from Gorgonzola which I do enjoy: a pancake filled with buttered wilted spinach (see page 94) and a few small pieces of Gorgonzola makes a good starter or light supper.

Gruyère

The other great Swiss cheese, similar to Emmental but, in my view, even better. Firmer and creamier, it has a wonderful sweet, nutty flavour – definitely one of my Desert Island Cheeses. Like Emmental, it has naturally produced holes, but they are smaller (approximately pea-sized) and more sparsely spread throughout the cheese. The rind is rough and coloured straw-yellow to rusty-brown and should be stamped all over with the word 'Switzerland' to indicate a genuine unpasteurized product of that country. Cut pieces of Gruyère kept for more than 48 hours should be wrapped in a cloth dampened with salt water.

Perhaps the best cooking cheese of all, the flavour imparted by Gruyère is strong and sweet, but not overpowering. It is a supremely versatile cheese, a fact acknowledged by cooks in both France and Italy, who use it widely in their kitchens alongside their own cheeses. It has a special relationship with Parmesan, which adds strength to its mild sweetness, and a 3:1 mixture of freshly grated Gruyère and Parmesan is one of the best of all basic cheese mixes for general cooking purposes. The combination is recommended in several recipes in this book, for sauces, soufflés, tarts and gratins. Gruyère is so widely used in cooking that it is often, and unjustly, overlooked as a possible item on the cheeseboard. Eat it occasionally on its own and you will understand why it is such a truly great cheese.

Halloumi

Another brine-soaked cheese from Greece and Cyprus, properly made from either ewe's or goat's milk, halloumi should be slightly less salty than fetta. Slightly rubbery when raw, it really comes into its own when cooked. Slices ¼ in/5 mm thick should be fried gently in olive oil, until pleasantly gooey but not browned. Serve at once with a dressing of chopped fresh mint, olive oil and lemon juice, accompanied by a few fat calamata olives, a simple tomato and onion salad, and a glass of chilled retsina. It's a dish to transport you straight to the olive groves of Greece.

Leicester

There is no need to call this cheese Red Leicester – there is no other kind. Bland when immature (and it is usually sold far too young), Leicester becomes a very worthwhile cheese when allowed to ripen for 6–9 months. A good mature Leicester is mellow and nutty, and ranks alongside the best farmhouse Cheddars, though it will always be a little milder. Look out for whole wheels of mature farmhouse Leicester in good cheese shops, and buy a slice cut off the block.

Cooking with Leicester

When you find a good one it makes an interesting change from Cheddar: try it in the Welsh Rarebit recipe on page 403.

Mozzarella

Mozzarella owes its fame to the international popularity of the pizza. Sadly, it owes its decline in quality to the same phenomenon. It is now made all over the world – production in Denmark is huge – and the factory-made product that you will find in most supermarkets is rubbery and tasteless. Even genuine Italian mozzarella is on the bland side, and only generally becomes interesting when it is heated to a gooey, stringy melt (as good on slices of fried aubergine as it is on a pizza). The only mozzarella of real interest uncooked is the original *mozzarella di bufala*, made from the milk of water buffalos and still produced in parts of southern Italy. Softer and more porous, with a pronounced flavour, it is particularly good cut into thick slices and marinated for a few hours in the very best extra virgin olive oil. Serve with freshly torn basil leaves and perhaps sun-dried tomatoes.

Mozzarella is a fresh cheese and does not keep well. It should be used as soon as possible after it is bought. It needs to be kept moist, which is why it is usually sold in plastic packages containing lightly salted water (vacuum-packed mozzarella should be avoided). If you need to keep a cut cheese for a day or two, put it into a bowl and cover with fresh milk. Keep refrigerated.

Mascarpone

A wickedly rich cream cheese, completely smooth and glossy, mascarpone is the Italian answer to clotted cream. It is usually served fresh with fruit and other desserts – it makes an indulgent accompaniment to any of the Fruit and Almond Tarts described on pages 360–1. Sweetened with sugar, flavoured with cinnamon, powdered chocolate, coffee or liqueurs, and served with a few *amaretti* or *cantuccini* biscuits, it makes a pudding in itself. It is also a vital ingredient in *tiramisu*. There are savoury applications too: mixed with herbs or grated horseradish, it can be used to garnish simply grilled fish or meat. A blob of mascarpone will also enrich a dish of fried mushrooms with polenta (see page 306).

Parmesan

Parmigiano-Reggiano is the proper name for this king among cheeses. The generic family of hard cheeses is called *grana*, and Reggiano's major rival is a cheese called Grana Padana. Both cheeses can be good, but Reggiano is reckoned to have the edge.

A good *grana* has a very hard, thick rind with a slightly oily surface. The cheese is traditionally split with a special blade, rather than cut open, so do not be surprised if when you ask for a piece of Parmesan in a bona fide Italian delicatessen you are presented with a rough-edged, rock-like hunk. The cheese is said to be at the peak of perfection when a freshly split piece reveals tiny droplets of moisture on its surface. This is called *con gocciola* (with tears).

Pieces of Parmesan should never be stored in the fridge for long, but kept in a cool cupboard or larder covered with a cloth or wrapped in lightly oiled paper. If you have to abandon a large piece of Parmesan for, say, upwards of two weeks, your best bet is to wrap it tightly in cling film and put it in the freezer. To defrost, unwrap it and return to a cool larder and the paper/cloth treatment.

Cooking with Parmesan

The superb, almost fruity flavour of fresh Parmesan makes many Italian dishes what they are. Pasta dishes and risottos would be nothing without it. Parmesan should always be grated as freshly as possible – even at the table directly on to your food. Besides being grated, Parmesan can be shaved with the blade of a heavy knife or even a potato peeler into wafer-thin slivers. This is the way to present Parmesan on top of a simple salad, a plate of freshly steamed asparagus spears, or a dish of thinly sliced *bresaola* (Italian cured beef fillet) or Parma ham. Parmesan has a wonderful affinity with good olive oil, and there can be few more delightful snacks than crusty white bread dipped in oil and eaten with a few shavings of this remarkable cheese. A more extravagant but equally wonderful companion is the white truffle oil from Alba. It is phenomenally expensive, but only a tiny squirt is needed (supplement with olive oil) to impart its heady fungal aroma to a dish. Try this blissful marriage of cheese and oil on a salad of rocket leaves and french beans, or a dish of artichoke hearts and new potatoes. If ever you should be lucky enough to lay your hands on a whole fresh white truffle, shave slivers on to the simplest of risottos, or just plain pasta dressed with olive oil, and add a few Parmesan shavings, for one of the greatest gastronomic treats known to man.

Pecorino

Pecorino is the generic Italian name for sheep's milk cheeses, the best-known of which is Pecorino Romano. It is a close-textured hard cheese, with a slightly dry-mouth feel, and an excellent tangy flavour.

Cooking with Pecorino Romano

The cheese is a sort of ovine equivalent to Parmesan, and in areas where it is produced its use in cooking may be preferred. Its pleasures are undoubtedly a little less subtle, but considerable none the less. It can be grated on to risottos and pasta dishes, and is particularly interesting if used instead of, or as well as, Parmesan in pesto (see page 105). Enjoyable on its own, with rough country bread and olive oil, it also makes a good aperitif cheese, accompanying salads, salamis and other antipasti.

Ricotta

Ricotta was traditionally made from the whey left behind when the curds of the milk had been taken for making other cheeses. Now whole milk is often added, giving a rather richer result. The cheese is generally encountered in the shape of an upturned pudding basin. The criss-cross pattern on the outside of the cheese is an impression left by the basket in which the cheese is formed. It is made from the milk of both sheep and cows, though ewe's-milk ricotta from the farms around Rome (ricotta Romana) is considered the most authentic. It is a fresh, soft cheese with a very mild taste, and its appeal in its natural state is a subtle one. When very fresh its pleasant granular texture and light tang make it a good accompaniment to sweet things, and it is eaten with fruit, honey or powdered chocolate, rather like mascarpone (see above), though it is not so heavy. There are also ripened and salted types of ricotta, some hard enough to be grated, but they are rarely encountered in this country.

Cooking with ricotta

Ricotta is widely used as a cooking cheese in Italy, especially for stuffing pasta and baking tarts, both savoury and sweet. My favourite ricotta pudding is the Ricotta and Pinenut Tart (page 402). When I worked at the River Café we used to make a very simple but popular starter when we had a particularly fresh ricotta Romana: a ¼-in/5-mm slice (the cross-section of half a whole cheese) was cut carefully so that it didn't crumble, and laid on a bed of warm Puy lentils (see page 301). The only adornment was a simple dressing of finely chopped fresh parsley, garlic, fresh red chillis and olive oil.

Roquefort

France's favourite blue cheese is made from ewe's milk, and ripened in the caves of Combalou where the temperature is constant, winter and summer. Its unique blue-green mould has a particularly fine flavour, which is spoilt in some cases by oversalting to prolong the life of exported cheese. Look for a Roquefort with veins evenly distributed almost to the edge of the cheese; being wrapped in foil while still maturing, the cheese barely has a rind. The texture should be smooth, and creamy, not crumbly. This is a cheese you should always ask to taste before buying. Only one Roquefort is still made in the time-honoured fashion, with the penicillin spores stirred in by hand. The maker's name is Gabriel-Coulet.

Cooking with Roquefort

Roquefort is as good a blue cheese as any for cooking with: follow the suggestions for GORGONZOLA above. Like many cheeses it goes well with celery (though not, I would hazard, in a soup – see STILTON below). The French like to melt a slab of Roquefort on top of a good steak – a pleasing combination but not a subtle one.

Stilton

One should technically call Stilton 'Blue Stilton', as there is an unblued variety. But it is the famous blue-marbled Stilton that is rightly regarded as the King of English cheeses.

Good Stilton should be velvety and close-textured, never hard or dry. The rind (which is not edible) is a crusty, rusty-grey colour, with whitish powdery patches. Look for even, blue-green marbling that goes almost to the edge of the cheese. The very best Stilton is made only from rich summer milk; the resulting cheese has a yellowish tinge, the colour of pale butter, and is best eaten still fairly young (11–13 weeks old).

If choosing a Stilton for Christmas, it is best to buy it at the beginning of December, or even earlier; nearer Christmas, many inferior and under-matured cheeses are unloaded into the shops. Some are even held over from last year, and have been deep-frozen, as part of our Stilton mountain.

Cooking with Stilton

Some years ago there seemed to be a fashion in restaurants for Stilton soup, and variations such as Stilton and celery, or Stilton and sweetcorn. I must admit I never tasted one that I liked. I once made a Stilton soufflé, as a savoury to be eaten with a glass of port. It was reasonably successful, and can be made by substituting Stilton for the combination of Parmesan and Gruyère in the recipe on page 402. Generally speaking, however, I find the slightly bitter note in Stilton makes it less agreeable in recipes than the other blue cheeses such as Roquefort, Gorgonzola and Dolcelatte.

Taleggio

A fine creamy semi-soft Italian cheese that comes in a rectangular block. It is rich with a mild but distinctly fruity tang. Look out for unpasteurized cheeses, as these are likely to be particularly fine.

Cooking with Taleggio

Slices of Taleggio, which can include the edible rind, are quite delicious deep-fried in breadcrumbs (see page 403) or melted in a hot oven on slices of grilled French bread. Serve with a salad of rocket or bitter leaves.

Recipes

Perfect béchamel sauce

A number of recipes in this book call for the use of a béchamel sauce. This is made by pouring warm milk on to a roux made with flour and butter. There are a few simple but important points to observe to ensure success. The flour should be cooked in the butter for a minute or two before you add the milk. The milk should be warm or even hot – the mixture is then less likely to become lumpy when the milk is added. Vigorous stirring, especially when the milk is added, will also help to avoid lumpiness. The béchamel should be cooked slowly and allowed to boil for just a minute – the flour will then have completed its thickening job, and if the sauce is too thick it can be thinned with a little more warm milk.

Purists would first flavour the milk by infusing it with a mirepoix of vegetables, and if you have the time, this is certainly worthwhile. To a pint of milk add 1 small onion, 1 medium carrot and 1 celery stick, all finely chopped, plus a sprig each of thyme and parsley. Heat the milk and vegetables in a saucepan and, when boiling point is reached, take off the heat, cover the pan and leave to infuse for ½–1 hour. Then strain the milk through a sieve before making the béchamel.

Quantities

To get a thick béchamel suitable for soufflés and gratins, I use 1 oz/ 30 g each of plain flour and butter per 10 fl oz/300 ml milk.

For a pouring or sauce consistency, use 1½ oz/45 g each of butter and plain flour per 1 pt/575 ml milk.

Cheese sauce

For perfect cheese sauce, stir 4 oz/115 g mature farmhouse cheddar, or 3 oz/85 g Gruyère and 1 oz/30 g Parmesan into ½ pt/300 ml béchamel, and stir until melted.

A béchamel for savoury applications should always be well seasoned with salt and pepper – and a pinch of grated nutmeg if you have it.

Gnocchi Verdi
(Spinach and Ricotta Dumplings)
Serves 4

I learned to make these while working at the River Café in London. They take a little time, but are not hard if you follow the recipe carefully. Do not be tempted to make them in a food processor (though you can chop the spinach in one if you like), as the resulting paste will be far too smooth. The dumplings should still have little curdy pieces of ricotta in them.

1 lb/450 g fresh leaf spinach
salt and black pepper
1 oz/30 g soft butter
2 oz/60 g fresh Parmesan
  cheese, grated
2 large eggs, beaten
3 oz/85 g plain flour, plus
  extra for dusting the
  dumplings
a pinch of grated nutmeg
8 oz/225 g fresh ricotta cheese

To serve with the dumplings
plenty of melted butter
more freshly grated Parmesan
  cheese

Wash the spinach thoroughly and discard the thicker stalks. Wilt it in a pan for 4–5 minutes (see page 94), with only the water that is clinging to it, and a good pinch of salt. Squeeze the cooked spinach as dry as you can in a cloth, and chop it finely (with a mezzaluna if you have one).

Put the spinach into a large mixing bowl with all the other ingredients except the ricotta, and mix gently with a wooden spoon, stirring rather than beating, until well incorporated. Then crumble in the ricotta with your fingers, working it into the mixture until it, too, is well incorporated. The ingredients should be evenly distributed through the mixture, but it should be rather on the rough side, not a smooth paste.

At this point the mixture should be covered with a cloth and thoroughly chilled, for at least 4 hours or overnight. After this you should find the mixture stiff enough to form into shapes. If you can get the knack, you can mould little dumplings by using 2 dessertspoons, scraping spoonfuls of the mixture from one spoon to the other to get a neat, rugby-ball shape. Alternatively, mould fat little sausages, about 2 in/5 cm long and 1 in/2.5 cm thick, with your hands. Whichever method you use, the finished dumplings should be dusted with flour and laid on a lightly floured tray.

To cook the dumplings, bring a large saucepan of water to a steady rolling simmer – not too fierce or the dumplings will break up. Poach 6–7 at a time, removing each batch with a slotted spoon a minute or so after they bob to the surface (5–6 minutes in all), and transferring them to a colander to drain well. Have ready an ovenproof dish, containing a generous quantity of melted butter. When each batch has been cooked transfer the dumplings to this dish, and keep in a warm oven. When all the dumplings have been cooked, pour more melted butter over them, and a good sprinkling of Parmesan, and return the dish to the oven for a few more minutes before serving.

Leek and Gruyère Tart
Serves 6

This is no mere quiche, but a very rich, creamy tart, with a light, crumbly pastry. (You can use your own pastry recipe if you wish, but the one given below, taken from Elizabeth David's *French Provincial Cooking*, is well worth knowing about as it is very simple, requires no chilling or rolling out, and so can be made at the last minute.)

First make the pastry. Sieve the flour and salt into a mixing bowl and work the butter into the flour with your fingertips. Add 2 tbsp of the water, work into the pastry and form into a ball, adding the remaining water only if the pastry seems too dry. Spread the pastry directly into an 8–9-in/20–22.5-cm tart tin with your fingers, as evenly as you can, pressing the pastry up the sides of the tin with your knuckles. It is bound to be a little uneven but, as long as there are no holes or huge lumps, this is not a problem. Prick the surface of the pastry with a fork, cover with foil or greaseproof paper, and fill with clay baking beads or dry beans. Bake blind for 15–20 minutes in a pre-heated fairly hot oven (200°C/400°F/Gas Mark 6).

To prepare the filling, trim and thoroughly wash the leeks, then slice them thinly into discs. Sweat gently in the oil or butter, tossing or stirring regularly, for 15–20 minutes, until they are quite soft but not browned. Spread the leeks into the blind-baked pastry case. Sprinkle the Gruyère evenly over them, withholding just a spoonful. Lightly beat the egg yolks with the cream, season well with salt and pepper and pour over the leeks, then sprinkle the last of the cheese on top. Bake in a pre-heated moderate oven (190°C/375°F/Gas Mark 5) for 30 minutes. Serve hot from the oven.

For the pastry
6 oz/170 g plain flour
a pinch of salt
3 oz/85 g butter
about 3 tbsp ice-cold water

For the filling
2 lb/900 g leeks (1½ lb/675 g trimmed weight)
1 tbsp olive oil *or* 1 oz/30 g butter
3 oz/90 g Gruyère cheese, grated
4 egg yolks
8 fl oz/250 ml double cream
salt and black pepper

Ricotta and Pinenut Tart

Serves 8

Part cheesecake, part tart – wholly delicious.

2 tbsp marsala *or* rum
2 oz/60 g seedless raisins
12 oz/350 g fresh ricotta
cheese
5 fl oz/150 ml double cream
4 oz/115 g caster sugar
2 oz/60 g ground almonds
grated zest of 1 lemon
4 eggs
2 oz/60 g pinenuts, lightly
toasted
a 10-in/25-cm blind-baked
sweet pastry tart case (made
according to the recipe on
pages 360–1)

Warm the marsala or rum in a pan and pour over the raisins. Leave them to soak for at least 2 hours.

Rub the ricotta through a sieve into a large mixing bowl. Cream together with the cream, sugar, ground almonds and lemon zest. Beat in the eggs, one at a time. (All this can be done in a food processor.)

Stir in the pinenuts, raisins and Marsala or rum, pour the mixture into the tart case and spread evenly with a palette knife. Bake in a pre-heated moderate to hot oven (190°C/375°F/Gas Mark 5), for 30–35 minutes, until firm and lightly browned. Eat warm or cool, with Vino Santo, the fortified Italian dessert wine, if you can get some.

Spaghetti Soufflé

Serves 4

This is an ingenious way of transforming a light soufflé into a rather more robust supper dish. It sounds curious, but it is quite delicious.

6 oz/170 g spaghetti
2 tsp olive oil
8 fl oz/250 ml thick béchamel
sauce (see page 399)
4 oz/115 g farmhouse Cheddar
cheese, grated *or* 2 oz/60 g
each of Gruyère and
Parmesan cheese, grated
4 eggs, separated

Cook the spaghetti in boiling water according to packet instructions. Drain as soon as it is *al dente* – do not over-cook. Toss the spaghetti with the olive oil, so that it does not stick together as it cools. Curl the cooked spaghetti in an even layer into the bottom of a lightly oiled 2-pt/1-litre soufflé dish.

Stir the cheese into the warm béchamel so that it melts. Draw off the heat and beat in the egg yolks. Whisk the egg whites to stiff peaks and fold carefully but thoroughly into the cheese mixture. Pour into the soufflé dish over the spaghetti and bake in a pre-heated fairly hot oven (200°C/400°F/Gas Mark 6) for about 25 minutes, until well-risen and browned on the top.

Serve with strong English or Dijon mustard and a simple green salad.

Deep-fried Taleggio in Breadcrumbs
Serves 4

Served with a simple tomato salad and a few green leaves, this makes a delightful starter – the cheese melts deliciously. If you don't have a deep-fat fryer, you can heat up a good ½ in/1 cm groundnut or corn oil in a deep frying pan or wide saucepan.

Cut the cheese into 8 slices about ½ in/1 cm thick. Dip each slice in first the milk, then the flour, then the beaten egg, and finally the breadcrumbs, making sure the final coating of breadcrumbs is thorough and even.

Deep-fry the slices, 4 at a time if there is space in your fryer, for just 1–2 minutes, with the oil at 190°C/375°F. Remove carefully from the hot oil with a slotted spoon (with a wooden or plastic handle). The cheese inside will be rather runny, but the breadcrumb coating should mean that it just keeps its shape. Drain well on kitchen paper and serve at once.

8 oz/225 g Taleggio cheese, in a block
milk
seasoned plain flour
I egg, beaten
3 oz/85 g fresh white breadcrumbs

Real Welsh Rarebit
Serves 6 generously

More than just cheese on toast!

Melt the butter in a saucepan, add the flour and cook this roux for 1–2 minutes. Add the warm milk by degrees, stirring to keep the mixture lump-free. Stir in the warm beer, also by degrees. Bring this beery béchamel slowly to the boil and allow to bubble gently for just 2 minutes, stirring all the time. Take the pan off the heat, add the grated cheese and stir until it is melted. Stir in the mustard and Worcester sauce, and season to taste with salt and black pepper. Leave the mixture to cool and thicken.

Toast the bread slices and spread the cheese mixture evenly over each. Lay the slices on a baking tray and place under a hot grill until browned and bubbling. Serve with more beer!

I oz/30 g butter
2 oz/60 g plain flour
8 fl oz/250 ml warm milk
8 fl oz/250 ml strong beer (brown ale *or* bitter), warmed
9 oz/255 g good farmhouse Cheddar *or* mature Leicester cheese, grated
2 tsp strong English mustard
2 tbsp Worcester sauce
salt and black pepper
6 large slices good brown or white country bread

CHAPTER TEN

Herbs

It is often the heady aroma and just-released flavour of fresh herbs that transform a dish from the 'interesting' category to the really sensational. For this reason a good cook will always have a ready supply of herbs to hand.

Whilst it is gratifying that supermarkets and even small greengrocers are now selling the better-known herb plants fresh as well as dried, there are drawbacks to buying them in this way. First, cut herbs, especially those with delicate leaves such as chervil, coriander or tarragon, quickly lose condition. They will not last for more than a few days at best, and, even if they look all right, they will not have the same intensity of flavour as freshly picked herbs. Second, they tend to be packaged in quantities that are either too big or too small for the purposes you have in mind. If you require only a small sprig of thyme for a mushroom omelette, then it seems extravagant to buy a hefty bunch, most of which will go to waste. If, on the other hand, you are making pesto (page 105), the amount of fresh basil you will need will, at supermarket prices, cost a small fortune.

By far the best option is to grow herbs yourself. This is not merely a suggestion for those who already pride themselves on their green fingers. Anyone can grow herbs, as most herb plants are easy to look after and thrive in our climate with minimal attention. And even if you don't have a garden, you can still grow herbs with ease in small pots or window-boxes, inside and out. Used within minutes of being picked, the taste and aroma of the still-living leaves is beyond compare. The fact that they have been nurtured by your own loving hand gives an extra dimension of pleasure to your cooking.

The next two sections offer basic advice on how to grow your own herbs, first in a garden, and second in pots or window-boxes. There follows an alphabetical guide to herbs and their uses, with further tips for the successful cultivation of particular herb plants. For the gardening advice in these sections I am deeply indebted to my mother, Jane Fearnley-Whittingstall, whose wonderful home-grown herbs I have cooked with often, and always with great pleasure.

Herbs in the garden

If possible, herbs should be sited close to the kitchen: you have to be a very dedicated cook to put on your wellington boots, put up your umbrella and tramp to the other end of the garden for a sprig of mint.

Many herbs are natives of the Mediterranean and, although most are frost-hardy, they need a sheltered situation and plenty of sun in order to thrive. Exceptions to this rule are golden marjoram, which needs a semi-shaded position to prevent the leaves from scorching, and chives, parsley and mint which will grow well in partial shade. For most other herbs a south- or west-facing bed protected on the north or east side by a wall or hedge is ideal. In a small area a low hedge of rosemary or lavender would provide enough shelter from cold winds; in mixed borders small groups of herbs can be planted in the lea of evergreen shrubs. Creeping thymes and marjoram can easily be grown in the cracks between paving-stones on a terrace or path.

Besides sun and shelter, herbs need well-drained soil. This makes them useful garden plants on sandy and limestone soils, but if your garden is on clay you can get around this problem by digging plenty of grit and organic material, such as mushroom compost, into the herb bed before planting.

Most herbs can be bought as small plants to set out and grow on in the garden, and some can be grown from seed. Garden centres and general nurseries have a selection of the more popular varieties, and others can be obtained from herb specialists, sometimes by mail order. It is possible to buy small pots of growing herbs from some supermarkets – basil in particular is often sold in this way. Whilst these do offer the benefits of truly fresh herbs, and will keep, if watered regularly, for a few weeks on a kitchen windowsill, they are not ideal for planting out as they have generally been forced under glass, and are therefore lacking in resistance and sturdiness.

Once your plants are established, you can increase the supply of shrubby herbs such as rosemary and sage by taking cuttings in late summer.

Growing herbs in pots and window-boxes

You do not need a garden to grow herbs. A small patio, a balcony, even a window-ledge will provide space for a few pots of parsley, thyme, chives and mint. Terracotta pots look better than plastic ones, but they dry out very quickly, so unless you are prepared to be vigilant and water twice a day in dry spells, put a plastic pot inside the terracotta one, or line it with polythene with a few drainage holes cut in the base. A general-purpose potting compost will provide a suitable growing medium, and frequency of watering can be reduced by mixing water-retaining granules, sold in garden centres, with the compost. An occasional feed with liquid fertilizer will keep the plants growing well.

If you are growing herbs indoors, as well as watering and feeding, it helps to spray the plants with a fine mist of tepid water in hot weather.

In order to persuade the plants to produce plenty of fresh leaves it is important to prevent them from flowering by picking off any flower-buds that appear. While a plant is young it can be induced to branch and become bushy by pinching out the tips of the main shoots.

Extending the season

Perennial herbs like mint, chives and fennel normally die down in winter and start into growth again in spring. However, they can be induced to continue growing through the winter months by bringing them indoors or covering them with cloches in the garden. In early autumn herbs growing in beds and borders can be dug up and planted into pots, whilst those already in pots are simply transferred from their outdoor positions to the greenhouse, conservatory or a light but fairly cool room indoors. The stems should be cut down to 1–2 in/2.5–5 cm in height to encourage new growth, and the plants kept watered and fed. Annual and biennial herbs (chervil, coriander, dill, parsley, summer savory) can be sown into pots towards the end of the summer, and should be ready to use about 3 months later.

Basil

(Ocimum basilicum)

One of the finest and most versatile of all herbs, and also one of the easiest to grow. Grown indoors, its sweet fragrance will fill your kitchen with the scent of summer. Its greatest friends are the Mediterranean vegetables – tomatoes, peppers, aubergines and courgettes – but it also combines beautifully with eggs and fish – red mullet, sea bream, langoustines and lobsters in particular.

The leaves are at their most fragrant when the plant is still young, 6–10 in/ 15–25 cm high. Pick and tear the leaves as near serving as possible before garnishing a dish with basil, to release its aroma at the last possible minute. This is especially important when using the herb in hot dishes, as the flavour is quickly cooked out of the leaves.

A recipe for the famous Italian basil and garlic sauce of pesto appears on page 105.

Dried basil provides a feeble shadow of the flavour of the fresh leaves.

Growing tips

Basil is a half-hardy perennial, but best treated as annual, as it is unlikely to survive frost in this country. Can be grown from seed in warmth indoors or outside in a sunny, sheltered position when the danger of frost is past. Do not transplant, but thin seedlings to 6 in/15 cm apart. Warning: over-watering can cause seedlings to rot.

In winter keep basil in pots on a sunny windowsill indoors. Leaves can be stored whole in olive oil or frozen (see PRESERVING HERBS on page 423). The best-flavoured varieties are common basil and Italian basil, which has plumper, slightly curly leaves. Alternative varieties tend to be less strongly flavoured: purple-leaved basil (decorative) and bush basil (very small leaves, hardier and easier to grow).

Bay
(Laurus nobilis)

Bay leaves, fresh or dried, are used in cooking all around the world to flavour stews, soups, stocks and marinades, usually with red meat and game but also with fish. The flavour combines particularly well with oily fish such as mackerel and herring: fresh fillets rolled up with a bay leaf inside are fantastic grilled, barbecued or baked.

Dried bay leaves are almost as good as fresh, provided they are not kept for longer than a couple of months.

Growing tips

Bay is a slow-growing evergreen which can be grown outdoors in a sheltered position, but is safest grown in a pot and brought into a greenhouse or conservatory in cold winter spells. Decorative when clipped as topiary pyramids or lollipop-shaped trees (clippings can be dried for use later), bay can be grown from cuttings, or you can buy a small plant to grow on. Alternative varieties: golden bay has yellow leaves, willow-leaf bay has long narrow leaves.

Chervil
(Anthriscus cerefolium)

Unjustly neglected outside France, the delicate, feathery leaves of chervil have a subtle, faintly aniseed taste which goes excellently with white fish. Like basil, it is best added to dishes at the last minute, as cooking will kill its flavour. To the juices of a baked, braised or poached fish, or to a good fish stock, add a little cream and reduce to thicken, stir in a generous sprinkling of finely chopped chervil, and you have a simple but exquisite sauce. Whole sprigs of chervil make a fine addition to a leaf salad.

Growing tips

A hardy annual, chervil can be grown from seed outdoors, or indoors in pots for a winter supply. It seeds itself liberally, making a pretty garden plant like a more delicate cow parsley. Sow outdoors in light shade at monthly intervals, then thin out to 6 in/15 cm apart. You can start cutting leaves when the plants reach 4 in/10 cm high.

Chives
(Allium Chesenoprasum)

Chives have all the bite of their cousin the onion, but none of the tears. They are most commonly used as a garnish, added finely chopped to soups and sauces just before serving. A chive mayonnaise is perhaps the finest way to dress a potato salad, and excellent also with cold poached salmon. Snip into salads of summer leaves, or on a tomato salad as an alternative to basil.

Growing tips
Hardy perennial. Sow seeds in the spring. Chives can be increased by dividing every few years and replanting bulblets in spring or autumn, in sun or light shade. The pretty purple pom-pom flowers are decorative, but non-flowering stems will have a better flavour. Lift, pot up, cut back and bring indoors for winter use. Chives make a good edging plant in the garden.
Same family: garlic (*A. sativum*), Welsh onion (*A. fistulosum*) and tree onion (*A. proliferum*).

Coriander
(Coriandrum sativum)

For my money fresh coriander has one of the most distinctive and appealing flavours of any herb. It goes particularly well with fish and shellfish, and enlivens the taste of dull, cultivated mushrooms, and slightly sweet vegetables, such as parsnips, carrots, pumpkins and squashes (see recipe on page 105 for Baked Butternut Squash with Coriander Pesto). Its flavour is so pronounced that it is best used without other leaf herbs, though it does combine well with garlic and the curry spices. Add whole or torn leaves to curries and soups as a garnish at the end of cooking.

If you are buying fresh coriander, take care not to confuse it with flat-leaf

PARSLEY (see below), which it slightly resembles. The aroma will leave you in no doubt.

Coriander seeds, which are used whole or ground to make a spice, have a completely different tase from the leaves.

Growing tips

Hardy annual. Can be grown from seed. Sow seeds in autumn or spring outdoors in their final position or in pots. Thin to 8 in/20 cm apart. If seeds are wanted, the plants should be allowed to flower. For winter use make a late sowing or freeze the leaves (see page 424). The feathery, fresh green foliage is decorative in the garden.

Dill
(Anethum graveolens)

The sweet aniseed taste of dill is most famously associated with the Swedish pickled raw salmon dish of *gravadlax*, and with another Scandinavian favourite, herrings pickled in dill vinegar. In fact it goes well with almost all fish, and can be added generously to any liquor in which fish is going to be poached or braised. Cucumber is another good companion to dill, and a delicious salad can be made by dressing ½ cucumber, finely sliced, with 1 teaspoon mustard, 2 tablespoons soured cream or yoghurt, 1 tablespoon finely chopped dill, a squeeze of lemon, and a pinch of salt and plenty of freshly ground black pepper.

If you do not grow or cannot find fresh dill, then the feathery fronds from the top of FENNEL bulbs (see below) can be used instead.

Growing tips

Hardy annual. Can be grown from seed in a sunny, sheltered position. Sow at intervals from spring onwards, away from fennel plants to avoid cross-pollination. Sow in pots to bring indoors for winter use. Dill is a good foliage plant, with yellow umbelliferous flowers like fennel. Being self-seeding, it is likely to spread.

Fennel

(Foeniculum vulgare)

The fleshy bulb of Florence fennel (*F. vulgare dulce*) – a different but related plant – and the pungently aromatic seeds of the herb are more commonly used in the kitchen than the feathery leaves, but this is no reason to disregard them. They have a fresh, aniseed flavour, very similar to another close relative, DILL. Fennel leaves combine well with pork and veal and, as an alternative to dill, with fish. When you buy fennel bulbs, do not discard any leaves that might be attached – chopped finely, they can be added to another dish such as the risotto on page 428, and all the trimmings of the bulbs can be added to a fish stock. If you grow fennel in the garden, you will need to cut back the luxuriant stalks at the end of the summer. Do not discard these either, but hang them up to dry. Placed on a barbecue, or laid on top of a griddle pan until they blacken, they will infuse a wonderful smoky aroma into any fish (ideally red or grey mullet, bream or sea bass), or pork or veal cutlets.

Growing tips

Hardy perennial. Can be grown from seed. Plant outdoors in full sun. Do not grow near dill as the two may cross-fertilize. In autumn lift a clump or two and grow indoors in pots. Leaves can also be frozen for winter use. Fennel makes an impressive, stately garden plant, especially in its bronze-leaved form. Self-seeding, it quickly spreads in its bed.

Horseradish

(Armoracia rusticana)

Not really a herb at all, but an edible root. I include horseradish in this section because it is used fresh as a flavouring rather than eaten as a vegetable, and because although it is pitifully hard to find in the shops it is extremely easy to grow. It is also very worthwhile.

The fresh root, washed and peeled, should be grated. It can then be mixed with a little double cream, or crème fraîche, and mustard to make a sauce for steaks, roast beef or smoked fish (particularly eel and trout). Mixed into mayonnaise, it is a great glorifier of the humble hard-boiled egg. See also the recipe for Horseradish Mash on page 112.

Growing tips

Hardy perennial. As horseradish has a tendency to run wild in the garden, it makes sense to grow it in a sunken tub or large plastic pot. Roots can be stored for several weeks in a box of dry sand or peat.

Lemon Grass

One herb that you will not be able to grow at home, lemon grass can be found in Oriental grocers and now in some supermarkets. It is widely used in Asian cooking, particularly with fish, and in this book is required in the Brackenbury's Spicy Mussel Broth (page 179) and the Thai Hot and Sour Soup with Squid from The Fox and Goose Inn (page 161). If you cannot find lemon grass a good strip of lemon zest is an adequate substitute.

Lime leaves

Another ingredient in Asian cooking, also available from Oriental grocers. The flavour is pungent and aromatic, and not dissimilar to BAY, which can, at a pinch, be substituted.

Lovage
(Levisticum officinale)

A useful garden herb with a good savoury flavour not unlike celery, lovage deserves wider recognition. The thick stems can be used as a vegetable, prepared as for celery; the pretty dark green leaves and young stalks are added to soups or eaten raw in salads. A small bundle of lovage does wonders for a chicken stock.

Hardy perennial. Buy a young plant or sow seeds in late summer. Divide roots to make new plants. Freeze leaves and young stalks for winter use.

Marjoram/ Oregano

(Origanum)

Recipe: The versatile *gremolata*, an aromatic mixture from Italy, is made by combining a tablespoon of finely chopped oregano with a teaspoon of grated lemon zest and ½ a clove of garlic, very finely chopped. It can either be used dry, sprinkled on food before serving, or as a dressing, stirred into olive oil. Traditional beneficiaries are *osso buco* (see page 210) and grilled fish. A variation is made with parsley instead of oregano.

The several varieties of marjoram, one of the more pungent of which is commonly known as oregano, are sweet-scented and native to the Mediterranean. In Italy oregano is the herb for including in pizzas, but is also used widely in all sorts of fish, meat and vegetable dishes, often combined with thyme. The most delicately flavoured variety, and that favoured by the French, is sweet marjoram. Dried marjoram keeps the flavour of the fresh plant somewhat better than most dried herbs.

Growing tips

Shrubby perennial. It is easiest to buy a small plant, though seeds can be sown in spring. To increase yield, divide or take cuttings from late spring to summer. Grow in pots indoors or outdoors as a front-row garden plant, trimming the plants in autumn to keep them tidy. Bees and butterflies enjoy the flowers. Sweet marjoram (*O. majorana*) is delicate and needs plenty of sun; it is most easily grown indoors, on a sunny windowsill, or in a greenhouse or conservatory. Oregano (*O. vulgare*) has a pretty golden form and pot marjoram (*O. onites*) is a hardy variety which grows well outside. All kinds can be grown indoors for winter use.

Mint
(Mentha)

The unmistakable scent of mint is one of the great pleasures of an English summer, and the perfect companion to spring lamb and young vegetables, in particular peas, carrots, broad beans and new potatoes. In the Mediterranean it is equally prized, and makes a good alternative to basil, chopped on top of a simple tomato salad. It also goes beautifully, again instead of basil, with marinated grilled vegetables – courgettes, aubergines and peppers (see page 120) – and in a salad of cucumber dressed with yoghurt.

Mint's versatility extends to combinations with fruit, particularly grapefruit, pineapple and melon, and of course in long summer drinks. A cooling jug of Pimms would be nothing without a few sprigs.

Of the many kinds of mint, those most commonly grown for the kitchen are spearmint and apple mint. Both are excellent, and the rounded, hairy leaves of apple mint do indeed have a hint of the eponymous fruit.

Growing tips

Hardy perennial. Hard to grow from seed, so you will need to buy a small plant from a garden centre. There are several kinds of mint, some decorative like the variegated green and white apple mint and the tiny-leaved, creeping Corsican mint. All will grow easily in light shade or full sun and are invasive plants; to restrain the running roots, plant in pots or in a bucket with the bottom removed, sunk into the soil. To increase the supply or to pot up a few roots for winter use, just dig up one of the rooted off-shoots from the parent plant and replant.

Parsley
(Petroselinum crispum)

Parsley is the most commonly used herb in this country, probably because it is so friendly. Its mild, grassy flavour benefits almost any savoury dish, fish in particular, and also helps to bring out the taste of many other herbs – hence its use as a vital feature of a bouquet garni. There are curly-leaved and flat-leaved varieties. The latter, known in some quarters as continental or Italian parsley, has the best flavour.

Parsley and garlic are one of the great culinary duos: heated together with a little butter, they will do wonders for almost anything that has lived in the sea and plenty of things that haven't, from frog's legs to chicken livers, spuds and snails. Add a fresh chilli, and replace the butter with good olive oil, and you have a fine dipping sauce (which doesn't need to be cooked) for prawns, langoustine or squid.

Cheap and plentiful (free if you grow it yourself), parsley in large quantities can be used to make a fine soup, either standing on its own, or with other fresh herbs (see page 430 for recipe).

Growing tips

Hardy biennial. Sow seeds from February to June outdoors in sun or light shade. Soaking seeds overnight in warm water is said to aid germination. For winter use bring indoors in pots, make a late sowing indoors, or, in the garden, cut down in September, water and cover with cloches.

Rocket
(Eruca vesicaria)

These delicious peppery leaves are not really a herb, but a cut-and-come-again salad plant. See Vegetable chapter (page 74) for culinary uses.

Growing tips

Hardy annual. For a continuous supply make small sowings outdoors every 3–4 weeks between April and September. Useful in winter as it grows best in cool weather, and seedlings are ready to cut 3 weeks after sowing.

Rosemary
(Rosmarinus officinalis)

The marriage of rosemary and lamb is a blissful one with which every English cook is familiar, but there are many other uses for this pungent, twiggy herb, most of them pioneered by the Italians. They favour it with beef, inserting it with garlic into a fillet for roasting, in much the same way as we do to a leg of lamb, and also with fish, especially red mullet, which is served with a rosemary and anchovy butter (simply cream 3 oz/90 g soft butter with 8 mashed anchovy fillets and 1 tablespoon of finely chopped rosemary). Scallops can be threaded on to a twig of rosemary and barbecued or cooked on a griddle pan. Whole new potatoes are delicious roasted in their skins in olive oil, with generous sprigs of rosemary thrown in for the last 10 minutes of cooking time.

Growing tips

A shrub, hardy except in very cold winters, rosemary needs sunshine. Buy a small potted plant and transplant to grow on. A beautiful evergreen, it flowers in early spring and off and on all summer, and is easily raised from cuttings (see above). 'Miss Jessopp's Upright' is the best variety for hedging, and grows to 3–4 ft/1m high. There are white- and pink-flowered forms and less hardy varieties such as 'Prostratus' and 'Severn Sea'. Rosemary can also be grown in pots, indoors and out. It will get too big for a window-box after 3–4 years, so take cuttings for replacement plants every third year.

Sage
(Salvia officinalis)

Sage is the offal-lover's best friend. Liver, sweetbreads and brains (see appropriate sections in Chapter 5 for cooking guidelines) are all transformed by the punchy, slightly camphorous flavour of sage leaves, a few of which should be finely chopped and mixed with the seasoned flour in which the offal is tossed before frying. A few more whole leaves can also be casually thrown into the frying pan for the last minute of cooking. They should accompany the offal on to the plate, and definitely be eaten. If you are deep-frying vegetables in batter (see page 119), a few sage leaves can be dipped and fried too, for just a few seconds until crispy. Sage also goes well with pork, veal and poultry. Chopped finely, it can be added to a sausagemeat stuffing for chicken or turkey.

Growing tips

Hardy shrub. Buy a small plant to grow on. Sage is a decorative plant which forms a low cushion of evergreen leaves. Purple-leaved (*S. officinalis* 'Purpurascens') and variegated forms (*S.o.* 'Icterina' and 'Tricolor') can also be used to cook with. Further plants are easy to grow from cuttings, but can become straggly unless trimmed regularly. Replace plants after 4 years or so. Can be grown in pots indoors.

Savory
(Satureja hortensis and *S. montana)*

Savory is an excellent all-round herb which seems to capture the flavour of several other herbs; it has notes of thyme, chervil and rocket. Almost impossible to find in the shops, it is very easy to grow, and guaranteed to provoke interest among guests who have never encountered it before. It can be used to flavour all sorts of stocks and stews and goes particularly well with peas, beans and lentils. A simple purée of pulses can be brought to life by a few finely chopped savory leaves stirred in near the end of cooking. There are two main culinary varieties: winter savory and summer savory. They have different growing requirements and marginally different flavours, but can be considered interchangeable in their kitchen applications.

Growing tips

Summer savory (*S. hortensis*) needs a sunny position. It is a hardy annual. Can be grown from seeds sown in April in the garden and again in pots in late summer for an indoor winter supply. The leaves can also be dried or frozen (see page 424). Winter savory (*S. montana*) is a hardy, nearly evergreen shrubby perennial and can be grown from seed and increased by dividing the roots.

Sorrel
(Rumex acetosa)

See Chapter 2, page 75, for culinary uses.

Growing tips

Hardy perennial. Sorrel is easy to grow from seed and can be increased by dividing the roots. New leaves will come to replace those you have cut. Leaves should be cut just where they meet the stem, and the flower-spikes should be removed as they appear, to ensure a continued supply of tender young leaves. For winter use cover with a cloche.

Tarragon
(Artemisia dracunculus)

A sophisticated herb beloved of French chefs, tarragon is none the less versatile and not hard to use. It goes well with fish and poultry, and is an essential ingredient for béarnaise sauce. For a simple but successful version (there are many more elaborate ones) of *poulet à l'estragon*, put a few sprigs of tarragon and a piece of lemon zest inside the cavity of a good roasting chicken. When the bird is cooked, deglaze the roasting tin with a splash of white wine, and strain the juices into a clean pan. Stir in 1 tbsp chopped fresh tarragon and 5 fl oz/ 150 ml double cream or crème fraîche. Reduce to thicken, season to taste with salt and pepper, perhaps adding a few drops of lemon juice, and serve with the bird. A similar procedure can be followed with juices from a cooked fish, or, using a good fish stock, to make a tarragon cream sauce for white fish.

Tarragon vinegar (see page 424) makes excellent mayonnaise and salad dressings.

Growing tips

Bushy perennial not reliably hardy in cold areas. It is important to get French tarragon (*A. dracunculus*) and not Russian tarragon which is confusingly called *A. dracunculoides* and has a much inferior flavour. French tarragon needs sun, shelter and good drainage, and does well in pots and window-boxes. It is difficult to grow from seed and seed sold as tarragon is in any case almost always the inferior Russian kind. Better to acquire some young plants of French tarragon and increase by division or taking cuttings (see above). When harvesting, do not take more than two-thirds of each branch or the plant may die. Bring a pot indoors for winter use.

Thyme
(Thymus vulgaris, T. serpyllum,
T. praecox, T. x citriodorus)

A powerful herb with a slight bitterness and good savoury flavour, thyme is an essential ingredient of a bouquet garni. But it also deserves an outing on its own from time to time. Unlike many herbs, its flavour infuses well during long, slow cooking, and a sprig of thyme is a worthwhile addition to many casseroles, in particular of red meat and game, and in the making of most good stocks. A sprig in the cavity of a roasting game bird, or a strongly flavoured fish such as red mullet, also pays dividends.

Thyme has an affinity with three other ingredients in particular: mushrooms, black olives and artichokes. Mushrooms stewed with a little thyme can be eaten on toast, or with polenta and Parmesan cheese, or made into a fine omelette. Black olives and artichokes are combined with thyme in the savoury tart on page 427.

Growing tips
An evergreen, creeping plant with flowers in colours from dark purple-red to pale pink and white, the shoots make new roots as they travel along the ground. Start by buying one or two small plants and increase by severing rooted shoots from the parent and replanting them. Some varieties have silver and gold variegated leaves. A good edging and carpeting plant, as it tolerates being walked or sat on. Can also be grown in pots indoors.

Herb mixtures

Combining fresh herbs is largely a matter of personal taste and what you have available – few herbs clash horribly, although as I have mentioned, the distinctive taste of fresh coriander leaves goes better with curry spices than with other fresh leaf herbs. The following reliable combinations are traditional in French cuisine.

Bouquet garni

A bundle of fresh herbs, tied together with string and added to soups, stocks and stews as a flavouring. It is removed at the end of cooking. The classic combination is 5–6 sprigs of parsley, 2–3 of thyme, and a couple of bay leaves. Rosemary, chervil, basil and tarragon can also be added if you feel they would be appropriate. A fresh bouquet garni is infinitely preferable to the dried product.

Fines herbes

The classic ingredients for an *omelette aux fines herbes* are equal quantities of finely chopped fresh parsley, tarragon, chervil and chives. Watercress and fennel leaves are optional extras. 1 tablespoon of each herb, half only for tarragon, is about right for two 3-egg omelettes. The same herbs can be stirred into butter sauces and cream reductions for fish and chicken.

Herbes de Provence

Usually sold as a blend of dried herbs (see below), this mix is likely to contain thyme, rosemary, sage, marjoram, basil, fennel and mint. It is used for flavouring Provençal *daubes* and ratatouilles. There is no reason not to make up a version of the mixture with fresh herbs.

Preserving herbs

The idea of growing your own herbs is to have a constant supply available all the year round, and the guidelines above explain how most types can be brought indoors and kept in pots during the cold months. However, if this seems like too much hard work you may prefer to use another method that enables you to use your herbs throughout the winter. Here are some suggestions.

Freezing herbs

Most leafy herbs can be frozen, and will be better than dried herbs for flavouring dishes. However, frozen leaves do not reconstitute well after thawing, so will not be an adequate substitute for fresh leaves in salads or as last-minute garnishes. They may be more usefully employed in soups, stews, pasta sauces and other cooked dishes.

To freeze herbs, lay out separate sprigs on a tray in the deep-freeze until they are frozen, then put them into freezer bags. Alternatively, you can freeze finely chopped herbs in water in ice-cube trays and bag up the cubes to use as required.

Drying

This is less satisfactory than freezing, as more of the flavour is lost in the drying process. Herbs that dry reasonably well are bay, thyme, marjoram, oregano, mint, dill, lovage and sage. Again, they are better employed in cooked dishes, such as soups and stews, so they have time to release their flavour and become tender. Nobody wants to encounter gritty dried herbs in their food.

To dry your own herbs, cut whole stems on a sunny day when the herbs are free of condensation or rain-drops. Either tie them into small bunches or lay them out on an open rack such as a metal cake rack. Place the racks or hang the bunches in a dark, warm, airy place such as an airing cupboard or above an Aga. When the leaves are completely dry and brittle (after about a week), strip them from the stems, break up with your fingers or in a pestle and mortar, and store in airtight containers.

Mint and other dried herbs can be home blended to make herb teas and tisanes – you'll have to seek a greater authority than me to get accurate recipes for such infusions.

Herb oils and vinegars

Making your own herb oils and vinegars is one of the pleasures of having a good supply of fresh herbs. The procedure is simple, and you can experiment with almost any herb you like.

For herb vinegars, a good white wine vinegar is warmed in a pan until hand-hot, the chopped herbs are added, and the vinegar rebottled with the herbs, capped tightly, and left to infuse for 2–3 weeks (ideally on a sunny shelf). The vinegar should then be strained and rebottled (with a small sprig of the herb, if you like, to remind you what it is).

Here are a few suggestions, with quantities of the herb appropriate for 10 fl oz/300 ml vinegar:

BASIL: 5 tbsp finely chopped

BAY: 6 whole bay leaves

DILL or FENNEL: 1 tbsp seeds, 2 tbsp chopped leaves (NB: excellent for pickling herrings)

MARJORAM: 2 tbsp chopped

MIXED HERBS: 1 tbsp each of chopped tarragon, chervil, watercress; 2 garlic cloves, lightly crushed; 1 small dried chilli

ROSEMARY: 2 good stems

TARRAGON: 2 good stems

Herb oils are even easier to prepare than vinegars: there is no need to heat the oil, and the bottle does not need to be strained, provided the oil is used up within 4 months. For a spicy, aromatic oil, good for dressing salads and grilled vegetables, add to a 27-fl oz/75-cl (wine bottle-sized) quantity of extra virgin olive oil: 2 stems of rosemary, 6 sprigs of thyme (ideally lemon thyme), 2 garlic cloves, lightly crushed, 4 small fresh chillis, 10 black peppercorns and a small strip of lemon zest. Cap tightly (cork in a clean wine bottle if you like) and keep for at least 3 weeks before using. Use within 4 months (or strain the oil and keep for up to a year in a cool, dark place).

Herb butters

Another way of preserving herbs is to cream the chopped fresh herbs with butter. The butter is then seasoned to taste with salt and pepper and moulded into a pat or roll from which slices can be cut. Herb butters can be kept for up to 1 week in the fridge, or for 4 months in a freezer. Their uses are a little limited, but they are always good on a piece of simply grilled meat or fish.

Try the following (quantities given are for 8 oz/250 g butter). The butter should be softened at room temperature first. The creaming can be done by hand or in a food processor.

CHIVE BUTTER: 6 oz/170 g fresh chives, finely chopped. For grilled fish and meat.

HORSERADISH: 3 oz/85 g finely grated fresh root (sieve butter after creaming to remove fibrous pieces, then shape and freeze). For steaks and grilled fish.

PARSLEY: 4 oz/115 g parsley, finely chopped, 1 garlic clove, very finely chopped, a squeeze of lemon juice. For grilled fish and meat, and boiled new potatoes.

TARRAGON: 4 oz/115 g, finely chopped. For grilled steaks, poultry and fish.

RAVIGOTE: 1 oz/30 g each of parsley, chives, tarragon, chervil and watercress. For grilled meat or fish.

The concept of herb butter is ripe for experimentation, and you should feel free to invent your own recipes.

Recipes

Artichoke and Thyme Tart
Serves 8 as a generous starter

This is a straightforward tart made with a savoury custard, but the powerful flavour of thyme permeates the creamy filling to delicious effect. I use whole sprigs of thyme, which make the tart look beautifully rough and rustic, but I suggest you don't actually eat the stalky bits.

Cook the artichokes in plenty of well-salted boiling water until they are tender (see page 47 if in doubt). Drain and leave until cool enough to handle.

Pluck the leaves from the artichokes and trim off, with a sharp knife or pair of kitchen scissors, all the edible parts. Put these in a bowl, squeeze over a few drops of lemon juice, and mash roughly with a fork. Reserve.

Using a sharp-edged spoon or a small vegetable knife, scrape out the chokes from the artichoke hearts. Cut the hearts in half and slice each half into ½-in/1-cm slices. Scatter these over the base of the tart case.

Lightly beat the eggs and egg yolks with the cream, stir in the mashed artichoke trimmings and season to taste with salt and pepper. Pour this custard over the sliced artichoke hearts in the tart case and scatter the chopped olives over the top. Break up the sprigs of thyme into short lengths, and scatter these over the tart.

Bake the tart in a pre-heated moderate to hot oven (190°C/375°F/Gas Mark 5) for 40–45 minutes, until lightly puffed and brown on top. Serve warm or at room temperature, with a few green salad leaves.

3 large *or* 4 medium globe artichokes
salt and black pepper
a squeeze of fresh lemon
a blind-baked 8–9-in/ 20–22.5-cm pastry tart case (made according to the recipe on page 401)
2 whole eggs, plus 2 egg yolks
8 fl oz/250 ml double cream
10–15 black olives (ideally calamata), stoned and very roughly chopped
5–6 good sprigs of thyme

Salsa Verde (Green Herb Sauce)
Serves 6

The recipe for this is infinitely variable. The idea is to bring in a bunch of herbs from the garden and improvise a fresh, aromatic sauce at the last moment before eating. The version below contains dill and tarragon and is particularly suitable for fish, either grilled and hot, or poached and cold. Horseradish and/or mustard can be included to make a *salsa verde* for boiled beef or tongue. For a sauce to accompany lamb, follow the recipe below omitting the dill and adding perhaps a small bunch of basil and a few mint leaves. Experiment at your leisure; it is very hard indeed to make a nasty *salsa verde*!

a good size bunch of flat-leaf
  parsley
a small bunch of dill
a small bunch of sweet cicely
  (*optional*)
a small bunch of chives
a few sprigs of tarragon
2 garlic cloves
4–5 anchovy fillets
2 tsp capers
a good squeeze of lemon
4–5 tbsp best olive oil
salt and black pepper

Pick over the herbs, discarding the tougher stalks and any damaged leaves. Wash them and pat dry with a clean cloth or spin in a salad dryer. If you have a mezzaluna (see page 22), put all the ingredients except the oil and lemon juice on a large chopping board, and chop until very fine, almost a purée. Transfer to a small bowl, add the lemon juice and stir in enough oil to get a thick, pulpy sauce. Season with pepper, and salt only if it is needed.

Alternatively, chop the ingredients finely in a food processor, trickling in the lemon juice and oil at the end.

Green Herb Risotto
Serves 4 as a starter

A particularly delicious and delicate risotto, this makes a fine starter on its own, or can be used to accompany fish or meat.

1 small onion *or* 2 shallots,
  very finely chopped
2 oz/60 g butter
8 oz/225 g arborio rice (see
  page 307)
1 pt/575 ml chicken, veal *or*
  vegetable stock
1 wine-glass white wine
1 quantity *salsa verde*, omitting
  the anchovies and capers (see
  page 427)
a few extra fresh herbs, finely
  chopped
salt and black pepper

In a medium heavy-based saucepan sweat the onion or shallot in the butter for a few minutes until soft but not coloured. Add the rice and cook for a further few minutes. Add a ladle of the stock and allow to come to a gentle simmer. Cook the rice until almost all the liquid has been absorbed, stirring occasionally, to make sure the risotto does not catch on the bottom of the pan. Continue to add the liquid by degrees, incorporating the wine towards the end of cooking, until the liquid is all absorbed, the risotto is creamy, and the individual rice grains tender with just a hint of chalkiness in the middle.

Stir the *salsa verde* into the risotto, which should become a beautiful pale green, flecked with tiny pieces of herb. Season to taste with salt and pepper.

The risotto should be served not piping hot, but *tiede*, with a sprinkling of chopped fresh herbs and a trickle of olive oil on each portion. Parmesan cheese is not necessary.

Nettle and Tarragon Soup
Serves 6–8

You could add a few nettle leaves to the Potato and Herb Soup (see following recipe) but since nettles are free I include an excellent recipe which exploits them more fully. April and May, when the nettles are young, are the best months to make this soup. Use stout rubber gloves to pick the nettles, and choose only the tips and top few leaves. Chives make a good alternative to tarragon, though the flavour is less distinctive.

Pick over the nettle tops, removing any damaged leaves or alien plant life. Rinse the leaves well and shake dry. Melt the butter in a large saucepan, add the garlic and sweat gently for 1–2 minutes. Before the garlic takes colour, add the onions and cook gently until soft and lightly browned. Pile the nettle leaves into the saucepan – the heat will wilt them, like spinach. Pour over the stock and return to the boil, and allow to simmer for 3–4 minutes.

Ladle into a liquidizer, puréeing until smooth (in batches if necessary), then return the soup to a clean pan. Strip the leaves off the tarragon stalks, chop them – not too finely – and stir two-thirds into the soup. Season to taste with salt and pepper. Reheat the soup without reboiling.

Lightly whip the cream, and stir two-thirds into the soup. Serve the soup with a small blob of the remaining cream and a pinch of chopped tarragon in each bowl.

8 oz/225 g nettle tops (a carrier bag approx two-thirds full)
3 oz/85 g butter
3 large garlic cloves, crushed
1 large *or* 2 medium onions, sliced
2 pts/1.1 litres light chicken *or* vegetable stock
2–3 sprigs of tarragon
salt and black pepper
5 fl oz/150 ml double cream

Potato and Herb Soup

THE BRACKENBURY

Serves 4

Served hot, this soup is a delicious winter warmer, but it can also be chilled and used as a summer starter. Use whatever fresh herbs you can get – but be judicious with strongly flavoured ones such as tarragon and oregano. Variations using just watercress, or sorrel, or parsley, instead of a mixture of herbs, can all be tried. The secret in every case is to have a good, fresh chicken stock, and to chop and add the herbs at the last moment, so they are at their most aromatic.

6 oz/170 g mixed fresh leafy herbs, e.g. parsley, sorrel, chives, basil, chervil, watercress, rocket, tarragon, oregano
1 onion, sliced
2 garlic cloves, chopped
1 leek, cleaned and sliced
1 oz/30 g butter *or* 2 tbsp olive oil
1 lb/450 g mealy potatoes, peeled and cut into 2-in/5-cm dice
1½ pts/850 ml chicken stock
salt and black pepper
soured cream *or* crème fraîche

Wash and dry the herbs in a salad spinner. Pick them over, putting the leaves in one bowl and the stalks in another.

Sweat the onion, garlic and leek in the butter or oil in a saucepan until softened, add the herb stalks and the potatoes, and pour over the stock. Bring to the boil, then cover and simmer for 20–25 minutes until the potatoes are completely tender. Rub the soup through a sieve or mouli-légumes, and season to taste. Thin with a little more stock, or milk, or water, to get the consistency you want.

Just before serving the soup, chop all the herbs very finely with a mezzaluna (see page 22) or in a food processor. Reheat the soup without boiling and stir in all but 1 tbsp of the chopped herbs. Mix these reserved herbs with the soured cream or crème fraîche and a pinch of salt and pepper. Serve the soup with a blob of the cream-herb mixture in each bowl.

If you wish to serve the soup chilled, leave to cool after liquidizing, then refrigerate for at least 2 hours. Stir in the fresh chopped herbs just before serving. The cream-herb mixture is also appropriate.

Index

Entries in light type are recipes, recipe ideas or cooking tips. Page numbers in italic refer to recipes written out in full in the recipe section of each chapter. (See also 'How to use this book', page 5.)

Macadamia nut, 315
Mâche, 75
Mackerel, 149–50
 barbecued with bay, 411
 marinated, 173–4
Magimix, 20
Mallard, braised with celery and orange, 270
Mandarin, 349–50
Mangetout, 76
Mango, 346
 and ruby orange sorbet, 373
Mangosteen, 347
Marinade:
 for fish, 142
 all-purpose for game, 279
 for mackerel or herring, 173
 marinated salt cod, 172
Marjoram, 416
Marrow-bone, bonus with oxtail stew, 249
Mascarpone, 394
Mash:
 horseradish, 112
 perfect, 89
McGee, Harold:
 author of On Food and Cooking, 25
 on storing vegetables, 35
McMullen, Philip, 7
Meat, 183–228
 buying meat:
  at the butcher's, 187–8
  by home delivery, 190
  from farm shops, 190
  in the supermarket, 189
  choosing meat, general remarks, 190–1
 flavour of, 192
 freezing of, 192–3
 organic, 186–7
 storing of, 192
 see also Lamb, Beef, Pork, Veal
Melon, 347–8
 sorbet, 348
Mezzaluna, 22
Michelin stars, 6
Microwave ovens, use of, 17
Millet porridge, 306
Mince:
 beef, 199
 lamb, 205
Mince pies, deep-fried, 373
Mint, uses of, 417
Molesworth, Nigel, 125
Mooli, with raita dressing, 76
Mozzarella, 394
Mulberry, 348–9
Mullet, Grey, 148
 braised in the Greek style, 174
Mung bean, 299
Mussels, 150
 spicey mussel broth, 180
Mushrooms, 77–9
 braised with polenta, 78

gratin, 78–9
 and potato gratin, with lamb, 214
Mustard:
 and cress, 75
 glaze for roast rabbit, 287
 sauce for sprats, 177–8

Navy bean, 298
Neck of lamb, with lemon and thyme, 218
Nectarines, 350–2
Nettle, 79
 and tarragon soup, 429
Niçoise salad, with salmon, 176
Nuts and seeds, 311–17
 alphabetical guide to, 312
 shopping for, 311

Oak leaf lettuce, 75
Oats, 306
 and banana milk shake, 306
Offal 229–50
 alphabetical guide to, 232–44
 shopping for, 231
 frito misto of lamb's, 243
 trio of rabbit's, 273
Olive, artichoke and thyme tart, 427
Olive stoner, 23
Okra, 79
Onions, 80–1
 choosing and preparing, 80–1
 gravy, for Yorkshire pudding, 226–7
 whole roast, 81
 sweet confit of, 112
Orange, 349
Ordering fish, 138
Oregano, 416
 in gremolata, 416
O'Sullivan, Kate, 449
Osso buco, 210
Owston, Anne, 9
Ox cheek, 234
 devilled stew of, 247–8
Oxtail, 243–4,
 with red wine gravy, 249–50
Oysters, 151

Pak-choy, 81–2
Papaya, 350
Parmesan, cooking with, 395–6
Parsley, 417–18
 butter, 426
Parsnip, 82
 and pheasant soup, 117
 fried in breadcrumbs, 82
Partridge, 269–70
 with savoy cabbage and pancetta, 270

Passion fruit, 351
 sorbet and ice cream, 351
Pasta, 310–11
 cooking, 310
 dried, 310
 fresh, 310–11
 wholemeal, 311
 courgette sauce for, 108
 radicchio sauce for, 114–15
 spaghetti soufflé, 402
Pastry:
 rough puff, 281
 simple crumbly, 401
 suet crust, 282
 sweet short crust, 360
Pâté:
 light smoked mackerel, 135
 bloater roe paste, 168
Peach, 351–2
 grilled, with crème brulée, 352
 with cardamom and sabayon cream, 374
Peanut, 315
Pear, 352
 and almond tart, 360–1
 poached in red wine, 375
Peas, 83–4
 canned, 83–4
 choosing, preparing and cooking, 83–4
 dried, split 301–2
 freeze well, 37
 split, purée of, with green peppercorns, 323
 split pea and bacon soup, 323
 split pea fritters, 322
Pease pudding, 301
Pecan, 315
Pecorino, cooking with, 396
Peppers, 84–5
 marinated, with salt cod, 172
 roast/grilled, 85
 roast red pepper and tomato soup, 113
 salsa rossa, 118
Perfect chips, 88
Perfect mash, 89
Pesto, coriander, 105
Petits pois, canned, 83-4
 in pasta sauce with pancetta, 83-4
Pheasant, 265–8
 ageing, 266
 choosing, 265
 cooking methods, 267–8
 freezing, 267
 hanging, 266
 value of, 254
 with apple, Calvados and cream, 267
 and bacon casserole, 285
 and parsnip soup, 117–18
 casserole, 268
 roast, 267
Physalis, 353